WALKING OVER THE EARTH

Walking Over the Earth

A Memoir by

LAUREEN KRUSE DIEPHOF

Edited by

FLOY BLAIR SITTS

Adelaide Books
New York / Lisbon
2019

WALKING OVER THE EARTH
A Memoir
By Laureen Kruse Diephof

Published by Adelaide Books, New York / Lisbon
adelaidebooks.org

Editor-in-Chief
Stevan V. Nikolic

For any information, please address Adelaide Books
at info@adelaidebooks.org
or write to:
Adelaide Books
244 Fifth Ave. Suite D27
New York, NY, 10001

ISBN: 978-1-951214-47-0

Printed in the United States of America

Contents

Introduction

I'd been roaming the world for five months when curiosity led the hotel manager in Tangier, Morocco, to question me, "What are you doing here?"

"I'm traveling around the world," I replied. "What do you think about me traveling alone in the world?"

He focused his eyes on me, lowered his head, and raised his eyebrows all at once. "I think you're either running away from something, or you're just a strange person."

"I'm not strange, and I'm certainly not running away from anything. I like adventure!" I huffed.

"How old are you?"

"I'm 75 now. I had my birthday a little while ago in the Orkney Islands."

"Oh, hmmm, you had a birthday while traveling alone." It was a statement, not a question. He rested his jaw on his hand, elbow on the counter, and studied me.

This one-minute episode happened right after I yanked the tiny suitcase on wheels out of the taxi, slung my camera over my neck, grabbed the computer in the other hand, and limped up the stairs to the lobby.

"I have a reservation," I said. I wanted to find my room and rest after the ordeal of getting there.

He pushed the paperwork toward me. I signed it and handed him my ATM card. He then handed me the key to the room and pointed to the elevator. I limped the few steps to the elevator, knowing his eyes were on my back, as were the eyes of many other men sitting in the lobby.

I got a lot of questions and curious looks during my adventure to 16 countries, many cities, and several tiny islands. I also saw a lot of interesting sights and met a lot of interesting people. Some of them thought I was strange, many asked questions, and all of them looked at me in awe.

Of course, as a woman traveling alone in faraway lands, I had to be careful to avoid those who sought to take advantage of me or do me harm. But more than anything, I met kind people who were willing to lend a helping hand . . . or foot, as in the case of the guy who stopped a train door for me with his foot. Once the door stopped, another gentleman followed the foot-placed leader by grabbing my suitcase and lifting it up and into the train, while another took my elbow and helped me board before we left the station.

What did I learn during my grand adventure?

There are good people in this world. This book will introduce you to some of them, along with the not-so-good people who make the journey more interesting. At least that's how I've learned to look at them. What else can you do?

Every person has a story.

This one is mine.

Unlike most books about travel and adventure, my story doesn't concentrate on just one geographical area. It's also not a short one.

It takes its time.

Also, unlike most authors of similar books being published these days, I didn't set out on my adventure because I was trying to escape something—or someone. And I wasn't searching for great meaning or some profound truth.

I certainly learned a few things along the way, of course, but this adventure was more about celebrating life than it was about trying to figure it out or escape it.

That said, my story will help you escape. There's nothing wrong with that. You will likely find meaning in my story, as well. And you will discover how to travel the world on a bare-bones budget. One way or another, I hope my story will help inspire you to get off the couch and live *your* great adventure.

No matter how young—or old—you are!

Chapter One

April, 2012

*From the Arctic Circle to the Sahara Desert and
points in-between, the free spirit begins her journey.*

I'm in Reykjavik, but where is the guesthouse?

The terrain from Reykjavik's Keflavik Airport put me in mind of
a moonscape. From the bus window, you see miles and miles of
rolling hills of black lava rock with low-growing yellowish grass
and green moss blanketing chunks of lava rock structures lying
helter-skelter.

The rocks of all sizes and shapes rolled out of the Icelandic
volcanoes years ago and stayed in place, forming structures whose
sole purpose from then on was to enhance a traveler's imagination.

Yesterday morning, after the flight beginning in San Francisco on Alaska Airlines and a change to Icelandair in Seattle, I arrived in Reykjavik extremely tired, and then I had to walk nearly
three miles to the Igdlo Guesthouse, dragging luggage behind me.
I had one hand holding a bag on top of a small, rolling suitcase,
pulling it behind me; my laptop computer in the other hand; and
a camera over my neck.

It was chilly but not freezing cold. My black raincoat and vest under it were just right for the brisk walk I took to find my first home.

Walking up an incline from the city airport/bus terminal where I was dropped off, and then crossing the street, I couldn't figure out which way to go, so I stopped a woman riding a bike and asked her where the Igdlo Guesthouse was. She told me to wait a minute. I stood on the cold sidewalk wondering if I should keep waiting for her or continue on down the street. She came back a few minutes later and told me to follow her, that she had found the guesthouse.

This was the first example of how often people would step up to help me along the way. It is also my first word of advice for travelers. You must never be afraid to ask questions, even in English first if you don't know the language. Pantomime works, as does pointing to a map, and finding a word in the local language dictionary works, too. A good dose of humor and smiles will go a long way. Learn to say "thank you" in every language.

Even before boarding a bus from Iceland's Keflavik Airport to Reykjavik, I inquired of a patient woman about one of the places I would be staying after the eight days I'd be at the Igdlo Guesthouse. I had worked out the next place before I left the U.S., knowing it would be in another part of Iceland that I knew nothing about. She also gave me some help, and I learned that the next place would be on the Arctic Circle in a fishing village of 500 people.

I finally found Igdlo, which is a Greenlandic word for igloo, and now I'm sitting in the community room writing of my experiences. I can report that the house, while it was difficult to find on foot, is clean and comfortable. Ingimar, one of the owners, is a complete gentleman and ready to help out in a moment. He has been called into service a few times already.

Expats meet expats.

I have met two other expats from other places in my Igdlo home. Mireia is from Barcelona, Spain, and works in Iceland for a touring company that takes Spanish-speaking people to various sites. She just climbed up onto a ladder and did something that turned on the Internet.

My other new friend, Gergo, is a young man from Hungary. All senior citizens should meet someone like Gergo. I met him yesterday, and while we were sitting in the community room, I mentioned that I had to go shopping for groceries. The kitchen was available for all guests.

"When was the last time you ate?" he asked.

I told him I had an egg salad sandwich sometime in the morning. When he heard that, he went to the kitchen and made a noodle dish with cheese and ketchup and presented that to me.

"Thank you, Gergo. I'm calling this Hungarian Rhapsody." It was delicious. I said, "I will need to get some groceries tomorrow. Is there a grocery store nearby?"

"It's several blocks away. I'll go with you in the morning if you like," Gergo, who became my first friend on the journey, promised.

I woke up at 5:30 a.m., wide awake and wanting to make coffee. However, the coffee maker grinds the beans and then makes the coffee all in one action and is quite noisy. Not wanting to disturb the house, I decided just to lie in bed for a little while.

There was a knock on the door, and without first putting on my glasses, I opened it and saw outlines of two men. They were Ingimar and Gergo wondering what happened to me. I was supposed to meet Gergo at ten for shopping. It was 10:30 a.m.

Well, they could breathe easier knowing I wasn't dead, only jet-lagged.

Gergo and I walked to Bonus, the grocery store near the shopping district downtown. I purchased a half-dozen eggs, a can of tuna fish, a small loaf of bread, a bread-like cake, a package of carrots, salad mix, mayonnaise, a container of coffee cream, a carton of yogurt, two apples (they were imported from the U.S.), a bag of potato chips, and Gouda cheese (from Holland). It all came to approximately $18. I'm going to make it last for the entire 11 days at this home. I took Gergo out for coffee to pay him for helping me out. At the coffee shop, all tables had bottles of water and tiny glasses for customers to enjoy a sip. Gergo carried all the groceries back to the guesthouse.

I washed out some things in the sink in my room. The water smells like sulfur, which is normal here. Heating buildings is cheap due to the natural sulfuric water that is available all over the island.

Ah, I met a local character.

Day before yesterday, I was sitting in the Mokka Coffee Shop downtown. A gentleman sitting near the door lifted his cup of tea as a greeting to me, and I smiled back. When I walked to leave, he met me halfway and said something in Icelandic. He first thought I was English, then learned I was American.

We agreed to meet the next day where I could interview him about his life as an actor. The next day at the appointed hour, I was in the coffee shop sitting next to a tall, young Icelandic woman. I asked her if she was a student, and we exchanged names.

"Oh, I knew you would be here. I'm meeting Kitel, as well. He's going to read what I wrote." She translated her fantasy piece into English for me, and then in walked Kitel Lassen with his friend, Gestur Gunnersson, who did much of the translating between Kitel and myself.

Kitel has a full beard, big smile, and seemed to know many people who walked through the door. In the 70s, he toured with the Innk Group Players across 19 countries, including the U.S., acting in five plays. He played an Eskimo. The playwright traveled with them, he said.

Kitel is an actor, poet, painter, and singer. He studied at the National Theater School, which is now called Iceland Academia of Arts and is the school where Asta Fanney Sigurdardottir, the young woman who sat with us, goes to school now. She invited me to a graduation exhibition on April 21st at the school. *Asta* means love, and *Fanney* means snowy Iceland.

While in the company of the three Icelanders, the two men told me many stories from their memories of American soldiers on a base near where they lived during World War II. One soldier took it upon himself to deliver fruit to Kitel's mother. His sister was very ill and food was scarce. Other stories they told made me proud of the Americans.

Yesterday, while on a walk again through the town, the rain, and fog, I met Gergo on the street. He walked with me for a while until he turned and went the other direction. Later, he said he had wanted to look at the hotel where he had applied for a job.

"I hope you get the job, Gergo. You are so kind, and I hope the manager sees that."

"Maybe kindness doesn't get the job," Gergo replied with his head down.

"Well, it should."

On the walk back to the guesthouse, I stopped into a pottery shop where I met the third generation potter. A Bill Clinton lookalike, he explained that the generational pottery business is a hobby of his now, and that he works for a prison full-time but comes into the shop to throw pots. The pots are beautiful and are purchased by collectors. He gave me the website: www. listvinahusid.is.

He showed me that each pot had the seal of the business on the bottom. The business was established in 1927.

About prisons in Iceland. The longest anyone would stay in prison is 16 years, and that would be for killing someone. Iceland does not have the death penalty.

Today is Good Friday and most stores, museums, and government offices are closed, so I'm going to take a walk to the other side of town. I'm quite sore but realize it's a good sign that I'm getting stronger. Sitting for many years as a photojournalist in front of a computer has left my body weak. So this senior citizen, traveler, explorer, and temporary expatriate will show how to get back into stronger condition.

Cured by a Viking

My goal today was to walk to the Saga Museum and the Perlan (Pearl) Restaurant that sits all aglow on a hill. The restaurant has a mirrored, windowed dome that can be seen from far away. The gourmet and pricey Perlan, located on the fifth floor, rotates so a guest can view the country in all 360 degrees. I opted for the cafeteria on the fourth floor, which was more affordable. We are fogged in, so the gourmet restaurant wouldn't have been a good choice, anyway, at least until the fog clears and the stores open again. Most everything has been closed during Easter holiday.

On the way to the museum, the heartburn I have been fighting reared its gaseous head, and I've been suffering.

I stopped at a Shell station to get directions, and while there, I looked around for something to curb heartburn. A Viking of a man assured me there wasn't anything in the store for heartburn but that he'd share his cure. He opened up a quart carton of milk, poured a glass full, and handed it to me.

"What do I owe you?"

"Nothing. I know what heartburn is like, so it's free to you."

I ask you, how is that for good customer service? The milk has actually worked for most of the day.

The same as in many other countries, I learned later, Iceland does not sell products such as Tums without a doctor's prescription.

The Saga Museum and the Perlan sit on top of a circle of six large geothermal water containers. On the first floor, with a headset tour guide, you can visit the earliest settlers in Iceland through a chronological history with lifelike replicas of Icelandic figures found in the Viking sagas. The figures and the stations within the saga were so lifelike, I felt I was watching the action of real people. This includes the burning of Sister Katrin, a heretic; the beheading of Jón Arason, a Catholic bishop; and a scene of the people who died from the notorious Black Death that led to the destruction of one-third of Europe's population. Ingólfur Arnarson was there with his wife Hallveig Fróoadóttir in 874 A.D., when Arnarson first arrived in Iceland from Norway.

Later, while on a walk again through the town, the rain, and the fog, I met Gergo on the street. He's still on a job search.

Viewing the city

Today, I walked nearly all day, and I'm happy to say my legs did pretty well until the end when I thought I couldn't walk one more step. All the coffee shops were closed, and it was cold. Then I found Yo-Yo, a yogurt shop.

There were many choices of yogurt and toppings. I walked in, and I think I scared the customers. Imagine a white-haired lady in ice-cold weather, wearing sunglasses, dressed all in black, limping in and shaking from the cold. I set my black purse down and took off my coat (wearing black under the coat, as well), and all the while, the three kids of a family sitting at a table nearby watched me.

After I got my dish of yogurt and sat down, one of the girls braved a smile at me. I smiled back, and then I guess I wasn't witchy-looking anymore. She broke the ice and warmed me up. Perhaps I appeared more approachable when my glasses changed from sunglasses to clear.

I had walked from one end of Reykjavik to the harbor and back. There were brief moments of sunshine.

I saw the Hallgrímskirkja concrete church, a famous landmark. The church houses a 5,275-pipe organ, which I heard demonstrated on my last visit to Reykjavik with my friend, Marilyn McCord, five years earlier.

The statue of Leifur Eiriksson, the first European to arrive on the land that later became America, stands in front of the Hallgrímskirkja Church. The 74.5-meter statue of Eiriksson was a present from the U.S. on the 1,000[th] anniversary of Iceland's first parliament. The gift was officially received by Iceland on May 3, 1932.

From the church, I walked to the harbor. Snowcapped mountains framed the opposite end of the harbor where large ships, yachts, and sailboats were anchored.

While in the Geysir Restaurant, I had a crepe with fish, rice, and vegetables. Three young ladies sat next to me. Two were from the States, one from Illinois, and one from Kansas. The other young lady was from Amsterdam where all three work for the same company. The lady from Illinois works in Switzerland, while the other two work in Amsterdam. It was quite refreshing to hear them talk and laugh.

You never stop learning, I've learned! Ingimar loaned me a book, and one of the first items I read in the forward was that modern Icelanders refer to Vikings as "ravaging plunderers" of the period of Scandinavian voyages, 793-1066 A.D. That is from the book *Iceland From Past to Present* by Esbjörn Rosenblad and Rakel Sigurdardottir-Rosenblad. My apologies to any handsome, burly, large men whom I ever thought of as plunderers.

Travel plans may be up in the air.

The sun came out today, and I will take a long walk to the port and near the Civic Center and the House of Parliament.

Several newcomers have joined me where I'm staying for another three more days. They seem like gifts to me, bringing their enthusiasm and friendliness with them.

There was some discussion between Gergo and Marianne, a laughing lady from Switzerland, as well as Ingimar, about where I'll be going in June. In Marianne's tour book, Thorshofn is listed as the loneliest spot in the world.

This is what I know. It's close to the Arctic Circle, and to get there depends on the weather. The person I'll be renting the place from may drive me either all the way, with a possible stop along the way, or straight there; it all depends on the weather. I may even fly to the nearest city and then take a bus the rest of the way. This evening, I spoke to Siggi, the owner of the hotel, about the travel plans.

I agreed to call him again in two weeks.

How will I get there? Not even I know, yet.

That's Iceland—unpredictable weather.

Yesterday was cold. How cold was it? It was cold enough for me to purchase a wool, Iceland-knitted, cardigan sweater. It is a blessing to wear. I then sat cozily in a French restaurant watching rainfall, rain that almost looked like snow. Leave it to the French to present chocolate cake as a piece of art. It was drizzled with raspberry and chocolate syrup, a dollop of whipping cream, a sprig of mint, a strawberry, and a yellow berry. The waitress couldn't identify the yellow berry, about the size of a marble.

"I've seen them before, but all I know is they don't come from Iceland," she added.

Today, the sun came out again, and now I'm too warm with the Icelandic sweater. Wait until tomorrow, for the weather is unpredictable.

I went to the 871 Museum. That number designates the first settlement of Reykjavik around 871 A.D. The way the museum is presented amazed me for Iceland's desire to protect its history. When the building was being excavated for the foundation, a whole log house was discovered under the ground. Instead of ignoring what they found or destroying it, the people in charge simply built over it. The presentation is genius.

Moving to a new home

Not often you walk into a guesthouse and hear live music, but that's what happened today. I'll be staying at my second home, the Salvation Army Guesthouse, until the end of the month. Every morning there are morning prayers. And today, a guitarist and a room full of people sang together as I walked in with my luggage.

The guesthouse isn't only for "down-and-outers" but for travelers, as well. It's a fundraising machine for the good works of the Salvation Army.

Beginning in September, guests will be students of the University of Reykjavik. The Salvation Army is making a change from renting to travelers to renting to students. I think students sound like more of a sure thing that could provide a steady income.

The room I chose is a private room, not bigger than a cell at California's Soledad Prison. It's clean and has ample room to put my belongings. I find that I'm dragging heavier weight due to the paperwork I pick up here and there. This is why I chose to get a taxi instead of taking the long walk, dragging along a top-heavy, noisy, rolling, two bags of "stuff."

I'm staying upstairs on what is called the first floor. The kitchen is on the second floor, with two refrigerators and angry notes taped on both, warning the food thief that not only is he a low-life, no-good, son-of-a-biscuit, but he must be made aware that now there is a hidden camera inside the new refrigerator. So there!

I went to the grocery store and purchased a pear; two tins of cream cheese, one with peppers and one with oranges; and crackers. I'll heed the written word on the refrigerator until the food police arrest the "no-gooder." I'll keep my food in my room.

I left the Igdlo Guesthouse with sadness; I could only wish I were a billionaire and could take everyone I met with me on the rest of my journey. For example, there were the young lady and her boyfriend from Spain, the Hungarian previously mentioned, a Chinese couple who live in Italy, the laughing woman from Sweden, and the owner of the guesthouse. I would recommend Igdlo as the place for anyone wanting a clean, peaceful, restful, and convenient place to begin his or her journey.

Not only was it a nice place, but also everyone had good stories about where they went, what they saw, and where they would be going next while in Iceland. Ingimar made all kinds of information available. Isn't it amazing the good people you can meet along the journey?

Yesterday, I took the long walk to the mall. During the time inside this shopping center, I heard American music—"Kiss Me Once, Kiss Me Twice" by Satchmo, jazz, and country music. By the way, I spotted Mexican food inside the food court.

It's freezing cold today. Thank you, warm sweater.

The sun came out today.

I walked to the Reykjavik Culture Museum and saw some impressive manuscripts made in the medieval and post-medieval eras. Some were part of the collection of Árni Magnússon.

There is a sad story associated with Magnússon. He was born in 1663, educated in Iceland and then in Copenhagen. Later, he was professor of Danish antiquities at the University of Copenhagen. Throughout his lifetime, he amassed a prized medieval collection of manuscripts, much of which was lost in a fire in Copenhagen in 1728.

Magnússon died a year later. His death made me wonder if it wasn't of a broken heart. It also reminds me not to put more importance on your personal belongings than on your life and on others in your life.

What was rescued of Magnússon's collection was sent from Copenhagen to the Icelandic nation as a gift from the Danes.

The museum rooms showcase the tools of the bookbinding business, the intricate and perfect printing by hand, and the designs made from the colored ink that was created by crushing rocks, minerals, and plants. Parchment from hides of animals was used for the written pages.

Now, when the computer doesn't do what I expect of it, I remember the tediousness of the scribes and the work they did to write stories and sagas. We have it made. I was once a scribe when elected twice to a high school girls' organization, and now I feel an affinity for those medieval scribes.

Later, I found the Noodle Station, a place where you can purchase a bowl of soup for only 650 ISK (around five dollars in Icelandic kronur). It was delicious. I walked on to the swimming pool and its two hot pots. Throughout Iceland, there are many pools with hot pots where you can sit and warm up, part of the Icelandic culture.

I gave the hot pot a good 15 minutes. Ingimar told me many people go to the pool before going to work in the mornings.

The hot water of the country is readily available, and cold water for drinking is good. There are no chemical tastes in drinking water whatsoever.

More observations of Iceland

Going swimming in Iceland is a social event that begins with first getting naked and taking a shower with soap. A monitor makes certain that no one enters the pool without a shower before putting on a swimsuit. The monitor was a woman around

60. She roamed around the locker room, and when she saw me, I must have looked confused. I didn't know her purpose in the room.

"Go to this shower and use soap." She pointed to the shower and the soap dispenser.

"Yes, of course," I said with reluctance.

"How long have you been doing this job, making sure everyone is clean?" I had to ask, while scrubbing off my dirty self.

"Thirty years. Some women foreigners resent it. They don't want to be around other people without their clothes. But we want to be sure the water is always clean."

The monitor was right about that comment, as I later read a letter to the editor in an English-language newspaper, written by a foreigner, expressing distaste of the cleaning process I had just experienced. Well, my thinking is, you're a guest in the country, and just as you would were you a guest in someone's home, you must conform to the rules. It's disrespectful not to. As travelers, we aren't in the country to make changes.

After the cleansing process, you put on your swimsuit and go to either the pool or one of the hot pots or the steam room. The hot pots range in temperature, and I've been warned not to stay in the hottest hot pot for longer than 15 minutes. I was also advised to get out often and cool off before getting back in.

Icelanders are friendly and helpful, but an outsider must make the first move. I've experienced that many times and again this morning. After I greeted a woman sharing the hot pot and small talk was initiated, I asked a question about the slaves of Ingólfur Arnarson, the man credited with being the first to settle in Reykjavik. He is also credited with beginning the first parliament.

The young woman gave me a history lesson about Arnarson. He sailed with his slaves, who came from Ireland, along the Icelandic coast from Norway. He threw two pillars out of the ship and told his slaves that wherever the pillars washed ashore, that is where he would settle with his family. After about three years, the long search ended on the shoreline where Arnarson settled, and that became Reykjavik.

The history also continues that Arnarson's stepbrother, Hjörleifur, who had sailed with Arnarson, settled in what became known as Hjörleifshöfdi. Hjörleifur's Irish slaves killed him. Then Ingólfur Arnarson hunted the slaves down and killed them in retribution. Vestmannaeyjar (Westman Islands) was named for the slaves.

Aside from the important history lesson from the young woman, I have also learned that tipping in restaurants and in taxis is not expected in Iceland. It's funny, however, to notice in one restaurant, I did see a "tip" jar with American dollars crammed inside.

A three-story bookstore here sells drinks and food, and a customer can take their purchases to any store location where there is seating and can eat and drink while reading magazines or books without purchasing them. Also, the library has several vending machines where a patron can drink coffee, tea, or soft drinks and eat snacks while reading.

I took it easy today and stayed close to my guesthouse, venturing once in the morning to my favorite coffee house that reminds me of Santa Cruz, California—cozy, mismatched furniture; uneven, hardwood plank floors; a cup of coffee with a free refill; and free reign to stay all day if you want.

I also walked to the bookstore previously mentioned and purchased a rolled up thing with cheese, cucumbers, tomatoes, peppers and lettuce.

Icelandic fashions and salty fish

It is 13 days into my yearlong journey, and today I took my usual walk around Reykjavik after first having morning coffee in a cozy place, joined by my new friend Gergo. Sitting by the window, it was fun to observe teenagers walking to school, laughing and kidding each other. The girls wore their fashions of tights under short-shorts or skirts, coats with fur-lined hoods, and boots of all kinds. The warm, woolen, hand-knitted sweater is the traditional fashion statement of the majority, however.

There is also the trendy look that is turning Iceland into a new high fashion center. I call it shabby chic—off-center cuts, one covered sleeve with the other one open, shirts over tops and over skirts and over lacy slips, with boots up to the thigh, and let's not leave the dripping fringe and woolen ruffles out of the mix.

On my walk, I made a reservation at the Information House for the Blue Lagoon. A spa about 40 minutes away from Reykjavik, the Blue Lagoon is where people bathe outside in the warm, healing, geothermal water.

I also made a reservation to see the opera *La Boheme* at the new opera house. Going to the opera reminds me of when, while in Germany, Juliane, my grandniece, and I went to see a German opera with libretto written in Italian. Not fluent in either language, she had printed a summary of the story in English for me before we left. It didn't take too long until I was confused with the story line. On a break, Juliane admitted she printed out the wrong story.

La Boheme will be sung in Italian with Icelandic libretto.

At the new, impressive, opera house, I ordered lunch—herring over rye bread. When it arrived at my table, it was a surprise to see that the sauce on top of the chunks of herring was purple. It matched the chair I was sitting on. It turns out that the sauce was made of beetroot. Not often do I turn back a meal, but this was so salty that if another fish had eaten it, it would have died.

To top it off, the butter for the extra bread had chunks of salt on top of it. Couldn't eat it, and I told the waitress it was just too salty. And no, I didn't want anything else other than a cup of coffee. When I paid the bill, the manager had given me a discount, and the coffee was free.

Toes saved me at the Blue Lagoon.

Ah, the Blue Lagoon. I felt I was inside a Maxfield Parrish. Steam arose from the azure water while I paddled around in comfort and amazement. The geothermal water was warm, with hotter currents circulating below and around. The warmest spots were easy to find; just follow the people standing in a group.

The setting is in natural surroundings with a bar you can waddle up to and get a soft drink or liquor.

It took a half-hour or more to get to the Blue Lagoon after everyone had been picked up from their hotels and taken to the bus station for the final ride. I met some nice folks from the States who had been in Germany at the wedding of their daughter.

Cold and damp air met us at the lagoon when we got off the bus. We walked through what seemed to be a wind tunnel with tall, lava walls forming the entrance. After taking the mandated shower with soap before putting on my swimsuit, the warm blue waters beckoned to me after the freezing walk to the edge of the pool.

"The HS Orka Energy Company extracts the geothermal fluid from its reservoir by drilling deep wells of up to 2,000 meters. The geothermal fluid, which reaches 240 degrees Celsius [464 degrees Fahrenheit], is then used to heat freshwater for central heating and to create electricity." (From the website www.bluelagoon.com.) The spa is located in a lava field in Grindavík on the Reykjanes Peninsula. Friendly people were everywhere, soaking up the warmth and feeling relaxed, until . . .

Wind suddenly blew so strongly, it made waves above the bubbling water. I lost my glasses to the wind, having put them temporarily on a plank while I slathered my face with silica mud. The silica in boxes at key locations is thought to make your skin soft and lovely.

"Oh no! My glasses!" I screamed.

Icelandic kronur and dollar signs flashed through my consciousness. Glasses? I'd first need an eye exam, then I'd have to purchase a new pair. How's that going to work with my traveling-on-a-dime?

A gallant man standing in the water next to me stammered, "Wait, wait, wait."

My hero found my glasses near his foot and brought them to the surface with his toe. They were toed-in!

Most people are good.

My headline, Most people are good, comes from my experience as an ex-pat and as an older traveler who travels on a dime.

There. That about sums up my adventure here, but wait, there's more. Walking around the city of Reykjavik makes me realize how small the town is when I run into people I have met. Take Gergo, the young Hungarian man, for example. Somehow we seem to end up on the same streets when out walking in the fresh Icelandic air. I saw him again today. He asked how I was doing with the pain in my legs when I walk. Back when I first arrived in Reykjavik, I couldn't go far without having to stop and let my legs recuperate. Day by day, I'm getting stronger. I can walk all the way to town, through town, and back around again with no pain. I let the legs rest for a day, which seems to help.

Then there's the nice young fisherman from Seattle who has been in Iceland for about three weeks and stays in the same guesthouse as I, and we have shared the same table getting on-line time with our computers. Just a few days ago, his mother joined him from Seattle. We met each other at the Blue Lagoon and again today in the streets of Reykjavik. His mother took a photo of her son and me. I'm sorry not to know their names, and that's sad, because we became friends for a few days. Seeing them together made me wish my sons were here with me.

I went to Mokko Coffee Shop, hoping to see the gentle-man-actor, Kitel, but he wasn't there.

There is a nice lady who works in the chocolate shop in the oldest timber-made house in Reykjavik. She's kind and patient when I go in there and pay for only one tiny piece of chocolate and snag a free sample, as well.

Yesterday, I sat next to two men at happy hour in the same coffee shop where I go nearly every day, and they waved at me today.

There is a disheveled woman who comes to the prayer singing every morning, and she has begun to recognize me when she sees me. I have seen her pick through trash. She has blue eyes circled with a lifetime of troubles, but she manages a smile.

Saw a sign advertising a menu of whale and puffin, along with the photos of these dishes. Puffins are the cute, fluffy little birds who sustained Faroese people for centuries with their eggs and, of course, their meat. Eggs were, and still are, secured out from the rocks, but now puffin egg-gathering is more of a hobby for the men who climb up to the puffins' nests.

I've seen a lot of life and have experienced kindness, and then I found the City Hall, a picture of architectural genius open to the community.

This is a city hall the likes of which I have never seen before. It sits smack dab on a lake with sculptures all around it. A group of women was getting a children's art project ready for an exhibition. I saw two men with baby buggies taking time with their babies, using their paternity leave privilege, and across the lake was a church. Inside the church, a funeral was attended by many people whom I observed coming out and standing around until the body was placed in the hearse and driven off.

It's heartwarming for me to see fathers and their babies nearly every day, walking and pushing the buggies. I saw a father working on his computer while a baby slept near him in the buggy. When the baby woke up and was a bit fussy, the father finished his work and began to leave. I couldn't stand not saying something to him, so I praised him for being a good father.

"It's normal here in Iceland," he said. He was on a paternity leave, which brings equality to the work world. A mother doesn't need to feel guilty for taking time off work to stay home, as both mother and father receive leave time. The father gets to bond with the baby, while the mother recuperates and gets ready to get back to work.

First day of summer

It's a holiday today, April 19, celebrating the first day of summer. There will be celebrations to honor the important day. There are two seasons, it appears—summer and winter. It's chilly, but the sun came out for most of the day.

Because it's a holiday, there is a lot of activity in the streets, beginning with a day of running. I went to the City Hall and saw people getting registered to run around the lake, and it was the same place where children's art was on display the other day. Children's art is the most natural and creative. Whoever runs the children's art program in Reykjavik needs to be congratulated.

A man, who said he was from New Zealand but who had an American accent, performed a show on the street that kept everyone enthralled. He first began by coming on the street "stage" in pajamas. His shtick was slightly risqué but hilarious. He had the audience in the palm of his hand with his jokes and his acrobatic skills.

He got two men out of the audience to hold a ladder, a man on each side. While he joked and while the ladder was balanced, he put his body into acrobatic maneuvers atop the ladder. This caused gasps in the audience.

Another French-speaking man further down the street played a guitar and sang French songs. The guy I saw earlier in the week who played the "saw" must not have received the memo because he wasn't anywhere today. He was reminiscent of the saw player, Tom Scribner, in Santa Cruz, California, who was so popular that when he died, an iron statue was made and dedicated to him. You can see it on the Garden Mall.

Someone just said hello to me and asked me how I was. I answered him in American slang, "I'm hanging in there." Then I laughed and told him I was fine.

He shook my hand and said, "Happy Summer. It's a great day in Iceland."

"Sure is."

Summer

I just finished a great day with the best bowl of *supa a dagsins*, soup of the day, and the best soup I have ever slurped—carrot, curry, and bits of ginger. It was just what I needed after walking in the cold weather, and I was told it was "all you can eat." Well, I went back three times and stopped just before the fourth time; I decided someone might be keeping score.

It's the second day of summer, and very early in the morning, restaurant workers were busy putting chairs and tables outdoors because, I repeat, it is summer! I observed people sitting at outside restaurants enjoying drinks and food, all the while wearing coats, hats, and scarves. Don't let anyone tell an Icelander that when it's summer it's too cold to sit outside.

"It's not cold to us," a waitress said.

My day began by talking to a gentleman just in from Montana with serious jet lag. Then I met an Italian at my favorite coffee place where Anna Asthildur gets my coffee to me with a smile. The word *Ast* means love in Icelandic, and *Hildur* is an old Icelandic name, she told me.

The Italian man, Cosimo, was there. He is an artist and recent graduate of a culinary school. He arrived in Iceland, I believe he said, 14 years ago as an exchange student, and he decided to stay. He likes the country and is now fluent in the language.

When he learned I was from the U.S., he remarked that he would be afraid to go to America.

"Why?" I asked.

"Because it's violent," he said.

"Did you learn that from television?"

"Yes, and from movies."

Moving onward . . . .

Here's a travel hint for those on a budget. If you really want to see the city, get on a local bus and stay on it the whole route. I did that this afternoon and got acquainted with the bus driver, Arnie. He stopped at a station next to a restaurant that is a convenient stop for the drivers. He invited me into the station and shared his thermos of coffee with me. His daughter was an exchange student in Denver a while ago, and he has visited her there.

"I saw Aspen, Vail, and other snowy places while there," he told me. I felt right at home talking about my old homestead.

When the bus was back at the original stop, he handed me a transfer and advised me to hop on number one.

"That will take a long time, and you'll see a lot."

On bus number one, the woman driver welcomed me, and when she, too, had a scheduled break, she told me we had just gone through the third largest Iceland city called Hafnarfjordur. It's located close to an aluminum factory, and there are many new houses being built for those who work at the plant. The houses are built on top of lava fields. She pointed out there is a place called Lava Gardens that consists of many large boulders of lava, most of which are covered with moss, and there are trails to follow.

But in Hafnarfjördur, you better watch out for gnomes, trolls, and elves, for they surely exist in the Viking area of the town.

"The houses are cheaper here because of the aluminum factory and the geothermal operation plant. There's also some pollution seen in the air at times," she told me. Today, however, it was clear.

I had learned from a coffee attendant I met that the ore for aluminum is imported to Iceland from Brazil, and then the final process is completed in Iceland and sold to Germany and the Netherlands, with most of it kept for use in Iceland.

Most Icelandic houses and buildings are covered with aluminum. The previous time I was here, my questions about why this is so were not answered, so this time I kept asking until I was satisfied. Houses and buildings are covered in aluminum to protect them, I was told. Something is needed to protect houses from the harsh weather.

"From the early days, back in the 1800s, there weren't enough trees to build houses entirely out of wood. My father-in-law remodeled his 100-year-old house and found sheets of banana cartons inside the walls," the coffee tender told me.

The bus took over four hours of travel and cost only around $3.00. And the bus drivers were good folks. Consider riding buses if you are traveling on a dime, as I am.

Americans want to take over the world? Really?

"Americans want to take over the world," so said an Icelander I met yesterday and again today at Shofan, my current favorite coffee shop.

Meanwhile, Gergo joined the Icelander and me in the corner of the room after I had greeted him and a coffee server I hadn't met yet. The coffee server had perfect American English language skills, and I mentioned that she sounded American. Turns out, she did live in the States but is Icelandic.

The Icelander who made that statement about Americans wanting to take over the world went on to make fun of Americans by doing an Icelandic version of John Wayne. He pulled his Icelandic fishing cap down to his eyebrows and crinkled up his eyes to look vehement. The smirking John Wayne then tried to tell me that all Texans are braggers.

Anna, whom I met yesterday, came in with a group of her young friends and waved at me. Later, Cosimo, the artist I also met yesterday, came into the coffee shop and stopped by my table to say hello and then good-bye on his way out of the shop.

Icelander John Wayne rambled on with his continuing education, now about the rudeness of the Italian artist who had stepped out. I have learned you aren't supposed to stand while speaking to anyone who is sitting down; John Wayne advised me of the rudeness of that practice. However, the Icelander admitted to me that he didn't like the Italian due to a past skirmish that occurred outside when the Italian had to hold the Icelander back.

The Icelander speaks many languages, which may be the reason he said, "No one should visit any foreign country without some knowledge of the language."

Ouch!

He rolled his own cigarette and wondered why I didn't smoke. He said he was healthier because of the tobacco he uses. He said it took a certain skill to roll your own, and I told him I could do that—"No sweat."

I remembered how my grandpa rolled his own cigarettes. So I took the paper in my hand and began to pinch the tobacco, and when I did, he kept telling me not to spill it. I was careful and put just the right amount in the paper, rolled it up, and licked one edge. I thought I did a good job.

He said it was fixable and that with a little bit of work, he could use it. Later, I saw him shake out the tobacco and redo it in another paper. I thought the one I rolled was okay, but then, I am an American.

Expat enjoys a night out.

I was out late last night for the first time since arriving in Reykjavik. I ventured to the Harpa Concert Hall and sat on the fourth floor on a chair that was part of one line of chairs that overlooked the stage. The opera *La Bohème* was beautiful. The lead singer received "bravos" from the appreciative audience.

The curtain calls were as good as the story line. Actually, the sets were designed without a curtain and moved around so creatively you didn't notice the changes.

The players began moving on stage and in the audience before everyone was even seated. Two players sat for a while up where I was sitting. At the beginning, those players joined the rest of the cast on the stage.

When the opera was over, I walked down all four floors, joining with hundreds of other folks. The theater, with a capacity of 750 people, was full.

I had planned on taking a taxi back home because I didn't want to be out late walking around. But the sky was still light blue with one star that hung over the harbor, and I walked home with about 100 other folks going the same way.

Reykjavik is known for its vibrant nightlife that comes alive around midnight; it was getting a good start by 11 o'clock.

Soon, I was on my way alone, with just a few more blocks to go, and I came upon a table with folks standing around. One of the gentlemen and a woman asked me if I would like a cup of coffee or hot chocolate. Sure, I said, and then I asked what was the purpose of standing there handing out hot drinks? They were representatives of the Hvitasunnkirkjan Church, telling all who would listen about the church and their services. There would be a service in English on Sunday at two p.m. It was a jubilant bunch of folks happy to spread the good news.

Back to Harpa Hall. The place became a controversial issue in the city because of the economic failures of the country, but according to what I have read about it, the hall has been credited as one of the reasons for the quick reversal of the country's financial troubles. The hall draws big names. One of those who lost his heart in San Francisco and whose lovely voice those in Reykjavik will hear is Tony Bennett.

Before the opera, I ate dinner inside the gourmet restaurant situated inside Harpa Hall. I had a dish of root vegetables. It is so hard to explain what that was, but I haven't tasted anything that delicious for a long time, excluding the curry soup of the other day.

The waitress, a delightful, smiling, young lady, spoke perfect English, and I had to ask where she was from. It turns out her father is the Ambassador from Uganda to Iceland, but before that, he was stationed in America, which is where she had spent most of her childhood.

Church and the flea market

Yesterday, I was expecting to hear from Siggi, the man who owns the place where I'll be staying up in the Arctic Circle, about when we would be leaving for the long trek. He wanted to leave earlier than I had expected, and I was to call him over the weekend. The call ended with him telling me to call back the following day, which is today. Right now, I am in limbo.

Yesterday, I was inside the community room at the Salvation Army Guesthouse, and Billy, a Salvation Army worker from both the U.S. and Iceland, invited me to attend their church, which is located within the same building.

I've heard music coming from there on occasion, but I didn't know what it was. However, I had met Billy earlier and again on the street with his auburn-haired, beautiful wife, Dorothy, from the Faroe Islands, and felt very welcome.

Salvation Army officer Margaret Saue Marti translated the message in the service so I would understand. She is from Norway, is fluent in Icelandic, English, Norwegian, and, I'm certain, other languages, as well. I was impressed that she could translate so quickly. Afterwards, in celebration of a church member's birthday, a table full of food was laid out for everyone. I had the sweets, of course, and two of the savory items, one of which was a cracker with salmon and the other caviar.

I also went to a flea market that day in Reykjavik and saw the usual. You know—books, clothing, shoes, DVDs, old videos, etc., etc., and then the unusual—horse meat steaks and roasts, dried fish, and durian fruit. The durian came from Taiwan, so said the seller, but it was frozen. He has never tasted it before, so I warned him not to let it thaw out. It smells so bad that everyone would clear out of the building. It is delicious to taste, however.

I finally broke down and purchased an Icelandic hot dog, a treat that is almost worshipped here. It's made out of cute little lambs and slathered with some brown sauce and mayonnaise. When the brown sauce dripped down my arm, I threw the whole thing out.

This morning, while waiting for the city to wake up, I strolled into the popular restaurant, Laundromat. I ordered a traditional breakfast of scrambled eggs, grilled tomatoes, and bread. It was good, and while there, I began to read a British magazine with an article about a woman reporter-turned-editor who was investigated for phone hacking. I think the people in the restaurant thought I would stay there all day. A library of books is shelved under the counter that wraps around almost to a circle. This restaurant should be called The Library.

Walking and observing

Intent on walking up to the Mokku Coffee Shop, I hoped to see Kitel one more time. Who should I run into on the way? It was the Icelandic John Wayne. I quickly told him I had an appointment.

So, at Mokku, in the middle of enjoying a delicious cup of hot chocolate, in walks Kitel—a bushy-bearded fellow with a devilish twinkle in his eye. He saw me and began to yodel. Yodel?

Well, I think it may have been the sound he made when he played an Eskimo the year he toured with a theater group throughout the U.S. about 40 years ago. Fifteen minutes of fame can spoil you for a whole lifetime.

Then he came over to me and began to sing. I left him singing his heart out, and I headed to the Reykjavik Library. Whom should I run into? Yeah, him again, the John Wayne.

"Was your appointment with the Italian," he asked? I assured His Jealousship that, no, it wasn't the Italian, and that I had to look something up inside the library, so, bye, bye. Those two have history between them.

This afternoon, after a long walk, I sat inside the Paris Cafe enjoying a bowl of leek soup and had the best seat in the house for the entertaining *Waiting for Godot* scene going on across the street on the corner. Two men, whom I have seen before, begged for money from people walking by.

The men, one with a crutch and another with an alcohol wobble, seemed to be enjoying their conversations while holding up the post office wall. When someone walked by, the one with the wobble would hold out his hat and ask for money. After someone walked by and didn't drop any money in the hat, the men had words to say to each other, and then they'd giggle. One time, however, after someone walked by with a disgusted look on his face, someone who must have said something that tempered the humor of the moment, Crutches gave the guy the universally understood middle finger salute.

When someone, and it was most often a woman, dropped money into the hat, Crutches would put his hand out to his wobbly friend for his share of the booty.

Little arguments went on for a few minutes, and then they were friends again. One man I saw dropped two cigarettes in the hat, and they both lit up, which momentarily took their attention away from their main purpose.

I was happy for the "rear-window" into the street theatrics.

Earlier, and what prompted my sore legs to sit down, was the long walk I took toward an area of the town I hadn't seen yet. It was several streets with tall, aluminum-covered houses, and one of those was the American Embassy. A young guard, who called himself a "newbie" because he'd been on the job a short time, told me I wasn't allowed to take a photo of the front, but if I walked a bit away, then I could do so. He enjoys his job and particularly likes his bosses. He gestured upstairs to the office.

It doesn't seem to matter how you walk throughout the streets; all roads seem to be within eyesight of the Hallgrímskirkja, the large church, which is a great big landmark not to be missed.

My friend Gergo is still in search of a job, as well as a place to call home. I read a news brief that finding an apartment in Reykjavik isn't easy, but Gergo is determined.

Tonight, I should have some travel plans from Siggi for the trip up north.

Up to the Arctic Circle

It's a wonder to me sometimes how I got to where I am. What turn of events would take me to a house overlooking the most awesome view of a fjord at the furthest end of the island of Iceland?

It began when Siggi, a tall, red-ringlet-haired Icelander, picked me up at the Salvation Army Guesthouse three days ago and took me to the town of Mosfellsbaer to his home on Dvergholt (Dwarf) Street.

We would leave the next day around noon to head up to Thorshofn, far up north to the Jorvik Hotel he owns at the Arctic Circle. Actually, we left at nine p.m. because Siggi had some complications that had to be settled before we departed. Meanwhile, I sat inside his home reading *Reykjavik 101* and getting acquainted with the smoky-colored cat.

I enjoyed the view of snowy mountains from the windows, as well as listening to the soft purring of "Smoky." We left while it was still relatively light, driving on roads where both sides were covered with lava-pocked rocks and bumpy hills of naturally growing wheat grass.

Siggi explained that the lumps of wheat grass are formed when ice sits under the grass and then melts, leaving mounds in small, grassy hills.

One area heavily laden with lava rocks in such formations led my mind to imagine they were carefully placed there, rock on rock on rock, by some giant artist who came out of the sky to create abstract art. Hey, that actually sounds like a saga, those folk stories Icelanders have been telling for generations.

We arrived late, after driving through rain and snow, at Gladheimar Cabins, where I fell fast asleep inside my knotty-pine room under a comforter that had been stuffed into the car with everything else that would be needed at the Jorvik Hotel. I will be at Jorvik for one month at least and may fly back to Reykjavik at that time.

The cabin—a two-bedroom house, fully equipped kitchen, living room with leather couches, awesome views of a river and mountains and ducks and geese—was made of knotty-pine walls and a wooden floor and is just one of many cabins that await weary travelers.

The next day, the journey continued on through a varied terrain, including dark hills with ribbons of snow, reminding me of gingerbread sprinkled with powdered sugar.

Then, Siggi made a turn off the beaten track, and I wondered if this was the turn I saw on the map that showed the route to Thorshofn? My question was answered with a surprise.

The Godafoss Waterfall!

White sheets of thunderous water dump down over rocks and empty into a blue pool. The water then cascades on into the Skjálfandafljót River. The Godafoss, meaning the Waterfall of Gods, roars down in north central Iceland.

It's cold up here.

Today is Sunday, and the town of 500 people is closed down. There was a little bit more activity in town yesterday but not much more. I took a walk through the little village and observed the fishing/harbor area, the little church on the hillside, the public school, and the houses that are spread about. The ocean was calm with ducks bobbing up and down and seagulls flying freely as they like to do.

It was cold, but I was comfortable with my Icelandic wool sweater and layers of clothing underneath. Back at the hotel, as I sat by the big window overlooking the fjord, it began to snow great big flakes that lasted about five minutes.

But today, it was about 65,000 degrees below zero. Exaggeration helps to set the scene so you'll believe me. I walked the opposite direction of the town, where I wanted to have a look at the airstrip I may be flying out of in a month. I didn't get very far after realizing I'd better go back and double my warming efforts.

With wool gloves and a stocking cap Siggi had loaned me, I started again up the road toward the runway that was not yet visible. The ocean was more active than the calm of the day before.

I had asked two men, who were dressed in yellow rain coats, where the airstrip was, and they said about one kilometer that way, and they pointed up the road.

The harsh wind blowing toward my direction was so cold, my glasses were frozen to my frozen face, and my hands matched. But by now, you know me, don't you? Can't give up, no sirree, so I forged on, taking my fingers out of the fingers of the gloves and putting them back inside like fists, and I pulled the hat down as far as it would go over my face with just enough space left to see.

I passed a few houses, and then there was nothing. Then up ahead, I saw an information sign in Icelandic and English that told about the area and what lay ahead.

Seems a Norwegian boat capsized many decades ago, and all but one person died. The boat is still visible, I'm told. I will get up there one of these days. A village close to that accident has long been uninhabited. I could only imagine it looks like what I remember of ghost towns in Colorado, but that Icelandic village would be much older.

By now, I could see the runway. The windsock gave the direction of the wind, and you betcha, it was blowing right on my face. The runway was on a light slope. It would have been fun to see the plane crabbing into the wind to land, slightly uphill.

Now, it was time to turn back away from no man's land, and on the way back, tiny pin drops of snow stung the exposed parts of my face.

From the window

It is so beautiful outside the big window while I warm up inside the Jorvik Hotel. It is bright red on one side of the fjord with lots of blue in the middle from the sky down to the water, and then there is a sliver of a moon and one star. The fjord is wide, and the water is busy tonight. It's been cloudy and dark most of the day, but just yesterday morning, the sun peeked through the clouds onto the water, and up until nine p.m., the sun was brilliant.

The scene changes just as fast as I learn about this magnificent part of our world. The varied bird life must know how blessed they are, for they are abundant and fly past the window for our entertainment. I must tell myself this is not a dream; I am really here on the Arctic Circle, and it is truly beautiful. The show outside is a gift for me. I relish the site and know there will be more days and nights like this.

The fjord water is moving straight out from the shoreline to the fjord. The wind is very strong and creating this phenomenon. I've never seen ocean water move so quickly the opposite way, with nothing coming back.

Tsunami?

I think there are waves underneath that we cannot see.

White flesh in a hot pot

Okay, I figure it was about 600 pounds of the whitest flesh you have ever seen. Flesh on three women who haven't seen the sun for a very long time. Six blue eyes looked at me as I, with my green eyes, slithered my flesh down to boil in the neighborhood hot pot. I sat knee-to-knee with strangers who didn't speak my mother tongue.

There are times like this I have to imagine that someone picked me up and plunked me down in unfamiliar surroundings just to see what I would do. I sat, getting warmed up, and that felt good. A young blonde lady came over and asked if I wanted to join in on an aerobic exercise class. Sure, I did, so I climbed out with the other white-fleshed women and men who joined us for an hour workout in the pool.

Then back to the hot pot to soak some more. A gentleman who works at the pool brought a pitcher of ice water and glasses for all of us so we wouldn't dehydrate. That sounds funny—don't dehydrate while you're sitting in water.

Then there were four women and a man in the pot. Soon, another woman wanted to get into the pot, and there was some discussion. The gentleman hopped out, and the woman took over the hot pot seat from him. I figured out it must have meant that there could only be five people in a pot at a time. I can see why; that's a lot of knees, ankles, toes, and derrieres.

Before he got out, the gentleman tried to tell me that he was a farmer. He searched for the English words to tell me he raised sheep. When he said "cheap," I baaed like a lamb, and he smiled and nodded his head. See, you can make yourself understood even if you must use animal sound.

Chapter Two

May, 2012

A gold earring led to chance meetings.

It's May 1, and a Labor Day holiday in Iceland. All the stores, schools, banks, and post offices are closed. But a celebration took place at the Thorshofn Town Hall honoring those who labor. It was then that I unexpectedly found myself celebrating with the mayor and other townsfolk.

The day before, after I missed the gold earring out of my ear, I planned to trace my path back to the pool. It's ironic that every time I lose an earring, I remember I had my ears pierced so that I'd stop losing earrings. I've lost more of them since the piercing. The same man who encouraged drinking water while cooking in a pot is the manager of the pool and the community hall. He assured me if the earring is found, he'll let me know.

"Go back there and have some soup," he said as he pointed to the back of the building.

"Soup? I just wanted to know about my earring."

"I know, but we're eating soup now. It's a holiday. You're welcome to go back there and have some soup."

Okay, that decision was easy. There was one man sitting at the table. He looked at me and said something in Icelandic. I told him I couldn't speak Icelandic.

"Well, then. Let's speak English," he responded and then moved down the table to sit across from me. That was Vilhjalmur A. Thordarson, a retired pilot who had spent a 50-year career with Icelandair.

Nice gentleman. He's been skiing in Colorado, places familiar to me, and he also drove down Highway 101 from San Francisco on his way to San Diego. He and his brother stopped in Monterey, enjoying the usual tourist attractions. He mentioned knowing John Steinbeck's writings and could understand the fishing industry as it must have been back in the day of the fish canneries. It's worthwhile to mention here that Icelanders love to read and are well-read. Almost everyone who learns I'm from Monterey County has mentioned Steinbeck. Vilhjalmur spoke about a Clint Eastwood movie that was filmed here, *Flags of Our Fathers*, a story that took place near Japan. Vilhjalmur splits his time between Reykjavik and a house some kilometers from the town.

While we sat together, others began to join the festivities. There were the aerobics instructor, some of the people I've met in the swimming pool, and other familiar faces. Vilhjalmur pointed out the town mayor and then motioned the mayor to come over and meet me.

Gunnolfur Larusson is the *sveitarstjóri*, or mayor, of the town of 500. He explained that the town commission, which meets twice a month, hires a mayor. The position is like the town manager of an American town. He invited me to come to his office whenever I wanted to. While I'm almost always with my camera, this morning I didn't have it because the mission was just to find the earring. Nice people and good soup warmed the day, but no photo.

After that, I took another walk all the way to the airstrip, and I didn't leave without the camera. The port has a tower that was empty of an operator, so I assume it operates as a non-tower. There were no planes in sight.

The biggest moment of the day, aside from meeting the nice folks at the hall, was the chance meeting with a group of folks riding Icelandic horses. I first saw them saddling the horses as I passed the farm. Then they galloped down the road, and I took photos as quickly I could get the camera focused. One guy stopped and asked me if I wanted a photo. He got his horse and another one turned around for the photo, and he spent some time chatting with me.

He was born and raised in the area and believes we'll probably see each other again in this town. No gold earring could have surpassed the day and the lovely chance meetings.

Traveling on a dime takes creativity.

Traveling on a dime requires the utmost in creativity. One idea is to find a place where you can cook your own meals. However, the downside of that is you miss the atmosphere of the area, its people, the environment, and the local food.

To discover the food of the people is to discover what they are about. Restaurants afford that possibility unless, of course, you only stick to your comfort zone.

An example of getting out of my comfort zone can well be the leg of lamb that sits inside the refrigerator of the Hotel Jorvik.

For almost two years now, I have gone back to a diet I had a long time ago, and that included the elimination of meat. It's been easy to stick with that plan, although when I was a guest at someone's home, I would break that resolve without any qualms.

So I'm not a full-fledged, dyed-in-the-wool vegetarian, as proven recently when I agreed with Siggi that I would go in halves with him on the lamb purchase. That will take me out of my comfort zone once again.

Staying in this hotel is another way I have saved a dime while traveling. That is because of the agreement I made with

Siggi that I would pay part of the rent and help out a bit for the rest of what it would cost to stay for one month.

There are two men who live away from this town but who will come here to work a few days out of the week. They work building the new fish production plant. I will be keeping their rooms and bathroom clean every week when Siggi leaves. I will also force a birth control pill down the throat of the cat once a week.

"If you forget the pill, I may end up sending you a box of kittens," warned Siggi.

These aren't big, labor-intensive assignments, and doing them just becomes part of the adventure of living as an expat.

The Hotel Jorvik (*Jorvik* means York in English) sits with a view of the Thistle Fjord. How the fjord got that name is anyone's guess. But the view out of a wall-sized window is awesome.

The ducks, geese, and occasional fishing boat returning down the fjord to the harbor are sights to remember. The scene changes often from complete fog to brilliant sun, from the sunset late at night to the moon reflecting on the water. The water moves with the whims of the ocean—sometimes rapidly in waves breaking close to the house and sometimes calm as a summer lake.

"Watching the fjord is like watching a fire," Vilhjalmur Thordarson said. That is so true. It stays the same and it changes, as well.

The hotel has many rooms to accommodate a group of people and would make a perfect spot for a writer or artist retreat. It's quiet, and the Wi-Fi has no glitches in the system; you can get on-line with little effort. I could see several creative people coming to dinner at the large table in the dining area.

Another way to save a dime while traveling is to enjoy the atmosphere of the area, not to hang out at only the tourist destinations where you're just going to see other tourists lining up to see what you can see in pictures. Go to a neighborhood coffee shop, sit down and observe.

A few days ago, I sat in a little restaurant/convenience store/ gas station and watched the lady prepare food for the day. There were the lamb, potatoes, and gravy for lunch, and brown bread with butter and coffee for breakfast.

Then I observed the customers coming in, asking questions, purchasing items, and eating their lunches with other friends. The camaraderie was fun and free to watch.

Walking to town and meeting the folks

On the way to the village today, it felt almost warm, but walking back, the wind was heading my way, and boy, was it cold.

The purpose of the walk this morning was to talk with the mayor. However, I learned from the two nice ladies who work in the office, Didda and Suala, that he went to Reykjavik and wouldn't be back until Monday.

Another purpose this morning was to get a good photo of the village from the edge of town. I saw the possibility of this the other day when I left the camera at home.

Also, I had planned to find a restaurant hidden near the fishing port. Siggi told me there was one, but I thought walking that way was off-limits to people not involved with the industry or the building of a new fish production plant that is going on now.

I found the restaurant, walked up the rough, wooden steps, and met Adalbjorn Arnarsson. He is the new owner of the restaurant he named Fontur, for the name of the edge of the island. He was such a nice man, and he, like many others, has seen me walking around town. He quickly made me feel welcome.

"It's a bit too early for lunch. I'll serve lunch in a half hour."

"Okay, I'll walk around and take photos. But I'll be back."

I've taken note that other people have begun to smile at me, letting me know they have also seen me in the village—the stranger in town.

I came back to the restaurant where Adalbjorn offered me a typical Icelandic lunch of fish in a gravy sauce made from the fish, with potatoes and salad. I know the salad had grated carrots in it and one other ingredient; I think it was celery root. I ate my lunch while workmen from the plant came in and got their lunch, as well.

I felt like the oddity at the lunch table, so I started conversations with some of the workers.

Birds and natural wonders

"Laureen, come and look out of the window! Hurry!" Siggi hollered at me while I was washing dishes.

I did, and there they were—two beautiful white swans flying past the living room window. Now, I ask you. Where else would I have seen swans flying past my window? Anyone who loves bird-watching would stay busy in Iceland, for the island has hundreds of bird species and categories under each species. Right now, while sitting at the window, looking out at the fjord and over about two inches of snow that continue to fall, I see a family of ducks in the water, and they are a variety of colors.

Two migrating birds flew into the area a day ago—the golden plover, or the *Pluvialis apricaria,* and the great northern diver. According to Dick Vuijk and his website www.iceland-nh.net, Iceland is the stopover for birds spending winter on the European continent. Birds nesting in cliffs, as the puffins do, are notable in Iceland and the Faroe Islands. In June, I'll be in the Faroe Islands and will no doubt see puffins and other species there.

Nature and colors abound on this beautiful island, with unbelievable sites of fast-flowing rivers; bumps of green and yellow grasses; blue skies (when it isn't snowing or raining); horses of all colors; red, aluminum house roofs; yellow, red, and purple flowers breaking through the ground; and glacier-formed valleys; with one remarkable site that must be shared.

Almost two weeks ago, on the way to Thorshofn, we ventured off the road a spell to an unbelievable site. I'll do my best to describe it.

Ásbyrgi is about a three-mile, horseshoe-shaped wall of stones formed around 3,000 years ago as a result of glacial flooding. It is protected inside the Jökulsárgljúfur Natural Park and is appropriately referred to as a natural wonder.

A natural wonder it is. We began to view the rock-studded wall, which is at least 100 meters tall, from the car window, and then we parked at the beginning of a long walk through a willow-lined pathway, listening to echoing sounds of bird songs.

When we got to the end of the trail at the curve of the wall, I observed waterfalls that flow gently down to a fast-moving, narrow river.

Going back and walking along the wall, our voices echoed in the clear acoustics created within the walls of the Asbyrgi.

It looks as if it were designed by medieval architects as a fortress to protect a castle. Not so. It was designed by nature, and in my opinion, it could be named among the natural wonders of the world.

Surprises

Woke up this morning really early to the sounds of a cat hissing and screeching. Smoky sat on the windowsill growling back at the offender. I looked out and saw a black and white cat ready for a fight.

I closed the window and settled back down until Smokey decided she needed to go outdoors to stir up some trouble. I let her out. About three hours later, screaming, growling, hissing, and scurrying around woke me again. The other cat was in my room. If the cat got loose in the house, I'd never get it out, and it would wake the others who were still asleep. So I closed the curtains around the black and white cat and pushed it out the window. I went back to sleep, and when I woke up, guess what I saw? Sprinkles of snow on the ground. Maybe that's what got the cats in turmoil.

Getting acquainted in Thorshofn (Þórshöfn)

On the way to visit the Mayor *(Sveitarstjóri)*, Mr. Gunnolfur Larusson, I began my walk on the snowy road and jumped back when I saw two teenagers in a car slipping and sliding, laughing all the way. An adult man driving behind them had an angry look on his face. When the two cars drove on down the road, I ventured across the road to the sidewalk, all the while telling myself, "I will not fall, I will not fall."

I was early for the 11 o'clock appointment, so I went into the Grill where the owner, Soley Indridad, greeted me. She had been gone for a few days to Reykjavik, so other women had taken over for her. She asked me who I was and what I would be doing in the town, and she seemed interested in my plans. I purchased a muffin called Aunt Mabel's—Original American Taste. Hmmm, I've never had a muffin with a burst of creamy caramel inside before. It must have originated somewhere in America, but not sure where. This one was made right in Iceland.

When it was time to leave, I made tracks in the snow to the City Hall and was greeted warmly by Mayor Larusson. He answered all the questions I had about the town, his job, and his hopes for the townsfolk.

"We are trying to make certain that everyone here has work," he said. He added that because of the fish production company now in the works, everyone is currently employed. He also mentioned that each family in town has two to four children, and he wants to make their needs a high priority.

The building of another harbor across the peninsula at Finnafjordur is another business he is working on with other folks. A larger harbor will benefit both communities and provide more opportunities.

Larusson then told me about a woman who once worked for the town to increase the number of its visitors, and he would make it possible for me to meet with her. He called her and made an appointment for us to meet later. He then gave me a pin with the logo of Thorshofn—a picture of a bird and a fish on both sides of the peninsula. I'll cherish it, for sure.

I met with Halldora, who is presently promoting the Guesthouse Ytra Lon Farm Hostel and the experiences being offered through the hostel. There is one other guesthouse, as well, plus the Jorvik Hotel where I'm staying. Halldora, the town's ambassador, gave a rundown of the reasons people should travel to the Langanes Peninsula, beginning with the variety of bird species.

"We have a rich bird life here."

Bird watchers would find it a paradise. She mentioned the northern gannet, which can be spotted from land only in Iceland.

"Usually, they can only be seen from the sea," Halldora said.

Other amenities found in the town according to Halldora include a car rental agency available from the city of Akureyi and managed by a local, the swimming pool, two hot pots, and the harbor.

"You can go to the harbor around four o'clock and see fishermen coming back from their trip," Halldora said.

"The town has many clubs with a variety of interests, which keep people busy with their hobbies, and there is also someone who does hair care and another person does nail treatment. I can have my tires changed and repairs on my car and the yearly checkup required by law, in this town," she added.

"Also in the town, you can find a health center with a doctor and a pharmacy, and an ambulance and police department, as well. And, we have an airport."

Siggi Magnusson, the owner of the Jorvik Hotel where I'm staying, had previously mentioned some of the town's features, also, and while looking outside the window that takes up most of one wall, he pointed out that from this vantage point, you can watch the sunset change its direction throughout the year until the solstice. At some point, you can see the sun set halfway down to the ocean and then watch it start rising again.

"This is because we're so close to the Arctic Circle," Siggi said.

Anyone interested in an Icelandic experience should not only stop at the capitol city of Reykjavik, but journey on to the town of Thorshofn *(Þórshöfn)*. No disappointments here, believe me.

Playing reporter

Today I met the police chief, Jon Stefansson, as he was driving out of the station.

"Hello, my name is Laureen Diephof, and I've been in town a while, and I want to write a story about this town."

"Yes, I know. I've seen you in town."

So now, I'm starting to see familiar faces, and now that they know what I'm about, they are smiling and waving to me.

Chief Stefansson keeps the peace in the four towns of Bakkafjördur, Raufarhöfn, Kópasker, and this town, Thorshofn. In all the time he has served in the law enforcement capacity, since 1984, he has never used his club or his mace. Since 1987, he has not used his gun, and he keeps it in the office. He does not own a taser.

"Are you saying there's no crime here?"

"My main job is traffic."

"Yes, I have seen people drive fast."

"And, I also keep people from driving drunk and with drugs."

"Is that a problem here?"

"Yes, a bit. People have too much to drink and then get in their cars and try to drive home."

"I've heard that the longest anyone can stay in prison in Iceland is 16 years. Is this correct?"

"Yes, that's the longest time, and we have many fewer people in prison than you do in the States."

"What if someone who has killed and served 16 years comes out and kills again?"

"Nothing," he said, and shook his head as if that never happens. "Good people live here," he added.

Chief Stefansson said he will retire in five years. He has two sisters living in the U.S., one in Illinois and one in Florida. He occasionally visits them, he said.

Before meeting the police chief, I had just come back from eating lunch at the Fontur Restaurant, which, as stated earlier, caters to the lunch crowd of people who work at the fish production facility now being built.

Lunch was lamb, potatoes, gravy, peas, and three kinds of salads. It was delicious and healthful. Coffee was served after lunch. Water is featured in every restaurant in Iceland and is usually the beverage of choice. Some restaurants put glass bottles of water on the table. Water in Iceland is plentiful and very tasty. It reminds me of the cold water we enjoyed while living in the Colorado mountains.

More surprises for me on this island

The wind is blowing strong, and the water in the fjord has been flowing south instead of north for the past two days. Being on an island out in the ocean brings all kinds of surprises. This morning, while looking out the big window, the water was blue and rolling, and a large fishing boat was making its way back to the Thorshofn port. I grabbed my camera, threw on my Icelandic sweater, slipped on my shoes, and ran outside to get a shot.

Later in the afternoon, I faced strong winds while heading to the hot pot, keeping my balance and trying not to fall over. The hot pot was a welcome and appreciated way to get warm again.

The day before, I walked back from the town a little different way and took photos from a different view of the hotel where I'm staying.

Today, it was time for me to change the bedding of the men who are working on the new fish production facility, and I had to give a birth control pill to the cat. I accomplished both projects and am off the hook until next week. Not a hard job at all, and the benefits are a tremendous view, a nice place to sleep, and an atmosphere of a small fishing village that I wouldn't be able to experience otherwise. The history of the hotel began when it was a summer home of Siggi's family until he purchased it from his mother four years ago.

Senior citizens, get off the couch and see the world!

Some people have said that I'm some kind of an extraordinary woman because of the yearlong journey I'm on. What?

Believe me when I tell you that getting on an airplane and flying to another country is not that difficult. Sure, you get tired dragging suitcases, getting your passport and ticket out, and sitting for long hours on an airplane. But once you reach your destination and rest up, it's easy. By the way, airlines are helpful in providing special care for those in wheelchairs or those who are sight-impaired. I don't use that helpfulness as of yet, but I will when and if needed in the future so I can continue to meet the good people in the world.

Not only that, the little glitches and unexpected events can be the most interesting part of the journey if you have a positive view.

Consider this. Americans are equal to the United Kingdom, according to the statistics on NationMaster.com, in that the average number of TV-watching hours per person is 28 hours per week.

If that doesn't alarm you, maybe this will. According to the A.C. Nielsen Co., by the time a person reaches the age of 65, that person will have spent nine years glued to the tube.

Here's another consideration. The Center for Disease Control claims that, on average, American men are 17 pounds overweight, and women are 19 pounds overweight.

When I faced up to the facts that I was overweight and in pain when I walked, even after half of a block, and that I was watching TV after working in front of a computer all day, and

I was no longer feeling the joy on the job, it was time to make changes.

I took out the TV, much to the chagrin of the company that provided the violence and porn into my personal space, and I made a plan to quit the job, learn about other cultures and their people, and improve my health.

I'm happy to say I have lost nine-and-one-half pounds, not only because I'm no longer gorging myself out of boredom and unhappiness, but because I'm walking every day and can now walk further. And the fresh air, ah! I have changed my attitude away from the bitterness I was feeling every day and have, instead, made up my mind that this would be the year where everything I experience will be done in an attitude of positive acceptance. So far, it's working, and I feel great.

Blue sky, blue fjord

The ocean and the sky meet today in blue. It's no wonder blue is the most favored color, some research has stated. The beauty of today's view almost made me change my favorite choice of color from red to blue.

I walked down the road in the morning, heading to the grocery store. Today isn't freezing cold but still cool enough for a coat, jacket, or raincoat. Raincoat?

Yes, instead of the mysterious lady in the brown and white Icelandic sweater, I opted for the black raincoat and black T-shirt, pants, and shoes. Now I'm the mysterious, white-haired lady who walks around town wearing black clothes and dark sunglasses.

Actually, one of the women in the restaurant/convenience store/coffee shop said that when I first arrived, people were wondering who I was and what I would be doing in this small town.

"That's not unusual," she said. "When someone gets a new car, for example, that's the latest news that goes around town."

On the way back from the store, I took a photo of the blue sky and fjord and one of the cutest little houses made of corrugated aluminum, with fetching lace window curtains. The house sits on the cliff overlooking the water.

Sugar in mashed potatoes

Yesterday, determined to head down to the little grocery store for lunch at the Grill and a soak in the hot pot, the wind pushed me all the way down the hill. There were times I had to catch my balance on the road. I walked on the road because the few sidewalks that exist were covered with snow. It was a wet, sloppy, slushy snow that turns to mud whenever the sun begins to melt it down. I don't have boots, to-boot.

I made it to the grocery store, purchased a few items, and put them in my bag with the swimsuit and towel, then hopped over the snow to the Grill. Every day the Grill Change to restaurant/convenience store/gas station puts out a lunch and keeps it under flame from around 11:00 a.m. until around 3:30 p.m. Today was the first time to treat myself to lunch there. I had time to kill before trudging back up the hill to the hot pot.

Today's lunch was a casserole with ground beef, spaghetti, carrots, and a cheese topping; a salad of grapes, red bell pepper, cucumbers, and lettuce; and a rhubarb syrup. I didn't know where I should put the syrup but dashed some on the plate. The meal also came with mashed potatoes that had a surprise ingredient. The potatoes were mashed with the usual milk, butter, and salt, and the surprise ingredient was sugar.

"Is this a typical way to prepare mashed potatoes?" I asked Hulda, the young lady who has been very accommodating toward me since I've been here, and who speaks perfect English.

"Yes, don't you like it?"

"Oh, yes, I do. It's just different than I expected."

I told her that in Holland, nutmeg is the surprise addition to mashed potatoes.

Hulda is a delightful young woman who agreed to print out my plane ticket for when I leave Thorshofn in about two weeks. She spent two months as an *au pair* in Spain and will continue on to Iceland University in Reykjavik to pursue a degree in physical care for the handicapped. We spoke for quite some time, while I worked up the spirit to tackle the uphill trudge to the hot pot.

Finally, I pulled myself and the bag uphill, facing the icy wind and a grey sky that was now freezing the slush into slippery, crunchy mounds of little snow caps. Now I felt it wasn't safe to walk on the road because of the ice. I made it, walked into the town hall where the swimming pool and hot pot are located, and announced, "This is summer in Iceland?"

In the Arctic Circle, you barely turn your head and the environment changes, almost as quickly as boys become men, it seems.

It is unusual weather; two different people have told me this. In fact, Siggi said he was worried about the tiny birds that flew to the area in search of the warm air.

In the hot pot, I soaked along with an Italian, a sprightly and muscled young man who will be in the area for two weeks. He told me through smiles that he'll hike in the peninsula and camp out. Camping out? In the snow?

That's right. He's all prepared with a sleeping bag, tent, and everything he'll need for the next two weeks. He works at a water park in the town where he lives in Italy and has long weeks of vacation, so he hikes in different locations every year. His work at a water park explains his perfect swimming stroke and powerful kick while swimming laps, which he did when he wasn't in the hot pot.

A young father and his boy of about three also stepped into the hot pot, and while the father ignored me, the little boy began to throw plastic cups of water out of the pot onto the floor. The father ignored him, as well.

When I finally felt warm enough for the last part of my journey, I got out, got dressed, and found the Italian in the lobby writing in his journal. That's a read I would covet.

Right now at 9:45 a.m., the area is fogged in, strong winds continue to roll the ocean in high waves, and the snow remains bright and white on the ground.

I have a screw loose.

I have a screw loose! That happened this morning when I tried to make my first cup of coffee. It's one of those deals where you put the coffee into a glass container, then pour boiling hot water on top of the coffee grounds, and then you press down a spring-loaded handle until the water is squeezed out of the grounds. Otherwise known as a French press, it makes a muddy cup of coffee. It's okay, not perfect, not Starbucks' quality but coffee all the same.

This morning, the whole thing came apart, and when I tried to figure out how to put it all back together with the spring and the filter and the rest of the pieces, I saw that it was missing a tiny screw. It may be tiny and insignificant, but my future here in this house with coffee depends on that little screw. It wasn't on the floor or the counter, and I even tried to wade a bit through the garbage until I told myself to stop that!

I went down to the grocery store and showed the manager what I needed. She couldn't help me but tried to find the words to tell me where a car repair shop is located, and where I could possibly get some help.

Then I walked catty-corner over to the Grill and ordered lunch. It was a crepe stuffed with rice, corn, and cheese, plus a salad. While I sat there, a table full of workmen sat next to me, and while I couldn't understand a thing they were saying, I realized how laughter is universal. They could have been joking about me for all I know, but their laughter made me feel good.

After lunch, I showed Hulda the part of the coffee pot I needed to fix. She also told me about the car repair shop.

So I'll go there tomorrow and see what they can do. Meanwhile, today is a holiday and most everything is closed, including schools, the post office, and town offices. I asked four people what the holiday was all about and no one knew the answer.

"It has something to do with Easter," Hulda said.

Boys become men.

Looking out of the big window inside the Jorvik Hotel where I'll be for another two weeks, I see turquoise and blue water that is slowly rolling to the shoreline. The snow on the mountains across the fjord is allowing some dark blue-black spots to peek out. Snow around the hotel is melting, leaving mounds of dark, yellow-beige grass trying to make a breakthrough.

Yesterday, the sun shone most of the day. It had been two days since I had been outdoors, and I took advantage of the sunshine to walk to the hot pot. I sat with a fisherman and his son and was later joined by another fisherman. The first fisherman said he often goes to another town to fish for the type of fish he needs for the market. We talked a bit about politics, and I mentioned to him that an interviewer on a radio station from the U.S. asked me if Thorshofn's city council holds their meetings in the hot pot, and I had said, "Sure."

Both fishermen laughed and said a lot is discussed away from the meetings, and probably some right there in the hot pot, but nothing official, of course. I then told them about the "Brown Act" whereby, in California, council members cannot meet apart from the regular council meetings.

The subject changed, and the first fisherman pointed out that the pool is 13-years-old. During the summer—whenever that is—the ceiling opens up. Large doors on the side of the building, where tables and chairs sit waiting for the summer crowd, also open to the outdoors.

The fishermen told me about the sports kids play in the town—a ball game I'm not familiar with, and swimming, volleyball, and soccer, called football.

When I left the hot pot, I sat down and drank a Coke, as I felt a little weak. Guess the time in the hot pot was overspent a bit.

Then, walking home, I observed about eight teenaged boys talking in a group on the street, wearing shorts and T-shirts. Soon they ran on down the road jogging around snow clumps. A man stood on the sidewalk, and I asked him if the boys were on a track team.

"No, they're on a football team, and they are just warming up."

"Will they just keep on running so they don't have to prac-tice?" I laughed.

"No, they know me, and they do what I tell them." His turn to laugh.

It was enjoyable to see the teenagers. They made me miss my sons at that age and my grandsons, as well.

In the Arctic Circle, you barely turn your head, and the envi-ronment changes; almost as quickly as my sons grew up, it seems.

The Night of the Golden Plover

The golden plover, a sight to behold by bird lovers in Iceland, is lip-smacking dinner to the cat. The day began with me at my computer answering messages, while Siggi, on his computer, kept looking outside to see yet another bird that has made its way up north. He started putting his bird photos on the website that will be launched in a few days, www.birds.iniceland.com. He is blessed with an artist's eye in photography.

"Look, there's a golden plover," he would say. Or, "Look! There's the oyster catcher," or, "Laureen, listen. Hear it? That's the great northern loon."

Man, oh, man, bird watchers get excited.

Then, "Look what's out there!" I thought oh, yeah, another bird.

"Hey, that's the Italian I met the other day," I announced, as he walked up to the door carrying equipment on his back almost as big as he.

He wanted to know if there was any room in the hotel, as he was so tired. Siggi told him no, but he was welcome to sleep on the couch for no charge. He also wanted to take a shower, and that, too, was granted.

The next event, while the Italian was in the shower, has two different versions, and I'll go with mine first. When I went downstairs to my room, what did I see? A golden plover scurrying, desperate to make a getaway from the cat that had brought it into the room via the window.

"Siggi, you've got to come and see this," I shouted. One time a big bumblebee flew around between the curtain and the window, so I expected him to be ready for something like that.

Oh no, the bird was now in the hallway, and then it ran back into the room fluttering its wings and fleeing under the second bed in the room, wings flapping like wind sails. Siggi tried to catch the cat and made a Bobby Crocker-like baseball slide to home base (I miss my grandson) as he slid under the other bed reaching for the cat. He got the cat outside and then picked up the bird and got it settled in the palm of his hand.

Okay, here's Siggi's version of what happened.

"I knew the Italian was taking a shower, and you exclaimed, 'Oh, wow!' and I thought it sounded like you were pleasantly surprised. She's caught the Italian in the shower, I was thinking. I thought I might just check it out, and then that's when I saw the bird and dove for the cat."

"Yeah, right, Siggi."

After Siggi got the cat outside and the bird settled in his hand, he told me to keep the cat inside my room, so I waited until the culprit came back in through the window. I closed the cat up inside her prison. Siggi was petting the plover's feathers, keeping it calm, while waiting to ensure the cat was locked in before freeing the bird. We waited for the Italian to come out of the shower so he could witness the bird's escape to its own environment.

About an hour later, and after many photos were taken and the bird was no longer stressed, it was time to release it. We stood outside in the cold wind while Siggi held the bird high in the air, and we all bid it farewell.

We heard a "beep" and observed its mate joining it on the ground. Together, they literally flew off together into the red-orange sunset.

Okay, you may think this is the end of the story, but it isn't. Not too long after the bird was released, two young German ladies came to the door looking for a place to sleep that night. Same story—no room in the inn, but you can come in and sleep on the floor, Siggi told them. The ladies were pleased with the offer and slept on mattresses Siggi brought up from the basement.

Otherwise, they would have had to sleep in the car. It's too cold for that.

The Germans left the next day for hiking in the northeast side of Iceland, and the Italian would catch a bus in the afternoon, heading back to Reykjavik.

I will always remember "The Night of the Golden Plover."

Changing scenes

The window scene from Hotel Jorvik changed in one day. The day ended with sunshine on Saturday, and the next day, the view changed when the fog rolled in early, accompanied by strong winds and then snow, and finally, a complete whiteout. An abstract piece of art in the form of ice crystals completely covered the large window.

Before the winds became too strong to go outside, I tramped on the grass to catch the waves in a photo, but I had to fight the wind to get back into the safety of the hotel. The waves grew bigger and bigger, and I thought of my son, Larry. Oh, how he'd love to pull on a wetsuit and catch a wave. Heck, I would have liked to have donned a wetsuit and just played in the waves.

Ducks disappeared for awhile. I assumed they hid out among the rocks, but they reappeared again. Guess when they get hungry, nothing will stop a good fisherman, be it human or duck.

Nighttime was tough on the cat I call Smoky. She wanted to go out of my window, which is her only outlet at night, but the wind yanked the curtains out the window like a sailing jib. The noise of the wind, the blinding snow, and the cold air made her afraid to jump. So she whined, questioning what to do.

When the window was open, the bedroom door clanged back and forth to keep the hard-working men in the hotel from their sleep.

So when she asked again to go outside, I pushed her out, and in a split second, she jumped back in. The next two times, I pushed her out and shut the window. She whined to come back in within a few minutes. That satisfied her for a little while, at least.

Then another challenge came this morning when I washed a few things out and tramped through about one foot of snow to the clothesline. It's just a few yards away, but the wind hampered the walk. I managed to hang up one T-shirt with about 15 pins, and the last time I looked, it was swinging around and around the line like a trapeze artist.

It's a great day for the hot pot, which opens up at four o'clock. You can bet your bottom krona, I'll be there.

A long walk

I went to bed in daylight last night. It was after 11:00 p.m., and at 3:30 a.m., I awoke to daylight again. I managed to sleep a bit more, and that was a good thing because of the energy it took to do what I did today.

I walked to the medical center to see if I could purchase those little pills that keep heartburn away. I walked in and noticed the Icelandic unspoken rule was in force—you must take your shoes off, which is appropriate in everyone's homes, as well.

The pharmacy part of the operation wasn't opened. Heartburn will have to wait. Anything to do with antacid medicine is not available over the counter. As I said before, this means not even Tums. It's considered medicine. I began a walk toward the end of the Thistle Fjord, which, if you reach the end, would be about 20 or so miles. Along the way, there is a farm, old church, museum, cemetery, and sheep with baby lambs grazing, all within five miles of the hotel. The refreshing breeze nurtured my soul with smells of the ocean, seaweed, and fish, and also a hint of rain. It was quiet except for my footsteps on the gravel and birds whistling signals to each other, the sounds that make Iceland a bird lover's bliss.

Cars passed by until I got beyond the airstrip that is about one mile from the hotel. The museum and church with the sheep were within eyesight, but they seemed to keep moving farther away, and cars grew scarce. I hoped that someone would stop and ask if I would like a ride, to further my resolve to reach my destination.

Later, a truck did stop, and the driver asked me something, which I'm sure was, "Would you like a ride?" I told him that the museum and church up there was my destination and asked if he could take me there.

"Yes, I will. Come and get in."

The seat was so high, I could not hoist myself up easily, and he told me something that I thought was, "See the hummingbird?"

I stopped, turned around, and was about to ask him if there were hummingbirds in Iceland. I sure didn't know that.

He then pointed to the handle and said again, "See the hummingbird?"

"Oh no, I thought you said, 'See the hummingbird?'"

"No, he said, 'Use the handle.'"

That got a laugh out of both of us.

He dropped me off at the church and museum and said he'd be back the same way in about ten minutes. I told him to look for me walking down the road. If he didn't see me, he should just keep on going, and I'd walk back.

I took photos of the sheep and the babies, as well as the church, which looks as if it is still being used as a church. I peered into the window and saw that all the pews were inside.

The museum building was freshly painted, but I didn't see any signs of museum life around it. The windows were too high to look into. A cemetery is located down a bluff, and from the bluff, you can see an old American plane that crashed there during WWII.

The sheep were cautious around me so I respected their space, plus I didn't want to overexcite them and make life difficult for the sheep handlers. However, a mother and her baby walked out of the area while I was there. I quickly and quietly walked out of the gate, while they kept a cautious eye on me.

Easy day today

It was a quiet day. We need that sometimes to regroup and get ready for what's next. I braced myself against the wind and headed off to the post office. My grandson, Brandon Crocker, will graduate in June from St. Ignatius High School in San Francisco, and I had to get my letter and the gift in the mail so he would get them on time. But I was about 15 minutes too early for the post office, so I went into the Grill and had a yogurt drink. Yogurt is popular in Iceland, and it is good. I spoke for a while with Hulda, the young lady who will soon head off to college herself.

Then I went back to the post office, but I was still early, so I waited inside the space between the automatic door and the main door and entertained myself by stepping on the spot that would open and close the automatic door. Childish, huh? Yeah, I know.

When the doors opened, workers greeted me, and like everyone else by now, knew who I was. After taking care of business, I left and took photos of the harbor, police department, Hulda at the Grill, the post office, and another aluminum-sided house.

I was shivering, and the camera shook too much for a decent photo. But I did go into the grocery store and purchased a darning needle and black thread to hem my pants that are way too long. I couldn't find a regular needle so went with the darning kind, and, by the way, if your eyesight isn't too good, those needles are easier to thread.

Later in the day, I took another walk the opposite way and heard the sounds of the loa birds calling to each other. They sound like cell phones ringing.

I'm on Iceland National News!

Can you believe this? I was just interviewed on Iceland National News! Now I will no longer be mysterious. I had gone into the post office to buy a stamp for a postcard of Icelandic horses as a birthday greeting to my daughter-in-law, Sue Crocker.

The post office was closed, so I meandered over to the convenience store, gas station, and the Grill. I just happened to be there when a cameraman and a reporter came in. They were there to interview a 14-year-old boy who has his own boat and goes out to the fjord to fish. Someone in the store told the TV reporter and cameraman who I was and that I, too, had been a reporter.

They took me outside and interviewed me. The reporter asked me what I was doing in Iceland and in this small town in particular. I told them I was writing a book about my travels. They had me walk into the store, sit, and write notes into my little notebook. Can you believe that this was another time I did not have my camera with me? Oh, well. The men came from Reykjavik to do the boy's story, but now they have one of me, as well. What a hoot! The boy, Jon Fannar Jonsson, has a small motorboat and goes out whenever the weather permits and fishes away his idle hours. He showed me with his arms the largest fish he ever caught. It was a codfish, about three feet long. His mother works at the Grill and was photographed serving coffee to me. Then they interviewed her about her youngest son.

The cameraman, Benedikt Nickolas Ketilsson, and the reporter, Johannes Kristjansson, had been out with Jon earlier in the day to videotape him in his boat before they came into the store.

Ideas for travelers

On another note, I've had people asking me how I travel on a dime, and therefore, I will tell you here how I have made all of this possible so far.

The dream to travel and meet the good people in the world began when a financial guru—well, actually, just a smart friend—sat down with me, and between both of us we figured out that my working was actually costing me money. I was paying dearly for the upkeep on my car, gasoline, and rent, plus long hours of work that couldn't be interrupted during the day. We saw that if I just lived on the social security and any other money coming in from writing, I would be better off. Requests for a raise over four years were fruitless.

So in January, I began to make a plan to journey as far as I could go in one year on limited income using creativity, ingenuity, and joy. While still working, I paid for the first three flights and the first three places where I'd be staying. Then with some small savings and a substantial gift, I was on my way. I also gave up my apartment, sold and gave away lots of items, and stuffed the rest into storage.

Following are traveling tips for those who want to travel on a dime. I want to encourage other people of my age to get off the couch and see the world.

It is not necessary to join every tour that is offered wherever you go. Pick one that would thrill you most above all the rest.

Listen to people share their lives with you—those from other countries and the people where you are visiting. The greatest gift of all is the people you'll meet along the journey, and that is free.

Take local buses around the entire loop. If you're lucky, the bus driver will point out important sites and give you inside information if you appear to be open to that. Ask for a transfer, and get on another bus.

Purchase food at a grocery store, and make eating in a restaurant a special treat.

Don't be tempted to purchase useless souvenirs. Take home photos and memories.

Never expect the same comforts you are used to. Be open and accepting toward your surroundings. Try things out—new food, local customs and manners, and look for the joy in everything.

Never, ever criticize the country, city or town you are visiting. That's the ultimate insult and will get you nowhere.

The only problem I have experienced is the negativity about the United States. Whenever a person opens a dialog with, "In America, they. . . ," I know I'm going to get a slice of negativity pie thrown in my face. Often, it's people who have learned about the U.S. on television or in Hollywood movies. But it's thrown at me as a fact. Don't take it personally.

On the other side, I've experienced Americans who have spent a week or so in a foreign country and then consider themselves experts on that country, often offering sweeping generalizations. Remember we all have lots more to learn!

Aileen loved nature; wish she were here.

Wow, the changes out here on this Arctic Ocean island amaze me. Just yesterday, Siggi pointed out to me that in the fjord there were light spots where you could see to the bottom of the water, even from inside the window. Ducks were swimming and birds were chirping; all was calm.

Today, I'm sitting at the same window, listening to the wind and watching the water breaking fast along the shoreline. And that is not all. It is snowing. Yes, those big flakes look like someone just shook a giant blanket and cotton pieces of lint are floating gently down through the air.

You might think the calm the day before was peaceful, while today, the water and the storm are angry, but in reality, it's nature at its best.

Today is Mother's Day, and it's a perfect day to remember my mother, Aileen Kruse, who loved nature. She found it fun to sit very still and watch ants in an ant pile until she figured out who was the queen. She would comment on how hard they worked and how amazing it was that they could carry so much weight on their backs.

She would marvel at the artistry of a spider's web, and she found a bigger gift if there was a sparkle of water on the web.

She would listen to the birds in the birdbath on the side of our house and always had a story about the birds that created havoc and the docile ones that waited their turn to bathe.

A new spring blossom lifted her spirits and the spirits of those around her.

I wish she were here.

I'm old news in this town.

Yesterday afternoon, I hot-potted it again and met a nice man with his two-year-old, adorable son, adorable until he became jealous of the conversation between his dad and me. He started throwing swim fins and other water toys at my head. His dad tried to divert him, as you would get a dog to go fetch. He'd throw something far away, and the little guy would go get it and throw it at me. He was finally subdued a bit when a fisherman got into the hot pot with us and began to play with the little tyke.

The little guy's dad told me about his job as administrator of the roads in the village and surrounding area. He said the biggest problem was the government, but he didn't elaborate.

He had also been active as a town council member and also helped with education in the schools, but he gave up public service to be more with his family.

He has lived in Denmark for four years and said in order to speak English to me, he had to first translate it into Danish and then back into English.

"That's the problem I'm having," he said.

His English sounded perfect to me. Those Europeans are amazing for how they can go back and forth between their own languages, English, and other languages. In the States, we're lucky to learn a little bit of some other language in high school, but nothing to qualify us as fluent. I wish that would change.

He had a big smile on his face when I got into the hot pot, saying that the townsfolk had been wondering who I was. That's not the first time hearing that, as others have said the same thing. My appearance in this town is old news now, and I'll be moving on in seven more days.

I've been told that the show I was interviewed for will be shown next week on Icelandic TV. Hope it happens before I leave. The fisherman who joined us in the hot pot was also part of another story, aside from mine, and he gave me what he thought was the time it would air.

Back at home, a German couple—she a blonde, blue-eyed, tanned woman—and he—a dark-haired, blue-eyed, muscular man, also tanned—stayed all night before they took off this morning for the rest of their tour through Iceland. Both are border control agents and gave me some advice about traveling through European countries and how to stay legal.

Another view of Iceland

Siggi invited me to go for a drive with him out to another beach and to a different view of the land, so I jumped up like a puppy and said, "Yes, yes, me, me! Take me!"

It was a great offer because the views were spectacular, and I met the retired pilot, Vihjalmur Thordarson, as well as his daughter, son-in-law, two grandchildren, and an all-white Labrador.

And, then, there was that flock of swans. How many times in one's life would you have a chance to see more than one or two at a time? And now, there were well over 20. We stopped the car, and for a while they just stood there and watched us. Then, when Siggi made some noise, a few of them flapped their wings, rose, and flew away in a circle. That was a moment never to be forgotten. It's a privilege to see them in their natural surroundings.

An abundance of driftwood was strewn along the road—all shapes and sizes, including large logs, all ocean-weathered. Some that landed there came from Russia.

"Not as much comes from Russia as before because they have better ways of working with the logs so they don't lose as much," Siggi said.

We stopped at a dark, sandy beach, and while Siggi jogged, I looked for sea treasures. I pocketed a few items for the bowl I have sitting in storage. These will join sea relics from Panama, Costa Rica, The Netherlands, and of course, California.

We ventured on toward Vihjalmur Thordarson's farm that sits on a lake near the abandoned U.S. Army radar station hill, Heidarfjall. It is a sad history that has ruined the drinking water on the farm, resulting from the stored American Army waste left over from the station and buried in the hillside. The U.S., according to Thordarson, has never attempted to rectify the damage done to this one small farm.

Vihjalmur's daughter, Margaret Vihjalmsdottir, and her husband, Egill Palsson, came back from visiting Thorshofn with their two children. They took a little time from their home in Reykjavik to visit her dad on the farm.

They made pancakes, and we all sat in the kitchen talking and smearing whipping cream and jelly on the cakes.

Egill is a theater professor at Iceland University, and he also directs professional theater all over Europe. Soon he will be directing a theater production in Denmark. Margaret is a known actress in Iceland and internationally, as well. She can be seen in part on YouTube in *Falcons*, a movie she co-starred in with Keith Carradine.

Vihjalmur, if you remember, is the retired pilot of Icelandair. He was busy working on the land when we arrived but quickly got out of his boots to be a great host.

Names are interesting to note. In Iceland, women are given their father's first name, as Vihjalmur, and then "dottir" is added to that to make the last name. Sons get their last names the same way, but "son" completes the last name, as in Vihjalmur's last name, Thordarson.

"She's a pilot." Vihjalmur motioned toward me and told his daughter and son-in-law about our common interest.

Wind and gnomes

It is a six-clothespin-wind today.

I washed some clothes out, and the long-sleeved T-shirt is barely hanging on the line with six pins. The jeans have already lost one pant leg, with three pins, to the wind. And yesterday, I started toward a different road than the two I usually tramp on, but the wind was so strong that by fighting it while walking, I must have looked like a drunk. I aborted that plan and went to the Grill for lunch, instead.

There I had a lamb chop, small potatoes in a sweet sauce, gravy, rhubarb sauce, and a salad of cucumbers, grapes, and red bell pepper.

Then I went to the grocery store, purchased a yogurt drink, and walked home where I stayed the rest of the day until I talked to the man who lives two doors down from the Jorvik Hotel where I'm staying. I also read eBooks that I ordered from Amazon.

Back to the neighbor. When I first got here, when it was snowing, raining, windy and cold, until now, when it is just windy and cold, I noticed some stone work and other creative handmade items on the neighbor's front lawn. He was outside working when I walked by yesterday, and I decided to stop a while and chat with him. He showed me the inside of the shed where he works on the stone and driftwood urchins and other fetching critters that grace his lawn.

"Here, take this. You can have it."

He handed me a small statue with a head and body made of river stone with glass eyes and stone ears. I had to turn it down because this senior traveler has limited space and must abide by the airlines' weight rules for luggage. It would be too heavy to lug around the world. But I appreciated the gesture more than you could imagine.

He learned his English, he said, by watching TV. However, his wife is from Ireland, so that must have helped. I haven't met her yet, but I did go back and get more photos. I hope to see him and meet her at least once before I head back to Reykjavik.

There are so many things I have learned to enjoy in Iceland, and one of them is you can buy a half-loaf of bread. The bread choices are good—those dense rye loaves that remind you of when bread was baked in an oven that also kept the house warm.

Another item I saw in the second largest city, Akureyri, was the red stoplight shaped like a heart. That would have been fun sitting in on the discussion when the city council decided their stoplight needed to be shaped like a heart.

Also in that city and in Reykjavik, as well, there are book-stores—large ones where you can sit and read, drink coffee, eat lunch, and stay as long as you want, all in prime city locations. Icelanders are known for their love of reading. I have just finished *Independent People* by Halldór Laxness, a 1955 Nobel Prize recipient in literature. All Nordic countries are known for their saga stories, folklore that includes little gnomes and other invisible people, and those books are abundantly available in Iceland's book stores.

Touring with Cathleen

Neighbor to the Jorvik Hotel, Cathleen Alfredsson, gave me one of the best days I've had since being in Thorshofn. I met her yesterday when I saw her husband, Solvi, working in his garage on the fetching little people he makes that enhance his front yard. I've wanted to meet her.

She graciously invited me into her kitchen for a cup of coffee held in a dainty teacup. She's Irish and has lived in Thorshofn for over 20 years and has raised two sons in the town. She considers herself Icelandic now.

Recently recovering from breast cancer, she was feeling good enough to take me on a long drive to key parts of the area, beginning in town and across the fjord to a farmer's house where the young farm lady welcomed us into her home. The cutest baby you could ever see kept us entertained. He didn't stop smiling at us.

Cathleen explained that this is the lambing season going on right now. Farmers are in their busiest season, shearing the back sides of the adult sheep and seeing to the health of the baby lambs. I can thank a lamb for the wonderfully warm sweater I wear nearly every day.

Cathleen drove slowly and stopped often whenever I wanted to take a photo, and that ended up to be about 50 shots of sheep, horses, a small waterfall, the clam dump, the harbor, a fisherman, and more.

A tall clump of rocks with a little shelf sat near the waterfall. She told me the shelf was used in the past for lanterns that were placed on it so the fishing boats could see they were close to the harbor.

The clam dump looks like a small, snow-capped mountain. Broken pieces of clamshells have been dumped there from the factory that is now closed. Cathleen, who worked at that factory for awhile, said the fishermen stopped fishing for clams, and the factory closed down. Town folks began to take the shells away for decoration, but the town has decided to do something with the shells that would benefit the town financially. She isn't quite sure what that is, but as it stands, it's illegal to take away the shells.

Cathleen drove around the soon-to-be, quick-freeze, fishing production plant to be finished in August. She showed me the current plant that turns fish into fishmeal, which is also a place where she has worked in the past. Her sons and other boys and girls in the town work during the summer months in the factory. I had seen many of them in the Grill, wearing the required hairnets.

Soon, herring will be the predominate fish caught, and the workers will work in 12-hour shifts, including kids beginning at 15 years of age.

By the way, Cathleen told me the Grill, as I have been calling it, is referred to as "The Shop." We were almost on our way back up the hill when she spotted a fishing boat coming into the fjord. I had previously told her I was happy with everything I had seen on my month-long stay so far except for not being able to watch a fishing boat unloading the catch. She turned and headed back to the harbor where the fisherman came in and was met by two examiners. They aren't in Thorshofn often but come in once every so often to greet a fisherman, ask for his papers, and look at the fish.

The cod was considered too small by standards, but since it was a small catch, the examiners approved it, anyway. One examiner lifted up a fish and said it was too dark of a color and then showed another one of a lighter color, which was more of the standard requirement.

The fish were brought up in baskets and dumped into another bucket filled with ice.

The fisherman, with a ruddy complexion, looked exactly how I imagined a hard-working fisherman would look at the end of a fishing trip—strong, healthy, and tired at the end of the day. Bet he sleeps well.

The tour with Cathleen ended at The Shop where we had a cup of coffee, and she greeted nearly everyone who came in.

After I was dropped off, I picked up my swimsuit and headed to the hot pot and swimming pool where I met the new headmistress of the high school.

A brilliant sunset closed the brilliant day.

Tomorrow is the last day here, and on Friday morning, I fly to Reykjavik.

Last day in the Arctic Circle

The word incredible comes to mind when I think over the past five weeks. It's the last day for me at the Arctic Circle in the little fishing village of 500 people, Thorshofn. The window in the living room of the Jorvik Hotel is a moving scene, changing by the minute. Ducks bobbing up and down in the fjord, talking to each other, and birds sailing past the window will live in my memory forever.

I have walked every day with only two exceptions, days when I decided to rest from the weather that often enveloped me in sunshine, snow, sleet, rain, and extreme winds. Sometimes, the change in weather occurred when on a walk; my sweater was my refuge.

Siggi, the owner of the hotel, has been so kind, expecting little out of me but to enjoy myself, relax, and choose to spend my day the way I want. I have learned much about his beloved country of Iceland, and I will miss him and his loving little cat I nicknamed Smoky, a real princess.

I'm going to miss the little village and its people who wondered, "Who is that white-haired lady with a camera taking shots of our town?" People have been kind to me once they learned of my intentions. I'm leaving and taking the mystery with me.

Today, on my last walk to The Shop, the owner gave me a hug and said it was a pleasure having me in town and in her store. She bid me a safe journey. The young lady, Hulda, who was mentioned earlier, left for a vacation in Spain yesterday, so our good-byes were said at that time. In the grocery store, the owner also bid me a safe journey as I purchased enough food to last until tomorrow when I leave on a small plane. By the way, traveling by plane is normal here and is close to the same cost as travel by car or bus.

In Thorshofn, I have met the mayor, police chief, fishing inspectors, roads administrator, fishermen, neighbors, post office employees, pharmacy manager, manager of the swimming pool and sports hall, the new headmistress, two restaurant owners, a retired commercial pilot, a movie actress and director, and many other good people. I have been interviewed for National Icelandic Television, and a radio station streamed an interview of me to the States.

The promise to myself that most people in the world are good was proved again.

Chapter Three

June, 2012

Landed back in Reykjavik on June 1

I left Thorshofn around 11:30 a.m. this morning in what I thought would be a small plane, but it seated around 12 people, including the 14-year-old whom I had met earlier in the week on a farm while touring with neighbor Cathleen. He was a great tour guide in the air, except at times when it was too difficult to hear him, even though he kept talking. One time, I did understand when he pointed down through the window of the plane to the edge of the water and said not too long ago, a polar bear happened to have been lost and ended up there. It was rescued and returned to its homeland.

We left the north part of Iceland, the Arctic Circle, where it has been cold even though it had warmed up a bit the last two days. However, landing at the Akureyi City Airport, the extreme weather differences were noticed immediately. We were in wool sweaters and coats, and the folks at Akureyi were in short sleeves and shorts. My wool sweater became a burden instead of the life-saver and good investment it was prior to our leave. While Iceland is known as a country with no trees, trees were plentiful and green in Akureyi. The grass was green, green, green, green everywhere.

Then those of us who went on to Reykjavik, after an hour wait, got on a bigger plane. Pretty stewardesses offered drinks and a small piece of chocolate. It took only 45 minutes of flying over two separate snow-topped mountain ranges to get to Reykjavik.

I am now in the Capital Inn, a hostel at the edge of the city where I'll be until June 11. I have already met four exchange students from Northeastern University in Boston who are studying at Reykjavik University.

Then there's a group of wild young men who warned me they are loud. I met the ringleader when he came out of his room looking for tape to mend his pink, plastic girlfriend. She was losing air and needed to get patched.

I offered my scotch tape and was invited into their den where they were primping for a night out. They were having a four-day stag party, which the English lad pronounced, "stig potty." I had to ask him over and over what he said.

"I'm speaking English to you, lady!"

"Okay, but you're not saying it right," and I gave him the American version. They said the four days in Iceland are in celebration of the groom who is getting married in September.

"Aren't you starting out a little early?" I asked.

"Oh, we'll have another one in September."

"Okay, then, I'm going to mention that in my book, and I want your names."

When I got settled into my room, I received an email from my flight instructor, Arngim Jacobsen, who told me he will be in the cockpit on Atlantic Airways when I fly to his homeland, the Faroe Islands, in ten days.

The Brits are celebrating . . . what?

Took to my room yesterday, but in the community room, which involves using the kitchen, the Brits were still celebrating. Five guys who are rambunctious to say the least.

No, they are not celebrating the Queen's Jubilee, but something akin to that, I suppose. Anyway, they took turns walking back and forth to and from the showers, through the community room, in just their skivvies. One had hot pink briefs. I felt as though I shouldn't be sharing in their joy, but when hot pink flashes before your eyes, what can you do?

They got all dressed up, including the gentleman who will be a groom in September, who was dressed as the bride. Oh, dear! Woe to the wedding party if these guys are the groomsmen. They left about 10:30 p.m. (generally way past my bedtime) for a night out on the town and came back in the wee hours of the morning. I woke up to the sounds of singing and a woman's voice from another guestroom shouting, "Don't you have any manners?"

I'll answer that. No, they don't.

Late last night, a couple from the States came into my room to sleep on the extra bunk bed. This is my first experience staying in a coed hostel, and it's quite strange to be so intimate with strangers.

This morning, I walked all the way to the mall to replenish my supplies, and whom should I meet there but the Hungarian, Gergo. We had been emailing this morning, and I told him I would be going to the mall, and he surprised me by showing up there. It's fun to see him again. We compared notes about our current sleeping arrangements, and it seems he's got a challenge where he is, as well.

"What makes someone want to sing at the top of his lungs before daybreak? Even birds don't do that," he stated.

I got back to my room after a taxing ride, taxing because the driver didn't understand where I wanted to go. However, he stopped the meter until he understood, in typical Icelandic friendliness. Now there's a jet-lagged gentleman from Seattle asleep in my room.

At the mall, I find it similar to American malls, loud music and lots of people. I went to the grocery store and heard the sounds of the 50s.

Prices here are about the same as in America with some items a little bit higher. Don't know what it's like for the Brits, and don't think they know themselves.

Murphy's Law

The heading Murphy's Law describes the kind of day I had today. It's an adventure, I have often told myself, even though I got lost, my legs were burning in pain, and I had to hire a taxi. Now I'll have to figure out a way to recoup the day's expense.

It's Sunday, and supposedly lots of stores are closed, I thought, including the shopping mall. But I didn't have any kronur left and had barely enough change to get downtown, so I asked the hostel receptionist where to catch the bus so I could get to an ATM money wall.

"Take number one," she said and half-way apologized for the distance it would take to walk. At the chosen bus stop, I waited for half an hour and finally stopped a red-headed woman with a runny nose and asked her if I was waiting at the right bus stop.

"Oh, no. Here, I'll walk with you and show you where you must wait."

We turned and went another way.

Another half an hour went by, and I kept asking people if it was a sure thing that buses run on Sunday.

"Yes, it will come in 15 minutes," a young skateboarder said. He came back in 15 minutes, and I was still there.

Then a large guy wearing black shorts, black T-shirt, tennis shoes, and black socks said he knew buses ran on Sunday but wasn't sure of the schedule.

"I haven't been on a bus for 40 years," he laughed.

Another man who left his apartment near the bus stop walked across the street to the recycling bin to dump his recyclables. When I asked him about the bus, his comment was, "It says here it should be here soon." He pointed to the schedule.

Then a young couple, students at Icelandic University, told me I should go to the other stop. (Remember, that was the one the runny nose lady told me was wrong.)

"It will be here in 45 minutes."

The nice young couple came back in their car about a half hour later and offered me a ride downtown, and when they dropped me off, they told me where to wait for the return bus, with three options. So I opted for the first one, and it took me to the shopping mall, which was open. Dang, I could have walked there first. I went into the mall and was again pleased to see that all major stores in Iceland have wrapping stations with free paper and ribbon. The customer has access to free paper and ribbon of their choice and use of necessary tools.

When I left the shopping center, I got lost, and my legs were hurting again. I saw two guys standing by a building and asked if one of them would call a taxi. Turns out they are radio guys and were on a break from being on air. When I told Asi Gudna of FM 95.7 that my name was Laureen, he got my name mixed up with the Swedish Lorene who won Europa 2012 singing competition.

After that was straightened out, he talked about his job. "Last night we were at the Harpa Hall recording a music awards show that Jon Johnsson won for male vocalist of the year. You can find him on YouTube," he told me.

Then, he had to hurry off for radio duties while I waited for the taxi. After a miserable and painful wait with no place to sit, a man came rushing to me.

"Did you want a taxi?"

I was waiting at the back of the building while he was sitting in the front with the meter running. He had seen me earlier in the wrong place and figured I was the rider.

I got the expensive taxi ride, and when I arrived at the Capital Inn and told the inn's host that I had gotten lost and had taken a taxi back, his comment was profoundly disturbing.

"Why didn't you just call here? We would have picked you up for free."

Lazy me

It was a lazy day and one where I recuperated and regrouped from several days of little sleep. We need to do that once in a while. But I began the day walking slowly to the Kringlan Shopping Center about half a mile up a slight hill covered with blue lupine and dandelions. Hey, don't talk bad about dandelions when you see them on a hillside coupled with lupine; the colors are the sun and sky.

At the shopping center, my goal was to find a pair of trousers. Icelanders' preference for tight pants or leggings with several layers of tops, one showing below another, is not what I wanted. I need jeans or pants with a wide leg at the ankle and definitely not too tight. The jeans I have worn here have gotten too big, and it's time to replace them.

"I'm not leaving here until I find a pair of pants that fits," I told the clerk. She vowed to help with my quest.

She got busy looking at possibilities for me and came back with an armload of trousers.

"I think you'll find what you want here. But if you don't, let me know. I have some other ideas."

I'm not a trend follower, and that's all right. The jeans are army green with the label "Boyfriend" and were produced in, you got it, China.

After the jeans purchase, I bought some cheese, bread, jam, grapes, and Indian tonic water to snack on later. When I got hungry and all that was left was the bread, I ate that with some good Icelandic ice water from the tap. I thought about prison food, where the guys in the "hole" are only given bread and water, and figured they were treated pretty well. Bread and water are good. However, it must be French bread, of course.

Tomorrow, I'll head down to the main part of the city and see what's going on.

Stinky feet

A big Swede is now sharing the room with the German guy and me. He took off his boots, and now the room stinks, and it's not Chanel Number Five. It's more like Stockyard After Five. The German closes the window because it's cold, and the Swede prefers that, as well. But I prefer to be cold with fresh air. The window is too far up for me to reach it, and it's across the room. Coed sharing is downright weird sometimes.

This hostel is far away from anything, and a car would be helpful. I've traveled by Moe and Joe (left foot, right foot) to get everywhere. I look forward to moving on in a few more days. When traveling cheaply, you have to take the good with the bad, the stink with the fresh.

You aren't going to get me; I cut my losses.

How long does it take a person to cut their losses and go on to what is best for you? It's taken me a lifetime, but I'm getting better.

I had to ask myself this morning, what is a 74-year-old woman doing in a tiny, hot room with three men, a German, a Swede and a Scotsman, all with stinky feet and all loud snorers?

It was difficult to fall asleep, and the bed from the bunk up above me squeaked all night. And the community room was noisy far into the night.

What caused the final decision to move upstairs happened when I woke up in the middle of the night. I saw an arm with a hand, fingers extended, hanging out over the top bunk. In my transition from sleep to wakefulness, I imagined it was trying to reach me. It was in silhouette, and for a minute, I forgot where I was.

I deserve better in my 74th year, so I requested an upgrade to a private room. It's going to cost me, but for four more days, I'll have some peace and quiet, and to my knowledge, no one will try to get me in the middle of the night.

Lost again, but I pre-empt the Queen

Got lost again but not as badly as yesterday. When you're lost but not in a hurry, it gives you a chance to reflect. I have found that every person I asked about what bus to get on, where to get off, or what path to take to get back to my hostel, gave me a different answer. Some were adamant about their clarity, while other folks just said, "I think you want to . . . ." Never trust directions from well-meaning people who begin with that phrase.

I wanted to go into the main part of Reykjavik and head to the harbor, so I got on the bus that I was told would take me there. It did, but what should have taken 15 minutes took more like over an hour because I boarded on the wrong side of the street. The bus driver was friendly and made certain that I understood exactly how to get to my ultimate destination.

Then when he stopped at the end of his route and before he began again to head back, he explained some of the terrain we were on. We were actually in another city that is called "Harbor Town" in English and is nicknamed "Lava Town." Housing in Lava Town, according to the driver, was increasing a few years ago, but it abruptly stopped in 2008, when the country went broke. Recently, construction began again. I found it fascinating how the lava rocks were used for landscaping purposes.

Other reflections

The bus driver told me the Capital Inn, where I'm staying for one more week, is known as "between life and death." That's because it sits between a cemetery and the fast traffic of the freeway. On another day, before I knew it was called "between life and death," I walked through the cemetery and was impressed with its beauty. Green grass and many bulb-type blossoms give the cemetery a cheerful garden atmosphere.

Two other charms of Iceland I like are clothing hanging out outdoors to dry and the small trash dispensaries connected to light poles in many places on every street. You don't see trash anywhere.

I did find the harbor that day, and I enjoyed the views of yachts, ships, and even a sailboat. I walked around the harbor neighborhood. I didn't take my camera with me on purpose, as I wanted to totally experience the walk without the burden of equipment.

News flash—the interview with me when I was in the Arctic Circle was shown on Icelandic National TV tonight, and while I couldn't hear it very well because people were in the dining room making noise, it was fun to see my answers written in Icelandic language. The kind person in charge of the inn preempted the English Queen's Jubilee party on the station I'd be on so I could watch myself on television.

Sorry, Queen.

Interview

After two days of getting on the wrong bus or waiting at the bus stop going the wrong way, I did it correctly today, and I got some unusual notoriety in a restaurant. A gentleman got up from his seat at his table and came over to me.

"I saw your interview on television yesterday, and I just wanted to say hello." He went back to his table and started talking to his friends. They all turned and looked. I waved and smiled.

Then when I went into a candy store to purchase some chocolate as a gift for my next hostess, the clerk also mentioned she had seen me on TV. I feel that I had my 15 minutes of fame.

More 15 minutes of fame

I figured my 15 minutes of fame were over in Iceland until I walked out of the Kringlan Shopping Center and on to the parking lot heading back to the Capital Inn. I saw a pretty lady on a bicycle with pink flowers hanging over the basket and flowers in her hair. I thought that's what I want someday whenever I go back home (wherever that will be in California)—a bicycle with flowers. I smiled at her and she smiled back, and I continued until I heard her driving back around me and then heading toward me again.

"Hello!"

"Hello!"

"I saw you on TV."

We spoke for a while. She was very friendly and had a comforting smile. I was surprised how much she remembered about what was said on that interview.

Neither of us had a pen handy, so I hope she will remember my email address and respond. Her smile made my afternoon.

The day began again with wrong information. I was told the shopping center opened at 11, but it didn't open until one p.m. However, some of the coffee shops opened up earlier, so I tried them all and had three cups of coffee.

Today I paid special attention to the phenomenon of human body language. On the way to the center, I stopped at a bakery and asked if they had a W.C., and the girl rubbed her nose, a dead giveaway she was not being truthful, and said, "No, we don't have W.C.s here."

I thought about the workers there. Guess they have to wait until the end of their shift and go at home. It would have been understood if the employee's words had been, "No, we do not have W.C.s for the public."

In one coffee shop, a man and a woman with English accents, hers American and his British, appeared to be at an interview for an on-line dating service. He, bald with big eyes and a moon-shaped face, sat up straight, obviously trying hard. She sat back, relaxed, observing the man.

Later, they walked off together. It was too early for the sunset, but they looked compatible walking through the mall.

I saw a mother and son involved in conversation, and a dad and daughter, as well, at another table. Both pairs were holding their counterparts' attentions, and I felt happy for the moments they had with each other.

On the way back, I met another lady who is staying in the hostel of the Capital Inn. She stopped and asked why she hadn't seen me, and I told her I had upgraded to a private room. She agreed it was a good idea.

Getting a whipping

What can you expect, huh? We're out on an island all by ourselves and subject to the weather. It has been warm, so I packed my Icelandic sweater away, but this morning, I brought it out again. It's cold. It's windy. However, I forged ahead like a brave Icelandic bird and hobbled to the bus station, the right one, and went to town.

It's not easy walking in strong winds when your hair is twisting around on your head and you cannot pat it down because the winds are coming from all directions.

It didn't take long to get to the post office and then a breakfast place for Icelandic pancakes. They look just like American pancakes, except with whipped cream. Whipped is the word today. Then it was a return trip back to the hostel by bus.

In town the other day, I took a photo of the Bad Taste Record Store. I didn't want anyone seeing me go inside, or they might think I have bad taste in music.

It reminded me of the "Careless Hair Salon" in Den Haag, Holland. Would you want some careless hair stylist to create a do for you? Perhaps they could make some money in Iceland taming windy hair woes.

I have one more day in Iceland, and then I head off to the Faroe Islands.

One last trip to town

Caught the bus for the last time and headed to the main part of the city of Reykjavik this morning for one last look before leaving, as I'll probably not be coming back again. There's more of the world to see.

There I was walking down the street and whom should I run into? The Mayor of Thorshofn. He is in Reykjavik "on holiday," as the British say.

"It's a small world," we both agreed. And then at the same time, "It's a small country." I didn't expect to meet anyone I knew downtown, but it's actually happened before, as I have met Gergo, the Hungarian, many times while in the city.

I left the mayor and walked up the hill to the Hallgríms-skirkja, a Lutheran church that stands high above all other buildings and is a landmark I have often used to keep my bearings.

There is an elevator that goes clear to the eighth floor, and then a few steps take you to the very top. This day was the third time to attempt to see below, free of fog, and the results were many good photos.

Coming down inside the elevator where a sign was posted on the outside door, "Only six people allowed to ride," the rule was violated. When several of us got into the tiny space, two more women wanted on and squeezed in, and that made seven human beings packed into a space like Monterey County's Driscoll straw-berries in a basket. We were so close that anyone could have leaned in for a kiss in any direction.

Everyone remained silent, which is always hard for me to grasp. Standing so close but not speaking, as if everyone were invisible, I had to break the ice. The Devilette made me say, "In how many languages could we say, 'Get me the hell out of here'?" That broke the ice and all of the people walked out laughing.

Then I went to Mokka Coffee Shop, which, rightly so, promotes itself as a Bohemian meeting place. Guess I'll miss saying good-bye to Kitel Lassen, as he didn't show up and take his regular seat.

I had Mokka's specialty, a waffle with whipped cream and jam. Remind me to buy a waffle iron whenever I get settled back in California next year.

The tourist season has begun in Iceland, and there are a lot more people in town with big eyes, their cameras hanging around their necks. The stores have created areas for souvenirs, and restaurants have their tables and chairs outside.

Tourist season brings out the people who seem to enjoy being on the street stage, including a guitarist and singer, barefoot and sounding good; Superman; a woman with an orange wig and a blue and purple satin outfit; and a Viking who was with a group singing Icelandic songs to the tourists.

When I got on the bus to get back to the hotel, there were two men sitting across from me, a bit inebriated, trying to figure out how to turn on the fresh air vent, but they kept falling until they decided the air was fresh enough. As for me, I was happy to get off the bus and take a big breath of air.

Tomorrow, I say good-bye to Iceland and fly off to the Faroe Islands with Arngrim in the cockpit.

Flying with my favorite pilot

I walked into the Icelandic Domestic Airport, and there he was. My favorite pilot and instructor, Arngrim Jacobsen, walked into the bedlam where passengers were getting checked in to fly to the Faroe Islands.

We greeted with a hug, and he led me all the way into the plane. What a privilege that is to walk into the plane with the pilot!

He had co-piloted Atlantic Airways into Reykjavik and would make the return trip, but this flight he would be with his student from Durango Air Service from way back in 1994—me!

It was thrilling to be asked to sit in the cockpit during the last 20 minutes and observe the action that kept Johan, the Captain, and Arngrim busy getting the plane ready for the landing, which, due to winds, meant changing landing directions to fly into the airstrip from another way than usual. It seemed as though there was a myriad of instruments to check, unlike anything in a small, two-seater Cessna.

Being in the cockpit and seeing the view is amazing. There were cliffs and huge rock mountains on both sides of our path, and the close proximity of those rocks to the airplane rattled my nerves, but with Arngrim in the cockpit, I really had nothing to worry about.

Then we flew into a valley and over the rooftops of the village houses and made a perfect landing.

After all the passengers left and Arngrim and Johan finished with their reports and paperwork, I left again with Arngrim, got my luggage, and walked past the fussiness of customs to his car.

He lives an hour away from the airport, and while we were driving, he told me he had taken the time off from work to be with me during my time in the Faroes. What a guy!

We got to his home, and I saw again his wonderful parents, Per and Eldrid, and their grandchildren, and we had a fish dinner. It's been five years, we all agreed, since I was in their home with my friend, Marilyn McCord.

Happy days ahead!

Under the sea to the Faroes

The Faroe Islands between Iceland and Norway are composed of 18 islands, with 17 of them inhabited.

On the way to Arngrim's home in Soldarfjordur on the Island of Eysturoy, from the Vágar Airport located in Sorvagur, we drove through the Vestmannasund, one of the subsea tunnels that goes right under the sea, and then we drove through two regular tunnels.

All along the one-hour drive, up on land, I saw sheep of many colors, an ancient breed native to the Islands, and charming farms, some with grassy rooftops.

There are harbors where fishermen take their boats out to sea as they have for centuries, and there are fjords bordered by tall, table-top mountains with emerald green grass below that showcase the stone ribbons that circle the tops of the cliffs.

There were many birds to see, including those I can see right outside of the kitchen window and all the way across the fjord to the Skali Village. Big fishing boats are in every harbor, including a Russian ship that sits alone in Soldarfjordur's harbor.

The next day, Arngrim took me on a drive to other villages. There are many colored houses, some with grass roofs, all standing on green grass.

Arngrim's parents, Per and Eldrid, take care of their grandchildren during some days, and at the same time, they provide the coziest atmosphere you could ever desire. Arngrim is the most loved uncle to his nieces and nephews.

Most everything is perfect. However, there was a glitch in the day when I went inside a bank to exchange Icelandic kronur for Faroese money and was refused. According to the bank teller, Iceland's finances are not yet secure enough to take the risk of exchanging them.

Well, thanks to Arngrim. He will buy the kronur from me and use them in Iceland on his many flights into Reykjavik.

Faroese family and recipe

I have seen Arngrim's brother, Runi; his sister, Eyd Venned; and several of his nieces and nephews coming in and out of the house, and some of the grandchildren have spent the night.

Tonight, I was fortunate to be invited to a beautiful home that overlooks the fjord and belongs to Arngrim's sister-in-law, Anna Jacobsen. She is married to Arngrim's oldest brother, Meinhard. Over a traditional-type dessert, I heard all about Anna's daughter, Maria Meinhardsdottir, and her education to become a physician. She was heading back to school tomorrow, and a goodbye party was planned for her. Her husband is also studying medicine.

"We have a close family and we live near each other. All of my cousins and close friends that I have grown up with stay in touch. My cousins are my best friends," Maria said.

She also had a close friend visiting with her. That was Judith Signhild Finnsson, and Judith explained that she, too, is heading back to school where she is working on a family and human services degree in Chicago, the city where her boyfriend also attends college.

This gathering is typical of what I have seen among the Faroese people and their close-knit families. A traditional delicious cake and other lovely dishes were served.

In the middle of the day today, when they have their largest meal, Eldrid cooked a dish I'm calling Sunfrid Jacobsen's Fish Casserole. Sunfrid is another of Arngrim's sisters-in-law, married to Rogvi, Runi's twin. It's a fish dish, easy to prepare, with a mouth-watering blend of ingredients. Arngrim translated the ingredients and changed the measuring units. Please see the back of the book for my best yearlong travel recipes.

Beauty everywhere

There is no end to the wonder that comes from the views seen from nearly every vantage point in the Faroe Islands. You can't help but stand amazed over the magnificent hills that rise straight up to meet the rocky ledges. Now that summer has arrived, brilliant green grass graces the hills almost to the top.

There is also the fjord, the avenue that fishing boats and ships take to go out to sea. I look at the fjord and see how the sun and water movement creates sparkling diamonds in the water.

It's sometimes very peaceful, but I have heard stories of the old days of fishing when there were only rowboats without engines, and many fishermen were lost to the sea. There are many memorials on the islands dedicated to those who never returned.

What brave souls they were, and still are, in my estimation. Even though the boats are loaded with technology and highly trained fishermen, it's still a rolling, roaring sea where they fish to bring food to the world.

Sheep wander and swing their long coats over the hills, some far up on the slopes, and you can't help but wonder how they keep from rolling down the hillside.

Speaking of sheep, Arngrim and I were at the top of a hill when a mother and two lambs walked toward us.

"They must think we're the farmer and will give them food," he said.

After they looked at us for awhile, they assumed we weren't who they thought we were, and they turned and walked away. I just know it's not my imagination; I'm sure I saw a disappointed look on the mother's face.

In my discovery of beautiful places, the Faroe Islands are on the top of my list.

The family of athletes

All of Arngrim's brothers and sisters and nieces and nephews have athletic abilities, and some have gone on to high achievements in their sports.

A recent example is Per's ten-member rowing team that picked up two first-place wins in the Klaksvík and Skalafjords. But let's not leave out the female six-person team, for they also placed first in the same two competitions.

The ten-man boat is the largest boat in all the competitive rowing events. The competition that Per's team won in the Klaksvikingur boat is the most prestigious win, and the latest recent win was the second time Per's team took first place.

Last year, Per and his father, Martin, were on the winning Klaksvikingur boat. It is unusual, indeed, for a father and son to participate in the same race.

The recent 1,500-meter Klaksvikingur race that Per and his team led ended with a time score of 6 minutes 38.24 seconds, followed by other boats with the times of 6 minutes 39.15 seconds, 6 minutes 39.18 seconds, 6 minutes 50.03 seconds. You can see the strength and teamwork required to row the distance in that time. (Fifteen hundred meters equal approximately one mile.)

A ten-member boat race is 2,000 meters; however, some fjords' lengths are shorter in distance, which causes a shorter race with different time results.

For those of us not familiar with the sport of rowing, www.kvf.fo can provide more information. Click on the green icon—3-2 (Sport), and then click *kapprodur*. This website featured highlights of the June 4 race, describing it in rip-roaring detail as an excited crowd cheered on its favorite team. The site shows lots of videos of races that occur each year in June and July.

Rowing competition began with the use of fishing boats similar to the style the forefathers used in the 1800s before fishing boats used engines. Rowing has become a national sport in the Faroes.

In the large boat of ten, five rowers sit side by side with a steerer in back giving information on speed and tactics to stay ahead. Male rowers may have a female person at the steering helm, and men steer for the women's team boat.

The folks who steer are animated, shouting and cheering the rowers on, and as stated above, the crowd is wild in anticipation.

"The rowing teams begin their training in January on machines, and on April 25, they put their boats into the water for the first time of the season," said Arngrim.

Through the grottos

Arngrim and I left from his home in Soldarfjord on the Island of Eysturoy and headed to the village of Vestmanna on the Island of Streymoy. There, we boarded a boat to view the cliffs and grottos on the west side of the village and further on into the sea. It was a sightseeing adventure that got us up close to, and then through, narrow, high rocks. We heard sounds from above.

Looking up, way up, toward the high-rise rock cliffs, we saw birds in their nests in the nooks and crannies. It's as if they have their own condominiums. This has been the life of Faroes' birds for centuries.

The boat accommodated over 40 passengers, with seating indoors out of the cold or outdoors on the top of the boat. For more adventurous people such as Arngrim and myself, the place to be was at the back of the boat. I had to drag my Icelandic jacket/sweater out of my luggage to prepare for the cold trip on the fjord.

The boat started out slowly while we received safety instructions from the boatman, then it picked up speed, and the village got smaller as we headed away. A blue and white wake splashed a trail behind us.

Soon, we were sailing inside a narrow strip with a natural, gigantic, rock wall on both sides, but just before that and all during the proximity of the cliffs, a commentator told us to look for the birds and their nests.

That's not all of the life on the cliffs. I was astounded to see sheep on the steep cliffs, as well. I can only assume the grass is sweeter there.

Breathtaking rock formations changed at each turn inside and at entrances and exits to and from the grottos. Trying to capture the whole experience inside a camera was trying at times, for everywhere I looked, there stood another spectacular sight and many birds flying around.

Before going inside one of the nearly enclosed, dark grottos, we were asked to wear protective helmets in case a rock came loose. We could see dripping water glistening on the sides of the rocky walls.

After the trip and when we arrived back at the Vestmanna, we took in the museum where lifelike figures told the story of the beginning of life on the Faroe Islands. A boat sails for two hours from Vestmanna every day, year round, depending on the weather. www.sightseeing.fo.

Stories from the sea

On Sunday, while on the way to the Faroe Island capital city, Torshavn (not to be confused with the island village, Thorshofn, where I stayed for five weeks in Iceland), we made a detour to the top of a mountain where NATO had a fully operating radar early warning system during the Soviet Cold War days. The purpose of the system was to detect Soviet airplanes coming too close to the Scandinavian countries and the United Kingdom. NATO operations are now closed, but the site is used, instead, for commercial traffic. It no longer monitors military traffic. Five years ago, when Arngrim took my friend, Marilyn McCord, and me to the top, the system was operating, and we were not allowed to take photos. We knew that we were being observed while on the road and the property on top of the mountain.

We continued on a two-hour ferry trip, passing islands and jutting sea rocks heading to the Island of Suduroy where we will spend the day and then ferry back to Torshavn. Arngrim and I walked around the Torshavn Harbor and viewed a large cruise ship that brought many tourists into the city. We also strolled around government buildings—a town municipality building and a red-brick-colored group of buildings with grass-covered roofs that has been in use since the 1700s, and the Faroese Parliament building. It is thought among historians that the Faroese Parliament is older than even the Iceland Parliament of the 900s.

An old sailing vessel called a smack was in the harbor and reminded Arngrim of the story of that same type of ship and the tragedy that befell his family and many people of the island.

Per, Arngrim's father, has stories to tell of his own adventures while working as a fisherman for 30 years in the same sea where his father perished before he was born. Per was born in August, 1932.

Per's father, also named Per, and his two uncles were fishing with seven other men from Soldarfjord. They were on a smack called the *Emmanuel* and were fishing between Iceland and the Faroe Islands and were on the way back to sell fish in the United Kingdom. They didn't get to their destination. Instead, they perished in a violent sea. On the same boat there were also nine other fishermen from other cities on the Faroe Islands. A total of 19 souls perished on the *Emmanuel.*

Another smack, the *Laura,* from Suduroy, was also destroyed in the same storm. Altogether, there were 20 men in that boat. Some were brothers, and some were fathers and sons. They left mothers, daughters, wives, and girlfriends waiting for their men who never came home.

For those of us who do not know the experience of rough seas, go to YouTube and look at Rough Seas Iceland—the red boat. Hope you don't get seasick.

Per's mother was 37 when she lost her husband and her two brothers-in-law. She was pregnant with Per and had five other children. She lived as a widow for another 55 years.

A tragedy such as this was not uncommon in the early fishing days in the Faroe Islands, and there are memorials honoring those men who never returned. One memorial rests in a small park close to Arngrim's home.

Per, a strong man today, spoke of working on a German boat for a few months where he and other fishermen taught the German fishermen how to split, clean, and salt the fish. His job on this boat began only two weeks after he and Eldrid were married in 1957. Now I would like to introduce this fine lady.

Eldrid's life on the Island of Eysturoy as a young wife and mother demanded strength of mind and body, a nurturing spirit, and plenty of endurance. She took care of the children and the household while Per would be out fishing, many times for as long as six months.

She is a small woman with a sweet face who beams out warmth to everyone who comes into the home—children, grand-children, in-laws, and friends. Even though I do not speak her language, even in our silence, she communicates a warm, welcoming spirit toward me. She works hard but moves around quietly performing her daily rituals, and always with good humor.

In the earlier days when the children were young, clothing was homemade, as there were no stores within proximity of the Soldarfjord where they live. It was possible to purchase clothing in the capital city of Torshavn, but it was difficult to get there.

"I made all the children's clothing with my sewing machine and by knitting sweaters, hats, and mittens."

She explained her early life while Arngrim translated and she sat knitting. Faroese women begin as children, almost out of necessity, but now they create works of wearable art. Her daughters show great talent in knitting. I call it "speed knitting," as they are fast with those needles. Eldrid's granddaughters will learn soon. She was making a hat for Solja, her granddaughter. Solja was named after the flower that in English is called the buttercup.

Arngrim further told me that in earlier days, boats would deliver the mail at certain stops along the fjord, but now, of course, mail is delivered to each household every day. Eldrid began to work as a caregiver for the elderly when the children were older, and she retired from that after 30 years on the job.

The names of Eldrid and Per's adult children are Sanna, Meinhard, Arngrim, and Eyd, and the twins are Runi and Rogvi. They have 12 grandchildren.

Traveling with two 40-year-olds

Hanging out with two 40-plus-year-old guys wasn't a bad gig for a 74-year-old. Being a mother of three sons, three grandsons, a brother, and no sisters, being around guys is never difficult for me, especially when Arngrim and his brother-in-law, Martin, both of Soldarfjord on the Faroes' Island of Eysturoy, were so kind.

We boarded the Smyril ferry with the car in the capital city of Torshavn after leaving Soldarfjord early in the morning and driving to Torshavn.

The ferry was complete with a cafeteria, television, Wi-Fi, and comfortable chairs. It was a two-hour, smooth ride where we passed the Sandoy Island, the island where Martin's mother came from, and two green rock islands called *dimun*—large *dimun*, which is inhabited, and small *dimun*, which is uninhabited. The one I saw very well through the window reminded me of an emerald stone.

"There are so many rocks and islands, and they all seem to have names," I said.

Martin answered, "All rocks in the Faroe Islands have names."

When we docked on the Suduroy Island, we drove to where Martin had an appointment and listened to Paul McCartney's music in the car. We ate lunch in the Tvoroyri Hotel, dropped off Martin for his stress test, and then Arngrim and I drove up to the north side of the island.

We drove through the lovely green island and saw a different terrain on the Eysturoy Island from anything I had observed in Iceland. One area had strange-looking rock formations that resembled tall columns. They almost looked human-built.

On the way to the village furthest north on the Suduroy Island, we drove through Hvalba and through many other smaller villages and their harbors. About three hours later, we picked up Martin and got the good news that he passed his stress test. Why not? He's a gold medalist in the free stroke swim meet in Island Games.

There was so much more to see. After all, there was the south side of the island waiting to be discovered by the three of us. Along the way, Arngrim wanted to find a cliff he had discovered on a drive by himself one time, and while we were heading up the mountain, the fog nearly made it impossible to see in front of us, much less find the cliff he wanted to show us. Arngrim stopped the car at a spot that looked like it might be the place. Martin took off walking up the hill to see if it was the cliff as described by Arngrim.

"It has an extreme drop down to the bottom, and there are many birds you can see," Arngrim had told us earlier. Martin kept walking, and we could barely see that he reached the top. Arngrim and I decided to follow. Then Martin disappeared.

"Oh, shit," Arngrim stopped still. Martin wasn't to be seen anywhere, and both of us had the worst feeling ever.

"Oh, my God," I said under my breath. But Martin popped up from where he had scrunched down, hiding from us for a moment.

Later, Arngrim said he was thinking, "Oh, Martin fell off the cliff. What am I going to say to my sister?"

If that was the right place, there was nothing to see because of the fog. So we traveled on and found an old lighthouse and farm. A cliff, similar to what Arngrim had been looking for, appeared, but not the right one. Still, it was impressive and scary. All around us sheep were grazing on the soft grass. By the way, the grass is really and truly as soft as it appears to be. It's like walking on a plush carpet. You only need to walk around the dark, marble memories dropped there by the sheep.

One other side of our trip was on a road that we should have taken in a four-wheel drive. What we saw when we got close enough was another old farmhouse and a lighthouse on the fjord next to the water.

Reflections on the way to Dublin

I'm so tired right now that if someone told me to stand in the corner, I'd fall asleep. It is 1:55 p.m. now in Dublin and 2:55 p.m. in Copenhagen where I left early today on a jet.

I think it may have been the lack of sleep that gave credence to the emotion I felt while on the way to Dublin. Challenges in the Copenhagen Airport should be part of this story, but like I said, I'm tired, and I don't want to go there in my mind and spirit.

Flying above the fluffy white clouds with an occasional strip of blue peeking through made me nostalgic, and I actually felt like crying but didn't really have a reason. Several times while looking out of the window, I saw rainbows in perfect circles.

I remembered that Don Watkins, owner of the Durango Air Service where I got my pilot's license, called it a "pilot's rainbow" after I told him of seeing a shadow of the airplane situated right in the center of the circular rainbow.

That did it! With a lump in my throat, I remembered those days when Arngrim patiently explained over and over what I needed to know to get that big machine in the air and down. He is a perfectionist, and that is exactly whom you would want as a teacher and exactly whom you would want to pilot the plane you're in. His attention to detail makes certain that everything goes as planned.

Take, for instance, yesterday. Arngrim mentioned to the head flight attendant that I was his friend and his former student, and it would be a treat for me to be invited into the new Atlantic Airways airbus cockpit that would take me from the Faroe Islands to Copenhagen.

She did more than that. She got an invitation for me to sit in the cockpit during takeoffs and landings. A lottery win wouldn't have surpassed that. And it was better than I expected. Thanks to the generosity of the pilots, Johan and Tommy, both born and raised in the Faroes, I was allowed to sit in the cockpit during the entire flight. But a bigger thanks goes to Arngrim for making it possible.

Arngrim began his dream of flying while attending a church camp during the summer months in the Faroe Islands. The landing strip was within eyesight of the camp.

"I liked to watch the airplanes land," Arngrim remembered.

Per, Arngrim's father, told me that when Arngrim came home from camp, he put his fist down on the table and exclaimed, "That is what I want to do. I will be a pilot."

His first attempt to get lessons at age 17 ended in a scam before he even got started. It was ten years later when he began to search again for a school, and that led him to Durango, Colorado. Meeting him and all the other young pilots from all over the world, and at a time when my husband, Will, was alive, will all go down in my memory as one of the best times of my life. This claim excludes giving birth to three awesome sons who have filled my life with joy.

I'll always remember the flying games at the Durango Airport when one of Arngrim's perfect landings earned him the first place prize. Will was flying with Arngrim during the competition. The pilots were to see how close they could get to a wide chalk-marker on the landing strip. Some got close to the mark, some landed before, and some landed after the marker. Arngrim landed spot-on the marker, with the chalk even showing up on the tires.

That was on my mind this morning as we flew through the clouds. I also realized, while dreaming and watching the clouds, that looking back at the finish of my year, certain people will stand out. I know Arngrim's family will be front and center. They taught me the importance of family support.

"If anyone needs any help, someone in the family is always there," Arngrim told me.

This is a special tradition in the culture of the Faroese people. And it extends to people not in the family, as well. That was evidenced many years ago when Per worked on the tunnels that are unique to the islands.

"My father was going to be working and would be away from us for a long time, so we all moved in with another family until the job was finished," Arngrim remembered.

I met one of the women of the family, a little girl at the time when her family hosted the Jacobsens. I met her at the rowing race that Arngrim's nephew, Per, rowed in and where he took first place.

But now, the journey has led me to the city of Dublin in Ireland, and I am in a hostel, where I am the oldest of about 50 teenagers who came in to stay for a few days. The man at the front desk, when I mentioned I would probably be the oldest person here, replied with, "Just don't dance on the table before nine p.m."

Euro games and theater

After being inside the hostel, my fifth home on my journey, for about one-and-a-half hours yesterday, two groups of German high school students arrived and set up a Euro football game-watching arena in the community room. Germany won the game with four points to Greece's one point. Every time a point was made, loud cheers erupted, arms flew up in the air, and one boy jumped up and waved a German flag. In a room with that much spirit, you couldn't help but catch it. I rooted for Germany, as well, but can't help but feel sorry for Greece. Someone wins, someone loses.

This morning, I took a tour on a hop-on-hop-off bus and saw lots of old world architecture and famous sites that included Abbey Street, Trinity College of 1592, The Custom House of 1791, and the Four Courts of 1785. The Four Courts building can be seen right out of my window. There is some restoration of the building going on now.

On my walk back to the hostel today, I saw an old theatre, called Smock Alley Theatre, which was built in 1662. Rich Veneza of New Jersey is an actor but is taking a break and working in the theatre in the marketing department. He graciously gave me information on the history of the theatre and let me look at a section of it, but not the stage, as they were in rehearsals for the next performance, *Another Twin*, by Lally Katz, which will run from Monday to Saturday next week.

John Ogilby opened this stone-constructed theatre as part of the restoration by the British monarchy and King Charles II in 1660, along with London's Drury Lane and the Lincoln's Inn Fields. The Smock Alley was the first custom-built theatre in the city and still remains in its original form.

Rich pointed out the ceiling filigree and said it was assumed to be placed there by the same architect who built the interior of the ship *Titanic*, but he couldn't substantiate that claim. It's beautiful and is seen on the ceiling of a huge room that is used for various other activities besides theatre.

Artistic Director Kristian Marken of the Smock Alley Players directed *She Stoops to Conquer*, a play that returned 239 years after it was written.

"Written in response to the polite, mannered comedies of the late 1800s, this play is an uproariously cheeky and bold farce that has lost none of its shine in the intervening centuries," said director Marken in the program booklet when the play began its run in May of this year. www.info@smockalley.com.

Aside from the trip on the bus, I took a short shopping trip to a grocery store and a stop at an Italian coffee shop for lunch and coffee. I'm in a tea-drinking world here, and while I prefer coffee, I aim always to do as the local culture does wherever I am, unless the coffee option is offered.

The woman in the coffee shop couldn't understand when I asked, "What is a toastie?"

"What do you want to know, love?"

"What is a toastie?" I pointed to the wall menu.

"I don't understand what you want."

"Okay, then I'll have a toastie. I'll have cheese, spinach and tomato." ("Whatever that is," I mused under my breath.)

"She wants a toastie with cheese, spinach, and tomato," she hollered to the guy making the meals. "Next person, please."

It turns out a toastie is what we call a sandwich. Now, can you imagine how you would explain to someone asking, "What is a sandwich?"

An Irish awakening

I tapped my toes, clapped my hands, sang, laughed, and listened to traditional music of Ireland. This was the making of the American hillbilly sound. It was a fun afternoon and a nice retreat from earlier in the day when I suddenly got caught in a rainstorm that soaked through my clothes. I was inside the Brazen Head Inn where six men entertained a pub stuffed with people. Beer and whiskey were generously flowing between the audience and the musicians.

Temple Bar is the area on the south bank of the River Liffey in central Dublin. At night, the area comes alive with nightclubs and bars. During the day, there are photo galleries and shopping opportunities.

The Brazen Head Inn is the same pub that housed such writers as James Joyce, Brendan Behan, and Jonathan Swift. It also saw the revolutionaries Robert Emmet, Wolfe Tone, Daniel O'Connell, and Michael Collins.

I couldn't help but feel like I was back in the 1100s, while sitting inside the oldest pub in Ireland, built in 1198. The men played traditional musical instruments and sang, sometimes melancholic and sometimes bawdy ballads. Every song had a story.

There were two drummers. One used his hand to beat out the rhythm on the drum skin, while another innovated a rhythm section by strumming with brushes on the wooden box on which he sat. Other men played an accordion and an electric violin. There were also two guitars and a spoon player. All of the men took turns singing. The spoon player/singer's voice was so good he could stand in for one of the famous Irish tenors. Their expressions while playing the songs showed the love of their culture and the hardships the Irish faced throughout the years. The bawdy songs were so spirited, they made the musicians sweat.

One man from Ireland, Kevin McHugh, sat in on one number, singing and playing his guitar. His foot hit the beat with his leg flying up off the floor.

I met and spoke with some of the people in the pub. They were locals, some from the States, and a couple from England.

I thought listening to traditional Irish music was one way to learn about the Irish culture, but dinner would be another way. I searched the area known as Temple Bar and saw that in this neighborhood, a person could find food from every culture on the planet, it seems, but I wanted a typical Irish meal.

I found one by asking a lot of questions as I passed Italian, Persian, Indian, pizza places, hot dog stands, other restaurants, and many pubs in this land of pubs. I ended up having a dish of grilled vegetables and mash. Mash was mashed potatoes over meat and gravy in a casserole dish and then baked.

Now I have been awakened to the life of the Irish.

St. James Hospital Emergency Room

I spent time in the St. James Hospital Emergency Room in Dublin today. Not to worry; it was to get a prescription for a medicine I was about to run out of. When I got there, a nurse spoke with me about what I needed and assured me a doctor would see me. Didn't think I needed to see one, but guess they have rules.

Dr. Darrough Shields, who, by the way, was easy on the eyes, had the nurse take my blood pressure and temperature, and when he declared me able to continue with the medicine, he wrote out a prescription, shook my hand, and told me to have fun on my journey. Before seeing the doctor, I sat down in the emergency room to wait my turn and then observed a sign that stated there would be a four- to five-hour wait.

The only real emergency was the heavy-set man who was lying on a few chairs. He came into the room in a wheelchair. An attendant tried to get him to sit up, but he wouldn't budge.

Finally, he said, "If you just leave me alone, when they call my name, I'll walk in. I'm not that sick."

The nurse did call him in, and he stood up and walked in, just like he said he would.

I only had a 20-minute wait.

After I got the prescription, I went upstairs to the pharmacy through the hospital entrance room and lobby. I have never, ever seen such a hospital. It's just like a city. There were cafes, restaurants, gift shops, and many fast-food places, as well. It was a most beautiful, spacious building. I wanted to trade the noisy hostel for a stay in the hospital.

Before going to the hospital, I finally got the directions there from the hostel receptionist after she told me she didn't know any doctors. I decided a hospital would be the place to help me. I got on the tram just in time. A man saw me racing to the door, and when the door started to close, he opened it with his heel. It reminded me of a soccer game I saw when a player made a goal with his heel. Good save!

Turning a glitch into a conversation starter

After the hospital, I found a printer and ordered cards with my name and email address. Unfortunately, the printer used an "i" for an "l" on my address, but I didn't feel like going back to wait, so I just accepted them. Now, when I hand them out, I change the "i" to an "l" with a pen and that alone gets conversation going.

This morning, I attempted to change two $100 bills and was turned down at the bank.

"No bank in Ireland will change your bills," said a man who seemed to enjoy telling me that. He said there are no controls over counterfeit bills and no way to determine if they are counterfeit. However, he did tell me of a travel agent about one mile away who probably would change them for me, so off I went down the mall, passing screaming musicians and many shoppers. I'm telling you, some people in this world have money to spend. I have noticed in the stores they are having lots of sales, including three-items-for-two-euro deals.

It was a change-making business and an information center I found, and I immediately got some euros, which went right away to lunch on the top floor of a department store. Guess that business trusts that this American wouldn't hand them a counterfeit bill.

Dublin has many department stores that remind me of two stores in California, Ford's old store in Watsonville and Holman's in Pacific Grove, as well as Denver's Dry Goods and Daniels and Fishers Tower. Ah, the good old days when you could shop and have lunch in a nice upstairs restaurant with all of your packages at your side.

By the way, the noisy Germans have left the building, as I will myself tomorrow. I'll be picked up by Peter Lyons to stay at his and his companion's house for three days in Dublin.

Dublin scenes

I met a teacher with a group of students from Germany. Thomas Petri is a Renaissance man who teaches English literature, German, and religious studies. He also makes musical instruments out of cigar boxes and weaves string bracelets for fun. Additionally, he is a lay pastor for the Baptist Church, and he wears a kilt.

Another gentleman, Manuel, from a town near Bologna, Italy, is in Ireland to learn English. We sat together during lunchtime. I heated up something I got from a store, and Manuel spent some time and created a gourmet-looking soup. Guess who doesn't like to cook?

I'm learning how to walk in this city and watch for traffic that seems to take aim at me. There are big letters on every sidewalk warning pedestrians to either "look left" or "look right." Those warnings are necessary in a busy town with tourists who are used to drivers on the right side of the road. I'm so cautious that it takes me a long time to convince myself I can now walk across the street.

One time, while looking for a shopping area where I could replace the second pair of pants that have grown too big, a kind woman walked all the way with me to the shopping district that was jam-packed with folks looking for bargains. The shops are extremely noisy with blaring music and loud voices trying to be heard.

Yesterday, after listening to the jigging sounds of Irish music, I walked around a bit and found Christ's Church Cathedral, Dublin, a piece of the original medieval wall, and much more. While walking on a flower-filled garden path, a gentleman asked me where I was from. I don't think I look too much different from any Irish woman, but I've been mistaken now three times for being Swedish, just as the gentleman did yesterday.

But once they hear me speak, they know I'm from the States because of my "accent."

Blue pajamas and blue sheets, and viewing the past

I am now in Abigail's Hostel in the Temple Bar district of Dublin, not too far from where I was when I first arrived here. This place looks cozy with several couches and comfortable chairs in the common area. Peter, my "couch surfing" host, brought me here after a great breakfast.

Peter and Jola, who live in the Mount St. Anne's Milltown area, took me for a long drive yesterday to see another part of Dublin. We first saw the rocky beach of the Bray Coast. While there were a typical beach and boardwalk as seen in many places in the world, this one has grass between the beach and the parking lot, which would accommodate people wanting to sit for a spell on grass before embarking on the rocks.

Peter said someone told him that rocky beaches, instead of sandy ones, are favored in some places because rocks are cleaner, and you don't get sand in your clothing, between your toes, and all over the place.

The water was calm, and from where we stood, we could see the small mountain where a path took walkers up to the top for a great view. A train travels around the base of the hill near the ocean. I found out later that we were only a block away from where my friend and romance writer, Kemberlee Shortland, once lived. I must ask her how much of Ireland influences her stories.

After spending some time walking near the sea, we then headed to the Wicklow Mountains National Park in Glendalough. It is a beautiful park with a lake and walking trails. I could imagine on a non-rainy day how families could bring a picnic lunch and enjoy the grounds.

Peter had spent time there as a youngster and pointed to the dense tree forest and flora, and said a trail would take him through the forest to the top of the hill. For more detail on this beautiful spot, go to www.glendalough.ie.

It was once a granite-mining village, according to Peter. Walking around, I could only imagine what it must have looked like back in the day when the miners worked and families lived near the lakes, the river, and the hills.

Nearby, there is an old village of stone houses and a protected cemetery with many large stones and crosses. It is the St. Kevin's Monastery of the sixth century. Still standing is the church and a partial gateway of stone.

The first night, after I had already put on my blue pajamas, Peter brought a bundle of blue sheets, a blanket, and a pillow for my bed.

"Isn't it nice to know that we have sheets that match your pajamas?"

Meanwhile, Jola had been getting ready to attend a wedding of a friend in Poland, to be accompanied by Peter. She modeled a green dress and then a purple one, both in the same style.

"Which one do you like better?"

"That's easy. The green one that brings out your gorgeous, curly, strawberry blonde hair."

"I picked that one, too," Peter announced from the adjoining bedroom.

They were exceptionally good hosts for the www.couch-surfing.com program. Peter has not yet "surfed" for a spot in the world, but Jola is experienced in couch surfing and in hostel living. Peter and Jola have hosted many surfers, and, according to both of them, they have had good luck with choosing guests.

"Wear eye shades when you sleep and put ear plugs in your ears, and you'll get a good night's sleep," Jola had advised.

Peter, a kind bear of a man, and Jola, a feisty pixie of a woman, entertained me with stories and prepared the best of meals. Peter, a rising star in the business world, will soon depart for Australia, as he has been recruited for a position there. Jola, an experienced world traveler with stories and good traveling advice, remains in Ireland for a time.

Both were kind to me, and that was grandly appreciated. It's just another example of how good most people are in this world we share. I liked their style of living, and, of course, there are always ideas to learn and put into place in my life.

Couch surfing

I want to tell you about "couch surfing." That is exactly what I did at Peter Lyons and Jola's apartment in Dublin. I heard about couch surfing from my new German friend, Nathalie, when we were both in the Capital Inn Hostel in Iceland. She has been couch surfing many times as a recipient and also as a host.

All you do is join up and post your profile and vacation schedule, and a host may contact you to spend three evenings in their home. After you have been hosted, both the host and the couch surfer can post their experiences and recommendations.

Peter explained how he and Jola host couch surfers.

"We do it for the one month of June, and go through the couch surfing website searching for folks we think would be fun to meet and host for three days. We thought you were an interesting person with your background as a news reporter."

I think my age may have surprised them a bit, as I was several decades older than they; however, that is nothing new to me.

Couch surfers never pay, and they are usually hosted for the evenings, but by day, they fend for themselves as visitors/tourists nearby the host's home. It is up to the host if they want to take the couch surfer to see sights.

It's nice, but not expected, for the guest to gift the host with a bottle of wine or treat them to lunch or dinner. It is what you would do if you were visiting a relative or a long-time friend.

Peter liberated me from the Four Courts Hostel and took me back to his apartment, where we picked up two women from Sweden. He returned them, after having hosted them, back to the airport. After arriving at the apartment, and back on the way to the airport with the Swedish women, Peter dropped me off in a part of Dublin where museums are many, and the famous Trinity College campus can be toured, along with The Long Room Library that holds 200,000 books. The room is 65 meters in length, with very old books that line the walls and go up to the enormous ceiling.

I also had bangers and mash for lunch at the Porterhouse Brewing Co. after walking the shopping district and listening to a few Dublin street musicians.

One man stood out as a fancily dressed doorman for a large department store. He appeared to be more than happy to get his photo taken.

It's a very busy district, and before I left the area, I had coffee at the famous Bewley's restaurant. This family-owned establishment has been around since 1840, and still has the original stained glass windows. The restaurant roasts its own coffee they produce from their own plantations located around the world.

After the first day, I took a tram back to Peter and Jola's home.

Playing reporter in Belfast

"The boy? The boy in the Belfast jail?"

That was just one of the very few lines I had while playing a madam in the Western Stage production of *The Hostage*. The play was based on the warring years in Belfast and was adapted from an Irish play by Brendan Behan. It involves a planned execution of an 18-year-old IRA (Irish Republican Army) member who was accused of killing a policeman.

There I was yesterday inside a replica of a prison cell. The bed and door came from the Armagh Women's Prison in Belfast. The devastating cell was one part of the Irish Republican History Museum that was opened in the Conway Mill complex in 2007, which coincided with the first anniversary of the death of Belfast Republican Army member, Eileen Hickey.

Eileen had been one of the women Republican POWs in the *Armagh Gaol* from 1973 to 1977. Upon her release, it became her passion to educate people on the history and understanding of the Republican struggle in Ireland. She collected artifacts and prison handicrafts that represented various phases of the struggle for Irish freedom. Items also donated by hundreds of individuals and families date back to the Irish struggles during the years of 1798 to 1977 and beyond.

The guide from Dublin to Belfast told us that Belfast is enjoying a calm atmosphere today. I could see that in the business of the street where I had an opportunity to play reporter.

The tour began from Dublin early in the morning. I'm not really fond of tours that much because my independent streak wants me to sometimes veer off to something that catches my eye, but in general, I tried to stay in my group. That didn't happen yesterday, through another glitch.

The Dublin bus stopped in the center of Belfast after we had seen a lot along the one-hour trip getting there. We were told to find a bathroom if we needed but to be back at the same spot by

1:55 p.m. to get on a Belfast bus that would take the Dublin folks and others on a more extensive view of the city.

I ran off to a department store, found a W.C., and thought I had a few more minutes to spend, according to my watch. When I came back, and after learning I had missed the bus because the pin that sets the time in my watch had been pulled out and stopped recording the time, I just stayed put and played reporter.

I interviewed people about their lives in Belfast. Everywhere I go, it just convinces me more and more that people are basically good. Behind me on the bench where I sat, little teeny boppers were lining up. By the end of my time warming the bench, they were lined up all the way to the end of the street in front of a music store. A mother of one of the girls in the front of the line told me the girls were waiting for Jedward to show up. For those not familiar with the Irish pop scene, let me explain that Jedward are 20-year-old twins by the names of John and Edward. They are from Dublin.

They were contestants on the Live X Factor show in 2010, and, while they didn't win, they have gained in popularity since then. The girl's mother told me that both of the boys have wild hairdos. I looked them up on the web, and she was right.

The mother seemed calm and relaxed while the teeny boppers behind me squealed in anticipation of Jedward.

"Is Belfast quite a bit different than Dublin, would you say?" I asked her.

"Oh, I wouldn't know, I've never been there."

"Oh, are you from another area? Dublin is only an hour away."

"No, I was born and raised here in Belfast, but I don't travel."

It's only one hour away; that isn't traveling. People in the U.S. commute to jobs that far and farther. I wanted to tell her this, but I'm sticking to my resolve not to criticize people of another country.

Other people sat and joined me in eager conversation. They wanted to know about my travels and about the U.S. But how I missed the bus drew the most comments. They were so sympathetic that I had to assure them I was okay.

"Oh, my goodness, such an independent woman."

"Aren't you scared?"

"Do you travel alone?"

These were just a few of the questions I got, along with big, surprised eyes, scratching heads, and stroking beards.

Then there were two 20-something men, Adam McBurney and Ryan Murray, who eagerly joined me in conversation, and they had a lot to say about Jedward. I think Jedward are more for girls, it seems. These two young men were so much fun to talk with that the time slipped quickly away.

Before, when I was asking around about buses, I told one young bus attendant that I didn't have any English pounds, only euros, and that I was thirsty but didn't want to buy the required five euros of items to get a drink of water. In just a few minutes, the young man handed me a bottle of water.

There were two doctors who joined the tour in Dublin. They were both from the States and were playing hooky from a medical conference. When the bus arrived back at the starting point in Belfast, the woman doctor assured me I hadn't missed much, that they were never off the bus, and when we arrived into town on the Dublin bus, we had already seen much of what they saw on the Belfast bus.

I honestly think I had more fun being with the people of Belfast instead of riding around on the bus.

Chapter Four

July, 2012

Cultural differences

Today, after sending off a letter to my credit union and a CD of Irish music to my son, Ron, I looked for a spot where I could sit and use Wi-Fi. The first place I came to would only allow 20 minutes, so I walked down to the Grand Central Bank of Ireland that is now called The Grand Central Cafe and Bar.

"Do you have Wi-Fi here?" I asked the bartender.

"Sure we do."

"Is there a time limit?"

"Absolutely not."

"Well, then. This is the perfect place."

I looked around for a comfortable chair, not a high table and a bar stool. I cannot stand to have my legs dangle. I found a table in the corner and sat down, but I found the table too high to sit comfortably with the computer (not a good desk), but I had committed to the place and had a look at the menu.

Breakfast looked interesting, especially black and white pudding. Chocolate and vanilla, right? Wrong.

Hmm, it was some kind of meat, and it was a lot of meat on that plate, but I did my best.

Meanwhile, I wasn't getting on the Internet as promised. Soon, a nice gentleman, Mark Billane, came over to ask me if everything was fine. I told him yes, it was, even though the meal was a bit different. I told him I wanted to experience everything the Irish culture has to offer, so I found it all very good.

"What is black and white pudding, anyway?" I asked.

And he filled me in. It is blood pudding, he told me, and also hinted that breakfast at three p.m. might not be the best idea.

Then he sat down, and we had a lively discussion on the differences between U.S. expressions and those of Ireland. After he sat for a while, I thought he was avoiding work, but he assured me all was okay, that he was the boss. Here follow some of our interesting exchanges.

"Restroom—why do you call it a restroom? Are you going to take a pillow down there and rest? We call it a toilet, because that's what it is.

"And our cars have a boot, not a trunk," he said.

I answered, "Yes, but we put things into it as you would a trunk. Boots are what you wear."

I added, "Jumper. You say jumper, and I look up to the top of a building to see someone jumping."

"We call a jumper what you're wearing."

"No, this is a long-sleeved T-shirt."

"We call sausages bangers, but we also call old beat-up cars the same name."

"Hmm, we call old beat-up cars, old beat-up cars."

"Mash is potatoes."

"Yes, I know now. We call them what they are—mashed potatoes." It went on like this for awhile, and I don't remember all of them.

Mark kept me so occupied with his humor that I almost forgot about using the Internet that never did work. Guess that's why he's the manager.

Americans as seen abroad

I'm still in Abigail's Hostel.

Since my traveling, I've heard Americans called bullies, dumb, and the latest one—weird. While thinking about being a weird American, I traveled by foot up and down a busy mall street and observed the people of Dublin.

First, there was a gentlemen banging a drum and chanting as he walked up the street flashing a big, silly smile at all who would look at him. Then he walked by a two-man jazz group. One man played a moody saxophone and the other a drum high hat. The two men heard the smiling drummer playing another beat coming up the street, and they generously changed their music to fit whatever he was doing. Eventually, the drummer playing another beat moved on up the street to continue charming the folks of Dublin.

Then I saw a five-person stone sculpture that many people seemed to be interested in as they stood staring at it. Being weird, I thought I'd go and see what the Dublin folks were admiring.

The people were not in stone after all. I realized they were alive, but thoroughly painted grey, when I saw the woman blink. They didn't change their expressions. Every time someone would drop a coin into a hat, the group would gently bow their heads in thanks.

Then I went into a pub for a bite to eat, sat down, and ordered a plate of grilled vegetables, which was very good, by the way. Two men came in for lunch, sat down, and both continued their business on their cell phones.

When one of the businessmen finished his phone call, being weird, I leaned over and said, "Is this a typical business lunch?"

"Yes, it is," he laughed.

"Why don't you just stay in your office and eat lunch there where you could still stay on the phone?"

"Then I wouldn't get to meet my friend." He smiled at his own incongruousness.

I journeyed on and observed an alleyway with artwork of notable faces of Dublin, and on the same walk, I saw three people sitting down with a blanket up to their eyes, holding a cup out hoping someone would drop a coin or two.

Some man I've seen all over town keeps hounding me. He asks if I would buy a magazine from him. I say no, and then he walks by my side asking me why I don't want to help him. I told him I didn't want his magazine, and he asked, "Where are you from?"

Being a weird American, I told him it wasn't any of his business. Sorry if this sounds rude, but it was just one of those days. He walked away from me with a disappointed look, but went quickly on to harass the next person.

Irish music reminds me of my Daddy.

Last night, I sat at a bar waiting for Irish musicians and dancers to come onto the stage. You know how that is. You make a little nest for yourself where you have a good view, and an hour later, other people come in and stand in front of you.

I nursed a glass of wine for one hour, after convincing the door manager I was too full for a four-course meal. He reluctantly sat me down at the bar.

"You know, if people came in without ordering the meal, the dancers wouldn't get paid."

He looked me square in the eye to tell me this. C'mon, the place was packed. Don't tell me your restaurant isn't making money off of the entertainers.

I have a feeling lots of money was made last night, and much of it went to the owner, but it was also enough to pay the entertainers. I have known many musicians who entertain at restaurants and make little money from it. When will artists get paid? Okay, enough of the rant.

The six musicians were a drummer, an accordionist, a penny whistler, a singer, a guitarist, and a banjo player. The instruments and singers entertained with what I call back-hills music or hill-billy. My dad came to mind, for this was his favorite.

My dad played the harmonica while my brother played the violin, and my mother or myself, the piano. We had some pretty darn good sessions. Later, I learned to tap-dance, and we added that to our repertoire.

My dad came from the back hills of Illinois and went all the way up to the eighth grade in what he lovingly called Red Oak College. His father died in a farming accident when he was a youngster, and he had to work on the farm. He joined the Army at age 17.

I now recognize how my dad worked hard for his family. Music was the center of our life, and last night, listening to the music and watching the dancers brought up fond memories of those nights when we entertained the heck out of ourselves.

No souvenirs for me

I won't be purchasing any trinkets on my yearlong journey. However, I did buy a CD of Irish music for my musician son, Ron, and I have sent it on to him. I travel so light that there isn't any more room, plus I'm on an extreme budget. I haven't lost much on the trip—only one gold earring, two towels, and an alarm clock. Not bad for over three months, huh? None of those were too important. Memories, my notes, and photos will be my souvenirs. The one towel I lost came from the Salvation Army store in Reykjavik, Iceland. I'm going to find another one today.

I'm also going to meet Michael, my next couch surfing host, later today. I plan on staying with him next week, if he approves of me.

Tomorrow, I'm off to my friend and romance writer, Kemberlee Southland, and her husband, Peter, at their home in Kildare.

The next day

Kemberlee and I met up at the Jarvis Luas (light rail tram system) Railway Station in Dublin. From there we went to the food court where she had Mexican food and I had Greek food. We then boarded the train for Red Cow where she had earlier parked her car after taking her husband, Peter, to work. He is a mechanical engineer.

Later, we got the car and picked Peter up at work, and then drove to their lovely home in Kildare near the Curragh. Curragh is a national park on 50,000 acres of all shades of green. Today, it was sprinkled with raindrops. A famous horse racing course is run on the Curragh, and it is also the home for a training base for the Irish Army.

We drove through the Curragh, and then on a narrow, winding road among the green trees, shrubs, and grass to their home where their collies, Daisy and Poppy, were eager to greet their mom and pop and visitor.

These two dogs are so smart that one of them can recognize the names of her toys and can fetch the correct one, even if it is way upstairs in another room. They are beautiful and add much ambience to Kemberlee and Peter's home life.

Kemberlee writes romance novels and is also the co-owner of Tigearr Publishing— www.tigearrpublishing.com.

Kemberlee and Peter have arranged to take me to see some of their favorite spots in Ireland, the country adopted by Kemberlee, who is originally from Carmel, California. Kemberlee met Irishman Peter Southland while a tourist, married him 15 years ago, and has lived in Ireland ever since.

It has rained most of the day, but my philosophy, "It is what it is," means that nothing can be done about the weather, so why complain?

Yesterday, before meeting Kemberlee, I met Michael Lyne, with whom I'll be staying next week. It is another "couch surfing" opportunity for me. We met up at Abigail's Hostel and walked to a photo exhibit, opening night, where we saw photographer David Monahan's documentation of the recent wave of Irish emigration in photographs taken just before their subjects' departures to different corners of the world.

"It is my wish to photograph people of all nationalities who have made the decision to move from Ireland for economic reasons," he said during the evening's open house.

His photos were large portraits of individuals, families, or couples in moods of contemplation of their futures, while they stand or sit near old suitcases.

After that, Michael showed me the castle near Temple Bar. It was once owned by the Queen and is now used for government purposes. We ventured on to a 50s diner for a snack. While we were walking the streets on the way to the diner, we saw a man with incredibly long hair tied into a braid that ran down his back, talking with a group of men. He could have sat on the braid.

"I dare you to go ask him how long it took him to grow his hair that long," Michael dared.

"Okay, I will." So I did.

"Excuse me. Sorry for butting in, but I'm curious about how long it took you to grow your hair that long."

"Oh, all kinds of people ask me that. I don't mind. It's taken 18 years."

"Well, thank you."

I went back to Michael and gave him the news. I don't know what Michael thought of me at that point. But we made plans for the day he'd pick me up after I spent time with Kemberlee and Peter.

Prior to the evening with Michael, I walked to the Icon Factory, an artists' cooperative that produces art and attractive products celebrating Ireland's cultural icons in literature, poetry, novels, humor, acting, and sports.

I met artist Aga Szot from Poland who has been instrumental in helping get the Icon Factory up and running. She explained the purpose behind the Icon Walk—to provide access to famous Irish creative artists, and to give a forum to the artists of today to reach an audience.

The Icon Walk features art that demonstrates not only those who have made Ireland famous for its culture, but also those talented artists of today whose art features the famous.

The current-day artists are invited to participate by showing their work in a tiny studio donated for such use, with the agreement that they will also honor a past artist with a current work. Much of that work is seen in large paintings along the Icon Walk. In the Icon Factory, there are many items for sale featuring artwork on souvenirs.

The Icon Walk clearly demonstrates the difference between the trash-strewn alleyway before, and after the work is put in the gallery, an artistic alley wall.

Gardens, castles, and shades of green

I was with my friends, Kemberlee and Peter, who took me to see beautiful sites near their home in Kildare, Ireland.

The first one was the Heywood Gardens in Abbeyleix. We drove down tree-lined lanes to Ballinakill and parked the car near the old stone entrance to a formal garden, a garden that featured a sunken pool. Stone turtles sat around the perimeter of the pool. All variety of flowers, colors, and aromas circled around the garden and kept all three of us mesmerized with the beauty and the many creative photo opportunities.

There were lots of stone filigree and gargoyles, which always pleases my eye.

Every day there is something to learn. Today, I learned that the word *kill* in Irish is church, and *ballina* is town. Together, it means church town.

We journeyed on to the Rock of Cashel by the way of many small towns. One notable town had the unusual name, Horse and Jockey.

"This is a well-known stop," Peter said and noted the large restaurant.

The route we took was the original old road. Traffic now goes on a relatively new freeway and bypasses some of the towns we saw along the old road, including Horse and Jockey.

According to Kemberlee, who, I learned, uses much of Ireland's history in her romance novels, the Rock of Cashel was the seat of the Kings of Munster. One king was Brian Boru in the tenth century. Kemberlee has taken special interest in this king and the history surrounding him for her new book to be published in 2014, *The Diary*.

"That is the year of the 1,000[th] anniversary of Boru's death," she said.

Our third stop was the Emo Court House and Gardens at Laois. The massive house was built in 1790 for the Earls of Portarlington. Built in the neo-classical style, the house has grounds that include gardens, a park, formal lawns, a lake, and huge redwood trees. The building, green grass, and statues were overshadowed only by a cute and very busy red squirrel who never stopped eating acorns.

After the Emo House, we went on to the ruins of the Rock of Dunamase, and then on home to let Daisy and Poppy out of the house.

Kemberlee and Peter live near the National Stud area in County Kildare, where Ireland's thoroughbred industry is home to magnificent horses bred, reared, and trained there. The Kildangan Stud owned by His HH Sheikh Mohammed bin Rashid Al Maktoum is housed near their home.

The baton of the expat has been passed.

July 10, 2012. I have been traveling for three months and seven days. I've seen a lot, learned a lot, and met some incredible people who have taken good care of me.

Kemberlee and Peter spent every one of their waking hours making me feel at home. They passed the "baton of Laureen" over to Michael Lyne in Kavanagh's, the Gravediggers' Pub near the Glasnevin Cemetery.

The pub was established in 1833, and if my imagination serves me right, not much has changed inside its dark rooms. Men stood at the bar and tilted pints of beer, laughed, and exchanged the latest jokes, probably doing the same as they did after work over 100 years ago.

Before handing me over on the last day, Peter and Kemberlee took me to see the Newbridge Silverware and the Museum of Style Icons. The exhibit featured the Hollywood clothing and memorabilia of Marilyn Monroe, Audrey Hepburn, Princess Grace, and many others. It also featured Michael Jackson and Elvis Presley costumes. Princesses Grace and Diana had window corners of their own.

We then went through several greenhouses in the National Botanic Garden of Ireland. A variety of flowers, cacti, tropical fruits, and ornamental vegetables were healthy and beautifully displayed.

Now I am in the main town of Ashbourne, Ireland. Last night, Michael took me to a local pub out of the usual tourist beat, and there I sat in a dark, low-ceilinged, concrete-floored, old building favored by locals. I drank one-half of a "pint" just to experience the way the Irish have been drinking for centuries. It will no doubt be my first and last.

Then we went to a little more upscale place called the Snailbox. There, we met the regulars—Smitty, a retired tax collector; Johnny Malloy, a pilot; and Phillip Foster, the dynamic owner of the establishment.

Smitty insisted I look at the hats on the ceiling in the other room, so to oblige, I did, and there they were, thousands of hats from all over the world attached to the ceiling and walls. If I would promise to send Phillip a hat, he would give me one of his with the Snailbox logo. I didn't promise to do that for three reasons. Number one—I don't wear hats like that. Number two—I resist feeling obligations for anything simple such as exchanging a hat. And, number three—I didn't want to carry a hat around for the rest of the year.

I believe in angels.

Several angels have taken good care of me while on my personal path to see how people share this world we live in. The last angel, gentleman Michael Lyne of Ashbourne, Ireland, put many miles on his car to show me the Ireland he loves. Michael is one of the kindest men I have ever met—patient, funny, intelligent, and always a gentleman.

He lost his wife seven years ago and is obviously still sad over his loss. But he has survived and continues to find joy in life. He has traveled extensively in the world and tells many a good tale.

The final drive we took in his car this morning, July 12, was to the train station to drop me off for my next stay in the City of Cork. He thoughtfully packed a lunch for me to take on the train and gave me a book to read.

I decided to treat myself to a hotel room today before heading off to the hostel in town in the morning. It was a good plan, for when I hit the hotel bed, I slept for three hours. A walk down the hill to a small mom and pop store rejuvenated me.

Here follow some of the sights Michael wanted me to see—Newgrange, Knowth, and Dowth, all seen near the Boyne River. All three are sites associated with the United Nations Educational, Scientific, and Cultural Organization (UNESCO).

The mounds (tombs), covered with grass, are close to 5,000-years-old. Amazing to see and to wonder how the people could build such structures out of tons and tons of large rocks and with such accuracy. The accuracy I'm talking about here just blew me away. A cave we climbed into was lit up with electric light so we could find our way inside, but when turned out, it was pitch black, as it would have been 5,000 years ago.

The passage, as it is called, is still waterproof after all those years. It was pointed out that the structure was constructed so that on the shortest day of the year, December 21, and for a number of days before and after, a shaft of sunlight enters the chamber through an opening in the roof.

According to the material provided, "The rays first hit the edge of the broken basin stone at the back of the chamber floor, and then, as the sun rises higher, the beam broadens and moves down the passage. The alignment is so accurate that there is very little chance that it was accidental."

Keep in mind this construction predates the pyramids! After a tour of the mounds, you can put your name in a lotto system for a chance to visit during the winter solstice and see first-hand how the light comes inside the passage. But there's no guarantee the sun will be shining that day, especially given the amount of rain that falls in Ireland.

The tour through the three structures lasted three hours, and since Michael has visited them many times, he waited for me in the coffee shop.

Trim Castle was another site that greatly interested me, as it was the site for the Hollywood movie, *Braveheart*. Now, why would that interest me? Well, it's because some shirttail relative did our family research, which resulted in the knowledge that I'm supposedly related to William Wallace. I must make that trip to Scotland, then. Agreed?

A German couple, whom I first saw at Newgrange, observed something that made the young woman laugh at me, and it's no wonder. At both sites, I couldn't find my ticket to get in, and my comment at both places, while I frantically searched in all of my pockets, was, "I have too dang many pockets." Each time, however, I let people go in front of me as I scurried around inside my clothing looking for proof that I had paid to get in.

An abundance of heritage sites, castles, and ancient ruins are there to be explored, and I saw so many of them, for which I am grateful to Michael.

We ended the day when we visited his 97-year-old aunt who lives in a retirement home. Sister Dominic, a nun in the Order of Mercy, is a vibrant woman, knowledgeable about Ireland, and has traveled elsewhere in the world, including the United States. With penetrating eyes, white skin, and wearing a nun's habit as she has most of her life, she showed interest in me and shared some of her travel stories. I loved talking with her—a wise woman and an angel, indeed.

Friday in the rain

I'm in the City of Cork, and the county seat. I arrived yesterday after a three-hour train ride. From the train station, I got a taxi and arrived at the Hotel Montenotte. The hotel sits on top of a hill in an upscale neighborhood.

I sat in the lounge writing and answering email messages and enjoyed a breathtaking view of the city lights as it got darker.

I got up late this morning and had breakfast in the restaurant, then checked out, got another taxi, and then checked into the Kinlay Hostel in the Shandon area of Cork. Here I go, back to hosteling. It helps the budget tremendously, but I must say, a nice hotel beats everything.

Over the ten minutes it took the taxi driver to circumvent the city's rolling hills and busy streets, he talked non-stop about what I should see in his city. I couldn't understand a word he said. I kept reminding myself we spoke the same king's language. He was a tall, dark-haired man who very seriously worked at getting my attention. I sat in the back seat, while he would turn to look at me and point out the sites.

As we were driving, I pointed to the sign of the hostel, the hostel that he was speeding past.

"I'm going to take you to the back of the hotel so you won't have so many steps," he explained.

I understood that and thanked him for his consideration.

When we got to the back of the place, he backed up into a long and narrow alleyway over cobblestones and finally stopped.

When I got my room, I was stunned to find out that it was on the third floor, which was really the fifth floor. Fifty-five steps up the stairs to my room, I counted. A young woman picked up one of my suitcases and helped me to the room, while I had another two bags and my computer bag to hoist up the rest of the way.

I'm sharing the room with two young women from Spain, a woman from France, and one other woman from Antigua.

Tired but rested up a bit after getting settled, I took off walking down the road in the rain to the busy section of town and immediately got lost when I wanted to walk back to the hostel. Some nice young man told me I was close and to keep walking that way; he pointed to the corner of the street and the bridge that goes over the River Lee.

As I walked back up the street on cobblestone and sidewalks to the hostel, I heard the bells and chimes from the Shandon Church. This church is known to allow anyone to play the bells. How fun! I don't know what the rules are yet, but whoever played at the time provided good listening music.

Then it was time to find a grocery store, so I continued down the street where someone in the hostel told me I'd find a store. I stopped and asked three guys who were standing and smoking near a pub. One guy was a large bald man with tattooed arms. Another was about in his 70s, with a red nose and matching red eyes, and the other wore a blood-stained white apron. When I asked about the store, they all spoke at once. I was happy they all pointed to the direction of the store because I couldn't understand what they were saying. They appeared to be happy to be asked, however.

People have asked me about the language spoken in Ireland, and to answer that, the language is English and Irish. Nearly everything you see, such as road signs, for example, is written in both languages. Schools teach both languages to children, and most people have knowledge of both. I've been told there are areas in Ireland where only Irish is spoken. Dialects are different, and accents make it easy for an Irish person to tell what area of Ireland the person comes from.

The city, from what I have seen so far, is beautiful, with the River Lee running through it. I've seen an opera house, the famous and very old English market, and many pubs and cafes in historical buildings.

It has been raining all day.

What a trooper!

People give many clues that they see I'm not a young chick. This morning is an example.

"You are such a trooper," the owner of the hostel said as I walked down the 55 steps to the reception area from the room I was given at the top of the building. The comment was the prize for making it up and down the steps at my age, I assume.

My trooper goodness continued throughout the day when I swore, even in the day's difficulties, I would never give up.

It was the trip to Blarney for the flower festival, a fundraiser for Dogs-for-the-Blind, that put my trooper goodness to the test. I was told to catch the bus down the road from the hostel and that it would be there every 15 minutes. But the bus didn't come in 15 minutes or even for one-and-one-half hours.

Meanwhile, people came by, and each time, I asked the questions, "Is this the right stop for the bus to Blarney?" and, "When does it come by?"

I found that when I flagged down a bus, on three different occasions, even the bus driver couldn't answer my questions.

Every single person had a different response, and then a couple stopped to help me, using their technology. The woman looked up the website for the bus company and got the phone number so the man could call and get the correct time on his phone.

"It will be here at 10:15. But if it doesn't, then you should walk to the bus station," he advised me after his phone call to the station.

"Isn't there such a thing as a schedule?" I asked.

He shook his head and shrugged his shoulders in an "I don't know" manner. His wife also shook her head. "Most people take cars these days," she mumbled. No kidding?

By now, my legs and feet hurt so badly from waiting from nine a.m., and, at 10:15 a.m., still no bus. Another lady stopped and called on her cell phone and got a different answer.

"The bus will leave the station at 10:30, so I think it would be better for you to get the bus down there," she advised. It looks as though walking to the station is the only right answer.

So, I limped to the station, got on the bus, and the driver advised me that he would come by again in Blarney at 3:20 p.m. for the return trip. But that didn't happen, either. Instead, it came one whole hour later while I waited on tired, sore legs for the bus in Blarney.

I put the whole annoying business away, for the rest of the time was enjoyable. The flower show was nice with various activities and good people to speak with. A couple makes jam from fruit, as well as liquor that was once illegal. I bought a small bottle to give to my next host and hostess in Macroom.

A field of birds tethered to their posts was on display by a man who trains the birds for rescue. Big owls, a turkey vulture, and other friends of the sky greeted people who oohed and ahhed at them. There was an animal petting area where I couldn't resist holding an eight-week-old rabbit that seemed to enjoy a cuddle as much as I enjoyed giving it one.

Barry Noyce was there weaving baskets from reeds. His wife, Sarah, doesn't weave but supports the weaver in his hobby. He gave me rules about weaving I'd never heard before, but that was after I told him proudly that I had made one basket myself from reeds around our house in the Colorado mountains.

Some other observations I've made so far—Americans' way of saying a house is "for rent" is "to let" here. Food "to go," as Americans say it, is "take away" here. "Mini-brekkie"? That's a small breakfast, of course.

Just musing here about common phrases. A phrase in common with America and other countries is, "No problem" in lieu of "You're welcome." When did "No problem" become the response instead of "You're welcome"? I say, "Thank you" to the waitress for serving me, and she says, "No problem." Did I have a problem? Did she?

Observations once I'm back in the hostel—persuasions of every type are represented on the walls in photos and posters, from Che Guevara to Martin Luther King, from Elvis to the Beatles, from jazz to rock 'n' roll. Oh, yes, and Einstein. Weren't they troopers? Shouldn't I send them a photo of this trooper for their walls? After all I went through today, I lived up to the word.

Angels!

More angels arrived today. I finally asked at the reception desk if a room could be located for me that wasn't on the top floor and was told that the only room was a private room on the first floor. Couldn't afford that, I told him, and trudged on up the 55 steps.

Later, when in the kitchen cooking eggs and mushy peas for lunch, the owner took me aside and told me the nice guy at reception told him about the chore I have "upping and downing" on the stairs, and that he would give me the private room for the same price as the room with seven other females. Angels? Yes, indeed! I believe! I believe!

Before that good news, I walked up the stone path to St. Anne's Church Shandon for the Holy Eucharist services. I arrived a bit early, and a gentleman told me a bit of the church's history. It is one of Cork's oldest buildings, almost 300 years old, and is the oldest church in continuous use today. The original stained glass windows and a christening font dated 1629 are still intact.

"The font was rescued from the original church that was destroyed in the 1690 Siege of Cork," the gentleman said of the font we were standing near.

"So after the fighting, then everyone goes back to church?" I sarcastically asked, and he nodded yes.

The material that was available reads that the first rector in 1772, Reverend Arthur Hyde, was the great-great-grandfather of the first President of Ireland. The eight bells in the tower were cast in 1750, and weigh over six tons. The weather vane at the top is a gold leaf-painted salmon, which represents the River Lee.

I sat at the very front row and couldn't see when to sit and stand, and because the seats are nice and soft, I couldn't hear people getting up and down from their chairs, so I probably didn't behave appropriately. Anyway, I did get communion, and when leaving the church, met some friendly people. One man knew all about Monterey and the famous people who live there, including Doris Day.

One other pamphlet available that I couldn't resist was one about the Mother Jones Festival in Shandon of Cork. I have taken some of the information from that source. A festival will celebrate the 175th anniversary of Mary Harris' baptism in the church. Mary Harris was otherwise known as Mother Jones. (I could have called my grandmother that, for she was Mother [Nellie] Jones and a believer in the abolishment of alcohol—she was an active member of the WCTU [Women's Christian Temperance Union].)

Back to Mother Jones, the union organizer. Her family immigrated when she was a child, first to Canada and then to the U.S. where Harris became a teacher. She married George Jones in 1860, and they settled in Memphis. The couple lived through the American Civil War and had four children.

Tragically, a yellow fever epidemic arrived, and Mary's entire family died within a few days of each other in Memphis.

Moving on in her life, she became active in union activities in Chicago during the industrial boom. She took an active part in the March of Covey's unemployed army in 1894, and became a union organizer for the United Mine Workers Union of America. She organized workers throughout America.She was outraged over the treatment of young children working long hours in mills and mines, and because of that, she lead the March of the Mill Children from Pennsylvania to the New York summer home of President Theodore Roosevelt in 1903.

Because of the courage she demonstrated, the miners began calling her Mother Jones. She was the only woman present at the founding of the Industrial Workers of the World in Chicago in 1905. Later, she became active in the Socialist Party of America, and she supported the Mexican Revolution. That got her an acknowledgment from Pancho Villa.

Mother Jones was known for her passionate speeches in defense of working people. She died on November 30, 1930, at age 93.

On August 1 of this year, Mother Jones (Mary Harris) will be recognized for the first time in her native City of Cork. Plaques will be presented, along with concerts, film exhibitions and a lecture at the Bells of Shandon. The Irish premiere of *Mother Jones, America's Most Dangerous Woman* will be shown at the Maldron Hotel on July 31. A whole week has been dedicated to honor Mother Jones, with music, bell concert, choirs, and bagpipes, to name a few.

I will be gone by then, but I cannot help but feel in awe of a woman who took her energies from what could have ruined her life to doing good for others.

More musing on my stay in Shandon

Sunday, today, was one of quiet reflection and a thankful heart for the people who are so good to me. I can hear the bells from my room!

Back to the lunch and mushy peas. I've seen that on menus and wondered about them. Then I found a small can at the grocery store. They are mushy and very delicious.

I was taken away in a paddy wagon.

Paddy Wagon. That's the name of the company that drives people to sites all over Ireland.

Before getting into the taxi to take me to the bus, however, the driver gave me some interesting tidbits about Ireland. I could have listened to him forever, but I would have missed the bus.

One tidbit he shared was the reason that people in the U.K., including Ireland, Scotland, Wales, and the many islands, drive on the left side of the road. It goes back to the horse transportation days centuries ago, he said.

"The people rode their horses next to the fence on the left side of the road, so the warriors could reach into their coats and grab their swords with their right arms."

I gave him some information that he didn't know, and it relates to the same reason. Men's shirts button on the other side than do women's blouses. That's so the warrior could pull open his coat and reach for his sword. Then the taxi driver told me why castle steps are wider toward the wall—same reason. When a warrior comes down the steps, he has more room than the bad guys coming up the steps, which puts him at an advantage.

The Paddy Wagon guide, Michael Kearney, was a delightful fellow who could be a "voice-over" talent with his fetching voice and thick Irish accent. He was easy to understand and offered up interesting historical information and even sang us a song. He's a banjo player and plays in traditional Irish bands for set dancing. Set dancing, called *Céilí*, can be seen on YouTube, he told me.

The town of Cork, which he pronounced "Cock," is a music town, he said.

Our first stop on the winding road in the Paddy Wagon was in the town of Kinsale. Michael explained the road was winding because of animals. Cows wore a path between the grazing land. People then walked on the path, followed by horses used for transportation, then finally the car.

Better roads were necessary because farmers brought butter to the main town of Cork, and from there it was shipped out. When that happened, the road became known as the Butter Road.

Michael showed us the two forts in the town of Kinsale. The large fort was called Charles and had chains strung between it and the smaller fort, called James, Michael said. The chains had spikes that would stop enemy boats from coming into the harbor.

Before we stopped in the charming town of Kinsale, Michael told us to observe the low ceiling in the older shops in the historical part of town.

"The people were quite small back in the 1600s," he said.

The buildings have been restored and fit close together in bright colors.

There was a turning point in the history of Kinsale involving drama of the English, the Spanish, and a family named McDonald. "It's a very important part of our Irish history," he said.

Let's go to the Blarney Castle.

The castle is 600-years-old. The Blarney Stone at the very top of the castle is known as the Stone of Eloquence. The story goes, as it has for 200 years, that if you kiss the stone, you will have the gift of eloquence and will never again be at a loss for words.

I climbed up the 100 or so winding stone steps, just as the men did 600 years ago, and got to the top. I told myself that I wouldn't bother walking all the way and then kiss the stone that must have thousands of germs on it after 200 years. But did I kiss it? Wait, and I'll tell you about it, one way or another.

Our last stop was at Cobh, which Michael pronounced "Coh." This city's harbor was the last port of call for the ship *Titanic*. On April 15, 1912, while out at sea, the *Titanic* hit an iceberg, and 1,514 people died in the disaster.

I thought about the *Titanic* a lot while roaming the town, viewing memorabilia in shop windows, including framed newspaper accounts of the ship, and I remembered Denver's own Molly Brown who survived the disaster and was credited with saving lives.

I knew where Molly Brown lived during her heyday, which was in a large mansion in Denver, my hometown. A movie and stage play were written about her, *The Unsinkable Molly Brown*. Debbie Reynolds played Molly in the movie version, and I saw the play in New York many years ago.

Long day in the fog

Got on the Paddy Wagon again this morning at eight a.m. and didn't return back until eight p.m., and I'm doing the same thing tomorrow.

Paul was the guide who took us to visit the Cliffs of Moher, one of the most popular tourist attractions in the area. These cliffs rise from the Atlantic Ocean, up to eight kilometers. From the cliffs one can see the Aran Islands and other well-known sites. That is, if it's not foggy.

The fog came along with strong winds and rain and concealed the cliffs, so we couldn't see much. However, the visitor's center offered a restaurant, shops, and an educational program.

Even though we didn't get to experience the cliffs, there was a lot to see along the way, both going to the cliffs and coming back.

Here are some of the sites we saw during a foggy day.

The St. John's Castle and Bridge in Limerick were impressive, as are the city and the university housed there. This city is where Frank McCourt lived and where the film from the book he wrote, *Angela's Ashes*, was made. I learned from Paul that some of the filming also took place in Shandon near the hostel where I'm staying.

One interesting fact pointed out to us was several bullet holes on a house that had been fired on there during the Irish Civil War in the years 1921-22.

Lahinch Golf Club has a bumpy and probably difficult course, although I wouldn't know, as I only tried golfing one time and gave up after the first miss. It sits on not just rolling hills, but on bumps and obstacles that seem to give professional golfers a chance to practice and improve their skills. I saw golfers out on the course in a drizzling rain, standing next to big fat cows that enjoy the grass in another way from the golfers, but are just as obsessed.

One of the final observations we saw on our way back to Cork was the Bunratty Castle and Folk Park. It is in Bunratty Castle where you could enjoy a medieval banquet and traditional Irish night. I'm told that back in the medieval days, the folks ate with their fingers, and no utensils were even known about.

"That sounds like fun," I said, and a man who was on the bus and playing hooky from a convention said, "Yes, and with a food fight, too."

I met two ladies who were also taking a break from a conference. Shannon is from Creede, Colorado, and had at one time lived in Bayfield, Colorado, where I lived for several years. Tracy, her friend, is from Florida. They were disappointed to find the Bunratty Castle closed due to a scheduled private party. They were ready to see the castle, eat dinner, and then take a taxi back to Limerick where they had been staying. They still got off of the Paddy Wagon, and who knows what they accomplished after we said good-bye.

I was fascinated with the rock fences, walls that outline farmlands. They are built without cement, a century-long tradition. We were told that if another farmer from the community walked by and saw a rock that had fallen down, that farmer would replace it.

The rocks are placed so that wind can flow through them but not to the extent that would ruin the land. The livestock are wary of attempting to cross them, as they will collapse. The walls are built without tools or, as mentioned above, mortar.

Okay, now's the time to confess about the Blarney Stone. I thought it was silly and certainly not something I'd find fun at all, but I changed my mind.

What did the guy who climbed Mt. Everest say when asked why he did it? "Because it's there," he said. My answer to that question about kissing the Blarney Stone is, "Because I was there." I got in line, and soon it was my turn. A man told me to lie down on my back and lean my head far back, as millions have done before me. Imagine the DNA on that stone.

"Farther than that, luv," he said, and I felt as though I'd fall through the space between the fence and the rock. But he held on to me while I did the deed that thousands have done for decades. Then a photographer got the shot, and now I have it, and so what?

Touring Ireland tirelessly

First, before getting into another tour, I wish to again bring you into the loop as to how and why I'm on this one-year journey as an expatriate, so here's the scoop.

My job as a journalist expanded, and my expenses expanded, but no raises came forth. Like a 35-year-old man's receding hairline, my income stopped growing.

The risks of taking a worldwide adventure were far less than the risks of leaving a job with no future.

Yesterday was one of those adventuresome days even though the guide that took a Paddy Wagon full of tourists said, "This summer is the worst I've ever seen." It has been raining nearly every day since I've been here, and while it began to rain some more yesterday, it ended with sunshine as we toured through Ireland's "Forty Shades of Green"—a song with lyrics inspired by Johnny Cash when he saw Ireland outside an airplane window on his way to a concert in England some years ago.

I want to give a few impressions of the long day's trip through the shades of green. In Killarney, we learned about Dr. Hans Liebherr, a man who became rich from the invention and building of a factory for a construction crane that would make transportation from ship to shore easier.

Through Liebherr's riches and his appreciation of the Killarney beauty, he built Hotel Europe and the Dunloe Castle near the town of Killarney and its largest lake, Lough Leane, near the MacGillycuddy Mountains.

For me, the most impressive view was that of the waterfall inside the Killarney National Park. A five-minute walk took us through a forest of moss-covered, massive trees and overhanging greenery. With sun poking through the jungle, and after following a stream, we suddenly saw water falling through the thick forest, tumbling down over rocks. It was loud and refreshing to see such massive amounts of water falling endlessly down a hill.

The smell of tree bark, fresh and decaying pine needles, and air sprinkled with rain water refreshed me after sitting in a bus.

Next, we saw "a view fit for any lady," words coined by Queen Victoria when she visited Ireland. She heard that the views from up above were beautiful but didn't want to pursue the trip to find out for herself, so she sent up her ladies-in-waiting. When they returned, she asked them what they saw. That is when one lady responded with the words that gave the top of the mountain notoriety.

I have to say, this lady (myself) found the view beautiful, but I feel sorry the Queen didn't see it for herself.

Many people have fallen in love with Ireland and return often for vacations, including the late actor, Charlie Chaplin. He would stay so often in a hotel in Waterville that he purchased a house there that his granddaughter still visits. Every August, there is a comedy festival in the town in Chaplin's honor. There is a statue of him in the town, too.

Charles De Gaulle visited the Sneem Village and found it peaceful, and spent lots of time there. The day we drove through Sneem, the town was getting ready for a carnival. We could see the top of another mountain and a ring fortress on one side of the road, and on the other side three islands called Bull, Cow, and Calf.

The town of Killorglin in County Kerry is wildly celebrated every year to honor King Puck. King Puck is a wild goat that is captured and brought into town and then put on top of a table high above so everyone can see him for the duration of the town's festival. After much humiliation, one of his horns is cut before he is delivered back to the mountains. The reason, according to Michael, is so the same goat will not be picked for the honor the following year. This tradition has been going on since the 1600s. That's a lot of goat to get.

The Ring of Kerry is a fort from the Iron Age, a fortress for families and their animals. Also old, but only from a modern point of view, are the ruins of a town that was left standing as it was during the potato famine of 1844, and beyond. People died from starvation, and some left and died on their way out of Ireland.

Stone houses

The stone houses seen all over the hills of Ireland are covered with vines and shrubs, but the farmers who currently own the properties where the houses are will never disturb them. According to Michael, they are left for the ancestors of those who perished or for those who immigrated to America. The government passed a law to protect the houses.

"You never know when an Irish person would like to return to his ancestor's native homeland, and he or she would always be welcome. No one has ever judged the Irish for leaving to protect their family. No matter how long you were away, it's always said, 'How long are you home for?'," explained Michael.

He mentioned the American Indian Choctaw tribe that heard of the plight of the Irish and collected money to send to Ireland. This put tears in my eyes. Over 150 years ago, moved by news of starvation in Ireland, a group of Choctaws gathered in Scullyville, Oklahoma, to raise a relief fund. Despite their meager resources, they collected $170 and forwarded it to a U.S. famine relief organization to benefit the people of Ireland.

It was a long but wonderful day. I wished I had spent a bit more time in the city of Killarney. Horse-drawn carriages, friendly people, and beautiful surroundings could make me stay longer.

While resting at a tea shop, two men sat nearby and started up a conversation. When I left them to get back on the bus, they bid me farewell. "Av a good day, luv."

I certainly did.

What is a firkin crane? I know.

There are unlimited chances to learn when you're traveling, as I often repeat, and some interesting facts may be found right around the neighborhood where you are staying. That is, if you take the time to walk around.

As you may know, my recent home has been in the Kinlay House on the Bob and Joan Walk, near the St. Anne's Church and next to the Hotel Maldron that was once a hospital. Skiddy's Almshouse is on the other side of Kinlay House.

The walkway called Bob and Joan Walk in the Shandon area of Cork comes from the history of the Green Coat Hospital School, built in 1716, and made for poor children to be educated. The statues called Bob and Joan were situated at the gatehouse of the school, but now they are housed inside the St. Anne's Church.

The first time I heard the Bells of Shandon, they were ringing out a classical tune. I thought they were so peaceful-sounding and wished to hear more. I did. They haven't stopped. After a while, I heard "Old McDonald Had a Farm" and then it was "*Frere Jacques, Frere Jacques, Dormez Vous.*"

Tourists are welcome to climb clear to the top of the tower and enjoy 360-degree views of the City of Cork. That's not all; they are allowed to play the bells. They ring out most of the day with various degrees of talent. Francis Sylvester Mahony wrote a poem about the Bells of Shandon, bells that first rang out on December 7, 1752.

The Hotel Maldron is a converted hospital and has a grave-yard in the backyard with large tombstones, tombstones so old that most of the names are no longer visible, I observed. People are free to walk into the graveyard park and rest on benches.

Skiddy's Almshouse came about when the wine merchant, Stephen Skiddy, in his 1584 will, bequeathed 24 pounds to the Mayor of Cork City to build houses for ten of the city's poorest people over age 50. According to what I have read in the website on Cork City's history, the Almshouse was first erected in 1620. In 1975, the houses were transformed into flats by the not-for-profit Social Housing Development Company and have become 14 housing units.

I don't just walk around on the populated streets, but I enjoy out-of-the-way streets and alleyways where small doors open to low-ceilinged flats. Windows are covered with lacy curtains with trinkets on windowsills.

I did some walking around this morning after going to St. Anne's Church and then the Cork Butter Museum that is just a few steps away from the church and near another building called The Firkin Crane.

"What the heck is a firkin crane?" I asked the man who took my money at the museum.

"Firkins are barrels, and the building had big cranes that lifted the firkins up to get them ready to transport once they were full of butter," the man with a large, red and shiny face said with a big smile.

That building has a leaky roof and there's no money to fix it, he added. Otherwise, it would be part of the museum and the history of Ireland's successful butter business.

Ireland has just recently seen an improvement in the economy, some have said, although I have observed many closed-up businesses and empty buildings. I think it is sad that something as historical as the butter business doesn't have the funds to showcase all of it. But the museum that is ready to show some of the butter development is open for visitors.

I went to the City of Blarney again on Friday. When I was there the first time, I found an old hotel that reminded me of an old Colorado Western hotel and thought it would be fun to take a break from the hostel and spend one night there. This time I knew exactly how to get there by bus and return with no horrendous waiting times.

I did what I always do—I walked around the town. The community had a soccer game going on in the park, and many people were cheering their favorite team. It turns out that the Blarney Castle Hotel, where I stayed, sponsored one of the teams, and they won. I felt for just a moment that I was part of the community.

"Did you wear your sunscreen?" someone asked as I crossed the street yesterday.

"Bad weather, isn't it?" another person said today because it was raining. Weather, even though there is nothing anyone can do about it, is the number one topic in Ireland.

They are the friendliest, most helpful, and most sensitive people I have ever met.

The Irish and the smiling pig

"Aw, darlin', is everything ol' roight? Kin oy hep ya?"

I stood at the end of the street carrying a small bundle of clothing I planned on giving to a second-hand shop. There are several in the city, and without pre-arrangement, I knew I'd find one somewhere, plus I had other chores to do.

"Oh, no, I'm okay. Do I look confused?"

"Oh, no, luv, I didn't mean to imply it. Where do ya want t'go?" the lady with orange hair and a worried look on her face, asked.

"I walked a different way than usual, and I'm looking at that bridge and wondering if I should walk over it to town, or should I go down the street and take the bridge I'm familiar with?"

"This is the end of Shandon, roight here, luv. Do ya need some hep, darlin'?"

"No, I'm all right. I'm just thinking about what to do next. Really, I'm fine." I convinced her, for she walked on and crossed the bridge. I followed.

I dropped off the few "tops" I had worn for the nearly four-month journey and then began to look for a bank to get some more euros. The day before, I purchased some "tops" or "jumpers," as they are called here. The stores shout in great huge signs—"70 Percent Off" or "Everything Must Go." I paid my last euros for six T-shirts and sweaters. It was a great deal for 40 euros. They are all bright colors as opposed to the dark, winter "jumpers" I started with on my journey.

I asked three men standing on a corner if they could help me.

"I'm not sure where to find a bank. Can you tell me where I could find one close? I don't want to walk too far."

"Sure, I can, luv. Go down there to the end of the street. Turn right and you'll find a bank on the left side."

I didn't know which man to look at, for all three explained and gestured at once. All three wore rumpled black suit coats and trousers. One wore a tie, and two wore caps that I've seen often on Irish men. I don't know the name of them. The other man had mounds of white hair, a pink face and pale blue eyes.

I realize that the comfortable distance between two people is closer here than in America. People stand close when they're talking to you. I have observed that while people-watching and from my own experience.

I found the Bank of Ireland, went inside and up to the window with my ATM card to get some euros from my credit union.

"We don't give money from those cards anymore, luv."

"How am I supposed to get money then, huh?"

"Use the machine to me left," the woman employee pointed back to where I came from.

"Oh, no, I've heard that those take your card, and when that happens, you cannot get it back. I cannot risk that."

"Oim sorry, luv, but I cannot hep ya here."

Well, doesn't that just put me in a pickle? What will I do if my card gets stuck? I have no more money. But I'd risk it, anyway, and I put the card in. It took it but gave me a message that my pin number was wrong. How can that be? Panicked now, I went outside and tried to remember the number. I had used another number that was associated with another system. Then, aha! I went back to the machine that scared me, put my card in, used the other number, and waited for what seemed way too long. But then out popped the money, followed by my card. Life is good.

Next on my list was to get my Omeprazole meds for the heartburn problem. It was no problem in Dublin or anywhere in Iceland to get meds over-the-counter because I had a note from my doctor for everything but the Omeprazole. I didn't think that was necessary because it is available over-the-counter in the U.S. But a woman in Cork thwarted my efforts.

"No, my luv, oim very sorry, but we cannot give ya that, for we have laws here."

"I got it in Dublin. Why not here?"

"Did ya have a prescription?"

"Oh, no, but I had a prescription for another medicine by a doctor, and I filled it and the Omeprazole at the same time. Maybe that's why they gave it to me, do you think?"

"Probably, ya right, dear. Sorry."

I went on to get a second opinion down the street at a newer-looking pharmacy. The other one was so old, it still had wooden floors and wooden shelves, not that it made any difference. Actually, I thought it was cozy and quaint.

"No, I cannot," the kind man, an attractive young pharmacist with greying temples and black hair, said. But he did give me another brand that he said should do the job as well. He said it was only a matter of time that Omeprazole would be over-the-counter, but just not now.

I purchased the recommended alternative and then walked around to find a restaurant where I could sit down and be served. Instead, I found myself inside the famous, old English Market and got carried away with the shops and the stalls. I left immediately, however, when, at the butcher counter, I observed a half a head of a pig that was pure white with a mouth that looked as though it was smiling. I got the heck out of the English Market and continued on to find a restaurant, but the pig wouldn't leave my mind.

Leaving Cork on Friday

One more day in Cork, and on Friday I leave for Macroom to visit with Tine and Dermot O'Hare. They are friends of my friends, Kemberlee and Peter Southland, whom I spent a few days with last month. I look forward to meeting them in person, as we have been emailing back and forth for a while.

Friday morning, I'll leave Cork for good but will take away fond memories of the good people who stepped up to help me whenever I looked confused.

I also want to give credit to the staff of the Kinlay Hostel, awesome workers who do everything they can to keep the place clean and make it run efficiently. It's a tremendous job to ensure a place as large as this operates smoothly, with people from all over the world speaking different languages, all with different needs and desires. The staff was very kind to me.

Losses have continued on my four-month journey. (Has it really been that long?) How I think they got lost—a gold earring went down the drain in the hot pot in Thorshofn, Iceland; a vest got lost in the back of a taxi (I think); and a pair of pajamas. What? How did they get lost? I have no answer for that one. But today, on my last trip into the city business section, I purchased another pair of pajamas.

Early this morning, I went to one of my favorite restaurants before anyone else had arrived, and I had a scone, clotted cream, raspberry jam, and a cup of cappuccino. While I read the morning news (by the way, the papers are still those large pages we used to know way back when), I came across a name and had to ask the waiter, who was from France, how it was pronounced. He got an Irish coworker to explain.

Blaithnaid Ni Chofaigh will be the morning talk-show hostess on television. The Ni part of her name signifies that she is the daughter of Chofaigh, the name of her father. I couldn't explain how to say that name in written form. You are on your own here.

One more day left in Cork

I went to town for the purpose of buying a box of chocolates for the Kinlay staff, as well as some rubbing alcohol. The only other thing I wanted to do was soak up the town for the last time. I took many random photos just for fun.

The alcohol would soothe the infected ear from an earring that was trying to make its home inside of my earlobe. I got the earring out and wanted to disinfect my ear.

"No, we aren't allowed to sell alcohol. I do not have a license to do that," the pharmacist stunned me with that answer. I couldn't believe in a country where it's easy to "get a pint," you cannot get alcohol to disinfect a small part of your skin.

I went to another pharmacy and had to explain why I needed the alcohol, and she offered me something that wasn't all alcohol but was an astringent of some type. Then she proceeded to tell me how to take some cotton, put the liquid on the cotton, and rub it on my ear lobe. I wanted to say, "No kidding?" but I was polite, instead.

Next, I found a different coffee shop/pub from the familiar two I have frequented for the last two weeks. This one was in an old building with small tables sitting in front of a couch that curved along two walls.

There was a gentleman sitting next to me, and one at the bar.

"Nice day, isn't it?" The man at the bar turned toward me and said.

"Yes, it's a bit warm, but you are right, it is nice."

"It's nicer since you walked in, luv," the gentleman at the couch said with a gentle chortle.

"Oh, you Irishmen," I said, and both of them laughed.

After my coffee, and after walking back to the hostel, I came upon two women who were getting dogs out of a van owned by Dogs-for-the-Blind, a nonprofit agency that trains dogs for the blind and for children with autism. One of the women had a large, happy-looking, curly-haired dog called a labradoodle. Guess you don't need an explanation to know that is a mix of a Labrador and a poodle.

I have seen many people in town, including several today who volunteer to train dogs.

Worthy of mention

While in Cork, I met a young American lady, Erin O'Keeffe, and her cute son, Liam, at her favorite restaurant, Fenn's Quay, for lunch one day. Erin is as original as what she creates. She knits, paints, cooks, writes, publishes, and has won competitions in many venues. I only saw her one time but was keenly impressed with how this American woman has made a name for herself in her adopted country of Ireland. She was introduced to me through our mutual friend, Kemberlee Southland.

Good-bye, Cork, I'll miss you.

I arrived in Macroom, and one-half hour later, I was line dancing.

I left Cork, but it wasn't easy. Here's what happened.

I got to the busy station around nine a.m., knowing that the bus to Macroom wouldn't be leaving until 10:30, but that was okay because I like to arrive early, drink coffee, have a bite to eat, and spend the rest of the time "people-watching." I am nearly always early everywhere I go.

I purchased the ticket and the lady told me, "The bus to Macroom will leave at 9:30 and at 10:30."

So, I had my choice. The 10:30 time would be perfect because Tine would be waiting for me at the Macroom station in one hour, so I continued to wait.

At 10:15, I waited outside at the platform where I was told, "That's where you'll get the Macroom bus."

But at 10:30, a bus going to the town of Tralee was taking passengers. I figured the next bus must be the Macroom bus. I continued to wait for ten more minutes and then went to the ticket agent and asked if the Macroom bus was late.

"Oh, no, that bus left."

"Was that the bus that said Tralee on it?"

"Yes." She rolled her eyes. I can't stand it when people do that.

"Why didn't you tell me the Macroom bus wouldn't say Macroom on it?

"It's right up there on the sign." She pointed to a moving sign.

"Yes, it is up there, you're right, but I was waiting outside where you said the bus to Macroom would be located."

Blank expression.

So I needed to let Tine, who would be waiting for me, know that I'd be late. I didn't have a cell phone, and there were no public phones anywhere.

"Do you have Wi-Fi here?" I asked the blank face. I was ready to open up my computer to get a message off to Tine.

"Yes, but it won't work unless you're a customer of the company."

"Customer? I'm your customer."

"No, the customer of the company that sells the Internet service."

Blank face didn't tell me that an Internet service was located against the wall next to the coffee concession, but a person standing by heard my dilemma and pointed to it.

"Over there, luv. That's the Internet. You can use it and pay with a credit card."

Well, all was good, except I didn't have Tine's phone number, so with my inexperience with the Irish keyboard, I typed up a convoluted message for my friend Kemberlee to call Tine, her friend, telling her that I would be an hour late because I missed the bus.

On the way to Macroom, I calmed down when I heard the nightmare of a fellow passenger, Niamh Cosman, an artist in sculpture, who had travel stories that made my morning a walk in the park. Niamh will eventually find her way to the States and to the Burning Man Festival in the desert where she is partnering in a sculpture event. I wished her well for her success in her travels and art.

When I arrived in Macroom at 12:30 p.m., Tine was sitting on a bench waiting for me. She had received the message, and by 2:00 p.m., I was line dancing with her and a group of ladies.

Macroom Angels

Dermot and Tine O'Hare are the next angels in my travels. They live high on a hill in the beautiful and quaint town of Macroom.

Tine and Dermot are middle-aged folks with many interests. Tine has been knitting all of her life and creates beautiful objects, including socks that Dermot sports.

"I have always had hand-knitted socks," Dermot, a native of Ireland, said. "My mother knitted my socks, and now Tine does." His feet were up on a coffee table with the objects d'art proudly on display.

Along with Tine, Dermot also creates, for the very couch and chairs in their living room were re-upholstered by none other than the man himself. You'll get an insider's view of his other talents, as well.

I went into town today with Tine, who is originally from Holland, and found a sweet shop. Candy is made the old-fashioned way and sold the same. You walk in and order the quantity you want. It is weighed, put into a bag, and you walk out with a smile on your face. After that, Tine and I walked to the Demesne Castle and near the beautiful Sullane River next to the castle grounds. Above us was an old stone bridge. We then found an Internet cafe, and while Tine went to visit a friend, Dermot kept the soup hot for us, and I posted a day's blog.

Dermot is a fabulous cook and even seems to enjoy it. Yesterday, he made a salad with pomegranate seeds and finely diced tomatoes and onions, mixed together and served on a plate with radishes and cucumbers, all on a bed of greens. Beautiful. Later, he served a dish of rice with chicken and two colors of bell peppers.

Tine stays busy with her activities and friends. She shared with me some of her creative artwork, including hand-knitted scarves, sweaters, hats, and baby clothing, and then she had photos of the many quilts she has made and has given away as gifts.

Both Dermot and Tine have created an art-quality, terraced garden of stone in their back yard. There is an abundance of flowers and plants.

On our road trip on Sunday, I was amazed at how many fuchsia flowers grow wild all along the roadsides. Those are plants we see in the United State that usually grow in pots.

Marketing and island hopping

Yesterday was fabulous, weather-wise, which is important to the Irish and the company with whom I spent the day.

Tine and Dermot took me to three outstanding places and lots of interesting sights along the way. While we were on our way to the Demesne Castle in Macroom, we saw Gougane Barra, Glengarriff, and Bantry. One site I found particularly interesting was the prehistoric trees that came up in the boggy area when the reservoir of the River Lee was created. They jut up from the bog randomly in small stump-like statues and are claimed to be over 5,000-years-old and perhaps up to 10,000. They are protected.

I learned from Tine, who drove most of the way to our destination, that the lovely shrubs that line the narrow roads are actually stone walls that have been covered with vines and shrubs through many years. So it behooves a driver not to get too close to the shoulder of the lane.

The Hermitage of Gougane Barra is a monastery built by a sixth century monk on the most peaceful site, with graceful trees, calm waters, and a place to take silent walks. The area, also surrounded by a forest of trees dripping with moss, still has the original stone cells where the monks slept. Also, there are the ruins of the original church that was later built on the site when Christianity came to Ireland, also centuries ago. A beautiful stone church from several hundred years ago is still in use today on the grounds.

Another sight that enveloped me with beauty and history was the Island of Garnish near the Glengarriff Town, where Maureen O'Hara resides. We took a boat from the land to the island and could see her home, and when we landed on the island, there were many places to walk in gardens and among sculptures.

One group of stone steps stood straight up. I looked at the steps and said I'd give it a try. I made it clear to the top.

My new friends, Dermot and Tine, have extended their hospitality by introducing me to their friends and the community. I've enjoyed Dermot's humor as he mixes up his wise cracks with the locals and they with his. Humor exchange is the nature of the Irish. Take, for instance, when we were getting our tickets for the Garnish Island. Dermot tried to get a discount but was thwarted by the ticket-seller's humor.

Then I offered, "How about a discount for an old lady like myself?"

His reply—"Oh, if I woke up every morning to a gorgeous woman as yourself, I'd let you in free."

My reply—"Well, for a compliment like that, I'll pay you double if you let me on your boat."

How's that for a quick Irish-type reply? I'm learning.

This morning, we went to the open market where we saw baked bread of all types, all kinds of olives, and a myriad of good-looking tidbits from Greece and other parts of the world.

Dermot purchased his favorites from the sellers, all with the usual bantering, some of it just too quick for me to pick up. Tine headed to her one-morning-a-week job as a volunteer in a non-profit second-hand store.

Chapter Five

August, 2012

Leaving Ireland

I'm back in Cork but just for one night. Tomorrow I'll be flying to Edinburgh, Scotland.

I left my friend Dermot at the house and trudged on with my luggage and Tine who would drop me off at the bus station, and then she would go on to the Macroom Library to attend her knitting group.

Tine and Dermot are the host couple extraordinaire, for I saw firsthand how they would raise their hands to volunteer where help is needed. While I was afforded a week of their good humor and care, they took in a beautiful dog, a golden Labrador mix, that is in training to be a guide dog for a blind person or as a companion for a child with autism.

They were to take the dog in for just a night, but when I left them, the possibility of one more night was up in the air. Both Dermot and Tine love animals, and that was evident in how well they cared for the sweet-natured lady lab.

Speaking of sweet natures, I met the close friends of the O'Hares, Tony and Betty, in their home, and then the day before I was to leave, Betty, Tine, and I met for coffee at the Castle Hotel

Restaurant. The restaurant was packed with people meeting for lunch.

Before that, Tine and I walked around the Demesne Castle and arch that are smack-dab in the middle of the business section of Macroom. A bridge nearby goes over the River Sullane, a tributary of the River Lee.

Macroom, a town of around 5,000 people, boasts that it is "the city that never reared a fool," and perhaps that has some credence to it, as Dermot informed me that Macroom was the birthplace of Admiral Sir William Penn, a British Admiral and father of William Penn for whom the state of Pennsylvania is named. No fool, he!

On the way to meet Betty, Tine drove through the winding road and lush vegetation that led to the Bealick Mill, a Heritage Centre. The mill was closed to the public, but a man who was painting told us to go on in, so we took advantage of his kindness.

The corn mill, with the Irish name *Bealach Leachta*, was the ancient route used by local saints with names like Laichtin, Gobnait, Olan, Inbarr, and Colman. The mill overlooks Leacht Mahan, with stones that commemorate the Battle of Bealach Leachta. This bloody conflict, won by Brian Boruhma's forces, was fought in the riverside plain in 978 A.D. Fighting among humans never stops, does it?

The present, four-story, stone building was erected in the 19th century and served surrounding parishes as a corn mill. The corn was transported to the Port of Cork for export. Oatmeal was also roasted on stone hearths prior to grinding. "Irish Oatmeal is still available and is recommended by famous chefs such as Darina Allen of Ballymaloe," according to the mill pamphlet. The water wheel dates from 1860.

Back to the City of Macroom and the city streets that wind around the busy section. Tour buses and large transport trucks heavily use the streets. You must be experienced to walk among the streets in Macroom. In light of that, I followed Tine closely when we had to cross the street. It's also necessary for a right-handed driver, and one who is used to looking toward on-coming traffic, to look the opposite way from the usual habit.

Today is my last day in Ireland, and while I'm eager to move on, I must say here that I have enjoyed the Irish folks who are friendly with the greatest sense of humor and a little "blarney" thrown in for fun. The beauty of the country, the side roads, and the lanes with dense vegetation will long be remembered.

On the fringe in Scotland

Here I am in Scotland, and to my surprise until just a few days ago, I came into the city during the biggest month-long event of the year in Edinburgh. It was the Edinburgh Festival that boasts the largest festival in two events going on at the same time that greeted me.

The Fringe Festival, with over 40,000 performances and more than 2,500 shows, is packed into 250 venues across the city. The Edinburgh Military Tattoo is the other event. The military presents international performers, military and civilian, that are set against the backdrop of Edinburgh Castle. Tickets are difficult to get. I won't even try. I'm not that interested in things military, anyway.

I got settled into a room in what will be my neighborhood for three days and ventured around in an area that includes, ho-hum, the Edinburgh Castle. Some neighborhood, huh?

Finding a room was difficult since there were so many people in the city at this time. I did find a room, though. Can't brag about it even if it is near the castle. I have to pay extra for Wi-Fi and television.

On the street, I saw a crowd of people inside a stone building and courtyard. I went in and was immediately approached by one young person after another who handed me postcard-sized cards advertising performances that would be going on in the building at various times. I learned that the courtyard, where people were enjoying food and drink, is the Pleasance Building, which houses theater, comedy, music, and children's events.

But that wasn't all, because everywhere I went, someone thrust a postcard in my hand with yet another venue. Then an angel appeared just when I needed a place to sit down.

She was standing in an African-inspired skirt and top at the steps of a hotel and bar. She began telling me about the wonderful food and the great place to stay and asked me if I'd like a seat inside.

"Yes, I would because I'm tired. But I don't want anything to eat or drink, so guess I won't be going in."

"Oh, no, you are never expected to purchase anything here in our lobby. You come right in and sit here."

She pointed to a huge, overstuffed chair that looked so inviting that I felt comfort before I even sat down. She began to tell me all about the hotel and the ambience they are trying to create. "It's a fashion place. All of our clothing, the fabrics used within the hotel, are all African-inspired."

Then the young lady with a bright smile and flashing brown eyes told me she was in her last year at Edinburgh University in the hotel/travel/tourism department, and when she finishes, she'll go back to Africa to help her dad in his safari business.

The big chair was an uninterrupted home for close to an hour until a nice young man asked me if I wanted anything. A "No, thank you" didn't alter his friendliness. He was a former make-up artist on films made in Poland, and while in Scotland with a film-making project, he decided to stay, and that was six years ago. He is now studying the same subject as the young lady.

The three-hour walk around tall and very old stone buildings on cobblestone and concrete gave me a real feel for the city. However, it is also the most expensive place I've been so far.

Edinburgh . . . looking forward to leaving

Edinburgh. Glad I'm leaving it. I vowed that during my whole year I would look only for the positives, so I'm struggling here. Bear with me.

I find it difficult to circumvent the city, but people do step up to help me. I cannot use my computer unless I pay for the Wi-Fi. The computer in the hotel reception has a keyboard I'm not familiar with, and it is a waste of time (read money here) trying to get to what I need. I had to use it so I could print out a document, but gave up.

Yesterday, a lovely lady in the reception printed the German Visa papers I need, for a small amount of money, so for that, I am grateful. However, I made a mistake on the paperwork, and now I need another go at it. There's a printer down the street from Starbucks, and they will print it when I email it to them, so for that, I'm grateful. I walked in the rain to get to Starbucks. I'm soaked, but at least I cooled off.

The inside of the elevator where I'm staying is so hot, it's like standing inside a coffin until it stops and you free yourself. Then the lobby is hot, as well. Thank God for the rain.

The breakfast where I'm staying is more than ample, but people shove you to get to the food as if it were their last opportunity to eat. The city is full of people. Big groups of people who are loud (no, they are NOT all Americans) stand in the middle of the sidewalks and at the entrance to doors, and they stop suddenly in front of you.

Pedestrians have no rights; however, to be positive, if you are standing, waiting for a walk light, it is safer to walk in numbers. That way, a car is more likely not to hit you.

I'm leaving tomorrow morning for a small town called Blairgowrie near the city of Perth. I'll be there for three nights, and then will move on to Inverness. I look forward to a small town.

There is always something to learn, and when I look back at the four days in Edinburgh, I'll find the answer. There were some good moments and here are some of them.

A street comedian was giving a performance. He was skinny, bald on the top of his head, with long, straggly, greasy hair that swung back and forth over his shoulders. He wore baggy shirts and pants, and his gig was to blow up balloons into figures, and then he'd bring someone out from the audience to help him with his skits.

A heckler, a little girl around five-years-old, kept shouting at him, handing him little pieces of stuff she picked up off the sidewalk. He would take it and drop it to the side, trying to ignore her. She persisted, shouting at him. She'd walk up to him, slap him, then run away. He ignored her. When she finally got the best of him, he handed her a piece of candy, but she came back for more. He then threw a piece of candy toward her and then another one further away. The crowd laughed, and so did the heckler.

The audience was enthralled with the comedian and his shtick, and when I observed the crowd, it looked as though they were trying to ignore the little heckler, as well. She kept it up until the show was over. I saw her mother walk over to someone she knew in the crowd and ask her if she watched her daughter's performance. A stage-door mother was born.

In the breakfast room, I met two interesting women. One was in town for the Fringe Festival with a group of performers. She has a PhD in technical theater. The other woman I met was with a college group of performers, as well. She is in her 50s, a mother of six grown children, and is back in college.

Finding Starbucks was like wandering out in the desert in the hopes the pond of water you see ahead is a mirage.

People lighten my path.

On the bus driving through a forest on the way to Blairgowrie, my home for four days, the flickers of light that flashed between the trees made me think of all the people who have lightened my path along my four-month journey.

There was that couple from Kansas I met while sitting on a bench in an Edinburgh garden. They offered me a mint, which I accepted, along with their good wishes. There have also been many people who have opened doors for me, lifted up one of my bags, flashed me a smile, answered questions, said something encouraging, and yes, there were many folks who mentioned the weather in their desire to be friendly.

Waiters, hotel/hostel cleaning staff, bus drivers, cooks, and taxi drivers have been awesome and inspiring. Take, for instance, James Calnan, a Satellite Taxi Company driver from Cork, who was so interested in my yearlong journey that he refused a tip.

"You're on a long journey, and you'll need the money," he said as he helped me out of the taxi and into the airport on my way to Edinburgh.

Edinburgh is a beautiful city with a fascinating history as seen in memorabilia, statues, and stone buildings. But at the time, it couldn't fit into my travel scheme. I am trying to scope out the culture of a country through talking with the folks I meet, the real people in the town or city. Edinburgh was too busy, too noisy, and too full of tourists looking at other tourists.

I was thinking today, while on the bus, how good most people are if you pay attention. I think Princess Diana was correct in her words, paraphrased here—"Someone has to go out there and care for the people."

It made me wonder how many world leaders really know the people they govern.

Now I'm in another town, and a beauty it is.

I met a couple at the Perth bus station who were also on their way to Blairgowrie, and they agreed to show me how to get to the Hotel Royal. When in Blairgowrie, they got off the bus, told the driver that they would get back on, that they just wanted to show this lady where to walk. Now, isn't that generous?

The business district is on winding streets with restaurants, department stores (the old-fashioned kind with curved glass windows and shelves of shirts, for instance), bars, coffee shops, and tea houses. I stopped in a teahouse this afternoon and saw four elderly, delightful ladies having tea in real porcelain cups and saucers and dainty bites to eat while talk, talk, talking. The hairstyles were bowling balls with little puffs of cotton glued to them. Sorry, but old-fashioned is nice in stores, but hairstyles, hmm. I shouldn't say that, however, because maybe that "look" is coming soon for me. Who knows?

Another delightful lady at Perth, while waiting for the bus to Blairgowie, began to talk to me about the weather, and after a while, she said, "I knew you weren't from here because of your twang and your color."

"Color?"

"Yes, you are tan."

Well sure, I guess, but only from the neck up. But twang? Now I'm listening to the Scottish accent and often ask, "What?"

Everywhere I go, I have to adjust my ear to the new dialect. Adjusting to travel is a constant. Everything is different—sink faucets, shower faucets, door closures, use of keys, elevators, stairs, up and down hallways, and countless differences in times for breakfast, times to check in and out, and always the complications of how to get where you want to go. But this is all part of the fun I'm having.

Traveling through Perth, I saw a church that struck me. It is for sale.

Hiya! Bagpipes and Blairgowrie

One more day in the beautiful town of Blairgowrie in the Perthshire District. It is 60 miles from Edinburgh and 16 miles from Perth. I leave tomorrow for Inverness where the Loch Ness Monster lives. Hope it doesn't get me.

This town turns out to have been a great choice for me, and I will miss it and the kind people who live here. There are places that, if I knew more about them, make me wish I could better adjust my time. I would have enjoyed a much longer stay in this town.

Last night, I got to see the small town in action. The pipers marched down the street playing bagpipes and drums all the way to a pie-shaped, flower-laden park near the center of town.

I first heard of this event from one of the pipers when I walked by a church and took some photos of it. A man was nearby, and I asked him about the church. He was so nice to tell me, a stranger in town, about the event in the park the following evening. It wasn't until I saw him last night that I knew he would be one of the pipers.

It was fascinating to learn about the music and the instrument, as the sound always seemed to be the same, but last night, I actually could hear the melody and the rhythm of the music.

A woman piper explained how she learned with a small pipe to begin with and then advanced to the real instrument. The heavy instrument is carried firmly on the shoulder. She blows into the pipe and presses the air bag at the same time. All while walking or marching.

A nine-year-old drummer caught my eye. He reminded me of my son, Ron, at the same age. I was producing fashion shows and recruited him once for a Christmas show as the Little Drummer Boy. I asked the little Blairgowrie boy's father if he'd take a photo of me with the boy.

At the park, I met a lady named Paulette and her niece who was visiting. Paulette gave me a brief history of Blairgowrie. Sitting on the bench with her, she pointed to four large brick buildings that were once banks. "This town in its early history had a lot of very rich people in it," she said.

Some of the riches came from farming berries, called Blairberries, named for the town, and another business venture was the jute factory that began in 1832, in the Oakbank Mill. She pointed out toward the river where the plant had been located. The town also had a flax spinning mill, also near the river.

The town is built on gentle hills with flowerbeds and hanging flower baskets all through town. The walkway near a park and the River Ericht is a pleasant way to spend some time.

Sergio, a young man who works at the hotel, walked with me to the River Ericht and around the park surrounding it. I probably wouldn't have found it had he not shown it to me. Sergio is a thoughtful young man who didn't mind sharing his time with someone as old as his grandma. Sergio is in Scotland from the Basque area of Spain. He gave me lots of information about his hometown of Vitoria, and now I want to see that area. He had been a steward for an airline company, and something happened to end that position. He wasn't clear what it was, but I could tell he was saddened and worried that he would disappoint his parents if they knew he was no longer flying.

One of the friendliest and most helpful people is the pretty, blonde, blue-eyed travel agent, Pauline. I am going to miss her. She provided help for my next adventures. I saw her sitting inside the travel agency while on a walk with Sergio. I finally decided to walk in and talk to her about my future adventures.

"I saw you in here and just thought I'd stop to ask you some questions."

"Oh, I know. It's like I'm sitting inside a fishbowl."

Pauline spent a great deal of time searching online for the best deals. She has been in business for over a decade. She has one worker who came in once while Pauline and I were on a computer search. A delightful woman, she was dressed up and excited about an event she would be going to later. I felt like an insider for a few moments.

Pauline would be headed in the next couple of weeks to the Monterey/Carmel area, and I gave her some of my ideas about where to stay while she visits my stomping grounds.

By the way, people greet each other here with "Hiya," which, I was told by a Royal Hotel worker, is a combination of "Hi, how are you?"

I caught myself saying that yesterday when I met the woman who had shown me where the hotel was located when the bus got into the town. She saw me in Blairgowrie yesterday and told me the library's location. I needed a reliable Wi-Fi situation, so that's where I am today.

I need to find a place to stay in Inverness, and so far, that has been difficult, but I'll get busy on that soon.

"I'll take the low road and be in Scotland before you." But where is the B&B?

Over green and yellow hills, farm houses in the distance, then a forest. The forest on our way to Inverness was dense with pine trees and other trees I cannot name. Then back came the yellow and green rolling hills, mowed grass, and farmhouses. We passed mountain streams, rivers, and lakes, and finally the bus from Perth came to rest in the train station of Inverness, a city that claims the Loch Ness Monster.

I left the Royal Hotel in Blairgowrie in the morning to catch the Inverness bus in Perth, but before I left, a lady stepped up to me in the breakfast room, shook my hand, and said, "I'm happy to meet a fellow Californian."

This was Maureen McLean, part owner of the hotel with her Scottish husband, Iain. She had seen me in the hotel before but thought I was part of a tour group. I only had a few minutes to spend with her and wished it could have been longer. She's originally from Fremont, California, was in the import business, and has traveled further and wider than I have so far. She met her husband in Scotland when she heard him play the bagpipes. After swooning over the sound and the handsome man playing them, they met, got married, and purchased the hotel.

"It's a lot of work. It was a mess when we bought it, and we've put a lot of money into it."

It is a charming hotel built in 1852, with a wing of superior rooms. I didn't get those, so I guess where I slept was an inferior room. However, my room was furnished nicely, very clean, and the staff kept the rooms up exceptionally. Oh, and I loved the town of Blairgowrie!

Now I'm in Inverness, a town in the Highlands with building-to-building stone structures and houses. My first job was to find a bank where I could get some pounds in exchange for dollars from my ATM card. I asked around for a bank and was pointed to a business section where I headed with my bag on top of a bag and my computer bag, camera, and billfold.

After trying several places, I finally found the Bank of Scotland, which was open on this day, a Saturday.

I then hailed a taxi and told the driver my destination.

His comment, "Oh, okay, that's about 60 miles away."

"Oh, no, then I need to find a bus."

"I'm just having fun with you. It's not far away."

I know that I must look like someone who can be kidded. This happened throughout the whole year. I can only think it must be my friendly, fearless nature.

Meanwhile, he pointed out the castle, the river, and other interesting spots, and before I knew it, we had arrived at the B&B where I'll stay for three days.

I rang the bell. No one came. I rang the bell again. Still, no one came. I knocked on the window, and a woman opened the door.

I told her my name and that I was the one who was booked into the house for three nights.

"No, you're not. No one has booked a room."

"But I arranged this place through your friend, Pearl."

I had to explain to her what took place before she agreed to host me, and this is the way it went.

For three days, I had been searching on the Internet for a place to stay in Inverness because I'm on my way to a very special place on my birthday, but I was having problems finding Inverness vacancies.

Yesterday, it was nearly all day searching online, getting messages that there were no rooms. Finally, out of desperation, I wrote back to a few people who had replied with a "no vacancy" and asked if they had any ideas for me.

One woman said there was a room in a hostel with three flights of steps.

"No, I cannot manage three flights of steps. Do you know of any other place?"

She did not.

But one note made me pay attention. Pearl said she had two days vacant, but for the third day, she found a friend (after sending out requests for me) who could host me all three days in her B&B, or as an alternative, I could spend two days with her and one day at her friend's.

I sent a reply email that I'd like to stay all three days in her friend's B&B. I also got Pearl's phone number from the receptionist in the Royal Hotel and spoke in person with her.

Pearl said, "Oh, I've already booked the room for you." However, Janet, friend of Pearl, said she was waiting for a phone call from me. I was not told she wanted a phone call. Eventually, it all got straightened out.

It's a lovely stone house with a small, attractive bedroom and a living room where I'll be served breakfast. The simple problem is that I'll need to write my notes, do some research, and check my mail in an establishment with free Wi-Fi. That's where I am now—a noisy bar/restaurant near the heart of town about a four-block walk from where I'm staying.

Word of help here. When booking a room and only the rental business pages pop up, and when you steadily get turned down that way, look for the name of the hotel and find their personal website. Then send them a note. Working without a booking agent sometimes is the best route, not always, but it proved to be the right way this time.

Beginning tomorrow, I'll explore the town of Inverness and perhaps wash my clothes in the neighborhood laundromat.

Helpful folks, lederhosen, and kilts

Just when I thought it was hopeless, people stepped up to help. It takes so long to find places to stay during the summer months, so I try to be prepared by booking a room in advance using the good old web.

In Inverness, finding a room in Scrabster, Scotland, became my mission. I'm almost ready to give away my next destination but won't do that until I arrive there. I have a sentimental purpose for the next place where I'll stay for a week or more.

Finding a Wi-Fi station has been a challenge until the other day. I walked past the Palace Hotel where a big, friendly Starbucks sign beckoned me in. I asked if I could use the Wi-Fi even though I'm not staying in the hotel.

"Of course you can," said the gorgeous young lady who made my cup of coffee. We laughed about accents, and she went one further when she told me her mother lived for many years as a youngster in the southern states.

"My mother asked her grandpa who, by the way, sired 12 children in Alabama, if he had enjoyed going to school." The young lady tried her best to repeat the family's oft' told story with a southern accent—"Gawd, no, ah, caint even spell cat."

I sat in the hotel lounge working on the Wi-Fi supplied by Starbucks and the hotel until I exhausted all of my possibilities on-line. But I had a list of names of hostels and B&Bs for the next place. I needed a phone, but mine is in storage in Marina, California, so why not ask at the hotel desk? They could only say no.

They didn't say no. The woman at the desk said, "Of course." I assured her I'd pay for the calls, but when I finished, the hotel clerk wouldn't take any pay.

This kindness of strangers has followed me on my whole journey so far. "Good People Everywhere" seems to be my theme song. Perhaps one of my poet friends will supply the lyrics.

Yesterday, while walking around the city, I saw three men dressed in German lederhosen. Why? I wasn't fast enough to get there to ask them.

It's amazing to me that in most countries, the original clothing unique to that country has been replaced by modern clothing and fashions, so it's refreshing to note that the Scottish kilt is still worn here by men.

"I have a question for you," I asked a taxi driver. "Do you ever wear a kilt?" (No, I didn't ask what he wore under it . . . c'mon.) He replied that his daughter will be married soon, so he'll don a kilt of his clan's plaid for that.

A cousin worked diligently on our family's genealogy. We have one slice of family pie that hails from Scotland. Supposedly, we're related to Robert The Bruce, or as my sister-in-law, Carol, calls him, Robert The Brute.

One-half of my family ancestral pie is German, however. So there you have it—lederhosen and kilts. But wait, I still have a bit of a French slice in me. Would a beret go with lederhosen and kilts?

Viewing the City of Inverness with a twang

Understanding accents is the challenge here in Inverness, as it has been all throughout my four-plus months on the road. Scottish accents are different from Irish ones, and parts of Ireland have their own accents, just as we do in the States. I'm often told I have a "twang."

This morning, I hopped on one of those hop-on-hop-off buses that take you to key sites in the city. I find that seeing the sights by bus shows you the places you'd like to go back to in person.

All along Bridge Street, key spots were the Tollbooth, Town House, and the Inverness Castle. Across the street, I saw a church and decided I'd go there when the bus stopped, and I did. St. Mary's Church was on the bus route, as was the River Ness, which I crossed over to get to town from the B&B where I'm staying. Other interesting sites were the Caledonian Canal, Muirtown Locks, and Nature Reserve.

The Inverness Castle sits on the top of a hill and is a visible landmark near the business section of the city. It also overlooks the River Ness. The latest castle, and there were many over the years on the same site, was built in 1836. However, way back in the 11th century, a structure on the same hill was used for defense.

A story has Mary Queen of Scots intending to visit the castle but being denied access for political reasons. She later hanged the governor who was the person responsible for denying her visit.

The Grieg Street Bridge is a suspension bridge. When you walk on it, you may feel you've been hanging out at a local pub. There is always someone who will bounce up and down to see if the engineers knew what they were doing, and that is just what happened. Boys will be boys, even when they are men.

The B&B where I'm staying is comfortable, and the owner is friendly and runs a cozy place. She served breakfast today, and it was eggs, bacon, sausage, cereal, toast, and a scone with three kinds of jelly. I opted out of eating the meat.

"It's almost three p.m., and I'm still not hungry," I twanged.

Staying in high-end hotel vs. more frugal options

Janet, the owner of the B&B where I stayed for three days in Inverness, takes great care of her guests. She is organized, supplies clean rooms, and serves an ample breakfast.

Breakfast today was cereal, toast, croissant, eggs, sausage, bacon, mushrooms, and steamed tomato. I again opted out of the meat portion; you must stop somewhere.

The house of the B&B is over 100-years-old, and Janet has lived in it for 40 years while working in the hotel business. When she needed something to do, she decided running a B&B would be easy. She makes it look easy. Wouldn't be my cup of tea.

Yesterday evening, I ventured to the top of the hill to the castle, and on the way, I met a woman who works for the Sheriff's Department, which is now housed inside the castle. The castle had been vacant for many years, but now it holds governmental business.

On my final day, today, there were two other guests in the B&B. The woman and I managed to speak pretty good Spanglish together. She is from Spain, and when I told her that at some point I'd be in Spain, all kinds of information fell out of her mouth. "You must not miss, don't forget to go," etc.

On the way to the business section where I'd find the Bank of Scotland, rolling my suitcase and bag and carrying my computer, camera, and billfold, I observed again the lines of poetry that were carved into the slate-stone sidewalks. They are at various spots in the city. It would be difficult to remember where they are if I wanted to go back, however. So I decided to take them all in, because it may be the last time.

As I took one last look at the city on my way to the bus station, there was some noticeable excitement. It is back-to-school day, and the kids are dressed in their uniforms, and all of them cross with a crossing guard at every street corner.

Meanwhile, as I sat inside of a hotel lobby, golfers were getting their suitcases out and ready for taxi rides to the airport. For those non-golfers who may not know, Scotland is the country that gave birth to the game. You can't go far without seeing a golf course. They all seem to fit perfectly into the green environment.

Note to travelers on a budget—it doesn't cost anything to sit inside the lobby of a high-end hotel if you have a lot of traveling on your mind. Most hotel lobbies are generous in giving use of the Wi-Fi, with usually a purchase of tea or coffee. This hotel is so fancy, it doesn't compare to the hostels and guesthouses where I usually stay. Traveling on a dime can be done, and I'm proof of that. However, don't dismiss staying at a high-end hotel if you can, for there are many amenities, and the rooms are so comfortable. For me, though, I just think you meet the most interesting people who are also frugal travelers when you stay at a less-than-high-end place.

On the bus ride from Inverness to the hotel where I stayed last night, my seatmate kept me interested in his passion for science and humanities. Christopher is an author of two books and is embarking on another book project regarding his thoughts on changing the environment through a consensus, not through domination.

He had a place all picked out to sleep—in a croft. He explained it to me later by email.

"The croft is in the village, Rogart, near Dornoch. The croft had two fireplaces and a peat shed to store the peat to burn. When I viewed it, one end of it was still a dirt floor, but the landlord kindly put some boards in for me. I went through a winter without central heating, and it was very cold at times. There has been a settlement on the site since the 12th century. It is made of stones but now has central heating and a slate roof. It could sleep four comfortably. It was a great experience for me, though I would have enjoyed a few more visitors. It was an isolated existence."

Isolation and cold sound like a challenge, and he accepted it and managed it well.

Living like royalty?

It remains a serious doubt that any modern royalty have stayed at the Royal Hotel in the harbor town of Thurso in the Burg of

Caithness in the northern part of Scotland. It's just a ferry ride away to the Orkney Islands.

I arrived through an old wooden and glass turnstile to the old hotel lobby that must have seen a lot of history. A receptionist greeted me, handed me a key, and said my room was on the second floor.

"Go through the doors, down the steps, turn right, and get on the lift." She pointed toward the doors. "Then, turn right after you get off, and go down the hall, through open doors, down the hallway, turn right, and your room is the last room." Directions came in one breath.

I followed the chosen route while pulling my burden behind me, readjusting it when it fell apart, and carrying my computer bag and camera in the other hand. Each door I went through was closed, and each door opened differently; some you pushed, some you pulled. I twisted and turned to get around and through each door.

At last, I found the tiny room. It had a small bed and a small TV with small sounds that came out of it. I felt like an overgrown gnome. After a call to reception, and after someone came to fix the TV but declared it unfixable, I decided to take a walk.

Stone after stone building, I came to a museum.

One of my favorite places in the world is a museum coffee shop. Most of them have a classy ambience. When I opened the door expecting the same, the first person I saw was a gentleman sitting at the table. I smiled. He gave me a blank look.

Someone was slamming plates in the kitchen behind the counter. No one came to help me, so I said, "Hello?" Ignored. "Hello?"

She came out, looked at me as if to say, what could you possibly want in here?

"Are you closing?"

"No."

"Can I get something here?"

"What do you want?"

"A piece of that delicious-looking cake and a cup of coffee."

"What kind of coffee?"

"What kind of coffee?" I was puzzled. Hmm, Costa Rican? German? Dutch? Folgers? She just waited until I figured it out. "Coffee with milk." I smiled, like I had won the trivia contest.

"Sit down."

"Okay."

I did as ordered. She brought out the cake and coffee and went back to the kitchen to continue slamming dishes.

After viewing the museum, I walked back to the hotel room. The floor in my room was in need of heavy duty cleaning, and the kettle had old water in it and was dirty.

The bed—it was like lying on a bed of rocks. Restless night and up early in the morning. Didn't I recently say that I travel on a dime? Well, this is an example of how that may be interpreted.

The taxi arrived. I got in by myself, chugging the suitcases into the back seat with me.

"Have you always lived here in this town?"

"Yes," the taxi driver said.

"Oh, it looks like there is a lot of activity here in this port."

"Yes, a lot of activity."

"Wow, I see a lot of lumber there getting ready to load on a ship."

"Yes, a lot of lumber."

Forgive my cattiness, but I couldn't help but wonder if the dish slammer is married to the taxi driver.

Then I was at the ferry in the harbor town, Scrabster. Ninety minutes of a ferry ride later, I disembarked in the Orkney Island town of Stromness.

Slate is used on streets, fences, roof tiles, and buildings. With all of it wet from rain, and being dark due to the absence of sun, it seemed mysterious.

I walked on the street looking for a building number, but there were none, so I stopped at a little flower/gift shop—a little corner of color—and showed them the address and name of the guesthouse owner.

"Oh, I know where that is. I'll walk with you." The shop worker, a pretty teenager, was eager to help. She took both of my bags and walked all the way to the guesthouse, where Jennifer, my next hostess, was waiting at the door for me.

Storming the Islands

Today was an adventure unparalleled so far. The event I looked forward to didn't happen due to the unpredictable Orkney Island weather. But the day was an unexpected adventure, anyway.

I got a taxi early in the morning from Stromness to board a plane at the Kirkwall Airport, about one hour away by car. The plane from there goes to the Island of Westray and then on to Papa Westray. The flight from Westray to Papa Westray is the flight I looked forward to, as it is in the *Guinness Book of World Records* for being the shortest booked flight in the world. We waited for over an hour for the fog to rise, and as I sat watching the blue of the ocean water and the green in front of the airport peeking through the fog, it began to look promising. There was one other passenger with the same goal as mine.

The plane holds eight passengers. We took off with seven passengers toward Westray, where the pilot said it was clearing up. But, "We'll see what it looks like when we get there," he told us.

At Westray, we dropped off two passengers and picked up two other passengers, but the two of us with the goal on our minds sat in the airplane waiting for the pilot who was inside the building, making calls for the decision to go to Papa Westray, or not.

A few minutes later, the pilot returned and said, "Looks like Papa Westray is still fogged in, so we'll go to Sanday," another Orkney Island.

After picking up and dropping off passengers on Sunday, the decision was to head to the Stromsay Island, where two people got off and two on, and then we headed back to where we started, Kirkwall Airport, where we dropped off all passengers except two. Those two were going to another island.

It was around noon by then, and we had been flying all over the islands, so I was a bit hungry and ordered a bowl of carrot and parsnip soup at the airport snack bar. "It will take about five minutes," the lady behind the counter said.

"Oh, that's okay, looks like I'm in no hurry."

Then the other passenger with Papa Westray and the shortest booked flight adventure on his mind came to me and said, "We're going to leave right away."

"Oh, no, I just ordered soup."

When it was brought to me, it was blazing hot and I had to slurp it fast. I did my best because we were boarding again. Gosh, I don't even know what carrot and parsnip soup tastes like, I downed it so fast.

We headed up to the North Ronaldsay Island and dropped everyone off and picked up two people.

"Well, looks like we'll make it to Papa Westray after all," the pilot announced with relief.

Well, sure, we landed at Papa Westray Island where I'll be for about six days, but the shortest flight? Maybe I'll try that going back. Or maybe I'll book a ferry, or maybe I'll be happy for the adventure I had.

The pilot was a former bush pilot, and I had guessed that right. He powered up the engine as he turned from the taxiway to the runway.

This morning, I left three days of bliss at the 45 John Street B&B in Stromness, Scotland. Kay and Neill Sinclair are excellent hosts. Kay presents breakfast as a work of art with homemade bread, jams, and jellies, all from her garden.

"I don't waste anything. I use it all," she said, pointing out the little pots of homemade goodness, including various examples of how to put rhubarb to use.

The B&B was spotlessly clean, and the bedrooms and community rooms looked as though they had just been refurbished. Not so. The Sinclairs just keep up with what needs to be done.

Sinclair is a name my brother Jack and I knew from old Doc Sinclair who lived across the street from us in the Barnum neighborhood of Denver. He'd get mad at the neighbor kids when a ball would land in his yard. Other than that, his strangeness was tolerated. His wife, Jean, was an accomplished painter. I still have one of her paintings.

While in Stromness, I took a bus around historical sites in the countryside where I saw the Neolithic village, Skara Brae, in Sandwick, one of the Orkneys' most remarkable monuments.

Flintstones, eat your heart out. The rock homes and village are just the way they were left 5,000 years ago. The village made of stone with stone furniture sits near a farm and an ocean inlet.

Skara Brae sits quietly surrounded by cows, mostly Angus, grazing; sea gulls squawking; and little motor boats taking fishermen out to sea, and I can't help but wonder what the people all those centuries ago ever thought the future would look like. They were intelligent human beings, and that is evident in what they accomplished with primitive means.

After I saw Skara Brae, we drove past the excavation where a photographer from *National Geographic* was on the site taking photos that will be in the magazine next year. At breakfast that morning, the lovely lady, Kay, who runs the 45 John Street B&B, told the other visiting folks and me about how her father is one of the volunteer excavators. She said the experts think there is a large structure on the Ness of Brodgar site, as the walls are thick, and they have found artifacts and continue to carefully expose whatever lies beneath the surface.

Next on the trip, we saw the incredible Ring of Brodgar. These are stones posted deep inside the ground. Some are tall and some are short, but they line up in a perfect circle. It's not known what motivated the folks all those centuries ago to build such a site, and the muscle and brain it must have taken to accomplish putting the stones deep into the ground in such a formation leave you amazed with wonder. This site is on the list of UNESCO World Heritage Sites.

This Ring of Brodgar is just one of the many Orkney Island sites you can see and still not see it all. I feel certain there is not an archeologist anywhere in the world who hasn't heard, seen, or worked in the Orkney Islands.

On the way to Stromness to get to the B&B a few days ago, the ferry traveled near the Old Man of Hoy, a natural stone that rises from the land right next to the sea; that was the beginning of the sites of wonders in the Orkney Islands.

The Stromness Island, as all the islands, is steeped in history, and the stone houses in Stromness where people live today are said to be reminiscent of old Norwegian villages, as the buildings face the harbor with streets of crooked slate and cobblestone. Pedestrians must move to the side of the buildings so cars can drive through. Big yachts and cruise ships come into the harbor in Stromness, as do fishing vessels.

I didn't get there by air, but Papa Westray is my next destination. And this was my ultimate destination in the Orkneys, where I'll stay the longest.

In the calm of the ocean I think of you.

I couldn't be much closer to paradise than I am right now on the Island of Papa Westray. It feels as though I've been here all my life. The people are warm and inviting, and the surroundings are serene.

I was introduced to how the islanders here purchase their groceries. A store, called the community store, that is connected to the hostel where I'm staying, has shelves and freezers full of almost everything anyone could want. I stocked up a bit and put my groceries in the hostel/community refrigerator and cupboards.

Last night, the island, with a population of 75, held their weekly "Pub Night" in the community room of the hostel. Margaret, a woman around my age wearing a head scarf and coat, played the accordion while her grandsons accompanied her, one on the drums and one on the guitar. There were two other guitar players and a man on the mandolin. They "oom-pa-paed" until the wee hours of the night. And before they gave up the night, one other gentleman joined the group with a Jew's harp that twanged away.

This Sunday morning, I got up at six a.m. to use the Wi-Fi. I sat like a pretzel near the telephone where one of the teenaged girls from last night told me the Wi-Fi was the strongest.

After I woke up again around ten a.m., I said good-bye to the nice Scot I met on the plane coming over, the man who was also hoping to make the shortest booked flight and didn't. He left later today, and since the sky is blue, it's no doubt he accomplished his goal.

I took a slow walk, actually more like a stroll, to the water's edge, past the church, the primary school, and the combination craft store and post office. I'll go see that tomorrow. I also walked near the Angus cows and Shetland horses I took photos of, and I found some happy-looking chickens that didn't seem to mind posing for the stranger.

While I sat on a stone in the peace and quiet, I thought about growing up and how my family took nature trips into the Colorado mountains. How my brother Jack would have loved to see this place.

A man from Paris, Andre Boudic, walked up the road as I sat quietly, and we talked for a while. He had just come back from finding a secluded beach where he went swimming. I'd think it would be cold, but he didn't mind.

"If it's what you want to do, you'll find a way," he said, about swimming and everything else. He works in theater as a technician, working with backgrounds and sets and doing other theater-related jobs, and he has opportunities to travel near and far for his work. But now, he is enjoying his second time in Papa Westray.

"I found it a peaceful place when I was here last time and knew I wanted to return. It's a great place to get away from city life," he said.

Two German ladies, both loving archeology, were thrilled with the activities they've found on the Orkney Islands and Papa Westray, in particular. They took a boat out to the Holm of Papay, an uninhabited island that has a 5,000-year-old tomb.

When I first went on my walk and observed the church, I was welcomed in and told to go in and take a photo if I wanted and also to come back to the church for two o'clock service. That I did.

I met Margaret again, and she gave me a brief idea of what life was like growing up on the island.

"We didn't have television until the 60s," she said. It wasn't until 1980 that electricity came to the island. Up until then, they used generators for power, and they used coal to heat their houses. "A lot has changed," she reminisced.

But change comes slowly, as children attend primary school on the Papa Westray Island and high school on the Island of Westray. High school transportation is the airplane or a boat.

At the church service, I felt part of the community, as they waited for the pastor to arrive from Westray on a boat. By the way, the church has a space designated for a doctor, a nurse, and for surgery.

Weird walking

It was a lovely walk this morning and then back again in the afternoon. Before I started out, I went to the Store, as the locals call it. I needed a small notebook, as I have filled up about five of them on this journey. Rachel, a lady I met yesterday on the road, was the salesclerk. She told me that I might find the tide high and might be unable to walk on the beach. I don't care. I've long adjusted to the adage, "It is what it is." My activities are not influenced that much by the weather. Unless, of course, it means I'm not getting off the island.

After seeing Rachel, I made my way to the post office/craft store. The first room had some yarn from the Orkney Islands and lots of little key chains and other bling, postcards, and homemade cards with photos of local views. A fellow from Germany runs the post office and store. He and his wife fell in love with Papa Westray when they were tourists. When they discovered a house for sale online a while later, they came back, purchased it, and, in a few years, they were the post office officials for the island.

I found another man I took a photo of yesterday as he hung up his clothing to dry on a clothesline, again this afternoon, but in person today.

When I walked by a large, stone building on the way to the beach, I heard faint music inside, and the door was open.

"Hello?"

"Oh, hello," the tall, curly-haired man said as he came to the door from the back of the building. He was wearing knee-high boots with corduroy pants tucked inside them, and a jacket.

"I'm a nosey person and saw the door open and just wondered what was happening in here?"

"Yes, you are nosey, and I can tell you're one of those weird Americans."

"Yes, I am very weird, and I'll be sure not to disappoint you. I'm also a former news reporter and very weird for that alone." This is one of many times I was called a weird American. I vow not to disappoint anyone and hope that my weirdness comes out strong.

It went like this back and forth for a while, for I didn't want to let him get the best of me.

He told me the community hasn't yet decided what to do with the building I had inquired about, but it has a beautiful view of the ocean and the Holm of Papay, an ancient, chambered cairn. That island is reached only by ferry and is uninhabited, as I stated before.

John Harper is the gentleman's name, and he hails from England. He eventually invited the weird American to his house for tea. He was the same guy I photographed yesterday, and he knew who I was.

"You were taking a photo of me, and you wore turquoise yesterday."

"Wow, just about everyone knows who is on this island."

"Yes, with only a few folks, you cannot hide here."

We walked up the road together to his two-story stone home, and in the front yard, I immediately saw an old wooden chair I thought would make a great photo. He laughed.

Inside his home there were small picture cards of famous paintings, and I was able to name two of them, Van Gogh and Manet, so that gave this weird American two points.

He asked if I preferred tea or coffee and I said coffee.

"That's right, Americans like coffee, and they drink it weak."

"No, not me. I like my coffee strong, please. By the way, I wasn't aware that Americans enjoy weak coffee."

Turns out he is a flight instructor, commercial pilot, and an aerobatics instructor.

We eventually found a meeting place regarding flying small planes, and we exchanged pleasantries. He has lived for 11 years on Papa Westray, and like everyone else, finds it close to paradise.

I asked him about the name Papa, and his remark was that no one really quite agrees, but it is generally thought that it came from a priest who would come to the island many centuries ago as a missionary. That makes sense to me.

After coffee and conversation inside the comfortable home, I continued back down the road.

How could one person be so blessed, I thought. I'm sitting on a bench writing in my new notebook, watching turquoise water break waves on the white, sandy beach. Out toward the horizon, I see Holm of Papay, and to my right under the white and azure clouds, I see the stone buildings I just passed. The seals are barking to each other, and birds fly all around me. I interrupted the daily plans of two rabbits. They both scurried into the tall grass.

On my walk, I spoke to the Shetland horses that greeted me at the fence. I have met cows, horses, rabbits, and chickens so far.

Walking through history

It would take another few visits for me to see everything on this small but history-covered island.

This morning, I got an early start on something I couldn't leave without seeing. I walked up the road and past the black Angus cows that eyed me on my way to the Knap of Howar, the farm museum, and then the mill. A big, brave, fat rabbit watched me without moving in the grass where he sat.

The Knap of Howar is a monument of the earliest North European dwellings known, dating back to around 3800 B.C. The two stone dwellings are considered to represent a Neolithic farmstead. The furniture and fittings include hearths, pits, built-in cupboards, and stone benches. You can almost hear one of the Flintstones saying to his neighbor, "Come on in and get yourself a chair." He would then point to a stone slab with a stone back to sit on.

After the greeting, Flintstone's neighbor would enter the house by a low, narrow passageway. I'm average height and I almost had to crawl in. With his height, my brother, Jack, would have needed to slither in on his belly.

The Holland farm

The house and Holland farm dominate the landscape of Papa Westray and are situated on a hill overlooking the ocean inlet.

This was the farm of the Traill family who ruled the island for three centuries.

At one time, the hostel where I'm staying housed the farm laborers and their families, who were more like servants, I have been told.

John and Annie Jean Rendall and their son, Neil, own the farm now. Neil and his wife, Joselyn, currently operate the farm.

A joiner—the person who puts together the wooden portion of a structure—and a blacksmith were employed full-time on the farm in the past, up until 1938.

The Old Bothy was the accommodation for single men servants until 1922. It is this museum I was interested in seeing. It is generous of this community to keep it unlocked and free to anyone. Museum artifacts and memorabilia have been donated through the generosity of the locals.

In this museum, you would see a bedroom, a fireplace, chairs, cheese-making equipment, clothing, and tools of many trades. I saw an old phonograph player and old records, dishes, and other items used throughout the years.

The stone barn structure on the property dates from the early 19th century. It is now used for dances and concerts. When I got inside, I imagined the barn square dances my parents attended.

The threshing mill

Horses yoked to the machinery in the mill tramp-powered the cone-shaped, stone structure of the mill. In 1899, a 17-horse-powered Campbell, with paraffin engine, ran the mill until a 35-horsepower Lister diesel engine, installed in 1954, replaced it.

Before the threshing mill was built in 1820, the sheaves were threshed by flail in the old barn, then winnowed with riddles between the doors so that the draught blew away the chaff. The grain was dried over a slow fire in the kiln before being ground into meal or made into malt for brewing.

The 17th century dovecote, which I thought looked like a huge basket, kept the larder supplied with pigeons and their eggs, both of which were used for food.

From the hilltop near the farm, I could clearly see fishing boats and the opposite side of the island, and then the plane came in and landed near the shoreline. Cows, sheep, and many birds complete the present-day reality of life on Papa Westray and all the islands.

Precious gifts

It is my birthday today, and I received the most precious gifts.

The Papa Westray Island folks have a community get-together every Wednesday in the community room, which is located inside the church and where the doctor's office is located. I got there at the appointed hour, and soon after, the folks came in and took seats at one of the tables covered with delicious cakes, cookies, scones, and cheeses. The cups were kept filled with tea and coffee. Conversation was soft and pleasant.

After the chairs were all taken, Jennifer, who expertly runs the town-owned hostel where I'm staying, announced, "I'd like your attention, please. A visitor on our island has a birthday today, so join in with me to wish Laureen a happy birthday." She brought a cake to me with five candles, and everyone sang. John presented me with a card that I circulated in the room. I wanted to remember this day and the lovely people who live here.

Afterwards, I went for a walk on the beach. The Frenchman, Andre, had told me he found a quiet place on the beach where he swims nearly every day. I wanted to find that spot and began following shoe prints, shoe prints that were then replaced with barefoot prints.

On my way, I picked up seashells, and when there were so many of the same kind, I realized how human nature makes us selective as something becomes plentiful. I got more particular in my search, and at the same time, I looked out at the ocean, and nearby there were about nine seals watching me.

Andre had told me earlier in the day that when he swims, there's one seal that gets really close to him. "I talked to him," he told me.

"What did you say?"

"I asked him what he would have for lunch today, and he replied, 'Fish.'"

The seals began watching me as I saw Andre sitting on the shoreline. Yes, I found his beach, and he was right. It was white sand and quiet except for the conversation between the seals and the conversations among the birds and the sound of the rolling surf.

The seals just stared at me while I tried to get my camera adjusted to record the scene. They would swim close, then get back together again, and then they stayed in one spot to watch me. I was in a zoo.

Andre left, and for a while, the seals followed him until he was off the beach, then they came back to watch me. I was in the water up to my knees.

I became distracted with my own thoughts, as I began to think about my life of 75 years, my childhood, and my brother, Jack. Even though he spent most of his life in the mountains, I know he would have loved the Orkney Islands and Papa Westray, in particular. He had said one time he would love to see the Orkney Islands, and one time even pointed to them on a map that was spread out on his kitchen table. Jack was the reason for my adventure to the Orkney Islands.

In continued deep thought, I briefly turned my focus downward, and there was the second gift—a heart-shaped rock in the sand. Was that a gift from my brother?

I made the shortest booked flight in the world.

The flight from Papa Westray Island to Westray Island in the Orkneys, north of Scotland, took one minute and 25 seconds from the time we lifted off from one island to when the tires hit the tarmac on the other. This is the flight listed in the *Guinness Book of World Records* as the shortest booked flight in the world.

I was lucky to get to sit in the co-pilot's seat, as arranged by John, the aerobatic pilot instructor who lives on Papa Westray. Other tourists from Ireland sat in back seats.

The flight was prepared as any booked flight would be, which included ticketing, labeling, and luggage handling into the plane. The trip was a small arc beginning on one island and connecting to the other. I am now the holder of a certificate rewarding me for taking the shortest booked flight in the world. It was accomplished on the second try. You never know if or when the fog will change your plans.

More of the Orkney Islands

There is much to love about the Orkney Islands, aside from the changing colors of the ocean and the sky, the green grass, the sheep, the cows, and the friendly people. The islands' people believe in fair trade purchasing and windmill energy, and they have good recycling habits.

My next plan would be to see Kirkwall. I knew I could stay at a hostel in Kirkwall for only one night. The rest of the time would be full with a group of folks who had long-time reservations. The night I stayed, the place was deserted except for me. Not a soul was in the hostel, not even workers. I was alone.

How would I get to the other place I reserved for two nights? It was a long walk, and I could manage that, but not with pulling my luggage over unpaved roads, bumps, and grass.

I waited the next morning for a call from the lady who runs the hostel who said she would find out from the B&B if they could pick me up. I waited until 11 a.m. for her call and was too hungry to wait any longer. So I put three men who I met outside in the morning in charge of my bags and trundled up to the same hotel where I ate dinner last night. The restaurant wasn't open so back I walked, hungry.

It was through the generosity of those three men, visiting campers, David Scott; his son, Hamish; and their friend, William McCormack, that I got to the B&B. The men were hoping they could camp on the grounds of the hostel where I stayed last night. They, too, were waiting for the same woman, the owner of the hostel, to get permission to camp there.

David loaned me his phone and I called the lady who obviously hadn't even tried to find anything out for me. Instead of waiting for her to help out and call me back, I left the key on the table.

David agreed to take me to the Old Manse B&B. He stopped someone on the way who knew exactly where it was. Sheila, a retired mail delivery woman, graciously accepted me and showed me to a room that overlooks the harbor.

After I got settled, I walked on the road to a restaurant called the Half Yok Cafe. The spelling is correct. The explanation given for that spelling is that it is a Westray term for a workman's "piece" of his time to eat and drink when he stops for a break. I opted for a panini with cheese and a chutney, passing up a *tattie*—potato.

The people who own the cozy restaurant also take folks on mini-island tours, so I signed up for a half-day tour tomorrow, which includes lunch.

Walking around a new place affords a lot of ways to fill your senses—the smell of the ocean, food smells from kitchens, the sites of animals in yards or in fields, birds who flock together in the sky, deciding who will lead and who will follow, and the insides of stores. It's fun to see merchandise you're not familiar with, the ingredients that go into the item, and how they are packaged and where they are produced.

After I did all of the above, including a walk around a grassy cemetery with old and new tombstones and a remnant of a very old stone church, I met the three campers who helped me earlier. They were on the road looking for the Half Yok Cafe, so I gave them the directions.

The Wife of Westray was discovered in the dirt.

She was found by a team of archeologists who used a fine brush to sweep away the dirt and sand around a farmhouse where she was buried. It was a 5,000-year-old Neolithic dwelling on the Island of Westray in the Orkney group of islands north of Scotland.

The little one-inch figure has prominent frowning eyebrows, small dots for eyes and a broad nose. Was it a toy, a piece for a game, or a religious artifact? Expert archeologists don't know. The figure was among other Bronze Age stones, beads, and skeletons that a team of archeologists has been slowly exposing on the farm.

"It was the first Neolithic carving of a human form to have been found in Scotland, and to date, it is the earliest depiction of a face found in the United Kingdom." So states *Wikipedia*. It was found in 2009.

A second "wife" was found later at another site. This one was almost three inches in length, but it was missing a head.

I learned about this from the Heritage Center in Westray Saturday morning. That was followed up with a trip to other sites on the island.

Robust and entertaining guide, Graham Maben, drove a van with three other people, a woman from Latvia, an English woman, and a retired interior decorator from London, and my-self. The decorator is a Scot, dressed finely in a cashmere sports jacket, freshly pressed shirt, wool vest and scarf, and he looked like he was going to a fancy place. He stood back away from the cliffs while Graham, myself, and the two other women got fairly close to the edge of a jagged, rocky cliff.

We saw hundreds of birds flying out of their nests and back in. Sheep graze so close to the edge, it's a wonder how they know if they took one more step, they'd meet their deaths.

From there, we were taken to the Noup Head Lighthouse. It was built in 1898, with the purpose to warn ships off the North Shoal. The light is now automatic so it doesn't require a lighthouse manager on site. I always thought from reading novels that living in a lighthouse would be romantic.

Graham was full of stories about his beloved island and shared them while traveling to the next stop. We saw the Nortland, or Balfour, Castle, built in 1560.

"It was a defensive castle," he told us. But the architectural filigree makes you wonder why it was made so beautiful while also made for defense—to charm the enemy, maybe?

Gilbert Balfour, who was appointed to a high office by his lover, Mary Queen of Scots, built the castle. From the outside, it appears as do many remnants of castles in other locations, but inside, there are features worth noting. They are the fireplaces, the kitchen, the sleeping quarters, and even a toilet place where a full bucket of royal waste would be taken out and dumped into the moat. Disgusting job, but someone had to do it. I had learned years ago that the moat was not only to keep dangerous people away, but it was also a sewer. This is where those dainty nosegays—tiny bouquets of flowers—came into being. Royal women held them over their noses while crossing the moat by chariot.

Graham took the three others to the Heritage Center, and then he took me to view the Holm of Aikerness. This is an island where sheep eat only seaweed. Fresh water and nothing else goes into their diet. The sheep were originally brought to the island about 760 years ago by Norwegians, and since then the Orkney folks kept the species, Ronaldsay sheep, alive.

"There are 120 sheep in total, 50 lambs, 40 ewes, and the rest rams," said Graham. The sheep caretaker will travel to the island when the sheep are ready to take in for slaughter and for other reasons, Graham said.

Walking your feet off to get to the music

I left the Island of Westray with a ferry-load of young musicians yesterday, and now I'm in Kirkwall Island in cold, rain, and wind. Maybe it's time to get the Icelandic sweater out from inside the bottom of my bag.

The ferry left at six p.m. with a leave-taking musical salute to the organizers of the weekend music festival that entertained not only Westray folks but those from nearby islands, as well. Bagpipers played as the boat made waves, and the young musicians waved good-bye to the folks on land.

Music was played at various locations throughout the week, ending in the wee early hours on Sunday morning.

Don't know why, but somehow I missed the grand slam music venue that drew folks in to listen to many kinds of bands the night of Saturday, but I did have two more chances before I boarded the ferry.

A woman on Kirkwall who, with one other organizer, got together a few music groups of teenaged musicians, along with a few older folks, had them "jam," as they say in American jazz parlance, the weekend away.

I left the Old Manse Bed and Breakfast where I was grandly spoiled with full breakfasts, daily room cleaning, a softer-than-ever quilt, and a sleep-easy mattress, and then had the rest of the day until I'd meet the bus to take to the ferry.

I left my luggage at the B&B and walked around a bit, eventually ending up at the Pierowall Hotel where I went the first night in Kirkwall to use the Wi-Fi. A lovely lady invited me in and even had coffee delivered to me. It was here she told me I'd have two choices to hear the music that day.

"A group will be playing at the Church of Scotland," she told me, and then right there on the Pierowall grounds would be an afternoon session.

"The Church of Scotland is a bit too far for me to walk up to, but is there a bus?"

"Oh, I'll find someone. I'll go call and get a ride for you."

It wasn't more than five minutes when she came and told me, "Janet will pick you up in an hour out there." She pointed to the street.

Janet and I, along with a crowded room filled with many island people, including some folks I had met on Papa Westray, were treated to an hour of music. There were young people playing violins, a string bass, guitar, drums, and piano. They introduced the songs they planned to play.

"Some of our music we have already played last night, but we're going to play them again, anyway," one of the teen musicians said, and he got a chuckle from the listeners. Not only did the teens entertain with classical music, three men pipers also played. Some of the pipers were members of the men's singing quartet that sang later.

After church, I rolled my suitcase and bag, computer and camera bag over rocks on a road to the Pierowall Hotel from the nearby B&B. I parked them on the side of the building and waited for the music. Everything is safe on the islands, and for proof, not a key was used at the B&B either for the front door or the bedroom doors. I felt safe leaving camera and computer and wallet anywhere there were people around. It's a refreshing way of life on the islands.

Helen and David Smith of Washington, D.C., also came to enjoy the music. They were folks I met during breakfast at the B&B. They learned I would take the same ferry that they would, and since they had a car, they invited me to go with them.

Slowly, the musicians arrived at the hotel and sat on the grass. They got their violins and other instruments out and began to loosen up with traditional Scottish music. All musicians played more than one instrument. Violins became fiddles, guitars were strummed, and a drummer beat the rhythm on a typical box drum like I had seen before in Ireland. Another drummer tapped a *bodhran,* a traditional drum used in typical Irish and Scottish folk music.

A fiddle player—and there were many—would begin the round, then others joined in, and the music went around and around. People tapped their feet, nodded their heads with the beat, and everyone smiled in wonder at the talent there is on these islands.

Every young musician became entranced with the music as they played, and when they finally stopped, a fiddle would begin again and the round would continue. Nearly three hours came and went, and the Pierowall Hotel folks filled a table with food for all. The food, of course, was all locally prepared with seafood, cheese of all kinds, and lots of sweets.

Then it was time for Helen, David, and me to leave. We got on the ferry and realized we were followed on by many of the musicians who live in Kirkwall. Others live on other islands and would take either a different ferry or the airplane.

Traveling by ferry and airplane is the only way to get from one Orkney town to another and is an everyday occurrence.

"I was happy to be here today, and while waiting for the music, I walked me feet off," said one partygoer.

"Luv." How will she spend a 12-hour day?

I have been called "Luv" so often that I'm really feeling loved. The Scots have a way with words, and Luv is only one of them.

I checked with a taxi company this morning because I learned in the Information Center in Kirkwall that Bob's Taxis would store my "stuff" until I go to the port to catch the ferry to Aberdeen. I leave on Monday.

The dilemma for me leaving at night is the note where the hostel states that no one can stay in the building after check-out at ten o'clock in the morning.

It's going to be an interesting day to see what I will find to do for 12 hours in the town of Kirkwall without spending any money, frugal person that I am.

"Can I help you, Luv?" the man asked while he was talking on the phone. I explained that I heard I could store my bags in his place. "Yes Luv, right there." He pointed to a dismal-looking room with a worse-looking bench and suitcases and bags all over the place.

"Are you telling me that it's a safe place for my bags, my computer, and my camera until I come back at the end of the day on Monday for the ride to the port?" I asked with my eyebrows up on top of my head.

"You can keep it in here." He pointed to the office that he had just left. "And if no one is here, just ring us up and someone will come over and get your stuff out, Luv."

That sounds like a better idea, I thought, but when I got back to the hostel, I realized there would be no way I could call for a taxi without a phone. So I sent him an email and hope he'll learn that Luv needs a ride to his place and then one to the ferry, which is close.

I had the rest of the day and the evening to figure out how to spend a lot of time.

I have noticed from the help I have been given in the town that most are very pleased to assist. I purchased some food at the grocery store but didn't have a bag to carry it back in and would have had to buy one, which seems so wasteful.

"Here, I don't need this. Take it," a nice woman in line said and handed me an extra bag.

I have also noticed so far in all my travels that there are never plastic bags lying around on the streets, in open fields, or on sidewalks. Plastic bags aren't used unless you're willing to pay for them.

I've also noticed an absence of dirty diapers on country roads or in the city parking lots.

And never, ever do I see shopping carts rolling into cars on the lot. It just seems that people are considerate of others.

But the question remained, how would I spend 12 hours in town before heading to the ferry?

A day in the Orkneys

The Orkney Strathspey and Reel Society played last night at The Reel in Kirkwall. The Reel is a restaurant, pub, and center of Kirkwall music.

Last night, nine people showed up to play violins, two people were on accordions, and one lady played the piano.

I sat near the group and heard the director, who also played the violin, give directions. The repartee seemed to make everyone laugh. I couldn't understand anything that was said except for one time. That was when someone must have asked where the song they just played came from, and all I understood was, "That's what it's aboot."

But I understood the music. The strings put me into the wide, open spaces in the Western United States, music similar to what was played in western movies. I saw red stone rocks, sagebrush, and in the distance, snow-capped mountains, and I heard the rustling of wind in the cottonwoods. The same melody was played over and over.

Then there was a waltz, and I imagined a man wearing boots, dusty cowboy pants, and a vest dancing in a saloon with a dance hall girl. Then the music suddenly switched to the "Tennessee Waltz." I almost felt at home.

After the group played a few numbers, three more violin players showed up. It was obvious all musicians were seasoned and playing for the fun of it.

The sisters, Jennifer and Hazel Wrigley, own The Reel and are involved in the program, Live Music Now, aimed at disadvantaged members of communities, including disabled and elderly folks. Prince Charles, a patron of Live Music Now, was a member of the audience when the sisters appeared in the Live Music Now's 25th anniversary held at London's Barbican Centre back in 1997, according to their website. The sisters have played in many other places in the world and have produced popular CDs.

Every night, there is a different musical venue, and some require a queue to get in.

After I listened until the group took a break, I walked down the stone street to the cathedral, a recognizable landmark. Last night, with lights on the cathedral and the full moon, this view completed my day.

This morning, I walked to the library, purchased a book, read the newspaper, and waited for lunchtime. One funny sign I saw at the library was, "Use libraries and learn stuff."

Can't leave the Orkneys or Scotland until I've had fish and chips, so I walked to the harbor and asked a man who was pushing a baby stroller if he knew of a fish and chips place.

"Sure, luv. You go down there, turn right, and you'll find two chaps with fish and chips."

The first place had a long line, and the second place didn't have seating, so back to the line. It didn't take long to order fish (which I've learned is most always haddock), one half-order of chips, and a cup of tea. It was good. I walked on down toward the cathedral and found a place serving Orkney ice cream and got a cone of rhubarb and custard.

Walking back to the hostel, which is crowded, by the way (I now have three roommates), I noticed a small, round, metal object fastened with a screw to the sidewalk. I see those often, and they always remind me of my brother, Jack. He was a surveyor and one time pointed those out as a marked spot placed there by a surveyor who measured the location.

Chapter Six

September, 2012

Am I odd?

It's Wednesday, the first of September. This means in two days, I will have been on the journey for five months. It has breezed by. Today it is raining again, and I've decided to stay in for a change and watch the Paralympics that will be broadcast on TV.

The weather has been mostly cool, rainy, windy, with even some snow, from the very beginning of the journey that started in Iceland. I continue using the philosophy about the weather that, "It is what it is." But I must admit that it's cozier to watch the rain come down when you're inside watching it from a window rather than walking in it, although, I've done plenty of the latter.

So many people have been curious about what makes a 75-year-old woman do what I'm doing. From the beginning, I didn't think anything about it was unusual, but I'm learning from people's comments that I'm an oddity.

To answer some of their questions, here goes. No, I do not get lonely, as I'm meeting people every day, all day long. There are people everywhere, and if you're willing to begin a conversation, you never know how you may have affected someone that day. It's for certain, people have had an effect on me. People love to talk about themselves, and a willing listener can learn much about our fellow human beings.

No, I never feel that I'm in any danger. I don't put myself in situations where I don't feel safe. I stay in hostels, B&Bs, cheap hotels, and in homes. With today's worldwide Internet, it is easy to check everything out before making a commitment. And if I have ever been in an uncomfortable environment, I remove myself immediately.

Isn't it expensive? Yes, it can be if you're not careful. In the beginning, I wasn't as careful as I am now. Staying in a hostel makes it more affordable because you can cook your own meals. Once in Europe, I've found the bulk of the travel money was spent on getting here. Traveling between countries is a little more affordable in Europe. I tend to stay in one place for a while, rather than going to one country after another and seeing and learning very little about each one.

Sure, I get tired. But I pick and choose what I want to do, knowing that I can't do it all, but I can get a reasonable assessment of the culture by visiting museums, shopping areas, historical sites, and churches. I've never been a tour-taker but have found that some half- or all-day tours make it easy to see and hear about a site and save a lot of time, as well.

What if you get sick, people have asked. That just blows me away. Who thinks about that? Isn't that almost bringing it on? However, I know that in most towns and cities, medical help is available, if needed. I wouldn't have begun an adventure like this if I thought I weren't healthy enough. I do have aches and pains, but I'd have those if I weren't traveling, so why not just go for it?

The only question I do not have an answer for is what are you going to do when you go back? I will finish up this traveling saga, publish it, and then, who knows?

A one-armed atheist helped me up the steps to the St. Magnus Cathedral.

He saw my hesitation at the steep steps and asked if he could help me. I took hold of his one hand and climbed up the steps. Then he followed me in and began chattering away. It seems he wanted to be my tour guide, as well.

I've learned if you listen well, people will give you their opinions, and it wasn't long until he shared that he was an atheist. Well, we're all the same people under the skin, but I really wanted to experience the St. Magnus Cathedral on my own.

"Thank you for being such a great guide," I told him, and he got the hint. However, by that time, it had begun to rain and I left. By the time I got back to the hostel, it was pouring rain, cold and windy, and I was soaked to the skin.

The next day, I got another try at learning the history of the Cathedral. In the ninth century, the Orkney farmers became afraid of the Vikings. The Vikings plundered, of course, but they also sought land; thus, Orkney became a Viking settlement.

Fast forward to the twelfth century when the Orkney Islands were ruled by cousins, Hakon Paulson and Magnus Erlendson. Magnus was drawn to a contemplative life after being educated in a monastery, but the King of Norway made an expedition to the Hebrides and then on to Anglesey in Wales, and Magnus was supposed to go along.

Magnus refused the order to fight.

"When the King asked why he was sitting down and not seeing to his weapons, Magnus replied that he had no quarrel with anyone there. 'So I'm not going to fight,' he said.

"'God will shield me,'" answered Magnus. 'I shall not be killed if he wishes me to live, but I'd rather die than fight an unjust battle.' Magnus took out his psalter and chanted psalms throughout the battle, and though he refused to take cover, he wasn't wounded." So states the information I picked up at the St. Magnus Center.

The story continues. Hakon and Magnus became disenchanted with each other, and after Easter in 1117, it was decided to hold a peace conference on the Island of Egilsay. It was agreed that each cousin was to take two ships each and an equal number of men. Magnus got to Egilsay first. When he saw eight warships, he knew he was doomed. Magnus said he'd go into exile or to prison for life, or be maimed or blinded, but Hakon didn't accept, and his chieftains wanted an execution. Hakon told the man who was chosen to kill Magnus not to weep because it wasn't manly. Magnus told him, "Don't be afraid—you're doing it against your will, and the man who gives the orders sins more gravely than you."

After Magnus was executed, his body was taken to Birsay for burial. A cult grew up around him, with people thinking him a healer. In 1129, the King of Norway granted one-half of the Earldom of Orkney to St. Magnus' nephew, Rognvald, but only if he would defeat Earl Paul, son of Hakon.

After Rognvald failed, Kol, Rognvald's father, told Rognvald to vow to God that if he gained victory, he would build a magnificent stone cathedral at Kirkwall and dedicate it to his uncle, the holy Earl Magnus. Rognvald kept his vow.

St. Magnus was canonized in 1137, and masons were brought to Kirkwall to begin the work. The red sandstone was quarried at the Head of Holland outside Kirkwall, and the yellow stone came from the Island of Eday.

After visiting the cathedral, I walked across the street to the Orkney Museum, which tells the story from the Stone Age through the Picts (earlier people from North Scotland, I was told) and Vikings to the present day. I found the Stone Age artifacts especially interesting. I'm always amazed at the intelligence of the world's early people.

I did one more thing today. I got a bus to the airport to pick up my certificate that testifies I flew on the world's shortest scheduled air service between the islands of Westray and Papa Westray, as authenticated by *Guinness Book of World Records*.

Accents

The gang-of-14 has left the building. The tour, "Wild and Sexy Tours," spent two days in the same hostel where I am staying, and two of the touring women stayed in my room. One night, there was an additional delightful woman, a naturalist for the government. She works with people in nature, teaching and researching. We talked for a long time before the two touring ladies came into the room. The 14 people, mostly young and college-aged, and young, upward-moving professionals, came from various parts of the world and seemed to enjoy themselves. They cooked their breakfasts and then took off for a day of touring.

Yesterday, the guide cooked a scrumptious-looking dinner. He must be a perfectionist, judging by the perfectly diced red peppers and onions. "It's not really part of my job to cook for them, but I like to do it," the guide, bus driver, friend, and cook said.

It's fun to hear accents from everywhere, even here in the Orkneys where the people are difficult for me to understand without constantly asking, "What?"

I'm including some Orkney expressions for your enjoyment.

Sook=suck. "No more sense than a sookan turkey," referring to a stupid person.

Sirpan=soaking wet. "Me claes is sirpan weet." Translated—"My clothes are soaking wet."

Lug=the ear. "He's no chaet fur lugs," meaning, "He has big ears."

Peelie Wallie=sick, off-color. "His face is gae peelie wallie." Translated—"He looks ill."

Buddum=bottom. "You couldna see the buddum for it wis eltit wae dirt." "The bottom was obscured from vision because it was filthy."

Then there was the man in Westray who told me he walked to the beach. "I dangled me feet in the sea."

Making something out of nothing/making the day good

Three times in one day I got some news I had a difficult time getting out of my system, so on my walk, I told myself that I am just one little speck in the universe and that those three problems were not even close to important in the wide scheme of life.

I vowed (this was on Saturday) that I would look for something good to happen, and I smiled all the way to the center of town. Smiling increases the endorphins, I've read, so in spite of looking like a silly fool, I smiled at everyone I saw.

A young waitress I met the first day I arrived, who served breakfast in a hotel, recognized me, and it was good to be greeted by her again.

I had a craving for Orkney ice cream and found the Sinclair Sweetie Shop, went in, and looked around. There was only one seat in the back and a man was sitting on it.

"Oh, I wanted some ice cream but I wanted to sit down. Guess I'll go find another place."

"You can have this seat," the man in the back of the room said.

"Yes, he's my husband and is just resting back there. Go sit there. It's fine," said the man's wife from behind the counter.

So I got my ice cream and went to the back. I noticed a sign on the chair. It said, "This is where you'll sit while you wait for the police to show up after you have shoplifted."

Another older man walked back, saw me sitting there, and asked if I'd like a cup of tea.

It turns out this man is Jimmy Sinclair, the father of the Sweetie Shop's owner and father-in-law to the owner's wife, and he often goes into the shop to help out.

"Hiya, Luv, can I sit here with you?" He was a medium-tall man, lots of white, wavy hair, and kind, blue eyes.

"Yes, please do."

Another chair was found.

I told him about the journey I was on and how I would be leaving soon. I learned he was from St. Margaret's Hope near Lamb Holm where the Italian Chapel was built.

I had wanted to see the Italian Chapel but resigned myself to the fact that I had seen enough and didn't find it absolutely necessary to fund a trip by bus or tour to see the chapel.

"Oh, you must see the Italian Chapel before you go. I will take you there." He smiled often.

We agreed to meet at three p.m. in front of The St. Magnus Cathedral. He treated me to a cup of tea before I continued my walk around the town.

At 3:00, Jimmy promptly arrived, honked the horn, and I climbed in. It was pouring down rain by that time, so it was good to sit inside.

Jimmy talked loudly and non-stop all along the way to the Italian Chapel. I learned he was the son of a farmer, was born in the house where he grew up, and he would show me the house later.

His Scottish brogue, while charming, made me pay attention so I could understand the history of the wide, open, green, grassy slopes, water on both sides of the road, and a one-and- one-half-mile bridge. The bridge was built with massive stones and concrete that served to close up the entrances of Holm Sound.

Previously, in 1939, German Lt. Commander Prien took advantage of the gap in the Sound, penetrated the Scapa Flow, and sank the British battleship, *Royal Oak*, which was anchored off Scapa. Prien and his men got out safely; however, over 800 men trapped inside the *Royal Oak* perished. This site is a protected gravesite so divers are not allowed to dive in those waters.

"Some of those who died were only 17- and 18-years-old," Jimmy said. I cannot fathom the sad loss mothers must have felt losing their sons. I will never understand war.

Sixty-six blocks of concrete, most weighing five tons and some ten tons, were placed all along the barriers, blocking the tide. They are called the Churchill Barriers, from Churchill's orders.

Suddenly, beyond the Churchill Barriers, we arrived at the Italian Chapel, a relic of Camp Sixty.

Italian men were captured during the North African campaign and sent to build the Churchill Barriers. The Italians made something good out of their bleak situation. They transformed the area with flowers and paths.

One worker/prisoner, Domenico Chiocchetti, had an imagination that really went to work. With secondhand materials and worthless scraps, corrugated iron and plasterboard, a thing of beauty was created.

Inside, there are tiles lining the walls that look authentic but are painted to look like real tile, and the altar was molded in concrete. The "glass" windows were painted on the wall.

The Mother and Child surrounded by angels are painted on the walls, and the ceiling is painted in soft colors. Outside, the chapel is painted white with red trim.

Fifty years later, in 1992, eight former prisoners of war returned to Orkney and celebrated mass, according to Jimmy. Chiocchetti was too frail to attend, but his daughter Letizia was part of the party.

Later, Jimmy drove past the stone house where he was born. The day ended on a good note while we drove back to Kirkwall. There was a rainbow, a reminder that in the scheme of life, we are just a dot in the universe.

I'm leaving on the ferry tomorrow, Monday, and I'm assuming there will be Wi-Fi available. However, I won't board until midnight and will sleep on the ferry during the night.

Organization—some have the ability; some don't.

It's ten a.m. When I woke up, I knew that my time was up in the lovely Orcades Hostel in Kirkwall. I figured since the folks at the hostel said I could store my luggage until ten p.m., by the time I got a taxi to pick it up, I would have 12 hours to fill until

I head to the ferry. That would give me about one hour inside 12 places, and that would include the library, coffee shops, the museum again, the cathedral again, second-hand shops, antique stores, clothing stores, the pharmacy, tourist shops, and the bookstore. Oh, and there is a pet shop that has a few animals I figured I could stare at for a few minutes, anyway.

After I had my coffee and watched a bit of the Paralympics on TV in my room, I loaded up my "stuff" and carried it down the stairs to check out.

I handed in my key and signed the guestbook where I raved about the wonderful place. "Thank you for making me feel at home."

Giera Bews, one of the owners, along with her brother, Erik, and their mother, Sandra, said I could stay a while longer in the kitchen and lounge if I'd like. This is apart from their rules, but Giera said that since I stayed so long, the rules could bend a bit.

The Bews run a lovely hostel. It's the best I've been to so far. I've been in other really nice ones, but Geira is so "hands-on" that it's unusually refreshing. She's a delightful, gorgeous young woman who wears sparkly outfits while she goes through the hostel, smiling and cleaning up after everyone. It is a tribute to her that she can stay positive around so many different personalities with their various cleaning-up-after-themselves capabilities. She reminds me of a young Audrey Hepburn. Her attention to details and the hostel's cleanliness make you respectful with the desire to do your best, as well.

The building is decorated inside with fresh paint and wallpaper, and there are books, games, a large TV in the lounge, and a "community" computer. Wi-Fi works everywhere all the time, and the kitchen is stocked with pots and pans and lots of equipment that would make a television personality cook happy.

There is nothing anyone could want that you couldn't find in the hostel. Even toiletries that are left behind have a place to rest, with a sign, "Please use." Nothing goes to waste. The whole operation is a study in organization.

Speaking of organization, I'm always working at it, but it is never easy for me. Don't know why, but I could stand still and a button would fall off my clothing. Take what happened inside the St. Magnus Cathedral, for example.

I went inside to take part in a Sunday service. Before I entered, I missed the pen I usually carry in a pocket. My notebook is nearly always in my back jeans pocket, as it was this time; I take notes everywhere I go. But because I thought I had nothing to write with, my goal to write about my experiences was hindered.

Before I left the hostel, I had put a 20-pound note in my pocket so I wouldn't have to carry my wallet around and so I would be disciplined with a limited amount of money. Then I discovered that the cathedral sells pens to raise funds, so I told a deacon I wanted to buy one. That created confusion because the money for the pen is put into a different account from the money for the church collection. But they would see that I could purchase the pen.

When I pulled out the 20, a bunch of coins dropped, and they endlessly twirled on the stone floor, along with a tube of lipstick. I bent down to pick up the lipstick, and its top fell off. Three people stepped forward to pick up the coins and the top of the lipstick. When I bent over to help, a pill fell down from somewhere and landed on the floor. I picked that up and put it in my pocket. Then my notebook flew out of my hand.

"Gosh, I didn't mean to make a grand entrance," I said, with my hair now covering my eyes when I stood up. They scrambled to pick up my mess and to make change for the 20 note. A woman came back with a handful of change and told me then to pay for the pen with the change.

After the "grand entrance," I sat down toward the front of the cathedral and waited for the service to begin. I was early. I

reached into my back pocket to get my notebook, and out fell a
tiny pen that was lodged inside it. It was a tiny pen that was given
to me by Peter Lynn, in whose place I stayed in Dublin, Ireland. It
was usually stored inside my wallet. How did it not fall out when
I dropped the notebook?

After a bit, while I sat among the rose-colored stone columns, listening to the organ, I began to wonder what a lady of
my age would have worn inside this same church 500 years ago,
listening to the same bells that were calling people to church
(which, by the way, are the same bells and have never been tuned
up for the past 500 years and still sound beautiful). Would there
have been any ladies of that era who would try to look organized
but who would have made a grand entrance such as I made? If so,
what would they have dropped?

Peedie post

I got to Aberdeen this morning at six a.m., and a voice like Robin
Williams waking up the soldiers in Vietnam told everyone with
cars on the ferry to "prepare to get your car." He also announced
that the restaurant and coffee shops were opened for breakfast.

When I boarded last night, I met my nighttime roommate at
the door of the cabin. We barely spoke, and since it was by then
after midnight, we both just got into our beds. The boat made
engine vibrating noise as it left the harbor, and then it rocked and
rolled over the waves.

"Hmm, it looks like all the buildings are made of some kind
of grey stone," I mused out loud in the taxi after exiting the ferry.

"Aberdeen is called The Granite City," the taxi driver said.
"Granite is a durable material, which makes the city buildings
look brand new."

"They do look new."

But then the St. James Church on the same street showed
up among the grey. The rose-colored stones of St. James Church

were quarried from the same quarry as were the rose-colored stones of St. Magnus Cathedral in Kirkwall.

I must add that the buildings in the City of Denver where my brother Jack and I were born were made of granite. My thoughts of him while walking around Aberdeen were as strong as those granite stones.

Now I'm in a hostel and have my own private room. It is about two miles from the center of the city, and because I couldn't get into the room until two p.m., I took a walk and got to see what Aberdeen is made of. Aberdeen is beautiful and busy. I have noticed that people in large cities show serious thoughts on their faces; some look upset, some depressed, and many are in a hurry. Traffic in all large cities I have seen so far in Ireland and in Scotland and even in some small cities is dangerous for a pedestrian. Vehicles rule!

Just this morning, I came upon an accident victim lying on the street, and emergency responders were picking him up to take him to a hospital. He had been hit by a car. I'm not surprised. There are just a few marked crosswalks, and more are needed, as are some stronger regulations to protect the pedestrian.

Anyway, good-bye to Scotland and to the *peedie* Orkney Islands.

I've been wanting to use the word *peedie* for a while. It's a special word used in the Orkney Islands to designate something small, such as a *peedie* cottage, a *peedie* horse, a *peedie* tour, a *peedie* lunch, etc.

I'm in Croatia.

I just arrived in Croatia, in the city of Split on the Adriatic Sea. I'm told it's beautiful here, so I'm looking forward to getting to the town in the morning.

I did see some of it on my way to the hostel, but it was in the dark. I met a lovely young lady on the bus from the airport. She lives close to the hostel, and she walked with me and even helped carry some of my luggage. See, another angel.

It's hot here. Didn't think I'd ever say that, as from the time I left California, I've seen more rain than in my whole life. I love cold weather so this will be another challenge for me.

First day in Split, Croatia

The challenge—it's hot and humid. I was raised in a cold climate and have spent much of my adult life in a mild climate, but the native Croatians tell me I'll get used to it.

I have to because I'll be here for two weeks.

Last night, the lovely lady I told you about yesterday showed me where the market would be held this morning.

Today, I got some money exchanged, about six Croatian kuna for every one dollar. Since all of my clothing is pretty much for cooler climates, I went to the market and purchased a pair of white cotton pants.

I also purchased grapes, blackberries, carrots, cheese, and some bread. As I continued on down the market, I noticed the fruit got cheaper and cheaper. Haven't I always said that every day is an opportunity to learn?

I walked with a woman who cleans the hostel.

"I have a degree in finance but left the country of Slovenia, and now I do what I need to do." She, as everyone I have met, is very friendly and helpful. She walked with me to the market and turned me loose. On the way back to the hostel, I was close but still wasn't sure of myself, so I stopped a man and asked him. He then walked with me and pointed out that the street where the hostel is located still stands where I left it only two hours previously.

At the market, most items are set in price, to the best of my knowledge, but I'll learn more about that as the days go by. Women and men announce their goods, but not loudly. They are very polite people, as far as I have seen.

Surrounding the market are the gates to the palace. There are four entrances, and I've seen one of them, the silver gate, so far.

Stones are crumbling, and buildings, in general, are in need of upkeep. Laundry hangs on the outside of apartments and houses, which I think adds color to the environment.

The language is Slavic in its roots, and it sounds different from anything I've ever heard. My little bit of Dutch and Spanish doesn't work in this land. I am quickly learning how to say thank you, something everyone should learn in a foreign country right away.

Children learn English in school beginning at age ten, and later, they are required to learn one more foreign language of their choice.

I had a strange experience in Aberdeen when I ventured to the airport. I had set the alarm clock to ring at 5:30 a.m. for an early check-in. The alarm didn't work (this is the second time), and I can't figure out why. Anyway, I jumped up, slammed things into my bags, and got downstairs in time to meet the taxi driver.

When I got to the airport, I was too early and had to wait. The old adage, "Hurry up and wait," works here. Then when checking in, I was told I had to put my computer and the computer bag with all the papers, into my carry-on bag. So this is when I sacrificed a raincoat, sweater, and towel to make room for the computer, etc. I managed to get the computer into the carry-on bag, but I had to roll up the bag to make it fit.

That seemed to be approved by the customs agent; however, when I went through the system, I had to take the computer out, as well as my vest, the lipstick in my pocket, my wallet and the computer case.

"Here, I'll help you. You don't need this." The agent shoved the boarding pass and my passport into my bag. "You can get that later."

"Will you go with me?" I laughed. I felt I needed someone to help me get through the requirements of the country. Each airline, airport, and country has different rules.

He just laughed at my nonsense.

At the airport, I had bubble and squeak for breakfast. What is that? If you're not British, I'll explain. It's a potato patty with various vegetables mashed together and fried.

The palace and other delights

Listening to Engelbert Humperdinck sing *"Cuando, Cuando, Cuando"* and sitting by the Adriatic Ocean isn't so bad. After taking a 45-minute bus ride and then a 45-minute walking tour, I was hot and my legs needed a rest, so I sat at one of the many outdoor drinking pubs and restaurant establishments along Split's promenade where you can see cruise ships and yachts. I ordered a dish of ice cream from a photo menu.

When the waiter delivered it to me, it looked like a mountain poured into a glass. Fruit on the bottom, ice cream on the top and a cup of whipping cream on top of that. What have I done? I took the top of whipping cream off and ate the rest.

I've seen many people smoking, and it's hard to remove myself from the smell. I think tobacco companies make a fortune here.

Prior to the ice cream indulgence, I saw the hop-on-hop-off bus by the harbor and got ready to board it. The bus parked right by a road guard that required you to either high-step over it or walk around it away from the bus.

I chose to walk around and then jockeyed for room in line, but once the bus door opened, a large, excited, Italian family of children, parents, and great everythings noisily pushed and shoved their way to be first on board. Kids screamed, cried, and whined, while mothers shouted for them to shut up. The rest of us waited for the tour guide.

We drove by the Beavice, a locals' favorite sandy beach, and then saw the huge Gripe, an indoor sports arena, and the Gripe Fortress, a 17th century fortification. While we were there, our tour guide mentioned some famous Croatian athletes, and after she pointed out the archaeological museum that houses artifacts from prehistoric times to the Middle Ages,\ the bus brought us to the massive seashell-like roof structure of the Poljud Stadium that was built for the Mediterranean Games. The stadium has a capacity for 35,000 people.

We passed other white, sandy beaches that warmed up to turquoise, sage, and periwinkle blue water. It made me wish to take a flying leap into the Mediterranean.

The final part of the bus tour was the government-protected Marjan Forest. We wound through the forest on roads that were busy with folks strolling and riding bikes, and some were even roller skating. It was the cool breeze here that felt good.

The guide gave us so much information on the history of Croatia that it's more than enough for a book, but a few things stood out for me. For instance, the Dalmatian dog was named for the area of Dalmatia from where the dog was first recorded to have come.

We then met our walking guide who took us on a 45-minute walk beginning at the promenade and heading to the palace. We learned that the palace was built for Roman Emperor Diocletian in the fourth century. Imagine walking on the same rock surface that was used those many years ago. The guide pointed out the inside where a modern bank kept the pillars still there in remembrance of the palace's history.

It's amazing to me that people still live in the palace. I actually saw a man hanging his laundry way up on the top of the building.

When the preservation began, after many centuries, the emperor's apartments formed a block along the sea front, and they were completely filled up with refuse.

Today, the palace with the four entrances named gold, silver, iron, and bronze, is a UNESCO World Heritage Site. There were many tourists walking inside where the emperor once reigned, and now you can purchase items from postcards to trinkets to hand crafted jewelry.

There are many photo opportunities inside and outside of the palace, of which I took advantage.

I had an interesting talk with Antonia Cevra. She works at the hostel where I'm staying and is educated in the history of the country, its politics, and culture. She told me that since the country's independence from Yugoslavia and the war that gave them freedom, the country's citizens have become in-between people. The country has its independence and is a democratic country, but who they are remains uncertain.

Antonia said in fun that Croatian people are thought of as lazy. I haven't seen that because the women who work in this hostel seem always to be moving around, cleaning up, and giving a myriad of directions.

Warriors, dogs, and cravats

On my way to find the Ethnographic Museum that was recommended by Antonia from the hostel, I stopped at a nearby and locally known drinking establishment. There are many bars that serve hot and soft drinks, as well as beer, wine, and hard drinks, but they do not serve food.

A woman sat at a table outdoors, and I sat at a table next to her. I was also near a table of gossiping local men, all three drinking tiny cups of strong coffee. I ordered a coffee with cream, and it was just that—coffee with cream, whipping cream.

The men were obviously debating a local issue, as one man with a mustache and wearing a Greek fishing cap was animated with arms in the air and his voice raised to a high pitch. His two friends leaned in to set him straight.

Then another man, older than the three, walked by and made a comment that made them all laugh. Salt and pepper hair, sunglasses, and a shadow of whiskers, he walked away but came back when one of the men shouted at him. He walked back, pointed his finger at a man, and said something that nearly doubled the men over in laughter. Oh, if I could only understand the language.

My goal this morning was to find a museum. After coffee, I attempted to find the way and ended up on the top floor of the palace where I could tell something was about to happen.

Two warrior-looking men stood at attention at nearby stairs, and then the crowd of people standing by heard the beating of drums. Soon, the drummer, also dressed like a warrior, appeared and continued to beat the drums. A man dressed in white accompanied by a beautiful woman walked onto the balcony. He probably represented Diocletian, the original builder of the palace beginning in the year 293 A.D., and she was, I believe, his wife. He greeted the crowd.

It was all so serious until Diocletian cupped his hand by his ear, and the audience quickly caught on and shouted greetings back. He put his thumb up. Then he said a word that probably meant something like "hooray." He waited for the crowd to say it and then chastised us for not saying it loudly enough. He continued to egg us on until he was satisfied.

It was all great fun and not expected.

It so happens that the museum I wanted to see was up the same stairs where the emperor stood. So I had to wait until the ruler left the balcony with his entourage.

The museum wasn't free as I was led to believe, but it was worth the price. There were rooms, all of them in stifling heat, that displayed the costumes of people from various islands in various times.

The layers of clothing made me wonder what the women wore during the summer months back then, as most of the costumes would keep them very warm. The docent said they wore mostly white blouses and white skirts, but still in layers, it seems.

While on the way to see the museum, I learned two things. One, the Dalmatia area (for which the Dalmatian dog is named, as I've mentioned) includes Croatia and other countries of Slovenia, Hungary, Bosnia, Serbia, and Montenegro, and, two, the cravat—in America we know it as an ascot—got its origins from the Croats.

During the Thirty Years' War of 1618-48, the Croatian Light Cavalry reached Paris. The Croats tied scarves around their necks to connect themselves to their country of origin. The Croatian style became popular among the Parisians—fashionwise they were even then—and they brought the cravat into vogue. They called it *"a la maniere croate"* which means, "in the Croatian way."

In the tie/cravat store where I picked up this fashion history, there were displays of ties designating certain areas of Croatia. I saw a few ties that also had little Dalmatians running about on the them. Cravats were also for sale in the small shop within an arm's reach of the palace.

A little man sat near the palace with a small accordion. He saw me and saw a potential tip, I think. He whistled, and down came pigeons from the roof. Some birds sat on his head, some on his shoulders, and some on the sidewalk. It was part of the act, and a good thing it was, as his accordion playing was mostly one note breathing in and breathing out.

Travelers, pay attention.

It takes energy to travel! There are reservations to make, questions to ask, lots to learn in different environments, and names of items you must know.

Then you have luggage to pack and re-pack and drag and lift, and there are items to keep track of (camera, billfold, tickets, reservation papers, passport, medical documents, computer, keys, etc.). You have to manage your money, keeping track of the U.S. dollar vs. the currency of the country, and you need to pay the correct amount wherever you are.

You must know what neighborhoods are okay to walk through and how to find the stores that sell what you need—food, drinks, toiletries, medicine, clothing, and other items when the need arises.

A traveler must use practiced judgment on whom to trust and from whom to walk away when asking for directions and other important questions that come up daily.

It's important to know where the Wi-Fi stations are, where the tourist office of information is, the best money exchange office, and the best places to eat on the dime.

Okay, that all seems workable, and it is, with a strong attention to detail, but that's not all. In every place I have landed— in hostels, hotels, guesthouses, B&Bs, and homes while couch surfing—the bathroom facilities take a certain amount of know-how.

In some instances, shower faucets can be most difficult. There have been times I ended up in an ice cold shower because I couldn't understand the faucet system, and other times, I could run a bathtub of water but not turn on the shower.

Most people are generous with their help, but once in a while, someone is too tired to answer the question or just doesn't care about it. That's when you move on.

Last night, I walked a different way than the usual trail through the market stalls and found a shopping center with a spacious walking mall. The sidewalks there and in most places you walk on in Split are made of a shiny white stone. I would think it is marble, but I'm not certain because the stones are well worn. I ended up at the end of the walkway in a wide courtyard with tall, pink-stoned and pink-painted buildings on either side.

The view from several restaurants and pubs from the courtyard is picture-perfect. I took in a lavender sky and deep blue sea with yachts, ferries, and sailboats that seemed to be floating on top of the water.

I sat down at an outdoor restaurant and observed a wedding party—the bride in white and others in pastel—walking away into the lavender sunset.

It was comfortably warm with a soft breeze. I sat down at an open-air restaurant, opened the menu, and realized I was out of my financial comfort zone. I ordered a meal of grilled fish and spinach with potatoes and garlic. Before that, I told the waiter that I heard about local olive oil and asked if they had some.

"Yes, yes, I'll bring you some with bread for dipping."

It was indeed delicious. I have a German friend who told me a friend of hers brought some Croatian olive oil back to her from Split, and she said it was so good she could almost drink it. She was right. The home-style baked bread was great, too.

Back to this morning. I didn't want to make the same delicious mistake I made the night before and find breakfast/brunch in a pricey tourist destination place. It was Sunday, and many stores and restaurants were closed, but I walked into a store to get suntan lotion and asked the clerk for a good restaurant, to which she barely replied but pointed to the direction where I had dinner last night.

"Oh, that's a bit expensive there."

"Ma'am, everything here is expensive."

"Do you know of a place where the locals go?"

"Yes, I'll tell you how to get there." She walked out the door with me and told me how to find a buffet. I did find it and ordered from an extensive menu—eggs, grilled red bell peppers, squash, bread, and oh yes, olive oil. It was delicious, and I will go back there again.

It was here that I began to feel a bit dizzy but recovered with three glasses of water. Dehydration should be one of the items to which a traveler must pay attention.

I went back to the store and thanked the young woman for her good recommendation. Her attitude changed instantly.

"Oh, I'm so happy you liked it, and thank you for telling me that."

I drank four more glasses of water and juice before I got back to the hostel.

On the way, where I stopped for a drink, I met a most interesting 93-year-old man who claimed, when he heard I was from America, that he had been a spy for the Russian KGB.

The seduction of the professor

"I was the man of the world." So said Professor Andrei.

I sat down to get a soft drink in an outdoor establishment before heading to the hostel yesterday late afternoon. A man who looked like my father sat in front of me. I could see him preening and adjusting his shirt, patting down his hair, and turning ever-so-slightly toward my direction. Long ago, I took a social psychology class in my major, sociology. The curriculum was on clues people send, and body language was one of those. If my intuition and brief study were correct, this gentleman would turn and ask me a question. He did.

"I'm so sorry, but I do not speak Croatian."

"Oh, well, I can speak English, French, German, and many other languages." He spread out his fingers and counted on them. "So I'll speak English to you, then."

"Okay, English it is, then."

"What?" He cupped his hand to his ear.

"I said English is okay, then." He affirmed that with a nod.

"Where are you from?"

"America."

"Oh, America, you said?"

"Yes, the United States, the State of California."

"I was a spy with the KGB."

"Really?"

"I have a long and very interesting life history. Would you like to hear it?"

"Well, sure."

"May I sit here?" He picked up his cane and strutted over to a chair at my table.

For over an hour, even when the waiter began to take the chairs inside the establishment, until the end of the restaurant's day, I listened to this man tell me what an important role he played in the world, beginning with his birth in Split 93 years ago.

Professor Andrei worked in Ethiopia, Ghana, Borneo, and once as a representative for Tito during WWII when a new harbor was being built somewhere. He also worked as an Italian interpreter when marble was being quarried and used for a palace in gold, marble, silver, and glass.

I couldn't understand everything he said, and when I asked him to repeat it, I still didn't get it all. But he kept going. He would stop, make certain he had my attention, adjust his shirt collar as if he were wearing a tie, and continue.

At one point in his life, he lived in Prague, and it was here he had a gallery of his artwork. He also had a language school in Prague where he taught English. He called himself Professor Joe, instead of Andrei, for the reason that Joe sounded more English, as opposed to Russian.

On one occasion, he said a young woman approached him and asked if he taught English, and when he replied, "Yes," she signed up and took many of his classes until he realized that she was sent to find out who he was. English teachers during the Communist days were hard to find, and the KGB grew suspicious.

"One time, we entered a train, and I sat close by. When she got off the train, I followed her and invited her for coffee. Later, she came after class with a gentleman and introduced him to me. He said he was a salesman in caviar, and the company wanted me, as an English translator, to develop the Russian company.

Meanwhile, another one of my students followed the Russian girl and discovered she and the man were involved in an underground organization and were selling weapons, not caviar. The girl who followed the Russian told me to leave them or I'd disappear. This girl became my wife for ten years," he said.

Professor Andrei said he was featured in the *National Geographic Magazine* for his paintings, and that several of his paintings, according to his business card, were in the private collections of Stewart Granger, Adlai Stevenson, and many embassies throughout the world. His work has been exhibited in New York City, Washington, D.C., Sydney, Melbourne, Toronto, Columbo, Split, Zagreb, Manila, Brugge, and Blankenberge. His card lists his personal addresses in Prague, Zagreb, and Split.

During his discourse on his active years in the world, there was mention of his wives, his "way with women," and his remaining virility. That was a clue that his interest was more than a passing greeting to a foreign visitor.

"It would be a pleasure to invite you to my place of residence to show you the *National Geographic* article and many other writings about me that I have framed."

I thought I would be scared to go with him to his apartment, not that he could hurt me, but that if he became too friendly, I might push him away a little too hard and he would fall, hit his head on something, and die. I would then be arrested for murder.

"I would love to see your work, but I really do not want to go to your house, but thank you, anyway. You are very kind and certainly a very interesting man. I'm so happy you shared your life with me."

"Oh, let's just leave it all here, okay? Please don't use my full name in your book. I'll trust you."

I used only your first name, professor.

I walked back to the hostel with a bit more confidence in my femininity and a smile on my face.

Strolling in Croatia

Yesterday evening when it cooled down a bit, I took a walk, the second one of the day, to see what the harbor looks like as the sun goes down.

Before looking at the harbor in the evening hours, I wandered through the Archaeological Museum and was impressed by the many findings from centuries ago and many during the Greek and Roman era in Croatia. Don't know why, but I've always loved stone filigree.

"I've lived here all my life and have never looked up to the top of the buildings to see what you see," Will, my husband, said when we lived in his hometown of Den Haag, Holland, back in 1999.

It also amazes me to see the beauty and the intelligence used in the early artwork, jewelry, glass objects, pottery, and tools.

After visiting the museum and later at the harbor, I sat at one of the many outdoor drinking establishments and watched people. At one point, a pop band played on a bandstand.

Food kiosks were abundant with such items as potato strips. These were cut into long curly strips, placed on a stick, and deep-fried. You can eat it as you stroll along the harbor. I opted for a grilled corncob on a stick.

Palm trees; sun creeping through pastel clouds; the sounds of the church bells; the view of boats, small and yacht-sized; and many people wearing white made up the evening before I returned back to face the four Australians who were making havoc in the hostel where I'm staying.

I will leave tomorrow on a ferry to the Island of Vis. It is one of many islands Croatia claims, including Hvar, one island we will pass while making our way to Vis. Hvar is a popular island among the rich and famous, I have been told. Just recently, Tom Cruise and his entourage visited Hvar.

I need a nice, quiet, fishing village where I can stroll quietly and dip myself into the ocean. I have reserved just that. I'll be in a hotel with a room to myself. I'm looking forward to doing whatever I darn well please, and that means waking up when I want, sleeping when I want, and so on. Hostels do not give you that pleasure. I also look forward to meeting some of the fishermen and their families.

Something's fishy here.

"They will clean the dead skin off of your heels, ankles, toes, and around your nails."

"Fish?"

"Yes, tiny, little fish called *garra rufa*, or Dr. Fish."

I was just walking around the Split Palace to return to the hostel after brunch in my favorite restaurant when a sign caught my eye. It said, "New Fish Foot Spa!" I stopped and asked the pretty young girl what it was all about.

"You want to come in and try it? It will cost 70 kuna for 15 minutes."

Well, I'll try just about anything new and different, using my long-life practice of also learning how to use good judgment. I walked down steps into a little room to see two tanks of tiny fish with benches around the tanks.

She disinfected my feet and said, "Roll up your pant legs and put your feet in."

Guess the little fish saw dinner right away, as they quickly went to work around my toes, the bottom of my feet and up to my ankles. The water was cool, and the fish tickled.

It felt odd at first, and then I got used to it and watched the little pedicure fishes go to work, swimming around my toes and up to my ankles, taking off the dead skin.

I laughed to myself when I thought of the old kid's song, "The worms crawl in, the worms crawl out, they play pinochle on your snout. They eat your eyes, they eat your nose, and they eat the jam between your toes."

After 15 minutes, she handed me paper towels and told me to dry my feet. I asked if there would be a discount if I stayed in 15 minutes longer, and she said softly, "I'll give you five more minutes."

That felt about the perfect time, and when my feet and ankles were dry, I noticed they were completely soft. One of my big toes got special attention because it had a black bruise from rubbing against my shoe, and the nail is working its way off the toe.

According to the young lady, this method is widespread in the Far East and in Europe. After a bit of research, I found that Japan and Croatia were first to introduce the method. The treatment has caused some controversy in some U.S. states, as it is thought to introduce cross-contamination. Experts do not seem to agree. Most experts say if clean, hygienic procedures are used, it is safe.

The young lady here in Croatia said the procedure helps people with skin problems. They have a man who comes in to treat psoriasis on his arm, with good results.

After my feet were "baby-bottom" soft, I decided I needed to keep them that way. I have been walking barefooted in the hostels, which helped to give dinner with dessert to the little fish, so I went to the outdoor market to purchase some flip-flops.

At the market, I bought a pair from the sales lady who, when I told her where I had just been, said she had heard about it and was anxious to try it out on the psoriasis on her feet. But she added that in Croatia, people don't have that kind of money for such a luxury. She has two jobs, the one in the market and one as a television reporter.

For the record, the fish cleaning cost me about 11 dollars. I figured that was about what I'd pay for a seafood dinner treat. So it was a fish dinner, wasn't it?

I was moved to another hostel this morning due to a large group moving into the other one. My bed was needed to keep the group together. Someone walked with me to the different hostel.

I put my stuff down and took off for the restaurant I like. Going back, I got lost trying to find the new hostel. I had to walk to the first one and get someone to show me the way again. I felt like a homing pigeon, going back to where I called home for one week.

I'm not going out the rest of the day but will re-pack and get my bags in a manageable way, as there are three flights of stairs to get out of the hostel. Then more stairs to get down to the street and a bit of a walk to the ferry tomorrow morning. With refreshed feet, it should be easy.

Happy on the Island of Vis

I'm sitting on my bed looking out my window on the Island of Vis. I'm enjoying the view of the mountains on the other side of the harbor and listening to the ocean waves break. It's been pouring down rain. I walked to the guesthouse with the owner's grandson. I'll be staying here for the next six nights.

The grandson met me at the bus stop and carried my luggage through rain puddles. I was soaking wet when I got here. It's so breathtakingly beautiful, and the sound of the waves is mesmerizing. How could I be any happier than I am right now?

Norma and Gail from Canada and I left Split at 11:00 a.m. on the ferry headed to Vis and passed the Island of Brac on one side of the ferry. The ladies were so kind to invite me to hang out with them during the two-hour ferry trip. Turns out we were all going to the same town, Komiza. Gail had heard, as I had, that Komiza was the nicest town on the Island of Vis.

The day began when I woke up at six a.m. in Split and couldn't get back to sleep, so I got up and perused the Internet until seven a.m., and then the gentle rain turned to bursting thunder, lightning, and then a downpour.

I thought the ferry ride might be cancelled until a kind couple from Japan came into the kitchen, and he looked on the website for the ferry company's email address. He sent off a question, and it returned with the answer that it would be "full steam ahead."

A lovely young lady from Denver University who stayed in my room with her friend, both on leave from a student program in Israel, helped me get my luggage down the stairs.

I was early, so I rolled my bag to a Croatian-style fast-food kiosk across from the harbor and purchased a *burek*. I was told that those were delicious and that I must have one while in Croatia. It was about three types of cheese in a pastry wrap, and then deep-fried. I think there were about 1,000 calories in it.

When Norma, Gail, about 50 other folks, and I got off the ferry in Komiza, we climbed aboard a bus and rode through trees and vineyards until we reached the top of a hill and then looked down to the village of Vis.

I found the silver lining.

Well, here I sit listening to the waves crashing near my window and to the screaming seagulls. I just came back from eating a crepe inside a very nice restaurant that also has an outdoor venue. I chose inside because of the rain, as all the tables outside near the building under a canopy were occupied.

I have found that in Croatia, men sit or stand in groups, and I don't see many women getting together like the men do. Where are they?

I purchased some food in an outdoor fruit stand, which was part of a small, indoor grocery and meat store. Both clerks were women. One man standing nearby shouted at me, "How are you?" I think he was trying out his English. The men with him laughed, and one man hit him on the head.

I said, "I'm just fine, thank you." They laughed. Really funny, huh?

I purchased some tomatoes, bananas, cucumber, red onion, blue cheese, and yogurt. I'll put all into a salad later. (Not the bananas, silly.) At another small market in the town, I saw some jars with something that looked like pickled gooseberries, but I'm not sure what they were and couldn't understand the explanation. The farmer also had wine in plastic Coke bottles. This is typical, as there are many vineyards in Vis and lots of homemade wine. I opted for a bottle. There are certainly fancier wines professionally bottled and more popular, but they are a bit expensive for one person to purchase, and I wouldn't feel it frugal to throw the leftover wine away, which I might not have to do with the smaller, less expensive home brew.

The Island of Vis is the furthest away from Split, and there is a town called Vis; however, I'm on the opposite end of the island. Komiza is nestled into a cove with rocks behind it and the ocean inlet in front. Sailboats and fishing vessels nod up and down in the bumpy sea near the harbor. They haven't moved because of the rain.

From what I understand, Vis wasn't a tourist destination until about 15 years ago. Not counting the restaurants and guesthouses, the island still seems unspoiled by tourism. However, in my opinion, the town's people seem only to tolerate the tourists. Maybe well-traveled tourists have expected too much?

I made my lunch with diced, vine-ripened tomatoes; cucumber; red onion; crumbled-up blue cheese; and a pale green bell pepper. The latter is common here. They are about the same color as the inside of a cucumber and sweet. The yogurt I thought I purchased for the dressing turned out to be pure cream.

So I put that together with a bit of the wine and some sea salt, and boy, oh boy, was that salad ever good! The wine is very tasty, and I must say the coffee with real cream and my cookie for dessert was definitely worth writing home about.

I am going to go out again in the pouring-down rain and take a package to the tiny post office I saw here. I have a jazz CD from Split to send to my jazz-playing, drumming son, Ron. I have sent him a CD from every country I've been in so far. Other than that, I'm not purchasing any souvenirs for myself or for others. I don't have the room for souvenirs in my luggage, and if my bags are overweight, then I'd have to pay for that, as well. I remember traveling in the past when sometimes I'd have to purchase another suitcase to bring back all the souvenirs. When I traveled with my late husband, Will, one time he remarked that it seemed our trip was a shopping excursion. We always had requests from people to bring back items. The airlines prohibit excess luggage now, anyway.

The post office was closed by two p.m. Many shops were closed, too. I don't know why. I stopped off at an information center and learned that a local bus is available that goes in a circle around several other villages. I'm going to try and get that bus on Sunday afternoon. No one really knows the schedules for certain, as they seem to change often, but it's worth a try, anyway.

I saw my two new Canadian friends, and we sat and talked for a while. Meanwhile, the sun came out a bit, and a few brave people got into the water on the beach.

The Wi-Fi wasn't working in the house, so I found a restaurant with Wi-Fi, and just before that, I looked out of my window and found the silver lining.

The smiling crazy lady

Last night, a group of seven men dressed in black tuxedoes and gold cummerbunds sang a cappella inside a large building. I guessed it was a community hall, but it had no chairs. The singers were recording their songs. People crowded for a standing space, and when I got tired of standing, I found a bench outside near the water where I could hear just as well. I sat next to someone who didn't acknowledge that someone just sat down next to him.

This morning around 11 o'clock, I went to a pizza place and brought half of a pizza home for dinner. Meanwhile, however, I met my two Canadian friends, and they invited me to meet them for dinner tonight. Thank goodness for them and their bright smiles, as I am finding this island beautiful, but the flies are friendlier than the people.

I thought maybe I was beginning to look like that crazy lady who smiles all the time. In my defense, it's been my experience traveling in various places throughout the world that if you're friendly, people respond to that. Not here.

I asked my Canadian friends what they thought, and Gail said her theory is that tourism is relatively new here, and the people haven't had the opportunity throughout their lives to respond to strangers. And, she continued, other people have left the island. The island seems to have more elderly men, fewer women (or they stay home, while some work in shops), and a handful of children.

I smile at people, and they just look at me with no expression at all.

The first day that I noticed this, I was buying something from a bakery. I said, "Hmmm, let's see, what shall I buy for breakfast?" and the clerk stood there without a greeting or a comment of any kind. I pointed to what I wanted, and she put it in a bag, and when I said, "Thank you" in her language, she didn't crack a smile.

"How was your day? Were you really busy today?" I asked her.

"Yes." She gave me a dirty look and turned away to put the money in the cash register.

The first encounter didn't go well, so I just figured she was having a bad day, or my cheerfulness was just too over-the-top, so I ignored it.

But as time went on, it became more evident that we tourists are invaders on their island. "But, hey, as long as they're here, let's make some money off of them," is how I assume they think. I could be wrong. Maybe they just come from a culture of shy people.

Once in a while in a restaurant, someone will smile ever so slightly. It's very strange.

I did meet a young woman in a Komiza restaurant who shared a friendly moment with me. Tina Sepetavc was working on an art project, and I was working on my notes. We talked a while and exchanged email addresses, and we both joined up as Facebook friends.

I went to the beach today and sat on stones, trying to make a comfortable spot near the water. Sunbathers were plentiful on the little space I chose, and some women bathed topless. A few folks got into the water.

I twisted, turned, and tried to get comfortable lying on a pile of rocks. At least the rocks are interesting to look at. There were many that I swear must have been swept ashore from an ancient ruin. I'd like to take all that I find home with me but cannot do that.

My friends found me at the rocky beach and sat down for a while but didn't stay long. I'll see them later tonight. Meanwhile, I'll keep being that crazy lady until I get a smile from someone.

Wikipedia told me about the people of Vis.

"Vis was at one point the main hideout of Josip Broz Tito, the leader of the Yugoslav resistance movement. The island was occupied by Yugoslav Partisans under the command of Tito and by a British flotilla in 1941 and 1943. At the end of World War II, the island returned to Yugoslavia.

"During the war, the island was mined. Allied fighter planes were based at a small airfield that was also used for emergency landings of Allied bombers, including an American B-24 flown by George McGovern. After the war, the Yugoslav People's Army used the island as one of its main naval bases.

"After Croatia became independent in 1991, its navy did not reclaim most of the facilities, and the many abandoned buildings are being used for civilian purposes. In 2008, 34 mines from World War II were cleared from the island."

Wikipedia's explanation may help outsiders understand the people better. After all, 1991, when Croatia became independent, is not that long ago.

By the way, doesn't understanding the culture of a people create peace?

Fishing

Thank goodness for my two new friends, Gail and Norma. They are both originally from Canada and are long-time friends ever since both were nurses together. Norma moved to Australia when she married a man from there, and that has been her home for many years. The two friends get together every few years and travel together.

"We travel very well together," they both said at different times. They share equally and even have a "kitty" that they pool their money into.

Last night, they invited me to go out to dinner, and we found the absolute perfect place on a beautiful evening, right near the inlet where small boats dock.

We ordered a fish that we looked at before it was cooked, vegetables, local white wine that was very good, and coffee afterwards. The food was perfectly prepared.

We "oohed and ahhed" at the view as it became darker and lights reflected on the water across the inlet. Small rowboats came to shore as we sat there. It was a perfect evening with good friends. We laughed a lot.

Before the dinner, we got together at a community hall where two artists, both in their 70s, displayed their work. One woman's work was the views of Komiza and a few portraits, as well. Another woman's work was a bit more abstract, and lovely.

Today, on my way back from buying a few groceries, I saw that the tall, concrete and stone building that is shaped like a pyramid, only narrower, and is 35 meters tall, was open. I have been curious about that building and was happy to see someone standing near an open door.

"What is this building?"

"A fishing museum."

"Is it open to the public?"

"Yes."

"Are you in charge?"

"Yes."

"Okay, I'll come back after I put these away."

I went back, and the young man told me that the building was built in 1585, in defense against the North African pirates, and also it was used for tax collecting. He explained that the lower floor where one enters was a salt storage unit. Salt was used during the early days to pay taxes. The building became a *komuna,* a community center, and from 1987 to present, it has been a fishing museum.

The young man warmed up to me a bit and told me I was welcomed to walk to the top of the building if I wanted. He smiled as if to say I probably wouldn't want to walk up all those steps. I did want to, and I did walk up those steps. There was an iron pipe railing, which made it possible.

At the very top, there was a clock that keeps accurate time. I stood up there for a few minutes and took photos of the town and the sea and some of the houses.

"Oh, you're up here," the young man said.

"Yes, I made it up all those stairs."

"Well, I just wanted to make certain you were here so I wouldn't close up and leave you up here."

"Are you closing?"

"Yes."

"Okay, I'll be down. I just want to take another photo here."

"Okay."

A few minutes later, midway on my way down the stairs, I heard, "Hello?"

"I'm here. I'm on my way down." I was tripping down as fast as I could.

"Okay, I just wanted to make certain that you were coming down."

What is it with these people here? Why did he let me in if he was about to close down?

I got down and thanked him for letting me see the lovely exhibit.

"Where are you going now?" I asked.

"Home."

Seeing the island with Borut, the bus driver

Today, I took a local bus ride around a few villages and to the bigger city of Vis and back again. I wanted to take this bus for two days now and had gone back and forth to the information building to make certain I would be getting on the right bus, as I've heard stories that some drivers don't understand what you ask, and the first thing you know, you're not heading to where you thought you were going.

But the driver, Borut, was so kind. When I got on the bus, there were two other passengers, a man and his grown son. They were headed to the first little town on the route. The son was eager to answer all my questions and ask some of me, too. It was the first unusual question that helped me firm up the reason people appear to be unfriendly.

"What do you think of the people here?" he asked, and I, not wanting to insult his country, said that I thought the people were shy.

"No, Croatian people are arrogant," he said. Then he continued with, "They are also suspicious of big, powerful countries such as the United States and the United Kingdom."

So now I have learned something about the culture of the little Island of Vis, which is what my whole trip is about—the understanding of other cultures helps to understand how everyone fits into the scheme of our world.

The bus driver pointed out the names of the villages we went through. Along the way, there were many vineyards and olive groves. At one point, the vineyards seem to have been abandoned, and the younger passenger said it was because the work was too hard without enough money generated to make it worthwhile. Also, many of the villages we went through are inhabited by people over 65, as young people have gone elsewhere.

We dropped off the younger man and his father and later picked up a man who flagged down the little bus. Another woman in another village waited near her house and waved to be picked up, as well.

Borut pointed out the runway that had been used during WWII by American and English pilots, and now part of it is used for a cricket club. Further up the road, the runway could be seen, and I believe it could be used if necessary. Borut said the country is thinking of fixing it up.

Further up on a hill, he showed me a memorial that was mounted to honor the fallen American and English pilots who used the landing strip during WWII.

The whole trip took 45 minutes and was well worth the little over three dollars and was just as much fun as a 20-dollar tourist trip.

There are gifts from traveling.

The best of traveling doesn't only come with the collection of souvenirs, postcards, photos, or even memories. The best is what you learn about yourself. I have learned something important over the past few days.

I've learned that my expectations exceeded what the island people wanted to give, and that once I stopped expecting something from them, I felt more comfortable in my surroundings.

I cannot go into an environment wishing for what cannot be, but if I let be what will be, everyone is better for it. So I stopped trying to get friendliness back. I relaxed and let it come to me if it would.

I know for sure, nothing can ruin the beauty of this island, and if I take anything away, the memory will be the shades of blue in the sky and in the sea; the burnt orange, tan, white and black of the rocks on the shore; the smell of the water; the sound of the ocean waves crashing near my window; and the good coffee at the coffee houses.

I woke up this morning with the view of a small boat and a diligent fisherman out getting his catch of the day. I can only imagine that he will take it home, clean it up, and enjoy the benefit of living in paradise.

My friends, Norma and Gail, didn't surface this morning in any of the coffee shops, and I miss them. A lady I thought was Filipino was from Singapore. She and her daughter and husband, who now live in Australia, left yesterday. They gave me a book they all finished reading, and I have started to read it.

The couple from Finland must have left the island, as well, for I haven't seen them, either. People come and go, and the islanders stay and watch. I can't imagine what tourism has done to their lives. I try to understand and have compassion for the people whose country claimed its independence only two short decades ago.

The zen of traveling

I have found the zen for travelers. Well, I think so," anyway. I have stated that I learned that my expectations exceeded what the island people wanted to give, and if I stopped expecting something from them, I would perhaps be better accepted in return. I went about letting what will be, be. Today, I decided not to "try" but to just be in the moment.

My Canadian friends who left the island had told me about a little sandwich place, and I went about looking for it. Much to my surprise, all along the way, a few restaurant workers smiled at me in recognition of my appearance in their establishments during the week. And when I got to the sandwich place, a mother and daughter greeted me with smiles. The daughter waited on me and put together a sandwich and then put it in a toaster and handed it to me. She told me where I could sit and order something to drink. A bit later, she came out and sat with me, and we began to talk about the Croatian people, her college studies, and my traveling experience.

Her name is aptly suited for her—Glloria Raci. She is finished with her college studies except for the dissertation on bilingual education for children. She told me that many islanders have come from Armenia and do not speak Croatian, which causes difficulty not only for the child but also for everyone. It's a problem and is something dear to her heart.

She, her brother, and their parents moved to Croatia from Kosovo about 20 years ago when the country was at war, so she is sympathetic to the language difficulties of immigrants.

Glloria has shiny black hair, dark eyes, and a clear complexion. She beams out of a smiling face friendliness and acceptance with a big dose of humor. Her ultimate goal is to work with children.

In the town, children run, ride bicycles, and play on the main street facing the harbor where the tourists and locals gather to drink, eat, and people-watch. While at the sandwich shop, I noticed two girls on a bicycle, riding back and forth, back and forth. An older-looking blonde-headed girl was pedaling a small, Asian girl who road backwards on the bicycle. Both looked confident in their chosen places on the bicycle.

Today, the little Asian girl crept up to Glloria to say hello, and it was then that I noticed Glloria's love for children was real. When the little girl left, Glloria said the little girl had been adopted from Taiwan, and this was her first summer in Komiza. She added that the little girl has assimilated very well into the new environment.

Glloria gave me another insight into the Croatian people. Some older people may feel a bit left behind or trapped in a lifestyle that doesn't have an interesting future. Young people go off to college, and most do not return. "The older people may be feeling a bit frustrated with their routine life," she said.

I had my sandwich, and Glloria told me to come back in the evening when she would treat me to a typical Croatian sandwich. And that I did. It was sardines, cheese, and a nice sauce inside toasted bread.

I sat and talked with her and met her brother who was waiting on tables for drinks, and Glloria took her turn at the sandwich counter. The family also has a jewelry store. Her mother was taking care of that shop.

In the afternoon, after meeting Glloria, I took a walk in a different direction and found the high school and the grade school by walking up a narrow walkway on a series of steps that were placed far apart.

Three little boys came walking down the steps, and when they saw me take a photo, one of the boys made a face. I thought that was so cute, and I asked him to do it again. The little ham that he is, obliged.

Also, on the walk, I came to a doctor's office while a woman walked down out of the building. "Do you remember me?" she asked.

"I'm not sure. Where have we met?"

"You sat next to me on the bus on that rainy day from the ferry to Komiza."

"Oh, yes, I remember you now."

"Have you had a good time here in Komiza?"

"Yes, once I got familiar with the people."

"I understand."

By the way, I learned that along with the choices of coffee—cappuccino, espresso, black coffee, coffee with cream, and coffee with milk, there's one called American coffee. "What is that?" I asked a waitress.

"Oh, that's just plain coffee in a bigger cup." Talk about cultural exchange.

I also learned the stone steps I saw all along the walkways in Split, and some in Komiza, are indeed limestone quarried from Croatia. The White House in Washington, D.C., drew upon a type of Croatian limestone to help build its white columns.

The evening was lovely, and I wish I could stay a bit longer now that I have a better understanding of the people, and by the way, a better understanding of myself. But this is my last evening in Komiza. I will leave on the ferry back to Split tomorrow around two p.m., stay all night, and then I'll be off to . . . .

One more hour

I took one last walk through the village of Komiza until it was time to leave. I either spent too much time there or not enough. I think it might well be the latter, as I met more people and saw more just in my last three hours there.

Take, for instance, Dragon, the handsome grandson of the woman I rented my room from. He wanted to assure me that Dragon means nice flower, not a fire-eating monster.

Dragon is leaving the island on the same ferry as I, and is returning back to Serbia where he was raised and where his parents live. He's an intelligent young man who has an insight earned from living in a war-torn country and also from studying interior design.

He is interested in interior design from the standpoint of using design to create a positive, clean, pollution-free world.

Dragon gave me his studied look into the differences between his country of Serbia and Croatia.

"The countries hate each other," he said, and further explained that the disagreement came out of a war many years ago and also a war just 20 short years ago. Croatia wanted freedom from Yugoslavia, and the Serbs sided with Yugoslavia during the conflict.

He assured me again that the fire-eating dragon of Serbia didn't include the citizens of the country, but the leaders. Isn't that the way?

He also told me something interesting about guns made in Serbia. They are sold to various countries across the world. Dragon is intelligent and uses the foreign language of English well, with few limitations. I hung onto every word, and I learned so much from this young man.

Before meeting up with Dragon, I walked around the village to see more of the houses and the many, many cats that live on this island. A veterinarian needs to volunteer their time to neuter and spay the cats, as there are many felines who scrounge around for food. I saw one with three legs and one with open sores. Being a cat lover, this was hard to see.

One more item to report is the T-shirts I see with strange phrases. It makes me believe that the U.S. is enamored by young people. Here are a few, and I will observe more and list them as I see them.

True Religion Brand Jeans California, Los Angeles Play California, Louisiana U.S. Repair Shop, and Denim New York City.

I'm in Madrid.

I was trapped in the London Airport most of the day, and I feel as though I walked ten miles just back and forth through the airport, going here and there so the authorities could thoroughly check the travelers into their country. But the adventure began in the Split airport, and it wasn't pretty.

I landed in Madrid about 6:30 p.m., and it's now 9:30 p.m. I had dinner and am now on the Internet, where for the first time during my five months of travel, I've had to pay for it.

A completed, complicated itinerary planned by a pro!

I want to shout out for my travel agent, Pauline Hill. I met her in Blairgowrie, Scotland, after I was just walking past her office. I decided to stop and ask questions. I ended up with a complete itinerary that was, by the way, a complicated one, and she worked it out, keeping my budget in mind. It involved ferries, buses, airplanes, and hotels beginning in the Orkney Islands, then Croatia and now Spain via London. She is a total professional. You would fall over if you knew how little I spent on the awesome itinerary. But the traveling exhausted me.

I had my *desayuno* and am ready to divulge my "Jerry Lewis" style of catching a plane.

First of all, I believe more and more in a self-fulfilled prophesy when applied to my personal travels. I make good judgments and try to be as organized as possible, but still, during transitions, I worry there is something I haven't done correctly or that I have lost an important document or . . . and it goes on. But I persevere and seem to overcome any obstacles that arise.

Take my trip to Madrid that began two days ago. I got on a bus in Komiza for the ride to the ferry in Vis. There isn't any direction to board the ferry, so following people who seem to know the name of the game is the rule. There were no "lifts" on this ferry, but there were two Croatian ladies who put their bags on a wooden plank and signaled that's what I should do. So I did, then walked up narrow metal stairs to a community room where I sat looking out the window for two hours. My book was in the bag, so that was my first mistake.

When the ferry arrived at Split, everyone seemed to know what to do, where to go, and how to get off the ferry, and all at the same time. This includes cars, trucks, vans and boats. People were walking between cars to get to the other side.

"I don't see my luggage here," I said to a man who was standing on the side.

"How did you come into the ferry? On the left side or the right side?"

"Oh, I entered the ferry from the left side." "I think" (a quiet afterthought).

"Well, then your luggage is on the other side."

"How do I get there?"

"You just walk in-between the cars."

"But they're driving off the ferry."

He wasn't concerned and left his position, leaving me to figure it out. So I walked between vehicles with my hand out to stop them from hitting me. Somehow, I got to the other side. No luggage to be found. I asked someone who seemed to be in charge of a storage closet.

"No luggage here," the man said.

I waited for all the vehicles to leave, and from where I stood, I saw my luggage alone on the other side of the ferry. I walked over, picked it up, and while I walked off, passengers for the out-going trip were arriving. I managed to be the last person off the ferry, and there were no prizes awarded for that until I saw the taxi driver with a sign held up, saying, "LAUREEN DIEPHOF."

I stayed in a lovely Villa Cezar hotel near the airport and met a nice young lady, Ane Deankovic, who had arranged for the taxi transition from the ferry, delivery of a dinner from a local restaurant, and a taxi transition to the Split Airport the next day. The young lady, a recent graduate from college with a degree in economics, said her summer job at the hotel was about over, and then she would try to find a new job. It's very difficult to find a job in Croatia, she told me. She was so good at managing the hotel activities, and I wished her well.

Now here's where the fun began. I got to the airport at the correct time to check in, I thought. One time I was too early and they made me wait, so learning from that, and taking that into consideration and also misreading something in the paperwork, I got a shock when at the check-in window.

"Am I too early to check in?" I asked the friendliest-looking counter woman, who was smiling and laughing with her co-workers.

"You are too late. You are going to miss the plane. Put your luggage up here," she directed, suddenly turning into Cruella De Vil.

Before I got to the check-in, from something I learned flying EasyJet, I knew that I had to put my computer into my carry-on bag with the computer bag rolled up inside. This makes that bag very heavy for my shoulder, and I didn't do that this time because, previously, I had to take the computer out for customs inspection, and I just walked on board with it in my hand and put it under the seat. No one said anything. I tried that this time.

"If you don't want to miss the plane . . . ," Cruella told me, and she took my booked-on suitcase over to the machine. The man overseeing that detected a battery inside.

"You have a battery inside the bag. You must remove it," Cruella frowned.

"Oh, that must be my clock."

"You must remove it." Cruella looked at me with disgust.

So, I tore into the bag, underwear going this way, tops that way, pants over there, and my Kindle fell out, but no clock. I was frantic. Out came winter gloves, the Icelandic sweater, wool socks, rocks, seashells, pajamas, and a hot pink towel.

"Oh, come on," I said. I left the Kindle out, thinking that may have been the problem. "Let them look at it again."

She pointed to the men who would give it a second look.

"No, there's no time, just close it up, and let's go."

I tried shoving my life back into the bag, and now the bag seemed too small to accommodate all the stuff I had just thrown out.

"Can you help me close this up, please?" I pleaded with the agent.

He did help me zip it up, and then I was on my way with Cruella's stiletto heels clipping on the tile, with me in tow.

"Do you have your boarding pass and passport?" She turned with that look again.

"Yes," I replied, trying not to let her bullishness win.

I handed the customs agent my passport, and she and Cruella exchanged words, leaving me out.

"Oh, no, my camera." Suddenly it was not hanging over my neck.

"Oh, yes, sure, of course, you left it back there." She shook her head and strutted off like a banty rooster.

She came back with the camera, a small bag with my paperwork, and a book.

"Okay, now, come on," she instructed, and figuratively took me, the dunce, by the ear and led me to the gatekeepers. I walked on with the computer bag and the other bag until I heard a voice.

"Attention! If you carry more than one bag on the plane, you will be charged extra."

I stopped in route to the plane, stuffed the computer and rolled bag into the carry-on, and walked onto the plane—not the last person—but close to the last one, and I sat at the tail of the plane, the worst place to sit, in my opinion.

I finally arrived in London. You have to walk about two miles to pick up your luggage and then another two miles again to go through customs before you can leave. The plane I would take to Madrid was at the opposite terminal, which required taking a bus, more steps, more walking, and by then I was so tired that I stopped in a restaurant and looked at the hostess with hopelessness.

"I'm so tired. I just want to sit for a while before I order my meal."

"Oh, this space is only for drinking. If you want something to eat, you need to go over there."

"Okay, then I'll just drink."

"Well, if you want to just drink, then you need to go over there and order it." She pointed to the bar counter. I sighed.

"Come on, I will help you. If you're hungry, let's go, I'll carry this." She picked up the bag and took me to a seat where I ordered lunch.

I felt like crying. But I recognized once again that there are good people in the world.

After lunch, it started all over again, walking, carrying the heavy bag, up the stairs, down the stairs, until I finally found the stopping place where I would wait to watch on the marquee when the boarding gate would be announced and where I had to walk at least ten more minutes to board the plane. That was successful.

I'm in a hotel, a reasonably priced one, that charges for Wi-Fi. I purchased 24 hours' worth. It's a good time to rest up. I met two nice men from Palm Springs who were traveling nearly as much as I am, and also a couple with their 20-year-old son from North Carolina who sat next to me last night during dinner. Talking to them made me feel normal again.

Lazy day

Today was the first completely lazy day in my five-month journey. It helps that I am far away from anything. Surrounding the Holiday Inn Express near the Madrid Airport are fields of weeds and a few buildings that look as though all life has stopped. Without a car or access to a bus, except for expensive taxis, I decided it was a good time to do nothing except look for a place to eat.

I had the breakfast the hotel provided and when lunchtime came, I went down to the restaurant to partake. I was told the restaurant only has breakfast and dinner. Dinner wouldn't be available until 7:30 p.m. I was hungry, and the snack machines didn't look inviting.

"There isn't anything around here, is there?" I asked the hotel receptionist on duty.

"Yes, go out that way, turn left, and walk for about five minutes, cross the bridge, and you'll find a restaurant."

I checked out what she said to make certain I understood.

So I walked out, turned left, and saw the "bridge" that was a concrete overpass stretching over an eight-lane freeway. When I got to the "bridge," I had to walk up two flights of stairs and then walk over the overpass to the other side. I kept thinking, I sure hope the engineers built a strong bridge and it won't fall just when I'm in the center of it. I noticed it didn't sway, so that was a good sign. Airplanes jetted low over my head, as the airport is just a few miles away.

When I got over to the other side, there were more stairs, and at the bottom of the stairs was a narrow iron gate with a fence that wrapped around a field and the restaurant that had a great big sign painted on the window. "The Lunch," it said.

The fence looked like it surrounded a concentration camp, but I continued on and found the restaurant where a waitress told me lunch wasn't ready. That was at 1:00 p.m., so I waited at a table. Soon, other people came in behind me.

I had fish with a mild green sauce, a salad, and rice pilaf. The salad was lettuce, pickles, olives, onion, tomatoes, and cucumbers, a great combination. I was proud of myself for ordering everything in Spanish, as the waitress didn't speak English. She looked relieved. Dessert was a tiny bowl of diced fruit.

The rest of my time was spent watching Spain Television and understanding only what I saw and once in a while, the words and phrases. I was a rejuvenated traveler and ready for the next adventure.

I moved to another hotel today, and at five p.m. I went to the welcome and get-acquainted party for the Vaughan Systems conversation project here in this hotel. Several other folks and I will be going to a small village where we will be treated royally for one week while we engage Spanish executives in conversations in English.

We are not allowed to use any Spanish whatsoever, and if we do, we will be asked to leave. That's not going to happen to me! I will be in the village of Gredos, and others go to another place. We leave at nine a.m. in the morning on buses and return back to Madrid on Friday.

The program promises to get executives up to speed with English through the Vaughan System's own curriculum. It will be interesting to see how we do.

During the party, I met people, mostly from England and Scotland, and an American couple who are expats in Spain, as well as two young women from India and a woman from Canada, along with others whom I didn't actually meet yet. One gentleman from England told me about his experience as a volunteer in the Olympics. It was really a lot of fun, he said, and he would surely do it again. He was a smiling fellow and a joy to talk with.

Tonight, I went to a restaurant with three women, Heather from England, Evelyn from Ireland, and Rhona from Scotland. Heather has had an interesting life, and she wears it well. She was in a sparkling top that matches her own spark. She has lived in Taiwan for five years to be close to her son, her half-Asian grandsons, and her daughter-in-law. She currently "nannies" for a wealthy couple for two children she says are wonderful kids.

Heather has traveled a lot in her life and just returned from the El Camino walk through Spain. She has told me all about it, and I'd like to try a portion of that long pilgrimage.

Rhona has been an educator and is eager to get down to the business of talking to the Spaniards. She stayed in another hotel from the one I'm in, as did Evelyn and Heather.

When I come back to Madrid, I will be staying somewhere, probably a hostel, and then I'll go to the Basque area on October first.

Does it seem possible that I've been on the road for six months? Not to me. That is, until I look at my bags. The one I book on the plane has holes in it, and the zipper on the carry-on is not working well, so I guess that's proof of how well I have traveled. I leave here at 11 a.m. for another hotel near the city.

Swanky resort with Spaniards

I'm in a swanky resort outside of the little village of Gredos, northwest of Madrid. It took about three hours to get here, passing open spaces of wheat and cattle. That part reminded me of New Mexico. Then we were on winding roads, driving through little villages. We saw the Wall of Avila, a national monument. That's where we stopped for a coffee break and then continued on until we got to our final destination.

I was in a bus with the Anglos and Spaniards. An Anglo must sit with a Spaniard to speak only English. After the break, we switched partners. Or they did, for at that time, I didn't have a partner, so I could enjoy the ride silently. We came to a mountain area that had trees shedding their autumn leaves in colors of gold, red, rust, and brown.

We got to the resort and left our luggage in a small conference building and went on to the main lodge, and by that time, it was raining.

We had a briefing about what our job was as a volunteer conversationalist, and the Spaniards got their briefing, as well. A tiny person with the name of Carlota is the master of ceremonies and an up-and-coming actress. She explained well and teased us all a bit. Then we had a delicious four-course gourmet lunch that we got to choose earlier in the day even before we left Madrid.

Our job is to sit with a Spaniard, all of whom are employees of a utilities company. Eva was my first conversation on the bus, and she explained that her job with the company is to check out discrepancies with energy output. Eva has a 13-month-old daughter, and I had the privilege of seeing a photo of the cherub.

The second partner was a nuclear engineer, and the next one was an engineer from Granada. He made Granada sound very inviting.

My room is upstairs in the main lodge. The lodge and my room remind me of houses in Colorado—rustic, open ceiling beams, and a dormer on the roof. The doors to get into the room are flush with the wall, so you don't actually see doors as you walk down the hallway.

We had a game of sorts to play in the community room where we chose partners and asked three questions. Then we had to introduce our partner to the rest of the people.

We all have a schedule to follow during the day, and we eat dinner at nine p.m. My friend, actor Sumi Haru, who made a movie in Madrid, reminded me that dinners are late in Spain. She is right.

I have a scheduled break right now for 50 minutes, and then I'll have a one-on-one conversation with a Spaniard. I'm really having fun.

The visit to the village and super salad

We had a breakfast worthy of royalty waiting for us in the restaurant room. The table was arranged as an art exhibit with all kinds of food.

We all met in the common room for the day's work. My one-on-one would be with Luis, who is a nuclear engineer. I actually met him last night at dinner. He looks like Anthony Quinn. Carlota, our actress/mistress of ceremonies, told me that Luis and I would go to the village with her so she could purchase some pens at the book/stationery store.

It was such a privilege to see the village of Gredos, a village known for the growing of beans. We saw the central courtyard getting the market ready for the day. By then it was a bit after ten a.m., and farmers were bringing their fruit and getting their vegetables ready, and a restaurant had set out their chairs in the courtyard for people to sit, drink, and people-watch.

The church, with gothic stone features, was built in the 13th century. We walked around it and saw a fountain in front. A tall tower features large bells. The town is quaint with old streets and stone buildings set close to the sidewalks. Going to the village was a surprise, so I didn't have my camera with me.

Carlota said there may be another opportunity. I sure hope so, as I'm dying to take photos of the charming village. Luis told me that many people have left the town for larger cities and better opportunities but keep their houses in the village for use during the summer.

"They have the best of both worlds," I said, and Luis agreed.

Yesterday, the one-on-one I had with Bart led to a funny story he told me about understanding English in an American restaurant. The waitress asked him if he wanted "supersalad," or that is what he thought she said.

He repeated, "Oh, supersalad. Yes, I'd like supersalad."

"What kind would you like?"

"What?"

"What kind of soup would you like?"

"I'm confused, I thought you said supersalad."

"Oh, no. I said 'soup or salad.' What kind of soup would you like to have? I will bring you the soup and the salad."

Then I told him the story of the day I had in Holland where I made up my mind to speak Dutch all day. I saw a woman at the train station, and we were making small talk and doing quite well if I do say so myself, until she told me she just had her hair done. I looked at her, and in perfect Dutch, I said, "Oh, yes, I can tell. It's very ugly."

I misused the word and ruined the lady's day until I realized my mistake and apologized.

After the visit to the village and finishing up the one-on-one with Luis, I went up to my room, and it was cleaned up. The bed was made, there were fresh towels, and the room sparkled in cleanliness. I'm spoiled.

Playing games and improvisation

Wow! I'm waiting for a call from a Spaniard. We are playing "lost baggage." I am the flaky customer service agent, and she will be the frustrated traveler. The call will attempt to get her to use English in a moment of distress.

That was fun! She was great in her role. She stuck with her intentions and made herself understood. Afterwards, we met in the lobby and had a good laugh over our improvisation.

The next project was a skit we would organize together in a group to present to the wider group on Thursday. We were chosen to be the performers because we won a contest, and the winning group was promised a prize. The prize was that we have to work out a skit. To win this so-called prize, we had to take one photo of a list of activities and be the most creative. To the task—get a picture of something on top of something. That had me sitting on top of a bar!

This all reminds me of my own theater experiences, of which there have been many, both as a performer and as an acting teacher.

It also causes me to remember the TV show I had years ago. I seem to be saying years ago a lot as I bring up former experiences. My experiences go on deaf ears, as I'm just an old lady reliving the past. I assume most participants think that. Anyway, it is fun playing these kinds of games again in a young atmosphere like those I had participated in in previous years.

Putting a spell on me

I remember asking my mother this question when I was a child—"Why do all the flowers feel the same? It doesn't matter what flower it is, they all feel the same. Why?"

"That's because flowers have the same cover over their body, just like we do. My skin feels just like your skin. All skin feels the same, just like flowers' skins feel the same. I'm glad you asked that question," my mother answered.

I wasn't sure for a very long time why she was glad I asked that question, but it has come to me over and over throughout the years. She wanted me to learn that we're all the same, but our personalities make us different from each other, as do the cultures of the countries we come from. Personality and cultural differences make the world an interesting place, as evidenced in the program I have taken part in this week.

The Spaniards have shared much of themselves, their intelligence, their eagerness to become fluent in English, and their interesting culture. They have been polite and friendly toward the volunteers who, in turn, have been happy to share their time in helping them acquire fluency.

Much time is spent in one-on-one conversation between an Anglo and a Spaniard, and then there are the fun and games, another way to learn. Take yesterday, for instance. We broke out into small groups and discussed the formula for making a presentation, as every Spaniard is preparing to present tomorrow. Then after a bit of that, one group gave a spoof on Shakespeare, which was hilarious. The players were all great, and it was fun.

Before that, however, my group performed our skit. I played Clint from New Mexico, whose ranch is close to the Texas border. With my southern accent, I told the audience that I was a cowboy and ruled a ranch, milked cows, and fed chickens. I was introduced as a "man" (I wore a mustache and cowboy hat and a gun) who was looking for a wife to "cook, clean, and cuddle."

There were three women contestants, all "hidden" from Clint. One was named Dolly; she was stacked like a certain Dolly we know as a country western singer. She wore a hot pink wig. The second applicant was a nun in complete black habit. The last one was a woman who was into witchcraft. She wore a black and silver wig and all black clothing, and she carried a bat (the animal).

I asked the witch if she could cook and what would she put into my sandwich, and she replied with all kinds of nasty critters and perhaps a bat or two.

The nun was asked how she looked, and she replied that even though she was covered up, he (I, Clint) would be pleased to see her "beauty-spot." That comment was greeted with lots of laughs, which made Clint realize, even though he couldn't see the ladies, she must be covered up from head to toe. Not very interesting, he thought.

What Dolly said when questioned about her best feature surprised the audience. In spite of her frontal display, she said that it was her eyes.

Well, when the commentator and her assistant asked who I'd chosen to marry and take back to the ranch, I, Clint, said, "One of those ladies is too weird, the other wears way too much clothing, and the other one was way too much woman for me," and I chose the assistant, instead. We both ran off the stage together. The audience applauded and laughed throughout the skit.

Much later, the master of ceremonies and actress, Carlota, and the program director, Marisa, arranged a *Queimada* for all of us. "That involves an alcoholic, special drink with fire," Marisa said.

Even though I was tired at 10:30 p.m., my interest was piqued enough to want to satisfy my curiosity, so I walked up to the small building where the programs are held.

Carlota was scooping up the drink with fire coming up from the clay pot and on the liquid. While she was doing that, a few people read items that put us into the mood of a ritual.

"*Queimada* comes from a Galician tradition. It is a punch made from Galician *aguardiente* (*orujo en gallego*), a spirit distilled from wine and flavored with special herbs or coffee, plus sugar, lemon peel, coffee beans, and cinnamon.

"Typically, while preparing the punch, a spell or incantation is recited, so that special powers are conferred to the *queimada* and those drinking it.

"*Queimada* is a pagan ritual that dates back to the 11th century, although sometimes it is believed to be an ancient Celtic tradition transmitted along generations. Others claim it was actually developed in the 1950s.

"In 1955, Titi Freire designed the clay pot in which the *queimada* is usually prepared, and the spell that is recited nowadays was written by Mariano Marcos Abalo in the 1960s.

"The goal of the preparation ritual is to distance the bad spirits that, according with the tradition, lie in wait for men and women to try to curse them. All occasions are good for a *queimada,* but typically the *queimada* ritual takes place during St. John's night or witch's night on June 23rd. The people who take part in it gather around the container where it is prepared, ideally without lights, to cheer up the hearts and to be better friends." This information was stated in the material handed to us when we walked in.

I think this would be great fun for a Halloween party. Please see the recipe in the back of the book.

By the way, as I mention in the recipe, the Spaniards have put a spell on me!

Oh, that American lady!

I don't know what it was that created the laughing hysteria in Luis, Alfonso, and Linda, but over dinner last night, we all laughed until our sides ached.

Two Anglos and two Spaniards were required to sit together for all meals, and we were to change who we sat with at every meal to give everyone an opportunity to meet each other and so that the Spaniards would improve their English by listening to every accent.

I guess my independence and spirit of adventure are a novelty among the Spanish people in general, but when Linda quietly asked my age, she blurted it out to Luis and Alfonso. Alfonso had already learned of my age, but Luis, when he heard, started laughing, and none of them stopped laughing throughout the dinner.

This went on until I finally had to tell them I was an American woman with a pioneer spirit. What else could I use as an excuse for my independent and adventuresome spirit, especially since it doesn't strike me as unusual in even the tiniest bit? Just because you hit a certain age, does that mean you must stop living and doing what you like to do?

Alfonso stated that his 67-year-old mother would never do what I'm doing, and not only that, he would question her safety while traipsing all over the world.

Yesterday, we played a game that required a group effort. We were to draw a name out of an envelope and try to get our partner to guess the answer. It could be a celebrity, an author, a musician, or a famous person in history.

I first had the name Batman and sang a bit of the Batman tune—"Da, da, da, da, da, da, da, da," and I'd point to Luis to fill in the "Batman," but Luis, my partner, didn't get the answer. Then I had the name Beyonce, and he got that one right away.

The next time around, Luis appropriately guessed Napoleon when I said he and Josephine married in the Notre Dame, and in spite of my saying Napoleon was Italian (what was I thinking?), Luis got it right.

We had a get-together later after dinner with Anglo presentations that were informative, some just plain fun, and all in English, of course. I also had two one-on-one conversations that I enjoyed very much, and I've had two today, as well.

Tomorrow is our last day, and we'll have one more one-on-one conversation, and then the program is over.

Eva, the first Spaniard I met on the bus going to Gredos, has left, as she has a meeting on Monday at work, and she wants to be prepared for that. Besides, I think she missed her little girl.

It was sad to see her leave, knowing our brief moment of friendship in the span of our lives is over. She is a sensitive and intelligent woman, and I will cherish my time with her.

Tomorrow, we will all go our own separate ways, and I will miss every one of them.

Doors open. Doors close. The next door to open will be after I've spent three days again in Madrid before I go to the Basque area.

Saying good-bye

I'm back in Madrid after a long bus ride from Gredos. Ellen, a volunteer from Ireland, sat behind me on the bus, and neither one of us slept, as most everyone else did, so we kept each other company pointing out that the small villages we drove through looked desolate.

For over one hour, neither one of us saw a human being. Then I spotted a man in green overalls at a car repair shop. The next time was at the pit stop. The "sleepers" got off the bus looking tired from waking up, and I was wide-awake, as I usually am while traveling. The problem is that I'm afraid I might miss something, so I cannot sleep.

Program Manager Marisa handed out the diplomas to each of the Spaniards, with the help of master of ceremonies and actress Carlota. Nearly every Spaniard had something to say about what they got from the program. We Anglos also received certificates of appreciation for the time and effort we put into helping the Spaniards become more efficient in English.

Revolución!

I'm back in Madrid in the midst of a revolution.

"We are having a revolution because the government is increasing our taxes and we have no job opportunities, and there are cuts in education and our public services," said one of the men I stood next to during the beginning of a protest near the Parliament building in Madrid.

"We want the government and the King to rewrite the constitution because it isn't fair to the people," the man continued.

The protest took place this evening beginning around six p.m. when people began to fill up the streets. Madrid police were ready for action, and the national police wore their riot gear. A helicopter circled above.

As the protesters were getting their signs ready to hold up and TV cameras were being set up, journalists walked around with cameras slung over their shoulders, and there I was right in the moment, but without press credentials.

"When people start walking this way, you should get ready to run away fast," the man told me. On Tuesday, he saw police charge the crowd and fire rubber bullets at demonstrators, and he expected it to happen again tonight. News reports stated that 32 people were injured, and several people were arrested during Tuesday's rally.

I climbed up on the base of a statue so I could see a bit better, and I got some good photos of the action. However, I have promised not to put myself in harm's way throughout this one-year journey, so when thousands of people started walking toward the rally and then blew ear-splitting whistles, I decided it might be a good time to leave the immediate area. One man I spoke to told me the words the crowd shouted were, "Fire them, fire them."

"The government is bad," he added, just before I took leave and walked across the street.

One of the men I spoke to took off on his bicycle to buy himself a drink, and he came back with a Coke for me. Another friendly person here on my travels.

For further understanding of the unhappiness shared by many Spaniards, I learned that Prime Minister Mariano Rajoy's administration plans to cut spending by $51.7 billion. To do this, he'll freeze salaries of public workers and reduce unemployment benefits. The common man, however, isn't the only group to feel the cuts, as the royal family will lose their funding by four percent.

Earlier, before the distraction by angry Spaniards, I took a bus tour throughout the gorgeous city like a good tourist. There is so much to see in Madrid that I will need to return after spending some time in the Basque area. The architecture, art museums, and statues are stunning, and only one day just plainly and simply won't satisfy my appetite. I did spend time in the Museo Nacional del Prado and viewed Spanish, German, Flemish, British, Dutch, and Italian paintings.

I saw some Rubenses, Rembrandts, and Goyas, to name a few. There were so many rooms and departments that you cannot see them all in one afternoon or even in one day. The Prado will be on my list to return to later.

Peace with a whippersnapper

What a day! It started late because I slept until ten a.m. That's very unusual, but last night I was on the computer until two a.m., and I was shocked to see the time in mid-morning.

When I got out on the Gran Via, my main purpose would be to find a cafe. I walked past McDonald's. No, won't go there. Then there was Dunkin' Donuts. You gotta be kidding—that's also a no. Then what pops up? Kentucky Fried Chicken! Are these Spaniards crazy?

Across the street, I saw the Nebraska cafeteria. Huh? Nebraska? It looked nice, so that's where I settled for breakfast. I had two cups of *cafe con leche* and had to pay twice. As in other places in Europe, you don't get a free refill. Then I had some type of fried bread sitting on top of a puddle of vanilla pudding, and on top were strawberries and kiwi fruit slices. Hmm, not bad. Then back in the hotel, up on the old, tiny elevator that causes me to say a prayer, hoping it won't stall, I regrouped and planned the day.

The goal would be to find the apartment Torre de Madrid on the corner of the Gran Via and Paseo de España. Why would I want to find that apartment building? Because my friend Sumi Haru stayed in that building while she was involved in filming a movie in which she had a feature role. I wanted to take a photo of the building to refresh her memory. So I started on the adventure by first going the opposite way down the Gran Via from my hotel.

After many stops for coffee and to ask directions, I realized that something was not right.

Several people told me there was no such place as Paseo de España, and of course, I argued with them. Why would someone who lived in Spain all their life not know there was a Paseo de España that intersects with the Gran Via?

Finally, a waitress went inside, and I guess she had a genie in there to answer all questions. She told me to go back up the Gran Via and head to—now, where did she say? I forgot!

I went into a rather fancy hotel and waited my turn in line to ask the important question, "Where is the Paseo de España that intersects with the Gran Via and where the Torre de Madrid apartments are located? Please?"

She got a map out and convinced me that, indeed, there was no Paseo de España, but there is a Plaza de España, and if I continue up Gran Via, I'd come right to it.

She was right.

So far, the morning was a very long walk going both ways, but it was also lots of fun, as I took many photos and watched a lot of noisy city action. One time, an ambulance tried to continue down a street, but cars wouldn't move. A motorcycle cop got in front of them and made them move so the ambulance could get through. Priorities are not for the ambulance?

Something else is noisy, and those are the flashing green men or lights that tell you in bird-chirping sounds that you'd better hurry and walk across. About three-fourths of the way across, the sound changes, and I swear they chirp, "You're guilty, you're guilty, you're guilty."

I came upon the Torre de Madrid apartments, which are located across from a park of statues and fountains. I took a photo of the marque on front of the building and thought it might be nice to take a photo of the inside, as well. Sumi would like that, I was certain. I got inside and saw the lobby and the welcome desk. No one was there, so I just snapped a photo.

Out of nowhere, a large and very young security guard bounced out and shook his finger at me and said, "No photos, no photos, no photos."

"Oh, I'm sorry. I didn't know."

"Delete it."

I had already begun the process when I picked up the camera to delete the photo, but he groused, "If you don't delete the photo, I'll call the police."

"Listen, you. If you see what I'm doing, you'll notice that I'm deleting the photo. And by the way, you don't need to call the police, and further, you don't need to tell me you'll call the police. See? Look at this." I shoved the camera up to his face and deleted the photo in front of his eyes. Okay, it might have been a bit dramatic, but I didn't want to go to jail, and I can't stand to be intimidated by some "whippersnapper" a few decades younger than I.

He finally smiled and apologized. We both communicated our deep and abiding friendship, but we didn't hug or kiss. I left.

I saw a white pigeon in the park that appropriately symbolized peace.

Chapter Seven

October, 2012

Stinky bus ride

I think it is so boring for me to tell you how tired I am, but I'm going to bore you and tell you I'm tired.

After five hours on the "garlic" bus and other annoyances, I arrived at Vitoria in the Basque area of Spain. The man sitting next to me must have devoured an entire field of garlic bulbs, as he reeked. I offered him a mint and he said very politely, "*No, gracias.*"

Then there was the greasy-headed man who sat in front of me. He had little spiked hairs all over his head, which made me think of a hedgehog.

Stinky got off the bus after about two hours, and then a big bear sat next to me. He was fat and wore brown and had been drinking. He also reeked. In about two minutes, the big brown bear fell asleep and leaned on me.

When I pushed him away, he snorted, and that made the hedgehog in front of me laugh. The little spikes jumped up and down on his head.

We drove through different terrain, including an area of massive rocks and then fields of wheat. I saw a house on a hill of wheat that looked exactly how I had imagined Spain.

When I arrived at the Vitoria station, Jose was there to pick me up. He's an absolute delight and loves to show off his town. I have already seen much of the "old town" of Vitoria tonight and look forward to more of it tomorrow.

Vitoria in Spanish Basque

Jose picked me up from the bus station in Vitoria in the Spanish Basque country and gave me the traditional kiss on both cheeks. He is a dynamic fellow who has traveled in many parts of the world. He's informed about the world's politics and cultures and has proof of his varied interests from the photos and artwork on the walls in his home. And best of all, he's a great cook.

He is rushing around every day with many projects including traveling to Africa on Saturday. I leave on Friday. Through the Couchsurfing International program, Jose chose to be my host for four days.

I have learned much about the political and cultural history of the Basque Vitoria City. Vitoria was founded in 1181, by King Sancho VI of Navarre, and it was called the city of Gasteiz Nueva Vitoria. Then in the 19th century came that little guy named Napoleon who was defeated at the gates of Vitoria in 1813.

During the years of the Spanish Civil War in the 1930s, the Basque culture suffered. Francisco Franco and his Fascist party wanted to rid Spain of all heterogeneity, and because of that, the Basque people were harshly targeted. Franco went further in his quest by banning the Basque language. The Basques lost all political autonomy and economic rights. Many Basques were imprisoned or killed. Franco ordered a Basque town, Guernica, to be bombed by the Germans in 1937. Several hundred civilians died. Picasso painted his famous *Guernica* to demonstrate the horrors of war. When Franco died in 1975, the Basques received much of their autonomy again, but this did not satisfy all Basques. This information was gleaned from websites, brochures, and from Jose's studies and recollections.

Fast forward to present Vitoria. It is characterized by its green and sustainable nature and was named "European Green Capital 2012."

Today, the government has brought back the Basque language into the schools, and all children are required to learn it.

Jose has memories of growing up in the town, including the recollection of a street he pointed out as we took a late night walk. "When I was a kid, and before this became a closed street and a walking mall, the rich walked over on that side and the regular folks on this side."

We strolled all over the "old town," which is laid out in almond-shaped streets with medieval architecture of which I just cannot get enough.

We went to a coffee house and saw his mother and about six of her "cronies" who drank coffee, talked, and laughed up a storm. They were all around 80-years-old and were having their daily, very noisy social time. Jose said the ladies get together sometimes more than one time every day.

Three of the ladies came over to our table and hugged and kissed Jose, one of their favorite sons. He obviously enjoyed the attention the ladies paid him, and he seems to deserve it from what I have observed.

Today, I walked back from Jose's place to the center of the medieval old town and sat in a town square where Napoleon was noted to have fought. Amazing to me that I could be sitting at the same place so many years later.

By the way, if you remember, my desire to see Vitoria grew from listening to Sergio, who worked at the Royal Hotel in Blairgowrie, Scotland, and who talked about his hometown.

The cathedral restoration project

I had the good fortune of going inside the Santa Maria Cathedral with a group of Germans, other interested people, and a knowledgeable guide. At one point, we ducked down and almost crawled through a small space to see the opposite side of the cathedral and high above where we had been just minutes before.

We donned helmets to explore the medieval passages, the cathedral's parapets, and the suspended gangways that workers use for the current restoration project.

It's generous of the workers, the city, and the archeologists to share the working project with the public.

The Santa Maria Cathedral was first built in the 14th century and has gone through many changes during the subsequent centuries. The tower, for instance, was built in the 17th century. There are three doorways decorated with statues and reliefs. The interior chapels reflect the Gothic, Flemish, and Italian Renaissance images, which include paintings by Rubens and Van Dyck. Gothic architecture is prominent.

The cathedral is undergoing restoration and has been studied by experts from around the world for its architectural curiosities, including those deformations it has suffered due to previous restorations, our guide told us.

Inside, we saw the huge archways, statues, and filigree as we toured throughout. It always amazes me—the intelligence of the medieval people and how they managed to create such a beautiful monument with limited resources and tools. They were hardworking people with tenacity. I was in "filigree heaven," for I can never get enough filigree.

Speaking of working hard, the guide took us to see the ice storage pit. It was huge, and I'm the one calling it a pit because I haven't learned its name. However, the guide told me that workers gathered the ice from the mountains and carted it down and dumped it into the pit. It was kept cold with blankets during the transport. Wealthy people had the privilege of preserving their food with the chunks of ice.

Along with the visit inside the cathedral, a young woman, Gladis, whom I met the day before, met me at the cathedral. Her friend didn't speak English, so they waited for the Spanish tour. They didn't see all of it, as I did, because they wanted to meet up with me again.

I met Gladis yesterday when I was close to the pharmacy at the time I was supposed to pick up the medicine I had ordered earlier in the day. I stopped to ask her exactly where the pharmacy was, and it turned out it was two blocks away. She is from Maryland but originally from Colombia, and therefore her Spanish is perfect, as is her English. We found a lot in common between us, including both of us knowing Aspen, Colorado, where she lived for a bit over a year. Another angel was there for me. She worried that I didn't have a small purse to carry everything over my shoulder. Her new Vitoria husband had warned her that there are people who grab and run, and to always keep belongings nearby. I solved her worries by purchasing a small purse that holds my billfold and a bunch of other items, and I can sling it over my shoulders.

She showed lots of concern over my well-being, and I assured her that I am used to traveling alone and that everything is just dandy. "I could never do what you are doing," she said. I've heard that so many times on this journey, and I always feel like saying, "Why not?"

Later, I needed to purchase a pair of pants because all the walking I do has again changed my clothing size. I found a department store, and it was full of pants that are slim to the ankle. Not what I wanted, and I got so frustrated because I couldn't get anyone to help me. When someone did, they said there wasn't anything like what I wanted anywhere in the store. I walked out of the store and sat on a bench.

Then I made up my mind that I would go back into the store until I found a pair of pants that would fit me perfectly. I began to look again until another angel walked up to me, and I explained what I wanted in my poor Spanish. She looked around and handed me several pair to try on. I found them, and it restored my faith in customer service.

Speaking of customers, I am absolutely dumbfounded to go inside a drinking establishment/restaurant and see people throwing their paper napkins on the floor. All around the bar you find paper trash, and it doesn't go at all with the "Green Capital 2012" recognition of the city. The city enjoys over 42-square meters of green space per person, and there are parks and lanes for walking and cycling. It's a beautiful city, and except for the trash inside establishments, the city is clean. I can only hope that after all the customers leave, someone stays into the wee early hours cleaning up the floor and dumping the paper into the correct recycling can.

Enjoying Basque pintxos

Yesterday was a day I'll long remember. It first began with a haircut by Jose's friend, Elisa. She cut my hair and styled it as a favor to Jose. Her shop was upstairs and had orange- and green-painted walls with lots of mirrors. I liked what she did with my hair, but when Jose saw me, he said it looked better before. Later, it fell out a bit and looked more natural. It is a good haircut.

Then Jose took me on a drive up to the Basque Ullibarri-Gamboa Mountain area where we stopped near a dam that provides water to Vitoria. I remember a boy at Lake Junior High and West High School in Denver called Johnny Ullibarri, and now I realize his family must have originated from the Basque area of Spain.

Our next stop was at Salinas De Lentz, a small village with a restaurant called Arrate. It was there that I trusted Jose to pick out a typical Basque-type lunch, which, by the way, is usually late in the afternoon.

The tiny restaurant was full of men and only two women. I was the other one. We had a reservation, or there would not have been a seat for us.

Jose spoke to the waitress who was wearing a shiny silver and black dress with lots of bling on her wrist. Jose tends to make everyone laugh, and she was no exception. I didn't know what he was asking, but when she left, he informed me that the first course he ordered for me was a crab soup. The waitress brought a big bowl and a soup scooper and began pouring it into my bowl. Jose told me I needed to tell her when to stop. Well, after the bowl was full, it was almost too late to tell her.

I enjoyed the soup, and next was a dish of beef stomach in a tomato-type sauce, after which came the surprise of my life, a black dish with black sauce and some small, black, puffy things floating in the sauce. They were octopus-stuffed tentacles in their own ink. Well, hmm, isn't there a first time for everything? I erased the black ink off my lips and tongue when I had flan for dessert.

We walked around the tiny village of stone houses, narrow roads, a large church, and one hotel. From where we stood, we could see a church in the distance where Jose and his former wife were married. We drove there, and Jose found mushrooms on the grounds and picked a paper bag full of them.

When we arrived back to Vitoria, Jose had heard there would be a group of couch surfers meeting up at a popular outdoor and indoor bar. We ordered a glass of cider and watched people for a while, and standing nearby were two college-aged kids. Gonzalo turned to me and asked if we were part of the couch surfing folks. I said yes and asked them to sit down with us. We didn't find any others; however, his friend, Laura, found a group of theater people, and she spent a bit of time with them. Laura and Gonzalo are both exchange students in the local college and are from Mexico. Both speak English. Gonzalo has black, wavy hair and brown-black eyes—a handsome lad, indeed. Laura has a smooth, peaches-and-cream complexion and long brunette hair.

There was plenty of local character in the crowd. Jose spotted a well-known chess player. He was a large man with a bushy long beard, wearing a hat over long hair. You could almost see his face. Then there were younger people smoking pot, families with little kids, and people of all generations and walks of life. Jose agreed it was a very popular place for people of all kinds to meet up.

After a while, when Laura came back to us, Jose announced it was time to leave and go somewhere else. Somewhere else was a crowded bar with a crowd of people inside and just as many people standing outside in front. It was there where we met Elisa, who joined the four of us. Elisa doesn't speak English. After a glass of cider, we moved on to another place, full of people inside and outside, as well.

Ane, another one of Jose's friends (all day long and on into the night he ran into people he knew), joined us. She is from Granada and spoke English.

Ane explained that what we were experiencing was called *pintxo*—a Basque tradition where a snack is eaten in bars or taverns while hanging out with friends or relatives. For one euro, you could order a drink, and a *pintxo* would accompany it. They were small items served with a toothpick to hold them in place. The first one was a mushroom on a piece of toast. Jose wanted to find out how the mushrooms were prepared but couldn't get the answer from the cook.

Our group of six moved on to several other places for other tastes of *pintxos*. "This takes place every Thursday," Ane told me. "Not on Friday, but maybe again on Saturday," she said. It's a social event that happens every week. Ane said she doesn't go out every time because she works and goes to school, so she needs her sleep. However, she wasn't working on Friday, so she went out to the *Pintxos* and found Jose and the five of us.

Our spontaneous, friendly group was having a great time together. The two college kids hung out with us for a long time until they got phone calls about where some of their friends were, and they left to join them. Four of us went on to one more place, and then we parted.

"The party lasts until two or three in the morning," Ane told me. So I'm certain Gonzalo and Laura watched the sun come up.

Today, I'm moving on to a hotel in the center of the old town where I'll be for a few more days. There's more to discover with the Basque people.

By the way, Basque is spoken more in the mountains in more isolated places, but a few people speak it in the city. Signage everywhere is bilingual. The Basque language is totally different from Spanish, and for as long as 1,000 years, no one has found the origin of it.

I will miss the dynamic, funny, thoughtful man, Jose.

This 'n' that

It is noon here in Vitoria, Spain, and I am in the hotel room by the window listening to the church bells. Since yesterday, after leaving Jose near the doorstep of the Hotel Centro Vitoria, where I walked through a passageway to the door, I have been resting. I have found with the arthritis pain in my legs, one day of rest will almost make them new again.

After I checked into the hotel, I did venture over to the El Corte Ingles Department Store and purchased some food for a few days of stay here and a CD for my musician son, Ronnie. It's a large store where you can find nearly anything you need, and it's always fun to try out my poor Spanish and watch the people wondering what the heck I'm saying. It's really nice when someone actually responds back to me in Spanish, and we hold a "mini" conversation.

Some notes about Basque life.

Food. The Wi-Fi wasn't working well in the hotel room, so I moved to a restaurant where I ordered a big chunk of tuna with a slice of egg on top, and with onions and peppers. A long pepper, which I have never seen before, joins the snack, which has been generously splashed with olive oil. No one uses butter here, as far as I have seen. Olive reigns in this region.

Actually, it's only one p.m. and a little early for lunch, so what I am consuming is more of a *pintxo,* but it will suffice as my lunch.

Bread, not an everyday need, but when used, is crunchy on the outside and softer inside, the way bread should be. And, you can find small loaves. You don't have to purchase a long loaf. Butter is never used with bread. If you must have something on it, use olive oil the way the Basques do.

Breakfast around nine a.m. is usually tea (coffee for me), fruit, and perhaps bread with something on it generously splashed with olive oil. Lunch is around two or three p.m. and is usually a big meal with wine. Stores then close for a couple of hours, except for the cafes, restaurants, and bars. Some of the restaurants close, as well. Dinner is anywhere from 9:00 p.m. to 10:30 or 11:00 p.m. Then you go to sleep with a tummy full.

Restaurants. You can stay as long as you want, and it is not unusual to spend hours, but you must ask for the check. A small tip is appreciated but is optional. You are not expected to tip the 15-20 percent, as in North America.

The restaurants I have seen in the Basque area are old with wood, marble, wrought iron, and mirrors throughout, including the bar. Tile or wood floors are prominent. So far, I haven't seen a carpet in a restaurant. The floors are kept clean except for the patrons who leave their napkins on the floor next to the bar, which I spoke about earlier.

Transportation. There are buses, trains, and many automobiles. I have yet to see a taxi in Vitoria. I've been told you must call one to get picked up. I've tried to get a bus ticket several times now online, but the information comes back that my bank will not honor it. This is false, as I've called both my credit union and my credit card company, and they say everything is fine, so I don't understand the problem. So far, however, I've been able to get a bus at the station, just not the seat I may desire.

The people. My impressions of the Basque people are that they are easy-going but excited when they talk, with liberal use of hands and arms. "The Spanish people cry," said Jose about his own people. He laughed once when we saw a table full of animated, laughing, and crying people. They are very noisy when they gather together and seem not to notice it.

The dress. The ladies dress nicely at work, and the "ladies who do lunch" are dressed in nice skirts, blouses, and scarves. Men are in slacks and nice cotton shirts. Men at work are usually dressed in dark suits with ties and white or pastel-colored shirts. There is also a casual attire with the use of jeans, boots, and scarves. I've seen so many scarves, both on people and on rack after rack in the stores. I don't own one.

Music. When I walked to one restaurant, there was an older man playing a soulful electric cello in the street. It was so beautiful, it brought tears. American music is favored. I've heard country western, Frank Sinatra, Tony Bennett, Lady Gaga, and others. The old man was playing, "My Way." Hmmm, I wondered if he expected that in his old age, he'd take his cello to the streets?

Royalty. Juan Carlos is the King of Spain. Duchess of Alba makes the news often. She is 86-years-old and has a husband, a 61-year-old, handsome toy-boy, Alfonso Diez. She is beloved and respected by the citizens of Spain for her generosity, but she is also humored for the much plastic surgery that has left her with a pasty-fleshy face, not attractive. She has been seen frolicking in the sea with her lover while wearing a bikini. Well, good for her! She's doing her life "her way."

Tortilla de patatas or Spanish omelet

I have included a recipe at the back of the book for this versatile Spanish tortilla. I had this dish yesterday, today, and many days prior. *Tortilla de patatas* is the most common gastronomic specialty you can find all over Spain and is often served for a meal or a party snack (*pincho de tortilla*).

There are hundreds of variations, even in one specific region, but the most common one is made with eggs, potatoes, and onion. While it's called a tortilla, it has nothing to do with the standard flour or corn tortilla found in the U.S.

Fracking and jazz

A Florida Park visit was on the agenda, mainly for a photo opportunity of a bronze statue of American jazz trumpet player, the great Wynton Marsalis. His statue stands next to a bench that has well-known names of jazz musicians and singers inscribed on it. The names are those musicians known throughout the years who have played in the jazz concerts held in Vitoria Gasteiz.

After spending a bit of time in the park, drinking coffee in the outdoor venue near the gardens, I walked on to the old town, where, by then, people were strolling in large numbers. That area seems to be the popular place for protests to take place during the day.

There was a protest last night, as well. I could hear the magnified voices and then drum beat, and I was beckoned to see what was happening. I walked to where the sound came from and found it was nearby where an open market took place earlier in the day.

A stage was set up, and there were several people beating large drums and calling attention to their disapproval of fracking. That was a new word for me, so I asked around and got some bit of information about fracking and the protest.

Fracking is a process that injects large volumes of water, sand, and chemicals underground to break rock apart and free the gas. The U.S. Environmental Protection Agency and many state regulators say fracking can be done safely, and the American Lung Association says it can help reduce air pollution. But scientists disagree. Some claim the process can pollute water and sicken residents.

I'm not certain what the others who gathered around were protesting; however, I did see a long train that would give folks a ride around the city, and while on the train, a politician's face appeared plastered about, advertising his fine virtues and the reasons to vote for him.

While on my walk, I found the spot where the instantaneous group of six got its start a few nights ago. You may remember I mentioned a great chess player? He was there on the outside of the building sitting alone.

I also noticed the many Basque words on signs and one in particular on a restaurant. A gentleman assured me that it was Basque and he seemed proud to tell me that.

I cannot say that I fully understand the political history of Spanish and Basque people, but just note that during Francisco Franco's regime, he suppressed the Basque language. When you do that to a people, their culture stands to get lost.

About half of the residents of the three Basque provinces speak fluent Basque, or *Euskara*, which is the name of the language. *Euskara* is seen sometimes in bilingual signage, and sometimes alone. You can sense the turmoil that was brought about during Franco's regime when the Basque people's desire was to maintain their language and culture. It is for this reason that the name of the city is always written as Vitoria Gasteiz, using both the Spanish and Basque names.

A regular day before moving on

It was a regular day for a regular person in Vitoria Gasteiz, Spain. Tomorrow is a day on the road again, so there were things to do in order to be ready to check out by ten a.m. mañana.

After getting chores done and returning back to the hotel room, I found the bed made and the bathroom sparkling clean, and I'm thinking, who would want to leave this?

But it continues . . . .

One thing I really wanted to do in the Basque area was to find a rural hotel in a small village, a private home, a guesthouse, or a hostel, but that has been difficult. I'm sure someone familiar with the area could pinpoint the perfect setting. When I was with Jose, we found a hotel in the tiny town where we ate that lunch with the ink. But the hotel was way too expensive. We found another one, even a bit nicer, for less in price, but it was on the busy road and not near a town or rural setting.

A gentleman who works in the hotel where I am now discouraged me, as many others have, by telling me, "Sure, there are little villages in rural areas with hotels, but that's very isolated."

"That's just what I want," I say, and that falls on disbelieving ears. People just cannot imagine someone not always wanting to stay in a city. I feel that I missed out on the experience of seeing life in the sheep-grazing areas and learning about the lives of the sheepherders, but I just didn't get there. However, the time in Vitoria was wonderful.

"Maybe on your way to Bilbao, you'll see something in one of the towns you'll go past on the bus," the man in the hotel said. He's probably right, but then we'll be zooming by it with no opportunity to stop and inquire. Like everything I've done so far, I'm thinking, "It is what it is." The journey includes everyday occurrences with the good, the bad, and the ugly. So far, it's all good, thank goodness for that.

In Bilbao, where I'll be in a hostel for a week, I'll be near the Guggenheim Museum that is touted as one of the most impressive museums in the world.

From *Wikipedia*—"One of the most admired works of contemporary architecture, the building has been hailed as a 'signal moment in the architectural culture,' because it represents one of those rare moments when critics, academics, and the general public were all completely united about something. The museum was the building most frequently named as one of the most important works completed since 1980 in the 2010 World Architecture Survey among architecture experts."

The Guggenheim features permanent and visiting exhibits of works by Spanish and international artists, so it has been on my wish list to see it. That will be the next adventure.

I've enjoyed resting up in a hotel, and now I'm ready to save some money and go back to a hostel. They aren't bad, but not as cozy as a hotel, I admit.

Today in town, I sat down at one of many outdoor cafes and admired the clear sky and air that made the tall buildings and churches look like I could just touch them from where I sat. The bells rang one o'clock, and the pigeons ran circles catching the crumbs I dropped for them. From where I sat, a faucet with clean water supplied people with drinks, and even a dog got into the action. Several people washed their hands, and one man washed his face.

Back to differences I want to mention between our country and most of the European countries. First are the floor numbers. Our basement=Zero, or Basement. Their basement=First Floor, or -1. Our First Floor=their Second Floor. Our Second Floor=their Third Floor.

Another difference is the way we write the date. Our way is the month/day/year. Their way is the day/month/year." It can be confusing for the first few times you see it, and then mistakes can happen, especially with transportation schedules.

The younger generation is the best.

I arrived at Bilbao by bus from Vitoria this morning. We traveled through a freeway with pine trees and other types of trees on both sides of the road. We saw rock formations, mines and vineyards, old farmhouses and many new ones, as well. There were good views from my window showcasing churches and buildings and lots of green. As we got closer to the city, the buildings got taller and taller.

I opened my computer to check a few things and had to check an agreement with the bus's terms to use their Wi-Fi. When

I arrived at the hostel, I went out to get something to eat. It was a tortilla, the kind I have described earlier. There were all kinds of them sitting on the counter.

When I opened my computer to write this short piece on how I got here, the main page from the bus popped up, and I couldn't delete it. After trying to get help from the front desk, we decided it was a computer problem, so I went about trying to fix it. There was a nice young man sitting next to me in the community room, and I disturbed him to ask for help.

Well, folks, there was another angel, for in about three minutes, he had the problem fixed, the one I had been working on for one hour. Don't knock the younger generation, for they are the best!

Meanwhile, the lady at the front desk is from Cuba and full of energy, and she is willing to go out of her way for me. It is amazing how great most people are if you give them a chance, and she's a good example. We will travel by her car to her little village tomorrow so she can show me around. Angels?

You betcha!

A day of art, design, and subway

The day began with instructions for the second time about how to get to Casco Viejo, the old part of town, by the subway. Yanita Napoles, the lady at the front desk, the one from Cuba, explained it to me yesterday, but just in case, I got the directions one more time this morning.

It all went smoothly, with me buying a five-euro bus ticket, which Yanita said should last for the whole week I'm here.

When I got off at Casco Viejo, I really didn't know where to go or what to do, so I wandered around and got the flavor of the area as the city began to wake up. I found an old cathedral and went inside. People were sitting on the pews praying and meditating. I joined them for a few minutes, then walked out where I saw a woman sitting on the steps begging.

Later, I walked up toward the newest part of town and heard a young man playing an electric violin accompanied by an older man on an accordion. It was soulful music. I wished the lady beggar had a talent to share, with the ability to make a bit of money instead of sitting on cold steps. It's not a very creative way to live, and it's sad.

On this journey, there are many remembrances of one country that help me out in another. One of those today was the hop-on-hop-off bus that, so far, every large and medium-sized city I've been in has had—at least one or more. Luck was with me when I saw a big red bus that said *Turista* on the side, along with the friendly words, "hop on hop off." I signaled for the bus driver, and he stopped for me. It wasn't a designated stopping point, but he was a nice guy. I observed people in Madrid asking for the bus to stop, and the driver would just shake his head and drive on. In fact, I was one of those persons on another occasion.

The tourist bus was 11 euros for the one-hour ride, and the ticket could be used all day long if I wanted. I asked the driver if he had a rate for a *señora vieja,* and he said the price for a *señora vieja* was the same for a student. We headed around the town with a commentator that I couldn't hear very well, but I kept asking the driver where we were. Then it appeared! Right in front of us down the street stood the Guggenheim Museum.

"Oh, that's the Guggenheim, isn't it?"

"Yes."

"That's one place I must see. I'll get off here."

"No, don't get off here. I drive right up to it. Don't worry." He must have told me not to worry a dozen times before the day was over.

After I saw all I wanted to see in the Guggenheim, I walked over to an outdoor cafe to sit, rest my aching legs, and get something to drink and a *pintxo.* Those little snacks are just perfect. Today, it was tuna fish on a roll with a thin pepper.

You don't find huge servings of anything here; even the dinners do not overstuff you.

I saw the most beautiful white dog and asked the man who was sitting at the cafe if I could pet it, and he smiled and said, "Yes," and then, "I speak English." Turns out his son works in Silicon Valley in computers and has for 18 years.

The dog was a cross between a wolf and a husky.

"We never have to give the dog a bath. She is always clean."

While I sat down with the gentleman and the dog, several other people approached and asked to pet the beautiful animal.

The Guggenheim is a masterpiece in design, and to me, the building is the art, more so than the collection inside.

I found the architect's words about his process in design fascinating. Architect Frank Gehry, a graduate of the University of Southern California with a degree in architecture, demonstrates his philosophy in his work, with the belief that there should be no line between art and architecture. He says in the auto guide the museum provides that he first begins free-flow sketching. Without picking up the pencil, the design just comes to him without any preconceived ideas, and then he goes back to the sketch and begins a plan.

The building has a moving, flowing, smooth surface. It sits right near the river, giving the feeling that the water and the building are the same. Gehry said he had a love of fish and a personal history with fish. As a kid, his grandmother would take him fishing, and she would put the catch in the bathtub until time to cook it. Gehry would play with the fish first.

Evidence of the lightness of water and the skin of fish can be seen everywhere on the outside of the building, with liberal use of titanium and glass.

From a website: to "The titanium cladding used is half a millimeter thick. Each piece is unique and has been designed with the aid of a state-of-the-art 3D design computer program.

The columns are linked by glass curtain walls for light transparency. In some of the more curvaceous and irregular exhibition spaces within the museum, the floor is constructed of cement with curved and twisted walls."

After visiting the Guggenheim, I found the hop-on-hop-off bus and the same nice driver. We talked a bit about the Guggenheim before he started to move. He said the Fine Arts Museum, in his opinion, has the better artwork.

"It's down the street."

"Oh, I want to get off down there at the Fine Arts Museum."

"No, you shouldn't use the bus. Get out here and walk." He told me how to get there.

I then toured the art museum where the artist Fernando Botero was featured. Along with Botero's fantasy and humorous art, there were artists such as El Greco, Goya, Gauguin, Barceló, and more. I couldn't pinpoint a favorite. I liked all of it.

I found the bus stop, and the nice bus driver took me right to the Casco Viejo subway. There was also a nice gentleman who said, when I asked to make certain that it was the right stop, that it was correct and that he was going that way, as well. He got off at the same stop and bid me a good night. It was a great day, as always; people make it so.

A day in my life

This morning so far, I only ventured out to the grocery store, and that's it. My roommate from Madrid told me the grocery store was a five-minute walk, and Yanira Napoles from the hostel reception said ten minutes. I figured 15 would be about right for me.

Off I went down the street to the crosswalk, for certain. I wouldn't try it without the crosswalk, as the hostel is close to the train station, the subway, and the industrial area. Car traffic moves quickly along—like it does in any big city.

Then up a hill to another street, and there was the cafe I found on the first day. I stopped in there to get a real cup of coffee, as the hostel only serves instant, and that is NOT coffee.

The man, who either owns the place or is the manager, greeted me warmly. He's a tall, handsome guy wearing wrist jewelry and some bling around his neck. His sleeves are rolled up to his elbows—guess that's for the elbow grease needed to wipe the counters and clean the cups, saucers, and plates. He moves quickly, serving, taking money, washing the dishes, and joking with the customers.

An older, large man stood at the counter eating a croissant and dunking bits of it from his fork into his cup of coffee. That looked good, but I settled for the *cafe con leche* and took it outside. I really like the small cookies or chocolate that accompany the coffee in nearly all European coffee shops.

After indulging in the coffee, I headed up to the grocery store. There were no sidewalks to walk on, so I wove in and out of cars and trucks to the store. It isn't a welcoming front door, but no matter, it has groceries, and that's what I wanted.

The store offers large baskets that you have to pay a coin for, but you get your money back after you're through using the basket. There are other, smaller, plastic baskets with wheels for smaller purchases. I took one of those and vowed to purchase only what I needed for today, passing up lots of other items. That took discipline. After all, I would have to walk back with it, and besides, I don't want to waste food.

I purchased a tortilla, the kind I've mentioned before, a salad mix, a can of tonic water, and cream for my coffee. It's unusual to me to find milk in cartons not stored in the refrigerator but stored on shelves near the Clorox and soap boxes.

One of those milk cartons would only add to the weight of the grocery bag, so I purchased cream from the refrigerator.

At the checkout station, you must either have brought a bag with you, or you must purchase one. This keeps the plastic from flying around on the streets and in the trees.

Yanira gave me the itinerary for tomorrow. We will leave the hostel at two p.m. and go to her small town where I can see a small Basque village. Then we'll pick up her mother, and they will take me to a travel agent and then back to the hostel.

She wants her mother to meet me because "You are unusual," she said. When I left on this journey over six months ago, I wasn't giving my age a thought. The journey wasn't about that. But now, because I hear so often how unusual I am, I guess I'm beginning to believe it. It's amazing to think that people my age assume they cannot do the same thing I'm doing.

Okay. Now I must tell you the reason for the travel agent. I will be in Granada next week. A gentleman who was in the Vaughan program is from Granada, and he told me that as long as I'm in Spain, I should see his beautiful city, and many people have agreed. But here I am in nearly the opposite end of the country, and how will I get there from here?

Yanira has lots of friends, and one of them is a travel agent. When both she and I got frustrated with trying to get an answer, the travel agent had the answer for us. One, I could fly there for over $200, or I could take a bus for around $50. My option, of course, was a bus ride. On Tuesday morning, I'll begin the 12-hour bus ride.

There will be a change of buses in Madrid and several short stops along the way. Guess I need to buy a book to read. I'm working on another exotic place to go after I leave Granada, as long as I'm in the area.

Americans. Are we loud? Obnoxious? Rude?

Well, here goes some stereotyping. While on this journey, I have heard people's opinions of Americans and always without my asking. I've been told that Americans are stupid, they don't know anything about geography, and they don't study their own government. Also, among the slings and arrows, Americans are loud. Americans are obnoxious. Americans are superficial. Americans are demanding.

Isn't it a bit rude to blast a person's country when the person is a guest? I think so. However, no matter what people say, I aim to make a good representation of America by doing my best to be polite, to understand the culture I'm in, and to accept people as they are. There are times I read a bit of jealousy in the words against Americans because, at the same time, I see where the American culture is copied.

Here's why this issue is brought up here. Last night, a bit after ten p.m., I went to bed. My Italian roommate was getting ready for bed, as well. We turned the lights out.

About half an hour later, three people came into the room, banging the closet doors, trying to figure out how the security worked on the doors, moving their suitcases and bags around the room, walking back and forth, and turning the brightest lights on in the room. Their voices were low; however, their actions were noisy and went on for a long time.

This morning at breakfast, the room was full of people. I asked Yanira where everyone came from, and she told me there were groups from . . . , and she named many countries, including the U.S.A.

"What? I didn't hear any American English in the breakfast room," I said.

"Oh, well, there are three of them, and they are staying in your room."

"They were noisy last night!"

"Well then, I'll have to tell them to be more respectful."

"Oh no, then they'll take it out on me tonight."

"No, we're in a hostel, and people need to be considerate of others."

We'll see what happens tonight.

The village on the top of the hill

There are many people I've met on my journey who will remain in my memory forever. Yanira is one of those persons. She is refreshing to be around, upbeat, and positive. She took me under her wing almost from the beginning of my checking into the hostel, and she took a keen interest in what I want to accomplish this year.

Yesterday on the trip to the top of a mountain in a town called La Arboleda, part of the itinerary Yanira chose for me, she gave me a bit of her personal story. Here's a lovely and healthy-looking young lady with two children and a great job, and she's a one-year cancer survivor.

"The doctors call me a miracle." She smiled as she drove through the valley after leaving Bilbao. All along the way, we saw cities below as our journey took us farther away. At one point, she stopped, and we got out of the car so she could point out the ocean, the mountains, and the cities we passed that were now below us.

We drove through the city, Valle de Trápaga, where she lives with her mother and two children, and then up the hill, winding around and around until we got to the top and a quaint little village. She confessed that there is a better road than the old one we were on, but she prefers the old one. Here's a woman who thinks like me, for sure.

The village is not on the regular tourist map, so I felt privileged to be there. Since yesterday was a national holiday, when we arrived, we saw men playing cards at a table near a bar. Later, another table of men played inside the bar.

She pointed out the restaurant, Zuhastieta, that specializes in serving beans. Beans were a staple for the men who mined on the hill, and when food was scarce, they ate beans.

Yanira was a manager of a fish market in the small town for eight years, so everywhere we walked, people gave her a hug and a kiss on each cheek. When I was introduced, I also got kissed on both cheeks. Yanira, while managing the fish market, was also working toward her master's degree. Her project was to produce a hotel in the town. We walked near the hotel.

Yanira and I met up with two of her friends, and we walked around the little village and saw a golf course that had horses grazing on it. It seems there's a rift between the farmers and the golf course. Farmers say the property belongs to them, and the golf course folks say it's theirs and horses have no rights to it. It looked to me like the horses were getting the best feed money could buy, but for how long, no one knows.

I wasn't clear who used the golf course because, as I said, it's not a touristy town, but golfers seem to be able to find a small course, one way or another. That old adage, "If you build it, they will come" appears to be true.

The village was built long ago during the early mining days when men lived on the mountain to mine for iron. There are still barracks that are now used for housing families, barracks the miners stayed in during the week. But on the weekends, and for those fellows who didn't live on the mountain, they got a train ride down a steep incline to the bottom of the hill.

And that is what Yanira had in mind for me. After spending a bit of time with her friends, drinking a cup of coffee in the bar, and walking and talking a bit, it was time for her to take me to the train.

It's a working train now, even though miners are no longer mining in the town. The townsfolk take the train for business that requires a bigger town or for numerous reasons, I suppose.

The track is steep, straight down, going through a corridor of walls of rock formations, flora, fauna, houses, gardens, and even a cow was spotted. I saw Yanira wave at me outside of her car. She hopped back in the car and met me down below at the bottom where the train stops and picks up passengers for the steep ride up the hill.

After the train ride and visit to the small village, we stopped at the town where she lives with her mother.

"I told my mother about you, and I want her to meet you," Yanira said. However, when we got to the apartment, her mother, while friendly, was sick with the flu, so we stayed long enough for a glass of wine, and they generously gave me use of the Internet telephone where I could call my friends in Soledad and my aunt in Sacramento. It was about the same time my sons would be at work, so I didn't call them, although I could have. Yanira is a generous, giving, loving, upbeat person whom I'm proud to call a friend.

Oh, and the noisy Americans must have received the message. They were quiet tonight.

San Sebastian, here I come.

Jose, who hosted me in the lovely city of Vitoria Gasteiz, told me I should not miss the city of San Sebastian, and just recently, I received an email from him.

"It's a pity if you missed the visit to San Sebastian." He also wrote about his bad start on his trip to Africa.

He was in the Heathrow Airport and said, "Heathrow is always problematic." Doesn't matter what airport in London, both are to be avoided, if possible, in my opinion. Seems there was a "stupid woman in security" who thought he had nitroglycerin in his bag, and she called the police, which sent him to jail for five hours. When he was found without nitroglycerin or any liquid for that matter, he had missed his flight and had to stay in London and leave the next day. He told me he arrived in Lusaka after a three-day delay. This shouldn't have happened to him, one of the nicest persons I have met on my journey.

Meanwhile, my new friend, Yanira, also told me I must go to San Sebastian, and she went further and told me exactly how to get there. I took the short journey and spent part of a day there. But my trip also was problematic, for when I got to the subway, the ticket I had purchased just to use in the subway wouldn't go through the system. I realized it must have run out of credit, so I went to the information booth to ask how to get more money on the card. A woman sat inside a closed-up booth with a thick window encasing her inside a bubble.

I have asked questions before to the people inside the bubble, and some of them have even come out of their bubble to assist me. Not this time. She kept telling me something, and first of all, I couldn't hear her well, and then, of course, I wasn't keeping up with her *español rápido*. I tried to get her to help me. She shook her head—the meanie.

So I went over to another booth, to the man inside the bubble. And before I got the words out of my mouth, he kept telling me to go to the other booth, for that was the subway I wanted.

"I just want to ask a question."

"Go over there."

"Please, can't you just let me ask a question?"

"Go over there," he pointed.

I turned and angrily walked back over to the first bubble, and that woman blew me off. She left the booth but did not leave before the second bubble man told her off. She went inside a building, turned and looked at me, and shut the door.

Now what? I'm never shy about asking questions from anyone at any time, and I saw a woman heading for the subway, so I asked her. Unfortunately, she couldn't figure out what I wanted. She smiled and also blew me off, like a bubble caught in a breeze.

Then I saw a young man who knew exactly what I needed to know. He took my ticket, put it into the machine, punched some numbers, and told me to put five euros into the machine. I did as he said to do, and out came a fresh card and the old one, to boot.

"*Gracias*," I said over and over. He smiled and said in English, "I'm glad I could help you. Have a safe journey."

I gave a dirty look to the man in the second bubble, and if that old hag had been back from hiding from me, she would have received one of my dirty looks, as well. I would have waved the ticket toward her bubble-face.

No, I wouldn't have, but it doesn't hurt to think it. Or maybe it does. Who knows?

I headed toward the stop where I'd get on the bus to San Sebastian, and I arrived at everyone's dream place about an hour and a half later.

The terrain on the way was green, almost as green as Ireland, and I saw sheep for the first time since being in the Basque area, and some cows, too. I got off the bus, and then I thought, "Okay, here I am. Now what?"

I saw a huge fountain and walked across the street over to where some protestors were standing and got a great shot of the fountain. All fountains in Spain work.

I stopped and asked a Black man if he knew where the main part of town was located and the beach, as well. He was friendly and pointed to the direction that was simply straight ahead. Traveling makes for quick departures, so I didn't get to speak with him long enough to determine his country of origin, but I was grateful for his help. On the way toward town, I came to the bus ticket building and got the schedule to return.

All problems solved, and now it was time to enjoy the city that is populated by 183,000 people.

According to everyone I spoke to before going to San Sebastian, I was told it had the best Basque food and was famous for it. Also, I was informed that the city had wealthy people living there and that the bay was known as the Pearl of the Cantabrian Sea.

San Sebastian's history began as a fishing village and a place that housed Napoleon's troops, troops that nearly destroyed the city. Queen Isabel II chose the city as the Royal Family's summer residence, and then it flourished.

The braggadocio was all lived up to, for I found the city full of wrought iron beauty, stone curbs, marble entrances, and a long, tree-lined pathway next to a river. And I noticed the fashionably dressed people.

"The city is in the north of the Basque Country, on the southern coast of the Bay of Biscay. San Sebastián's picturesque coastline makes it a popular beach resort. Adding to the seaside environment, it benefits from hilly surroundings easily available, i.e., Urgull (at the heart of the city by the seashore), romantic Mount Ulia extending east to Pasaia, Mount Adarra, rising proud far on the south, and Igeldo, overlooking the bay from the west." From *Wikipedia.*

I had to catch my breath a few times when walking quickly on the boardwalk near the beach where surfers were catching waves. People sunned themselves while lying on the sandy beach, and the air was fresh and cool.

It was a long walk and a long time since eating breakfast, so Basque food was the next search. That was easy. There were restaurants everywhere, and since it was nearly three o'clock and the heart of the lunchtime hour, I wandered into an outdoor restaurant where the waiter handed me an English menu without my even asking.

I had for the first course, shrimp and something else stuffed inside a pastry that was covered with sesame seeds, all sitting on top of a sauce. The second course was fish, also sitting on top of two types of sauces, and one of those was pumpkin. I also had bread and red wine that was included in the package.

Dessert? Well, get this. It was called fried milk. There were other options available, but why not fried milk, huh? Why not? It came in a dish on top of a creamy sauce. It was like a pudding with a fried top and bottom. It didn't disappoint. But please, do not ask for the recipe or how to prepare it. I have no idea.

I returned to Bilbao with good thoughts of San Sebastian.

Town tree

Ever hear of a town to honor a tree?

The Basque town of Gernika (Guernica) certainly does. The town honored an oak tree trunk by keeping it in a pillared memorial on the grounds of the Assembly House.

And why is this tree so important? The story began centuries ago. It is reported that from the 14th century, Gernika was the meeting place for the people of Biscay. Each parish sent its representative to discuss common problems that arose within the territory. The meetings were held under the "Tree of Gernika" and were called the General Assemblies of Biscay.

But in 1876, the old laws that governed Biscay were abolished, and not until 1979, was the General Assembly recovered. The tree, therefore, represents the living symbol of the history of the people living in the Basque Country and of its unification.

I saw the oak tree and then went inside of the Assembly Chamber where the meetings of the General Assemblies of Biscay are held. The building represents the tradition of a relationship between public life and religion, and the space was designated to combine both functions. "We are, therefore, before a Church-Parliament, although the ecclesiastic aspect has currently been relegated by politics. Both the altar and the holy water fonts are still maintained as witnesses of bygone days." So states the information available to the public.

The walls are covered with paintings of the Lords of Biscay, and the interior seating is formal and covered in red. A chandelier hangs from the ceiling.

Another larger room houses the history museum of Biscay. A stained-glass window serves as a ceiling. It was the 1985 work of the craftsmen from the Vidrieras de Arte and represents the symbolism of the tree as a meeting point.

While I took a few hours to get a feel for the town and its people, I asked a woman if she could recommend a restaurant, as up to that time, only taverns were alive with people, and I wanted food.

She pointed to where I should walk and said I'd find a restaurant, so that's what I did. The restaurant she pointed out was full of laughing, mostly men, taking a break and having a bite to drink. So I walked on and saw other establishments doing the same. One man told me I could find a restaurant at the end of the block, so that's where I headed until the woman who gave me directions grabbed me by the arm.

"No, not there. That place is for bikers. Come to this place." She took me inside where I thought the merriment was about drinking, but I noticed there were tables of diners, so I guess I misunderstood the atmosphere. She told the woman in the kitchen to take care of me, and that woman told her waitress something that I couldn't hear.

The lunch at three p.m. was the last supper for me here in the Basque country, and it couldn't have been tastier. The way it works is there are several choices from a menu that isn't written down. You choose a first and second course, a drink, and then dessert. The busy waitress brought me fish soup, delicious, and then another fish dish. It was perfectly cooked and reminded me a bit of trout almondine.

Dessert was a bowl of fresh fruit. The merriment continued inside the establishment while I sat on their outdoor court. The Spanish people take their two-to-three hours off from work very seriously.

The typical merriment of the Basque people has some sad history that must have created a vast change in their lives, beginning with the Civil War that lasted from 1936 to 1939. The war was created out of the left- and right-wing factions since the Second Spanish Republic was formed in 1931. There were four periods of the Second Republic—provisional government, left-wing government of Azaña, and the two-year period of conservative governments. The elections of 1936 led to the Popular Front winning and becoming powerful, with difficult relations between left and right wings. Sound familiar, Americans?

Sides were chosen, and the *coup d'état* took place against the government of the Popular Front headed up by General Franco.

The National Front had the support of the German Air Force, which was organized by Major General Goering. Goering needed a testing field.

Now fast forward to the air raids that were conducted on civilian targets. Between the Italian and the German air forces, the town of Gernika was destroyed. It is believed that over 200 people were killed (some historians claim the number is much higher), and many of the buildings were leveled. That's enough of the sad history.

When I arrived into the town, the usual Monday market was in full bloom with stalls of fresh fruits, vegetables, flowers, honey, canned produce, nuts, and more, and a flea market with the usual items on display. The colors of the produce matched the vibrations of the people and the loud music. This market has been bringing people together in this venue for centuries and is of great social importance.

The market and other fiestas and town events caused me to wish for more time there in Gernika, but tomorrow, I move on, taking what I have learned about the heart of the Basque people with me in fond memories.

I want to thank the women in the hostel for making my stay in Bolueta successful and for their help with directions and activity ideas. Joana Revilla, the hostel manager, spent some time in Chicago. Maiteder Estevez is Basque, and that is where she got her first name. And of course, thanks to Yanira. They are hard-working young women who seem to take pleasure in making a nice atmosphere for travelers.

Granada

Granada, October 16.

I left the hostel at 8:30 a.m. by taxi. A hostel worker called it for me a bit earlier than my original intentions, but I was up and ready, so why not leave?

At the bus stop, a gentleman saw me walking with my two bags and the computer bag, with a camera and purse slung over my shoulder. He followed me to where I thought the bus would stop. He motioned for me to watch my bags. I sat down and put everything near me, and when two Middle Eastern men walked up, he looked over at me and winked. I took that to mean he thought that extra caution was necessary.

Then he began to talk to them, and I could tell by the body language and facial expressions, the men were being asked surprising questions, and they were doing their best to answer. A woman dressed in a red shawl and head covering joined them, and she began to argue with the man who thought I needed protection.

It all blew over when the protector lost his confrontational stance. The Middle Eastern men must have disarmed him, and whatever that was about came to an end.

The bus took me to Madrid (the protector sat in front of me) with one break along the way, through greenery, pine trees, rolling hills, sheep, gardens, crops, and cattle. I actually saw a sheepherder moving his sheep down a road. That put me back to Vallecito, Colorado, where we would have to move our car carefully through the herd of sheep while on the road to Durango.

In Madrid, I had a two-hour wait in the terminal and needed a restroom. I couldn't leave my luggage, but the restrooms were upstairs. I could see that the escalator wasn't working, and I couldn't see dragging my luggage up there or finding an elevator, so I sat and opened up the computer to use the Wi-Fi.

A gentleman in back of me tapped me on the shoulder and asked if I knew the password, and I did, from asking a bus driver a bit earlier.

He appeared to be a professional person in a three-piece, pin-striped suit—like what my dad wore for about 15 years—and he carried a briefcase. I asked him if he planned on staying there for a few more minutes, and he said, yes, that he would leave in half an hour for Barcelona.

"Would you mind watching my bags for a minute? I need to go upstairs."

"Of course," he said and moved to my side of the bench, while he kept working on his computer.

It took me about ten minutes, and I was back. I thanked him. Later, he got up and moved to the bus heading for Barcelona, turned, and waved a good-bye to me.

Then it was time to board the bus to Granada. A bus sat in front of me with the ultimate destination and the name Granada on it, but so far, a driver didn't appear. I saw a Black man standing near the bus, and I asked him if he was also waiting for the Granada bus. He said yes, and then, "We should just sit here and wait." I couldn't tell where the man was from based on his accent, but he seemed to know what he was doing, and we moved over to the benches.

"Yes, good idea. I wonder where the driver is?"

Other people who looked at the bus sat down, as well. But time went on, and it was a few minutes past the time to leave. With a question on my face, I looked at the man who had directed me to the bench. He looked at his ticket, leaned over, and showed it to me.

"We're going to the same place. See? My ticket is just like yours. So you might just as well sit and wait." He looked at me as if I were a "nervous Nellie." I tried to explain to him that I had missed a bus before when I thought I was waiting for the right one, and it turned out to be another one.

"Look," he said, and pointed again at his ticket, as if to say, "Dummy, stop worrying."

Well, the people I saw who were looking at the first bus began to move to a bus parked in back of us, and I decided to go look at it.

"I'm going to look at the bus over there." The man laughed at my silliness.

"Is this the bus to Granada?" I asked the driver.

"Yes, Granada."

I had taken all of my luggage with me, and I didn't look back. Instead, I just put the bags in the luggage hold, as did everyone else. Soon, the man came along, looking a bit sheepish. I just smiled at him and shrugged my shoulders.

On the way to Granada, I was reminded of Southern Colorado and Northern New Mexico. Miles and miles of ranches, wide open spaces, an occasional windmill as described in Cervantes' *Don Quixote*, a rest stop here and there, and then huge rock formations.

I spotted greenery of trees and bushes on rolling hills before the sunset when the sky turned fuchsia, orange, purple, and flashes of gold. Soon trees were silhouetted on distant hills. After a break, we got into Granada, and a taxi took me to the hostel where I found my room would be up four flights of stairs, with the last two twisting as if it were a castle. I asked for a different room and was told I could get one the next day.

This is the next day, and for eighty dollars more, I'm on the first floor, which is the second floor according to Americans' way of counting floors of buildings, and there are still stairs, but fewer.

Breakfast was a bowl of pureed tomatoes, bread for toast, olive oil, jam, and small cupcakes. Coffee tasted like it was made inside a dirty pot. The building is very old but of pleasing architecture with windows and shutters, old door fixtures, and lots of wood, marble, and tile. The hostel is on a tiny street near the center of town. I cannot wait to begin the exploration of the city so many people have told me about.

A night to remember

I headed out at a little after eight for a nine p.m. flamenco concert, and as I got closer to one of the city squares, very near where I'm staying, screeching noises got louder and louder. It sounded like a thousand carts of some kind in need of oil on the wheels. It got louder and louder, and I could no longer hear the crowd of people that by then was headed into stores for shopping. The noise was hard on the ears; it was that loud. Then I was right under the noise, for it was in the trees near the square and fountain. What was that noise? People seemed to be going right on with their business, ignoring the deafening sound.

"Are those birds I hear?" I shouted in English to a young guy standing near the square, and he replied back in English, which surprised me as much as what he said.

"Yes, they come here every night. They nest in the trees."

"How long has this been going on?" I shouted.

"All the time," he shouted back and laughed.

"I mean, for years? Or months?"

The man, who looked to be around 30-years-old, responded, "As long as I can remember, and I was raised in this town, the birds have been here at night."

The sound and the idea that so many birds would congregate on one central place and make so much noise, and always at night, just amazed me. Everyone else seemed not to notice—for there were stores open and things to buy.

That wasn't the end of the amazing night, however, for I continued on down the walkway to another, bigger square. I've been on this one several times today. It is very wide and covered with limestone rock tiles. It is decorated in-between with a red rock of some sort and also marble and another black stone. The whole square and very long walkway are shiny, and while the walkway is beautiful and unusual, it is somewhat slippery if you're not careful.

Now, after hearing birds and walking to the building for the concert, it was time to go in and find my reserved seat for the flamenco entertainment.

Someone helped me find the correct seat, and around 9:15, the concert began with two chairs sitting in the middle of the stage with microphones set before each chair.

Two men were introduced. Flamenco guitar music began, and, as it did for two-and-one-half hours, the guitar set the scene of the story with an introduction/solo, and then the singer began the story in passionate and energetic singing. There were many singers and various styles of presentations, but most began by sitting, until the passion in telling the story became so animated that most singers ended up standing. Some couldn't help but stomp their feet to the beat.

The music slides around the scales, not in a typical eight-note octave, but somewhat like opera. In flamenco, the singer passionately expresses himself until he reaches the peak of the story, and that is when the clapping begins. Toward the last part of the concert, as the music became even more passionate, people began yelling, "*Olé, olé.*"

I remembered that Jose in Vitoria told me once that Spanish people cry when they talk. They move their arms, and they are so emotional. I saw what Jose meant, for the men who sang nearly cried over the stories they told in song. The final singer held a note so long, I thought he might faint. That brought the crowd to their feet in a standing ovation.

There were many acts with singer and guitar, and then a dancer came on the stage. Her feet moved faster than a train on a track. She picked up her black skirt and lace ruffle, and then she moved her hands up in the air with fingers that had a life of their own, and she held a serious look on her face.

As I mentioned, the concert went on for two-and-one-half hours. The packed house enjoyed this fundraiser for a group that serves a mentally disabled population. There were several clients enjoying themselves in the audience toward the front of the stage.

After the concert, I walked back to the hostel, passing a few people, and a few passed me. I came upon four drunk Brits heading somewhere after lifting a pint or two or more.

It is safe here late at night, and even some restaurants were open to serve dinner.

When I sat inside the theater and saw the painted ceilings and decorated walls, and as I enjoyed the plush, comfortable chairs and the music began, I remembered how blessed I am to be on this journey.

Fleeting moments of friendships

The people I meet on this journey come into my life in fleeting moments and become lasting memories. There were two people like that today, not counting the street dancer.

I wanted to check out the cathedral to see the beauty that has been promised by several people, but also to find the place where I would catch a bus to Alhambra on Saturday morning.

On the way there, I passed several vendors of interest. First, the darling little elderly lady wearing a cotton dress and an apron, selling flowers on the corner. It is my bet that she's been successful at that corner business for years. She caught me taking her photo a couple of times and even mugged a bit for a shot.

There were several stalls, each with 50 or more baskets of teas, herbs, and spices. One basket had cannabis root. I asked the vendor about that, and he said it's not to smoke; it's to drink, and it would help you sleep.

Further on, an accordionist played, and another man sat next to him moving his arms around and jiving as best he could while seated on the stone walkway. A fellow with an impressive movie camera was recording the music. It was too good of an opportunity to miss, so I got my recording working, as well.

When the bearded guy on the ground saw me filming, his arms moved faster, then he jumped up, pushed his cane away, and began flailing his arms around, slapping his leg and his shoe, snapping his fingers, clapping his hands. His long, white beard went one way, and his head went the other. He performed for the camera and even did a bit of "dirty dancing" for my benefit. Then the poor old guy got tired and sat down. It wasn't a cold day, but it looked as though he had on several layers of sweaters and jackets. He must have turned up the heat inside of all that clothing.

The accordionist didn't stop; he continued to smile, enjoying the moment. I put some coins—probably about two dollars—into the hat and walked on.

The cathedral was closed until four p.m., just like nearly everything in Spain is closed until the magic hour of four or five p.m. when stores open again and people move about on the street until late at night.

I saw the hop-on-hop-off bus and went up to talk with the woman who seemed to be in charge. She told me how much it cost and that the ticket would be good for two days. I said thanks but no thanks, but then I turned around and said, "Okay, why not?" There is nothing but time in my day, and those buses take you all over town, so it was the thing to do at that time.

The lady and I got into a conversation about traveling, jobs, and going after what you want in life. Dolores Perales is a teacher on leave from teaching due to economics in Spain, and she is happy with the job working for the bus company, selling tickets and answering questions all day from people like me. She is fluent in English. "I want to do something different. I wish I could get a job teaching in California, either English or Spanish, for a school year," she told me. We talked for quite a while until the bus came and more people lined up behind me with questions.

She told the bus driver to take good care of me, and she handed me a map of Granada. I can't help it. I looked at it and announced, "Oh, I'm in Spain?" Talk about breaking the ice with people; that did it.

I got my seat, plugged in the earphones, and followed the automatic guide and the map. There was a young woman from China sitting close to me, while others were up above on the seats upstairs. She moved to another seat where she could see better and smiled at me. I did the same. We began to talk, and when we got to Alhambra, she walked there with me. We couldn't get in without a ticket, and the only way to get one is to be there at seven a.m. We stuck together the rest of the trip and laughed a lot.

"You are like a naughty little girl," she told me when I snapped a photo of a lady whose hairdo reminded me of a rooster. It was maroon-orange and stuck out all over her head. Encouragement like that just turns me loose. Isn't it fun to meet someone and immediately start laughing? We were two little girls in grade school. She is from China attending college but doesn't like it. She told me the professor she has for English is boring. Her English is very good, and her Spanish is even better.

"Why aren't you in school today?"

"I don't want to go."

"Why?"

"It's too boring. I want to change schools."

"Oh, so you're taking a day off, then?"

"Yes, something like that."

The bus arrived again from where we had stopped and continued until we reached the Carthusian, a former community of monks. The bus driver told us the last bus would arrive at 5:10 p.m., and it was 4:50 p.m. then. We walked up the steps to get inside but were informed there would be a fee to pay, and since we didn't have enough time, we decided to just go back and wait for the bus.

"Oh, no, the bus is here already."

"Can you get down there and tell him to wait for me?"

She took off down the steps and over the rough stone walkway, got on the bus, and waited for me. The bus was ten minutes early and was ready to leave when she got there. I told her it was important to trust yourself and not rely on what anyone says, that I had missed a bus one time because of wrong information.

"Do you know about the local buses? Can you get one and take it around the city, as well?" I asked.

"Yes, I've been on all of the city buses."

On the way back to where our trip originated, she admitted to having been on the round trip that day three times and had even slept on the bus. Not only that, it was the third day she made the same trip.

When we parted, she gave me a hug. "That was fun. I hope to see you again sometime."

I sensed a lonely young lady.

I almost missed seeing the Alhambra.

I looked forward to the trip to the Alhambra (which means "red castle" in Arabic), and, as many people had told me, the tickets are hard to get; some have been reserved months in advance. There was one opportunity left for me to get a ticket, however, and that meant I had to be at the main Alhambra gate long before it opened at 8:00 a.m.

The ticket manager told me to catch the first Alhambra bus at 7:00 a.m. in order to get into the front of the line. In only this way, a few people without advanced tickets might be able to get in.

Getting up early meant I woke up nearly every hour on the hour until it was time to get up and get dressed. By 6:00 a.m., I was on the way to the bus that would be in front of the large cathedral.

It was dark when I left, and it remained dark for the next two hours. In the dark, from about 6:10 a.m. until 7:45 a.m., I roamed the street up and down. There were no open coffee shops, but there were many young people who I assumed were walking to college classes. A couple walked up, and we discussed as much as possible in Spanish, and then she switched to English, for the woman had lived for five years in New York City, as had her husband for eight years.

Then another lady joined us. She was Ana, who is from Argentina and is fluent in English since she is an English professor in her country.

The couple, Ana, and I finally boarded the bus and then kept each other company. All four of us huddled under the couple's umbrella as we waited under the hard rain in front of the gate that would open at the magic 8:00 a.m. hour.

Once we got into the gate with our tickets, Ana and I went one way together, while the couple went another way. Ana and I found a hotel on the way to the site, went in and sat down in the lobby. Old photos and mirrors and pottery and statues sat on shelves before us as we sipped our coffee from porcelain cups and saucers. After having stood in the rain for nearly an hour, my legs needed the rest.

Then Ana and I began our tour in the rain, first in the watchtower, then other buildings, and then in a museum. After about two hours of climbing up and down steps, I avoided the very last steep corridor up to the top of the tower and sat down, instead. Ana waved to me from above.

We saw gardens of raindrop-covered flowers in bloom on the grounds, which are near the cathedral that is located in the center of the city's Muslim area and dates back to 1523.

"I've seen enough. If you have, also, then I think it would be fine to leave," I suggested to Ana.

"Wait, I think we've missed something."

"How can you say that? We've been walking and climbing for two hours."

Ana asked a man standing inside the cathedral, and I observed him discussing something with her and describing a direction. She came back to me and announced that we had missed the most important site, the Alhambra Castle itself.

"What?" I asked. "Wasn't that what we just saw?"

"No, it's over there."

We walked over to a spot that I had seen earlier that was cordoned off to the public, and Ana pointed out several people with umbrellas waiting in line.

"That's where we want to go," she instructed me.

We went right up to the front of the line to show our tickets, and the ticket taker told us our tickets had run out of time. That was a surprise to Ana and to me, as well. Then she remembered that the couple we had been with had mentioned something about paying close attention to the time on the ticket or we'd miss out on seeing the castle.

The ticket man told us we could go to an office and get the time extended. To make this task shorter, we walk-ran up some walks, down and up some steps, in and out of buildings, asking questions and getting lost until we found the tiny office.

The lady in the office asked Ana why we were late getting to the castle, and Ana later told me she answered by saying we had been so enamored with what we saw that we had lost track of time. She's good!

We got ourselves back up to the front of the line, and to the dismay of everyone in the long line, we were told to go ahead and go into the castle. I had thought for sure we would be punished and told to get in the back of the line again. And if I had missed the Alhambra Castle, I would have kicked myself all the way back to America. How stupid would that have been?

The Alhambra was a fortress, a palace, and a small city, and it features elaborate Moroccan interior with tile work on walls, filigree on the ceilings and arches, pillars, and baths in a series of courts. There are pools, and there is a lion room where water squirts out from the lions. The Alhambra dates back to the 14th century and is the work of the two kings, Yusuf I and Mohammed V. Since the 16th century, the palace has been designated as the *Casa Real Viejo*, the Old Royal House, to distinguish it from the Christian buildings.

The Alhambra has three areas that are often found in Moslem palaces. There is a reception salon, as well as the royal apartments called the Chamber of the Lions, previously mentioned. These are the work of Mohammed V. The third area, the Arab Baths, is symbolic of the city's religious turmoil centuries ago. Muslims built the baths for their belief that water is a symbol of purity. Christians believed the baths to be decadent and heathen-like, so most of them were destroyed. The Moorish life in Granada gave social importance to the day-to-day life in Arab-era Granada. This is evident in the architecture, music, food, and culture in general.

After we had, indeed, seen all there was to be seen, Ana and I went to a restaurant near the grounds and had chicken, gazpacho, and wine. After that, we got on the bus that dropped us off where it had picked us up bright and early that morning. We said good-bye, and that was the end of another great but fleeting friendship.

Just missed a jazz night

Walking a different way today on side streets, I saw the most interesting—and a bit hidden— shops, restaurants, and a little specialty school such as for music and dance, and also a little theater.

It was a restaurant across from a park that piqued my interest. It was called The Bohemian Jazz Club. The name alone called to me.

As I approached the front door, a young man walked out, and I said, "I didn't know about this place. No one told me," as if he were guilty.

He laughed and said, "Well, go on in."

"Will there be music tonight?" I wanted to plan my night in that place.

He asked someone, and they said no. That's too bad because this is my last night here, and jazz music would be a perfect send-off.

Inside, my disappointment waned, as the reception room was full of shelves with thousands of old books, including some classics, and it was fun to stroll among the shelves.

Room by room, I saw that the place was filled with antiques—typewriters, old radios, juke boxes, hats, and even a grand piano where two women were sitting, using it as a bar. There were two other pianos in use holding other antiques.

The walls were papered with jazz and photos of musicians—young, old, classic, and bluesy. There were old movie stars hanging in frames, from Mae West to Mary Pickford. I saw James Dean, Alfred Hitchcock, Frank Sinatra, Marilyn Monroe, and on and on all over the walls, without an empty space left. There were posters of concerts and news releases and even a poster about the sinking of the ship *Titanic*.

It was dark, and even at that, people sat reading and doing homework.

I couldn't have seen it all if I would have spent one complete day there. However, one thing I didn't see that I actually looked for, was a poster about the Monterey Jazz Festival.

One of my favorite events to cover when working as a reporter was the Monterey Jazz Festival. I was grateful to be part of the media who could stroll around and take in various musical venues during that jazz week in Monterey.

I think if the Bohemian Jazz Club had one more tiny space left on a wall, I'd send one of my reviews and maybe a photo or two.

Tonight, I pack because I have a bus trip tomorrow.

Jeronimo in the neighborhood?

You never know what you'll find on any given day, but I'm open for surprises. It has been a habit of mine when I don't have much of a daily plan, to take a street and walk as far as it will take me. After that, I take another street and do the same again. This has taught me a lot about various neighborhoods and how they can change from opulent to fortuneless in a matter of a few steps.

Yesterday, still in Granada, I walked all the way to the river and found statues and buildings I hadn't seen before that lined the shiny stone path away from the business section. There was one shop open (it was Sunday), and it sold chocolate. I went in and sampled a variety of chocolate and purchased some. I know now what gave me a stomachache this morning.

Then I walked the opposite way, and when I got close to my neighborhood near the park where the birds sing all night in the trees, I heard what sounded like gunshots or fireworks. I then heard drum beats, so I followed the sound to a crowd of people watching a parade.

There was a solemn-sounding marching band, several priests in black robes, lay people in full red gowns, and young men swirling some smoking, sweet-smelling incense. There was a statue of the Archangel San Rafael being carried on a platform by people who were hidden under it. It appeared to be floating down the street.

I stopped and took a photo and then a video of the production. There was a man standing near me, and on a whim, I spoke to him in English and asked him what it was all about.

"It's some sort of tradition in Granada. I'm not quite certain."

"It's a religious one. I can tell that with the priests," I offered my two-cents' worth.

Then I saw men with dark suits and official-looking military or diplomatic-type badges and appearing very important, standing to the side, watching.

"Have you seen the Jeronimo?" The gentleman I'd spoken with put his fingers to his lips and kissed them, signaling his Italian heritage.

"The Jeronimo?" Hmm, the only Geronimo I knew about was an Apache American Indian, but I kept that thought to myself.

"Yes, the Jeronimo. It's a monastery—just down there. Walk to the end and turn right. It's on your left." He kissed his fingers again.

After taking enough photos, I followed the Italian's suggestion and walked into the cathedral. It was opulent, to say the least, and here I am now, kissing my own fingers.

The monastery has two cloisters, each built around a garden. The walkway and the rooms, possibly where the priests have lived in the past, were dark, open spaces. A feeling of reserve came over me, until I ventured into the worship room, and I was overwhelmed.

The high ceilings were covered with paintings, as were the archways and all along the walls. Covered in gold leaf, sculptures in the background adorn the main worship area. The construction began in 1504, and I observed many square stones with names of priests who must have lived there from the 1600s.

There were richly decorated Renaissance interior features—coffering, scalloping, and sculptures galore. The monastery worship area certainly offers a backwards look through the early years of Granada and the opulent era, where gold met architecture.

I walked through it and really wanted to lie down and take photos of the ceiling, for you don't see art that beautiful unless you're in a museum. I have a special liking of cherubs, so I did my best to get close-ups of them. I leaned back as far as I could without breaking my neck.

When I walked out of the monastery, the parade and the sound of the drums and horns had continued on down the street toward another neighborhood.

Look up at the art while I watch the road.

I'm sitting in the bus station this morning in Granada and will wait in the coffee shop until it's time to catch the bus to Algeciras.

Picture this. I have a suitcase on wheels, a stuffed bag sitting on top of that, a purse over one shoulder, a camera over the other shoulder, my laptop bag in one hand, and I'm walking to the table holding my glass of *cafe con leche*. I feel like a contortionist.

Someone suggested I get a backpack, but I do not think it would hold all my stuff, and if it were a larger backpack, it would hurt my back. As it is, I wake up nearly every morning with a backache, but after walking for a while, it goes away.

"Don't worry" is a standard comment here in Granada, used for just about anything. So, I'm saying that now. "Don't worry!"

The lady in the hostel called a taxi that arrived in a few minutes. The driver was a young woman. I was so happy to see a woman driving—and one who could speak English—that I jumped right up in the front seat, something I learned not to do in Costa Rica.

The driver, who looked barely old enough to drive a car, learned English while living in England. She liked a comment I made about a four-story house that was painted pink with white trim.

"That is so pretty. It looks like a cake."

"You are a very creative person. I drive by that place all the time, and I have never thought of it as a cake. But now, I will."

During the nearly five-hour bus ride, sitting next to Tom who is from Australia, the time went quickly by. We had a lot to talk about, and by the time it came for us to part, I felt I had made a friend. We got into the same taxi, and he was dropped off first.

It was only about a two-minute drive to his hostel, while mine was nearly 15 minutes away. We drove and drove and drove, and finally, up near the mountains high on a hill, we came to where I'd be staying for three days. I hadn't had anything to eat, and the lovely lady in reception packed a bit of a lunch for me for a very reasonable price. I find that I'm far from the city but within walking distance to the bus stop. Soon, I'll go shopping for the next few days.

This place is nothing like I expected. The bus is across the freeway from the hostel and is too far for me to head right straight back to the same bus station to pick up some food. But the reception lady told me about another small market if I just walk down the road that's the freeway, then I'd come to a restaurant. The market is up a hill from there.

Here's the truth. I walked down the freeway facing cars and trying to stay out of their way; however, a ditch next to the freeway prohibited my walking further away from the traffic. Fortunately, most cars gave me a wide berth. I then found the restaurant that seemed to be about one mile away. I went up the hill from there, up, up, up the hill, over rocks, pits in the road, and dogs warning me with big white teeth that I was taking chances.

I found the little shop with a step-up to a window where I could look in and see that most everything for sale was large— large bottles of this and that. I purchased a tomato, some cans of tuna, and bread. I'm all set for two days' worth of dinner, as breakfast comes with the deal here.

I walked back, this time up a front road until I came to the end, and then I had to get back on the freeway. So I swung the bag out at my side whenever I heard a car coming so they could see me. What I learned at an early age, to always walk against the traffic so the cars see you, didn't work here. It was a busy freeway, and I would have to cross over to walk on the correct side, only to have to cross the freeway again to get to the hostel.

I have discovered I'm the only person in this compound! There is a swimming pool, a tennis court, and a lovely place to see the view of the ocean and mountains. Everything is closed down.

Tomorrow, I'm going to the Gibraltar for one day, and I bet there will be much to write about. I hope to see some monkeys.

Monkeying around with monkeys and friends on the Rock of Gibraltar

Yesterday marked one of the best days so far on the one-year journey. You could probably say it began on Tuesday, two days ago, when I met Tom Johnstone, from Australia, on the bus heading from Granada to Algeciras.

I believe there are no accidents, especially when Tom was my seatmate. Seats are reserved and assigned.

We chatted the whole four hours to Algeciras, and the next day, he accompanied me to the Rock of Gibraltar. It was there where we met three other people, and we all became instant friends.

But first, let me say, it is pouring down rain—thunder and wind today—and I'm trapped inside a spa-like convention facility. There must be room for 200 or more people here. It has been the worst mistake of my journey so far.

When we got to Algeciras on Tuesday, Tom was dropped off in the city where he made a good judgment call and stayed in town. My place, however, was so far away, I cannot get to town (grocery store, bus stop, port) easily. Yes, there are buses, but as I mentioned, the bus stop is on a busy freeway that I must walk across. Since it is storming right now, and since it's difficult to see outside, I'll stay inside this place today. I leave tomorrow, thank goodness.

By the way, I am still the only person staying in this resort. I have been given no special privileges. I slept a few minutes past breakfast because of a sleepless night and was told there would be no breakfast for me. That means I had to purchase a packed lunch. There are also no kitchen privileges and only a microwave, which is off-limits, as well. The cafeteria was closed up. I do have a French press coffee maker and some ground coffee.

Okay, that's enough of that challenge, so let's go on to the great day, yesterday.

I met Tom at the bus stop after the bus ride from the freeway, and together we traveled by bus to the border between Spain and Gibraltar. After searching and asking a question of a taxi driver who pointed out the walkway to the entrance of the border, we arrived, got our passports stamped into Gibraltar, the Colony of Great Britain, and continued on.

We heard a man speaking to a couple, also from Australia like Tom, about touring the rock in a van with him as a guide, going to the top where taxis cannot go, and also where it would take several hours to walk.

"That's what I want to do," I said to Tom.

"You could save some money if all four of you go together," the guide who heard me said.

We turned and looked at the couple, and we all agreed without further delay. It turned out to be one of the best decisions in my journey.

"Will we see monkeys at the top of the rock?" I asked the driver.

He replied with humor, "If you don't see any monkeys, I'll give you your money back. Yes, you will see monkeys."

We found our way to the top of the Rock of Gibraltar, but how did the 200-plus monkeys get there? According to everything I have read and accounts from the guide, the tailless Macaca sylvanus monkeys' arrival to Gibraltar still has experts guessing, and so far, no one knows for certain. One theory is that they came at a time when Europa and Africa were joined. Another is that they were brought over to the rock by the Moors during their centuries-long occupation of the Iberian Peninsula. There are those who believe they were introduced to the British as pets and then allowed to go wild on the upper slopes of the rock.

Sir Winston Churchill, upon learning the numbers were diminishing, intervened, ordering their numbers to be replenished. Thus, continues the saying, "Gibraltar will cease to be British on the day there are no apes left on the rock."

There are centuries of history of the rock, the caves, the monkeys, the city, and the wars, so that to spend one day there wouldn't be enough time. Tom said he's going back there after his upcoming trip to Morocco.

The guide took us to several viewing places where our new friends, Kim and Keith, and Tom and I took photos of the city and the bay and one of the tunnels, before we got to the monkeys.

All of a sudden, there they were—monkeys walking among the people, sitting on fences and rocks, watching us make fools of ourselves. The monkeys played and rolled around on top of vehicles. We were instructed not to touch them, as they will bite. Also, be careful about rummaging around in bags because they may think you're about to feed them. That was also a no-no. But dear monkeys, is it fair that you can jump on us and bite us, but we cannot touch you? C'mon.

Kim screamed and jumped when a monkey used her head as a bridge from on top of a van to a rock.

It was difficult sometimes to be somewhere close to a monkey without causing it to get nervous and lean over to hit you or bite you. They were everywhere, and I have many photos of monkeys on vehicles, on fences, watching us, and with their babies. On the way out, I saw a cat.

I walked close to get a photo of the cat, and another guide scared me on purpose with a loud, "Meow." After my surprise, he told me there was once a Gibraltar cat who gave birth to kittens, and one of the monkeys nursed one of the kittens and took care of it.

More of Gibraltar

Harvey and Kim have been friends all their lives, as their families have known each other throughout the generations. Harvey works in Gibraltar and had agreed to take Kim and Keith on tour for part of the day. Tom and I had met two days earlier and decided to see Gibraltar together, and that's when we met up with Kim and Keith. They then invited us to go with them when they would be joined by Harvey.

Before we met Harvey, all four of us sat in the town square and had a delicious lunch. While we sat there, Tom saw a camera chip under a chair a bit away from us. He picked it up and asked around if anyone had lost one, and when the answer was no, he took it into the restaurant. No sooner did he do that when a couple from Norway came looking for it. Tom was the man of the hour when the couple found he had turned it in, and they insisted on having their photo taken with him.

After lunch, we met Harvey, who is the most interesting fellow. He works with nuclear submarines for the government of Gibraltar and England. I hope this is correct, as hearing exactly what he does was not always easy. He did explain it a bit, and it seems to be something for which he first gained the knowledge while doing submarine work in the British Navy. We met him at the tunnel from the city square away from the port.

We toured a museum that was established in 1928 by General Sir Alexander John Godley who was the Governor of Gibraltar. In his desire to reform and restore Gibraltar, he created the national museum after he got permission to use the ordinance house, which had chambers of Moorish bathhouses and was also used as a semi-underground stable. The museum was opened in 1930.

It's an unusual and most interesting museum, and it has a gift shop full of books about Gibraltar. At the end of the tour, I began speaking with the woman who ran the shop and took admissions to the museum. She was born and raised in Gibraltar, as were her parents and her grandparents. They had some ancestor of Spanish heritage, and I noticed she used both a little Spanish and English mixed together, which is not uncommon in Gibraltar. I mentioned this to Harvey, and he told me that is where the word "gibberish" comes from.

When I looked online before even leaving the U.S., I knew somehow I'd get to Gibraltar and was surprised how in travel forums, folks generally weren't eager to see Gibraltar. One person even said, "All you can see there are monkeys." That's exactly what I wanted to see. It's an interesting place to visit, and not one of the regular sites everyone sees. I am happy to have had the experience.

Heading to Tangier, Morocco

It took 12 hours, but I'm in Tangier, Morocco, in Africa near the Strait of Gibraltar. Friend Tom of Australia sent me an email about his previous day getting here, so I was forewarned and even given some instruction. His journey took four hours.

I left the Albergue Inturjoven Hostel by taxi at 9:00 a.m. for the 11:00 ferry from Algeciras. My ticket originally was for the 8:00 ferry, but I thought the 11:00 sounded better since it had rained all night and was foggy in the morning.

When I got there, I went right up to the information window and asked what I was supposed to do first in order to catch the 11:00 a.m. ferry. She said, "There is no 11 o'clock ferry."

"What? Here are my papers. I was told last night that I could catch the 11:00 and not the 8:00, and here is the name of the man who told me that." A woman at the hostel had made the call.

She looked at the paper and gave me the first dreadful news. "The 11 o'clock ferry has been cancelled. Now you have to take the two o'clock."

"Two o'clock? What will I do here for five-and-one-half hours?"

"You can go up there to the cafeteria." She pointed to the escalator.

"I have all this stuff. Is there a lift somewhere?"

"Over there," she yawned.

"By the way, do you have Wi-Fi here?" (It's pronounced "we fee" here.)

"Yes, upstairs."

I trudged to the lift, the elevator in American terms, and arrived upstairs to a cafeteria and another large, adjoining room that was vacant.

I got *cafe con leche* in a glass on top of a saucer. These saucers do not have the usual indentations that saucers in the rest of the world have, so the small glass slid around. There began what I thought would be a five-and-one-half-hour wait. But there were more setbacks.

First, I decided to look up the address of the hotel in Tangier, so I could be prepared when I got there to give it to the taxi driver. The little red notebook wasn't anywhere to be found. I had looked at it in the taxi to make certain I had the words written down in Arabic, those words that would help me say, "No, thank you" and "Leave me alone," if needed. I can only think that I must have left that little red notebook in the taxi or that horrible hostel.

I have several red notebooks, and two of those were with me but not the one I needed. So, now I needed "we fee" so I could get the address of the Tangier Hotel off of my email address, but no one could help me find the password to the system.

Now it was getting close to one p.m., and I needed that address before I left. Don't know why, when, during transitions, I make so many poor judgment calls, feel disorganized and worried I'll forget something, lose something, or do something unintentionally illegal for a tourist. And, it's a self-fulfilling prophecy every time.

"Do you know the password for Wi-Fi?" I asked several people whenever I saw someone walk nearby.

"No" was the usual answer.

I went back downstairs with my entire luggage and asked again. The unconcerned woman at the information desk said you had to pay for it, and to do that you had to go upstairs in the waiting room.

So back upstairs I went with my things and looked around for a place to pay. There was a strange-looking wooden box that said Wi-Fi on it, with a slot for money. Honestly, I thought it looked fake. I thought of *Candid Camera*. It didn't say how much to put into it, so I put in two coins, and they came back. Tried again; they came back again.

Now I was starting to panic. I pulled most everything out of the carry-on bag, including underwear, medicine, papers, you name it—but not the right red notebook. Then I saw a man who looked like a professor sitting with his computer, and I asked him if he knew the password. He only spoke French and handed me a bottle of water.

"No, thank you. I need the password for my computer to get online." I did manage to understand that he was working on something but not online.

There was a Moroccan lady sitting nearby waiting for her husband, and I asked her if she knew the password for Wi-Fi, and she didn't understand me, but somehow I communicated to her that I had to find the name of the hotel in Tangier before I left on the ferry.

"Wait. My husband will be back." She got me to understand those words in some kind of language.

He did come back and spoke a little bit of Spanish, and he understood my dilemma and said, "Let's go. I'll help you."

We went back to the box, and he figured that it was useless, so downstairs again, where he asked inside two shops, and neither person at those spoke English to understand what I needed. Finally, we went to another ferry ticket window, and he asked the Moroccan lady if she could speak English to help me.

She could, and she got my email address up and found the email about the hotel, and I wrote it down. I thanked her and the gentleman for saving my day.

Ready to board. I juggled around to be first in queue at the check-in station, so I wouldn't have to stand long. But I got tired of waiting and noticed that others were getting tired, as well, so we all sat down on benches until a man opened up the customer window, and we all got in line again.

He looked at passports, which became the first of many times throughout the day that passports had to be shown. He stamped the ticket and handed out two boarding passes. By then it was after two p.m., and no ferry had arrived.

However, a group of us became a little village. There was a lovely Moroccan mother who lives in London with her two sons.

One of her sons, a delightful little boy with the most fetching smile, was in a stroller because he had mobility issues, his mother said. The other boy, age 11, was almost as tall as his mother and was polite and sweet to his mother and brother.

There were also two young couples from the U.K., another couple from Denmark, a movie star-looking Frenchman, the French professor-looking guy, and myself.

The mother began talking to some other Moroccan women about the delay, and they didn't seem to know anything about it. We all just stood around in the queue talking in various languages, wondering why someone didn't tell us what was going on.

It became 2:30, and still no ferry had docked. Around 3:00, the Moroccan women and the mother of the two sons spoke, and while they did, other people began to leave. I learned that those who left were going to leave on another ferry from a different company. The mother with the sons followed suit. Soon, however, they all came back because the original company wouldn't refund their money.

Somehow, someone heard the ferry was ready, and we would leave at 4:00. But we didn't. We waited.

Finally, at 5:00, at the usual next scheduled departure, we boarded the boat along with the other regularly scheduled 5:00 passengers.

The boat left at 5:30. Our little village stayed close together and helped each other. Someone was always there to assist me with my luggage, and someone helped the little boy in the stroller up and down stairs.

When we arrived at the Tangier port, people with cars were first off the boat, then our little village was next. We made the mistake of going down the wrong staircase, and all of us had to go back up and, you guessed it, wait.

Finally, someone from the ferry company opened a door for us and pointed to metal stairs that I believe could have easily been called a ladder.

Then there was the bus to get on, which was free and took us to the terminal where, once again, for the fourth time, we showed our passports. We waited on the bus for one last passenger who had a huge trunk and was trying to move it herself. The French professor helped her drag it on the bus after someone from the ferry company offered her a cart.

At the terminal, there was a choice to make—take a taxi to the city or take a bus. I opted to follow the young folks and go by bus. We all gave our farewells to the lovely mother and her two sons, and the rest of us waited in pouring rain for the bus.

Before the bus, I got a little bit of dirham (Moroccan money), so I could pay the bus and the taxi later.

I got on the bus, and the driver smiled at me and handed me a ticket, which I put in my pocket with the change he handed back, and I sat up front with my bag, which was soaking wet and had my computer in it, on top of my lap.

A man got on the bus and asked everyone for their tickets. I searched my pockets, my billfold, my purse, my brain, and I couldn't find it. Meanwhile, there was an argument between the man and a passenger, which ended when the passenger paid the bus driver. I was next.

"I can't find it," I said, and I must have looked like a wounded animal.

The bus driver saved me; he told the ticket taker he remembered me.

While we drove to Tangier about 55 kilometers away, the driver laughed and talked to two men who sat on the steps near the driver, and I observed the driver texting, as well.

We got to Tangier, and I got a taxi to the hotel. I woke up this morning and went downstairs for breakfast.

Two men were sitting in the lobby, doing nothing. The room was quiet.

"Yes? Can I help you?"

"I just want breakfast."

"It isn't time yet."

"What time is breakfast?"

"Eight o'clock, ma'am."

"Oh, I'm still on Spain time. Sorry."

Now I know there is a two-hour time difference. It was six a.m., and I have heard the amplified morning call for Islamic prayers.

It is now eight a.m., and I'm finally heading for breakfast.

Seeing Tangier with a guide

"Don't go very far away from the hotel" were the hotel manager's words. There are coffee shops up and down the street, and I'd be safe in any of them, but they are full of men. Not many women are seen here, and if seen, they wear the long robes and head covering. I've seen other women in western dress, however, but not as often.

I took his warning seriously and didn't go far away alone.

One morning, I took an early walk around about two blocks, and at one point, I arrived at the port where the ferry docked, and I took a photo of the port.

I found a grocery store down under another building and made some purchases. While at the cheese counter, I spoke English to a man from Tangier who told me I should go to Marrakech.

"It's very beautiful and safe. You should see it before you leave Morocco. It's the best city here."

I then found a large coffee shop and ordered coffee from a nice young waiter and asked if they had Wi-Fi there. He came back with an Arabic newspaper with the code written down on it. He had asked another customer to do that for me.

Later, back at the same coffee shop, now with my computer, he offered me a seat, but I needed a place to plug the computer cord into for electricity.

The waiter asked another man, whom I assumed was the owner, and he motioned for the waiter and me to go upstairs.

The waiter plugged the computer into a TV set that was situated high on the wall, and I was ready to open and begin writing. The balcony room where I sat alone comes close to circling the whole bottom part of the building. A huge crystal chandelier that almost takes up the entire space above the room hangs over the bottom floor. Upstairs, the walls are painted a bright salmon color with filigree trimmed in white, a common color choice here in Morocco.

I ordered lunch in French, my coffee in Spanish, and I said thank you in Arabic.

Lunch was hard bread cut into triangles with cheese, a dish of spiced olives, and a small cup of yogurt.

When I arrived back at the hotel, the manager said he would arrange a guide for me, as I mentioned I wanted to see the old town. "Don't go alone," he advised again.

I did venture onward to another neighborhood early the next day. I got into an area and couldn't figure how to get out. Men sat around watching me, with questioning on their faces.

One man with a beard and a cap asked me something, but I didn't know what it was.

"No," I said, figuring that with my head shaking sideways, I would be understood. He walked away, and then another man came up to me, trying to sell me something.

"No," I said.

A man who spoke a bit of English asked how he could help me.

"I'm trying to figure out how to leave this area."

"Go down that road." He pointed to a place where a few men were sitting, watching me.

"I think I would like to find a taxi." Some men heard that, and right away, they all wanted to get a taxi for me. I'm certain whoever would have won that contest would expect a tip.

"Can you please call a taxi for me?" I asked the man who offered to help.

He did call one, and I had an awkward wait while I was being sized up and approached to buy this, or this, or this. Looking back later, I think the men were just dumbfounded to see me by myself, but I was not in harm's way.

Today is Sunday, and I went on a tour of the city with the guide, Chariff. He explained that the country has been celebrating the Festival of Sacrifice. This age-old festival commemorates the prophet Abraham's willingness to obey God when he envisioned he was to sacrifice his son. Sheep are slaughtered according to humane Islamic guidelines, and then every bit of the animal is used in meals or in other ways.

On the tour, I saw a pile of wool off of freshly slaughtered sheep, as well as hides that would go to tanning companies. Horns and bones go elsewhere. Any leftover meat that families cannot finish goes to charity, Chariff told me.

When we left the hotel and started walking up the street, I observed Chariff looking toward some men up ahead. They were just standing around, seeming to be animated in discussion. He didn't say anything, and I know he wasn't aware that I observed his concern. We turned and walked down another street. He didn't know me well enough to understand my skills of observation honed from my reporter days.

Chariff and I went through the new market and the older market, called Medina. On the way, he pointed out the Kasbah, the Old Portuguese Fort, and the wall that is left from that. We saw narrow streets and narrow walkways along houses. The narrow walkway is room for one person.

The scent of food and spices surrounded us from the houses sitting right on the pathway and up and down many steps. A fountain and a park separate the city. Tangier can be roughly divided into three distinct sections—the old Medina, the Kasbah, and the new city.

Chariff explained that the fronts of houses aren't impressive-looking because the Moroccans are humble people and do not want to be seen as flaunting what they own. The doors were similar and in ancient patterns.

I yearned to see the inside of a Moroccan house and asked if that could be possible.

On our way, we did stop into a house converted into a B&B that was owned by friends of Chariff. The B&B was right on our path, and we went all the way up to the top of the house where we could see the ocean and across the bay to Spain, and on the other side of the rooftop was the city with mosques, old and new.

I had a feeling that, while Chariff was a great guide and guard of me, he had more experience than being a tour guide, and I felt a bit like he might have been expecting me to make a mistake that might be offensive to the Moroccan people.

I noticed his concern when a woman I saw dressed in all black and bent over, standing near an old building, smiled at some children who gave her something and then ran away. I thought she would make a great photo, but Chariff said she had a problem, and it wouldn't be dignified of me to take her photo. Of course, I understood that.

Before this, I was inside of the Anglican Church, which was about to begin a service. I was allowed in to take a photo of the front worship center. Chariff, a Muslim, was willing to take an hour out of my time with him so I could attend the service. But I declined that kind offer, as I really wanted to see the markets and learn about the interesting history of Morocco.

"Morocco was the first nation to recognize the United States," Chariff told me.

From *Wikipedia*: "Relations between the Kingdom of Morocco and the United States date back to the earliest days of U.S. history. On December 20, 1777, Morocco formally recognized the colonies as a unified sovereign nation. Morocco remains one of America's oldest and closest allies in the Middle East and North Africa, a status affirmed by Morocco's zero-tolerance policy toward al-Qaeda and their affiliated groups. Morocco also assisted the U.S. CIA with questioning al-Qaeda members captured in Afghanistan, Iraq, Indonesia, Somalia, and elsewhere during the administration of George W. Bush, 2001–2009.

"Formal U.S. relations with Morocco date from 1787, when the United States Congress ratified a Treaty of Peace and Friendship between the two nations. Renegotiated in 1836, the treaty is still in force, constituting the longest unbroken treaty relationship in U.S. history, and is home to the oldest U.S. diplomatic property in the world."

As we walked along the pathways and the streets, people Chariff knew would greet him with a wave, some men with hugs, and all with an obvious respect. He is one of 13 children. Part of our walk took us through his neighborhood.

On a narrow pathway through the Medina (old town) residences, Chariff pointed out that Tangier was home to many well-known people, including the artist Henri Matisse, Malcolm Forbes, Barbara Hutton, and others. Just a few years ago, the film, *The Borne Ultimatum*, starring Matt Damon, was filmed on the streets in the very old part of the city where we walked. We saw the market stalls of fruits and vegetables that come from local farms. Chariff said he remembers not too long ago when farmers would come to the city on market days on mules and carts to sell their wares.

We stopped off for a drink, and I was introduced to the most famous drink of all—a mint tea. It was so delicious that I want to go get some right now. It is served in a glass of hot water with tea, sugar, and mint leaves stuffed down into the glass.

I learned a bit about tipping here from Chariff. I paid for the tea, and the server put my change on a small plate, which I've seen done many times before. I took my change, and Chariff handed the server some change.

When we got outside, I asked him about that, and he said everyone likes to be tipped, and he saw that I wasn't going to leave the change, so he did it for me. Now I know a bit more tipping etiquette than before. I am a reasonable tipper and have given a tip many times; however, I had read that tipping in Morocco wasn't expected.

We walked a good three hours up and down steps and on ramps and in narrow streets and pathways where, without my great guide, I would have been lost without question.

When we returned back to the hotel, Chariff sat down in the lobby. I paid him for his time and also included a tip. It was just the amount of money I had on hand.

"I know this doesn't express how well I enjoyed our time, but I didn't get enough money out of the ATM machine."

He mentioned the amount like it was very small. It must be tough training these American women who insist on traveling alone. I paid a good amount for a whole day's time. However, it ended at three hours instead of the eight hours that was the original plan, so I feel he was rewarded enough. Anyway, I am grateful for the time he spent and the information he gave me about his country.

Last day in Tangier

Today is my last day in Tangier. It has been a fascinating five days. The hotel manager explained when I arrived that the city was quieter than usual because of the yearly "Festival of the Sheep." It took me a while to understand the importance of this holiday. I didn't think the city seemed all that quiet for the first few days, but today, I saw the difference.

The city is busy, as I learned once I got outside of the hotel. I checked out and walked across the street to the place where you can look out and see the cruise ship that had just come in and unloaded a lot of tourists, mostly from the U.K.

I had brunch, which was a cheese and mushroom om-elet inside a fried bread sandwich, a small bowl of a variety of delicious olives, and a small salad. I ordered fresh squeezed orange juice—yum. After that, I ordered the usual Moroccan tea served in a metal teapot for one person and drunk from a glass. The teapot is hot, so the handle is covered with a "cozy." The teapot is placed over a metal plate that is covered with a matching cloth.

Now let me explain walking across the street. At street corners, there are pedestrian-marked places that no one adheres to. People walk across the street with cars going up and down the street, with few breaks in between. If you wait for a break, you'd never get across the street. So I waited until someone else began to walk across, and I piggy-backed on their bravery. There was no way I could walk out in front of fast-moving cars, taking a chance they'd stop for me.

I could see first-hand how drivers get around people when I sat inside the taxi. I could swear my driver would hit the person who just jutted out in front of him. So far, I haven't seen any accidents, and more importantly, I have survived!

After brunch, I waved down a taxi, something you must do very aggressively, and went to the Kasbah Museum. Kasbah is the word for fort, and this one is the former sultan's palace (where Portuguese and British governors also lived) and has recently been completely redone. The new focus is on the history of the area from prehistoric times to the 19th century, most of it presented in seven rooms around a central courtyard. It at one time housed Malcolm Forbes' military collection of toy soldiers, but the building was sold to the Moroccan government for a history museum.

Inside are rooms of artifacts and wall maps of old trade routes. A garden is found outside the museum and is full of plants, trees, and Moroccan art—pillars and pots and Arabic calligraphy.

When I arrived, a young man, who obviously wanted to be my guide, approached me, and I told him politely that I wanted to be on my own. Meanwhile, some folks from the ship came in, and I spoke to some of them regarding their RV caravan trip.

I walked back out to get a taxi and was confronted again by the same young man. Finally, I told him, à la Greta Garbo, "I want to be alone." He said something that sounded as if it could be a swear word, but whatever it was, he got the message and left me alone.

Most Moroccans guess I'm German, which is one-half correct, but I'm an American, and that gets some surprised looks.

I got into a conversation earlier with the manager about my traveling alone. It is unusual, since in Morocco, most people my age sit at home and are looked after by their children.

"I see my mother every day, and if I'm out of town, I call her six or seven times a day to see if there's anything she needs or if everything is okay. My three other brothers do the same."

"What do you think about me with my travels?"

"I think you're running away from something, or you are just a very strange person."

"I just like to travel, and I am an adventurous person" was my reply. I added, "I like to see how other people live in other countries."

The manager gave me a blank look.

While in a taxi going back to the hotel from the museum, there were two women beggars near the street, and the taxi driver gave one of them a coin. I opened up my billfold and did likewise to the other woman.

Later, another mother and a boy, barely two-years-old, if that, were begging for money, and when the boy got some, he quickly handed it over to his mother. It is sad to see tiny children begging for their daily bread. The boy was the cutest little guy, and that got the attention of the women nearby. One young woman couldn't resist giving him a coin and a smooch.

Speaking of smooching, I have noticed the way men greet each other. They hug and kiss each other on both cheeks when they are good friends. Some, if they are not standing close enough for the hug and kiss, wave and put their hand on their heart. That is a beautiful gesture.

I am working at staying busy, for I leave on a night train at nine p.m. and will sleep on the train all the way to Marrakech. I was allowed to leave my luggage at the hotel lobby while I stay busy until time to get a taxi and head to the train station.

The introduction to Tangier has opened my imagination to art and design with fabrics, tile, and use of metal. I was told that many people ship carpets, chandeliers, and other goods back to their homes so they can decorate Arab-style. I wouldn't mind doing that, but my luggage carries a minimum of stuff, and I'm on a limited budget. Perhaps when I am motivated to pick up some items from Morocco, I'll do so at World Market.

The blue town

The town of Chefchaouen had been mentioned to me by three different people, and because of what they said, it sounded too alluring to pass up. I knew it was high up in the mountains, the houses were unique, and it was very "old world" in its ambience. I caught a taxi to the bus station to purchase a ticket. I had been told the bus would leave at ten a.m., and it would take two hours to get to Chefchaouen.

I crossed the fast-moving traffic to approach the ticket office where the agent said the bus wouldn't leave until one p.m., it would take two hours to get there, and the last return bus would leave at six p.m. That would be two hours to get there and three hours to look around. I went for it.

The bus climbed the mountains past little villages and donkeys and mules carrying packs, past pottery and tile shops, cafes, restaurants, bus terminals, gas stations, women washing clothes on the rocks in the river, and many people walking around.

After about one-and-one-half hours, we stopped and picked up some other passengers in another town. A lady sat next to me. She smelled terrible, and it got worse. We drove past a foul-smelling dump alongside the road. The refuse was not covered up, and it reeked.

I think the dump may have triggered the lady's sickness, although she may have been sick before boarding. She proceeded to throw up three times into a plastic bag. I handed her a towelette that I had put into my purse at the last minute. She accepted that. Her face was grey-green.

When she began to throw up, I nearly gagged myself, but I held another towelette close to my nose. What I had understood—that it would take two hours to get to Chefchaouen—was wrong. It took over three hours. When we arrived, I had one-and-a-half hours to look around the city. Unfortunately, the bus left us off at the station, not near the city. I wandered around a bit wondering what I should do. I was hungry, too. I couldn't get any practical wisdom from anyone. When I asked how to get to the town, it drew a crowd of men, each vying to be the one to take me in their car up to the top of the mountain where the city was located. They must have seen dollar signs on my forehead.

There was what looked like a hotel and restaurant across the road, so I crossed over and asked a gentleman if he had food there. He said he'd make me something to eat, but it wasn't really a restaurant. I went back to the station and again began asking for a restaurant, how to get to the city, how far away was it, and could I make it back to the bus on time? Deaf ears.

I went back to the so-called restaurant, and the man made me a fried egg and cheese sandwich. If I had anything unhealthy growing in my system, the penicillin on the bread cleared it up after the first taste. I left the bread and ate the egg and cheese.

When I paid him, he acted as though he couldn't understand what I was telling him in Spanish about the bread being bad. I also needed a bathroom, and he showed me where one was. Let me be discreet here. When I was a skier, I could snowplow pretty well. That's when you put your feet in a particular spot and crouch down slightly, just as I needed to do in that bathroom. It was difficult. Need I say more?

However, sitting outside at that place, eating that (gag) food, gave me the opportunity to see where the taxi stand was and how people used taxis to get to the top of the mountain. I went up to the stand and met two young men who understood I wanted a taxi but that I had just a little bit of time.

A conversation like that draws people like flies. Again, there was more help than I needed. A taxi—just a taxi—was my wish. One came breezing by, and the two young guys flagged it down and told the driver what I needed. It turned out that he understood a bit of English. He agreed to drive me up to the city and around it so I could take photos.

The man had a lovely, soft voice and a great laugh. I liked him immediately. He stopped up on top of the hill so I could get out and take a photo of the blue city down below. He drove through the town, up and down the streets, while I looked at blue houses and blue buildings. There wasn't much time left, but I got to see the essence of the town. It would have been fun to stay in Chefchaouen for a few days, but the taxi driver drove quickly, and soon my visit to the blue town was over.

The bus was there, and it was time to head back down the mountain in the dark.

Chapter Eight

November, 2012

Train ride to Marrakech

Marrakech, from what I've seen in the first few hours of my arrival, is everything people have told me.

I arrived after an all-night train ride from Tangier to the Marrakech train station and found the station unique in its architecture with touches of exotic Moroccan art in the decor.

After a taxi ride to the hotel, I moved into my room and then took a walk around the business section of the city, which is nearby.

I want to describe the hotel lobby where I am using Wi-Fi. A long seating area, somewhat like a couch, sits along the entire three walls. The seating is maroon with beige tile-like trim, and the "skirt" under that, in the same colors, is a large design that exemplifies Moroccan art. Cushions in the same motif line the back of the seating area. Those designs in the cushions are large and circular, and the cushion is fringe-lined. There are four coffee tables made of wood with stone tops. It could be marble; however, the color is maroon and beige, as well. There are several little stools here and there for extra seating. The walls, the ceiling, and the archway into the lobby area are covered with designs made of small tiles. The windows have draped maroon swags with see-through beige curtains. There are huge copper and brass pots sitting in the area, and the counter top is a grey marble. The lighting is dim, with the use of small chandeliers.

I remember in fashion design that the rule to combine items together is to find the unifying element. In the sitting area, maroon and beige is the unifying element, but the tile treatment is of all different colors.

I wasn't disappointed with my room, as it has the same exotic Moroccan ambience. I have a balcony off of the room overlooking the street below.

The train ride was right out of a movie. I got a first-class ticket. That didn't take me long to wonder what the second-class would be like. The bed in the cabin was comfortable enough, and the sheets and pillowcase were clean, but the bathrooms—oh, well, why go into that.

My cabin mates were two nice young men. One, a Frenchman, has a job where he organizes tourists on helicopter trips to the desert. There, they sleep in tents and hike around and then eat a gourmet meal at a formal dinner table. He showed me the website, and it looked like fun.

The other mate was a Japanese man who is on a European tour from Japan, studying other universities. He would go next to Amsterdam and then on to Germany.

Neither one of them spoke much English. We had some good laughs trying to explain ourselves using sign language and pantomime.

I wrote on my computer, which surprised me with Wi-Fi working for a few minutes. I showed them that I have three sons and three grandsons, and wrote, "Me with you two in this cabin reminds me of them." I then had that translated into French and Japanese. That made everyone comfortable, and we got along great.

The train took us through an arid land and wide-open spaces with few houses, all with flat roofs. I saw a sheepherder with his sheep, several donkeys, and horses with carts.

We slept through the night. I had been warned that during the night, if you're not careful with your belongings, they could disappear. I noticed the Frenchman slept with his computer next to him, so I did the same thing. It was slipped under my pillow.

In the city so far, I've seen horses and carts but no camels yet. According to the Frenchman who makes his home here, it's not unusual to see one-hump camels, horses, ostriches, and monkeys.

He wrote down several places he said I should see.

There is a lot to explore, and beginning tomorrow, I'll sign up for some tours.

Oh, by the way, the second language here is French.

Amazed in Marrakech

Everything amazes me; and at the same time, I'm not surprised. I woke up this morning and said I didn't want breakfast, but I would like orange juice and coffee—lots of it. I'm nursing a cold, and today I will take it easy and drink lots of liquids, for tomorrow is an adventure waiting for me.

What surprised me today? I was told to go upstairs for the juice and coffee. I didn't even know there was a large loft-type room upstairs. It's lovely and overlooks the huge chandelier that I'm learning is a common decoration in Morocco's buildings.

Yesterday in the morning, trying to get my first cup of coffee, I ventured down the street and found a hotel, a little bit fancier than the one I'm in.

I asked for breakfast and was directed to the upstairs. Up there, I saw a large pond with water jets in the center and a lookout over the city. But that wasn't all. There were some steps that went even higher to the rooftop. There are many rooftop restaurants, I've learned.

On this lookout, a band plays music beginning at eight p.m. I haven't gone anywhere alone like that here, yet. However, I'm discovering this city is safe, and people respect your personal space. Sure, they try to sell you something, but usually a "no thank you" a couple of times seems to work.

Absolutely the only thing that scares me is crossing the street in fast-moving traffic. The only rules are to weave in and out and don't get hit by a car, a horse and carriage, a donkey and cart, a motor bike, a bus, a van, or a taxi.

Another surprise is the American music I hear mixed in with typical Moroccan music. While on the train, just before disembarking, I heard, "Stand by Me."

Yesterday, I found the hop-on-hop-off bus at the corner, and a nice young man explained everything very clearly in English. The first bus would take me to the old, historical Marrakech and the afternoon bus to the newer section of town.

The bus first took us down the main street called Mohammed VI, named for the King, who is the grandson of the first King Mohammed. Mohammed VI was crowned in 1999. He holds a PhD in law.

Some of the conditions he is credited for improving are poverty, corruption, and human rights. He enacted a family code, which granted women more power. I got the feeling that while many people respected him for his position, there was also political discontent for some of his policies.

Women wear long robes covering their bodies, and some wear hoods and scarves to cover their faces with only eyes to be seen. One woman tried to sell me some bracelets, and I noticed that while her face was covered, she wore kohl, or dark eyeliner, around her eyes.

The bus took us past the Moroccan-Italian theater, which seats over 2,000 people.

The automatic guide furnished on the bus pointed out the Marrakech arts and music festival that attracts entertainers, artists, and visitors from all over the world.

The arts festival features the Berber culture. "The Berbers are an indigenous ethnic group of North Africa west of the Nile Valley. They are continuously distributed from the Atlantic to the Siwa Oasis in Egypt, and from the Mediterranean to the Niger River." From *Wikipedia*.

The tour guide, while we were in the ritzy section of the city and in view of mansions, said many well-known people have purchased homes there. There was a golf course near the mansions.

Later, we passed the King's Palace where he stays once in a while, and we were warned that it was strictly against the law to take photos of the entrance and the guards.

I behaved, although it was difficult. I noticed once when I walked past the entrance and smiled at the guards, I got dirty looks.

There were several gardens we drove by, and at one of those, camels were seated, eating and anxiously awaiting someone to sit on them for a photo-op. I choose not to do that. I have taken a camel ride in Egypt, so why do it again?

Gardens, we were told, are popular places for family picnic get-togethers. One of the prettiest gardens I experienced was a memorial garden in tribute to the fashion icon, Yves Saint Laurent. It is called the Majorelle, named after Jacques Majorelle, the artist who created it. The shade of cobalt blue is used extensively in the garden and in its buildings. The garden hosts more than 15 bird species, fountains, and cacti.

The garden also houses the Islamic Art Museum of Marrakech, whose holdings include North African textiles from Saint Laurent's personal collection, as well as ceramics, jewelry, and paintings by Majorelle.

The garden, pools, bridges, trees, overhanging shrubs, and sounds of birds mesmerized me; a peaceful place, indeed. It was in the gift shop that I determined this would be the place to purchase something blue for my grandson Michael's birthday, November 2. I found a blue-covered journal book for him.

I was so captivated by the garden and the tearoom where tea was poured into the cup from high above, as well as the museum and the gift shop, that I missed the last hop-on bus, so I had to take a taxi. I was far away from the hotel.

Seeing the Sahara by camel power

The song, *Midnight at the Oasis*, by Maria Muldaur, rang true to me, for there I was smack dab in the Sahara on a camel. I thought I wouldn't be riding a camel because, as I said earlier, I've done that, so why spend the money to do it again? Well, this was different.

There are many opportunities to take tours, go with guides through the city, take a hop-on-hop-off bus, and I have done all of those. But when the manager of the hotel presented me with a package that included a Moroccan dinner, breakfast, entertainment, and the opportunity to sleep in a tent in the Sahara—oh, and there would be a camel ride—I signed up.

So yesterday, at seven a.m., I met a van that took me to the old Medina where I got into a different van of English speakers. Another van was full of French speakers.

In our van were two young doctors, a man who will begin work in the parliament in Wales, and two German girls on a break from tourism school, a school located within walking distance from where we lived in Den Haag, Holland. There were also two Americans; another couple; a computer genius; a city planner; a retired engineer from Boston, originally from China; and a single woman traveler, me. One American, a fireman, told me he had come to the country directly from New Jersey, where he had been working 60 hours a week in the flood and fires. His hometown, Sea Isle City, New Jersey, was in the eye of the storm, Hurricane Sandy.

"I'm happy to get away from there and do something different." He was visiting his girlfriend who is in school for the summer in Spain.

We got on the long, long road to the Sahara, passing mud-brick houses, walls of various brick and stone, villages with women in their long robes and head scarves, and men in their robes and their head gear made of scarf material and wrapped in such a way that they become hats. I was told the different ways of wearing a hat indicate the tribe they are from.

We wound around and up the mountain through pine and palm trees and rocky outcrops. Women in the isolated villages strolled with packages on their heads. Little boys controlled donkeys that lugged loads of goods on their backs. Women who lived near a river washed their clothing and laid it out on rocks.

Village homes and buildings are made from the resources near them. I am always amazed at how brilliant human beings are in efforts to create beauty and to be practical at the same time.

Our driver would stop every so often for our bathroom breaks and drinks.

We finally wound up at the Aït Benhaddou Berber village, where the last of the Berber families live. It was at this village that the movies *The Gladiator, Prince of Persia, Jewel of the Nile, Kingdom of Heaven, The Four Feathers, Samson and Delilah, Legionnaire,* and *Lawrence of Arabia* were made. Our guide was an extra in many of the movies, as were many of the villagers. He said he could be clearly seen in one picture. He is a handsome, movie star-looking guy, and it wouldn't surprise me that movie moguls would notice him.

I had a difficult time maneuvering up the high steps in the village, but there was always someone who took my hand and helped me. I'm ever-so-grateful for their help. At one point, the movie star led us over a stream of water on rock stepping-stones. I looked at them and just knew I couldn't get from one to another, as they were too far apart for me. He turned, saw me, headed back over the stones, gingerly took my hand, and with great strength in his arm, he led me to the other side.

A bit later, we arrived at a place where the camels were waiting with their handlers, who also assisted during the night and the next day. This is where the surprise came for me, and for the reason the Boston man said I didn't do my homework. He was right.

I kept asking if we would need to take all of our belongings or leave them in the van. No one answered, and I assumed we'd take a little ride, sort of like a small pony ride you see in country fairs in the U.S., and that would be the end of the camel experience, and then we would go wherever the tents were set up. Not so.

"Just climb over the camel, slowly," the handler said. I couldn't get my leg over the saddle. My knees don't work like they used to, and this was evidence I would need help. He picked up my foot and put it over the saddle to the other side. I sat up, and the camel got first on its front knees and its hind legs, then its head jutted up, and I bounced backwards.

Now we were all ready for the little trip with the camels, but boy, was I ever not prepared for what happened next. Everyone got on a camel, and we were tied camel-to-camel in a line. Actually, there were two lines of camels, and we set off down the road. The little ride I thought we would experience turned into a three-hour night ride through the desert by starlight.

I didn't know we were going on a long ride like this. I left my bag and everything inside of the van—my medicine, my toothbrush, and everything. I had my purse and my camera with me, as those are always within my watchful eye.

It seems the group knew it would be a ride to the tents. But they, too, didn't realize it would be that long.

When we finally arrived, everyone was dismounting the camels with no problem and limping to the community tent. I was still on the camel trying to get off of it.

"I think I could use your help," I said to one of the handlers.

"Put your leg over the back here." He pointed to the rear of the camel that was now sitting down. "But be careful, don't get your leg too close to its tail."

"I'm trying." My brain knew what to do, but it wasn't getting the message to my leg. However, since the handler left, I was alone at the mercy of the camel.

I slid off the beast, and my leg followed. I landed into deep sand. The computer guy saw my dilemma, came to my side, took my hand, and got me up and over to the community tent.

The tent roof was made of bright splashes of colored material, and there were lamps hanging down. Benches and low stools were padded, and shades of reds, oranges, and yellows were scattered here and there. One of the handlers, a charismatic fellow, sat down after we all had tea and asked where we were from and what were our names. He spoke good English and French, as well.

He brought out the dinner in pottery bowls with pointed-top covers, called *tanjins* (tangine in English). First course was a soup, and the second was a typical Moroccan stew with lots of vegetables.

Bowls of orange wedges made up the dessert.

After dinner, we sat around a fire under a black sky illuminated only by the stars and the dim lights of the community tent and the circle of tents where we'd be sleeping. The handlers entertained us with their percussion instruments and songs. Then they gave everyone an instrument to play in a community effort.

By that time, I was exhausted. So I found the tent assigned to me, opened up the door flap, and climbed under a heavy blanket that felt more like a rug. Two other people came in a bit later. The tent was pitch black inside. At one point, I needed to use the restroom and had to feel my way to my shoes and stumble quietly to the door. I couldn't count on support from the tent walls. But I found the tent opening and my way to the restroom that was lit up with one light bulb. When back to the tent, I simply sat near the mat on the floor, and on all fours, crawled to the mat and under the blankets.

We got a wake-up call at six in the morning to watch the sunrise and then had breakfast of bread and some kind of thick, white butter that I thought was cream cheese, and a syrup-like jelly, and coffee or tea. The handler poured the drinks with the pot held high.

We walked around a bit and then heard our camels protesting. They were going for another ride and complaining like hell. The sounds the camels made began with "moo" and ended in a high growl. I was mortified when I discovered where I fell last night. It was smack dab into a pile of camel poop. No wonder the handler left me to my own resources.

We knew our muscles and bones would get another workout, but we all assumed it wouldn't last as long. It did.

Once, on the way back, one of the guides saw that a date picker was at work, so he picked some up for us and gave each person a freshly picked date.

About three hours later, we were back where we started the previous day.

The man from Wales helped me out of the van that left us off at the Medina. The man from Chicago, who kept us all laughing when we weren't moaning, had quickly rented a motorbike. He drove it up to show me.

"Good for you. Have fun," I shouted at him and began looking around for a taxi.

I'm back in Marrakech at the hotel now, and I'm sore everywhere. Did I find my oasis in the Sahara? Time will tell.

The King is coming.

King Mohammed VI arrived in Marrakech by limo and an entourage and headed to his palace at the same time our group arrived back from the Sahara. We saw a commotion above with crowds screaming and waving and with warning sounds that he was on his way.

There were police and guards of all kinds in their uniforms. I would have loved to have taken a photo but didn't relish the idea of spending time in a Moroccan jail.

I noticed something different a few days before the King arrived, and that was the street decorations that hang over the streets and light up at night. A taxi driver told me the words' meaning—"Welcome to Marrakech, King Mohammed." In Arabic writing, it looks like part of the artwork.

The trip to the Sahara took us over the Atlas Mountain Range, and parts of it reminded me of the trip from Durango to Montrose, Colorado, over the town of Ouray, which is dangerous all the time but especially in the winter, as the road is narrow, and it's a steep ravine below. I cannot imagine it would be any different over the Atlas Range.

This and that

Most people speak French to me at first. Some know a little bit of English but not much.

I have been advised to not eat anything from street kiosks or carts but only at legitimate restaurants.

I've seen olive orchards, date trees, and men and boys in robes with donkeys, either riding them or walking with them. Most every woman I see wears a robe and headdress, with once in a while, western clothing, but still with the headdress.

Pigskin is never used; pork is not eaten.

You see mostly men in coffee shops.

Water is always served with coffee, some in plastic bottles and some in small glasses. Bottles are recycled in an organized program.

There are sections of Marrakech that are popular with the "jet set."

The water system is unique in Morocco, which still maintains the 11th century underground canal system.

The City of Marrakech is called "The City of Happiness" because of all you can find in the city, beginning with the Jemaa el-Fnaa Square, which has been listed by UNESCO as a World Heritage Site. In this square, you can enjoy the rich popular culture of Morocco that flourishes in music, folklore, and food.

When our group from the Sahara arrived back to the Square right after the experience of the King's arrival, it was bustling with activity. It was crowded with people enjoying the many offerings.

I had to take a taxi back to my hotel and flagged one down, beating someone else to the ride, but the driver obviously didn't know my hotel across town. He looked at the card from the hotel. He gave me a price, and I said that was too much, and I began to leave. Someone else overheard the conversation, came over, and told me it was fair because the city was full of people and it was nighttime.

I still said no and got out of the taxi.

The man who was at the defense of the taxi driver asked me what I was willing to pay. I said a very low number and he said no.

Meanwhile, another taxi driver got into the action and said he'd take me for the negotiated price. He looked at the card with the name and address of the hotel and started the drive.

He laughed when I told him the other taxi driver didn't know the place, but shortly after that, he stopped the taxi and said, "Here you are."

"No, this isn't the place. I thought you knew the hotel." He waited for me to find the card, and I showed it to him again. The hotel was close by, but that taxi driver didn't know where it was, either.

Double dare

The plan was to be in the center quad of the Medina in Marrakech. I thought I was waiting at the right corner for bus number one. I asked a man shopping at the newsstand if it was the right place for the bus, in minimal French. "*Le bus por Medina?*"

But the bus never came, so I asked him again, and that time he said no. Then I asked the man who runs the newsstand, who had seen me waiting there, the same question, and he said no, that the stop was three blocks that way. He pointed down the street.

I finally caught the bus and asked a young girl who was on it if it was the correct bus to get me to the Medina quad. She spoke a bit of English and confirmed it was correct, and better than that, she was headed to the same place, and we could get off the bus together.

That worked. We walked past about 20 or more horse-drawn buggies that were stationed near the quad. The carriages were upholstered in bright colors and adorned with flowers.

The girl on the bus was dressed in western clothing, like many teenagers I had seen in Morocco. She lives with her grand-mother, I learned, and attends college.

I walked around the quad and looked at some of the goods for sale in the kiosks, but of course, I'm not in the market to purchase goods, although there was much temptation—bright colors of materials, shoes, bags, jewelry, household goods, and spices galore.

The snake men were in the center of the quad getting ready to play, sing, and charm the snakes. I began to take a video of the action but was stopped.

"If you take photos, then you must pay," said one man who stood with his face about two inches away from my face.

"I wasn't taking a photo. I was taking a video." I stood up to his bullying and think this surprised him.

"If you use your camera, pay me. Pay me."

Well, I assumed he didn't know that in the U.S., anyone in the public could be photographed. But the rules are different on the streets in Morocco, or they are made up on the whim of the entertainer. However, I do understand that street musicians should be paid.

I gave him some coins, and he looked insulted and said it wasn't enough, so I put some more coins in his hands. He suddenly became my new best friend.

"Where are you from?"

"I'm from the United States."

"Where?"

"California."

"California—Orange County—Disney in Florida."

"Disney is in Florida and also in Southern California."

"Hollywood."

"Yes, Hollywood is also in Southern California."

That about ended the conversation, and a hand shake secured our new friendship.

A snake handler came over to me while the gang of musicians played and invited me to put the snake on my shoulders. Well, he didn't invite me—he just put it there.

I think it fooled them a bit when I didn't protest. Snakes don't scare me if I know they are not the kind of snake that kills you. I was pretty certain the snake handlers out in the public didn't use killer snakes.

After that little bit of fun, I was asked to put some more money into the pot. This time, they wanted paper money. Well, it was fun, so I gave them about $5.00, which would give each of them one dollar.

The snake handler held the snake with its mouth turned toward his mouth, as if to give it a kiss. When he put the snake on my shoulders, I made the same motions, while I had one of the musicians take my photo. It was fun playing "one-upmanship" and surprising the men and an audience.

As I left, they played another song for me, and I headed back to the bus stop with my mission complete. They waved me good-bye. It entertained lots of folks who formed a circle around me. I'm certain I was an oddity for a few moments. Could that count as my 15 minutes of fame?

I knew the musician felt he had taken advantage of the American lady, but the once-in-a-lifetime experience was worth the total of six dollars to me, so we were even.

King Mohammed VI arrives

"Keep your window shut and the curtains closed all day today," the hotel manager advised me when I came back from a morning walk around the "hood."

"Why?"

"The King will be driving down this street, and the police told us to keep all windows closed."

"Okay."

I said okay because I didn't think there would be a possibility to argue against King Mohammed VI's wishes. I did as told. Later, my curiosity drove me to find a vantage point to view the King. I walked down the end of the street to a restaurant on a corner intersection and asked where King Mohammed VI could be seen driving out of town.

"His majesty and the entourage will drive down the street," the restaurant hostess, who spoke good English, said, and she pointed to the corner from where we sat outside, and she added, "around the next corner and to the side of the hotel down there at the end of the block."

"That's where I'm staying." She smiled at my surprise. But that wouldn't be right below my room, I realized. I sat and ate my lunch, drank two delicious small teapots and glasses of mint tea, and waited.

No King.

I walked back to my hotel and every so often, I peered out from behind the curtains, just in case the King might alter his route and pass by my room. Later, I heard sirens and horns honking, and I assumed the King was making his trip out of town. I missed seeing the King because the route was changed. But that was probably the way it was planned; stay safe, and don't go the way the populace expects.

I later took a long walk to the theater and new opera house. All along the way, there were men trying to sell me something—a watch, a ride on a horse-drawn carriage, a taxi ride, a place to sit inside a cafe, and an umbrella—all this in a matter of a few blocks. Once, when it would be necessary to walk across a busy intersection, I stopped and asked a man who just walked across facing me if he would mind walking back across the street to help me.

He said in French, "*Bien sur, je vais vous aider*"; he'd be happy to help me. But when we got to the curb, there were two Muslim ladies there in their black gowns, and I said I'd go with them. The gentleman said something to them in Arabic, and they agreed to walk across with me, laughing all the way.

Every time I make it across the street, I figuratively pat myself on the back. It's the worst possible traffic free-for-all I've ever seen. Even when at an occasional green walk-light, vehicles don't stop for pedestrians.

The Cultural Center/theatre and soon-to-be opera

Horse-drawn carriages are seen in the city as regular means of travel—not just for tourists. I tried to hail one down, but the driver waved me on. It was full, anyway. I don't know where I would have sat.

When I got to the theatre/cultural center, a few men loitered on the steps, and inside, a woman was sitting on a chair in the dark lobby. She didn't smile and barely answered me when I asked if I could look inside. Was she in charge? Or was she just sitting here? I didn't know, so I just walked in.

"English or French?" a man suddenly standing next to me asked. I looked at him with the palms of my hands out, questioning why he wanted to know.

"I am a concierge."

"Oh, are you an official concierge for the theatre and cultural center?"

"I will show you the theatre and the opera." Well, there was something I didn't quite believe about him, so I took a photo of him.

"No. No photos of me."

He threw his arm up, but I thought I had a good shot. Later, when looking at the photo, I saw that his arm hid his face.

He seemed to be in a hurry and impatient with me when I would stop and take a photo. I was quite glad when the "tour" was over. He left after I gave him a tip of about $1.50. Not a bad gig for ten minutes. I learned from the disappearing tour guide that the opera is in the process of being built and will be finished in about three years. It will have a stage that will rise from the basement to the theatre floor.

The theatre is already up and running and currently show-cases theatre and musical venues, as it has been doing for several years. The garden appears neglected with an empty pool and un-maintained plants. I believe the whole area is being revamped and will be an impressive cultural center for Marrakech and all of Morocco.

Men and women in Morocco; my conclusion

Meanwhile, I have been enjoying the morning breakfast routine in the hotel, and this morning, I sat at a table of gliders. They were very nice people from Australia.

I have been in Morocco long enough to have formed an opinion about the attitude of men toward women. Men treat women as though they are just slightly invisible but still there to be seen when the men want to look. Women, I have been told, cover themselves up more as a cultural phenomenon than for the Islamic religion, although that is the traditional reason. The women with the traditional robes and hidden faces are demonstrating their modesty. It's a different culture from the western world and takes a while getting used to. A western woman being too friendly may be taken a different way than just the desire to be friendly. It may look as if you are aggressive or as if you're flirting.

My friendly nature sometimes gets taken the wrong way, as evidenced with the man who sells tobacco from his perch on the sidewalk from eight a.m. until ten p.m. every day. I have always been cautious not to present myself as a bit higher in the realm of society, and I allow people their dignity no matter where they are in life.

I walk past him every day, sometimes two or three times. I began smiling and greeting him, and today, he made a motion for me to stop. He made a clicking noise and then pursed his lips and made a kissing sound toward me. Yuk.

I realized that he had misread my friendly nature, so I will be avoiding the tobacco man until I leave here. This means when leaving the hotel, I'll go to the corner opposite of my usual walk, then cross the street and continue down the sidewalk the usual way, but across the street from the tobacco man so as to avoid him.

The folks who work in the hotel and restaurant are gentlemen and seem to understand the western woman a bit better than the average Moroccan.

However, I have observed that the maintenance people are women, and the men have the desk jobs and/or are waiters and bartenders. There are exceptions to my observations throughout the city at various restaurants, and changes are slowly coming about, but in spite of the King's attempts at giving more credence to women, in general, men rule.

The day begins with a stomachache.

The day began with a stomachache.

I'm leaving Morocco on Monday morning via the train to the Casablanca International Airport with one changeover.

At three p.m., I will fly to Madrid on Iberia Airlines and change in Madrid to a plane going to Málaga, Spain. I'll be one week in Málaga, and from there, I'm flying to Zurich, Switzerland, where I will stay with a woman, couch surfing, for a few nights.

I made the flight arrangements online, and I needed to print the tickets. I found an Internet cafe where the gentleman agreed to print out the flight from Málaga, Spain, to Zurich, and that was accomplished.

But I still didn't have the flight ticket from Casablanca to Málaga, and time was running out. The itinerary had a note that said, this is for your information and is not the ticket. You cannot board with this. You will receive an email ticket and that is what you need to print and take with you to the airline.

Bright and early this morning, I went to the Internet office, and it was closed.

I went on to the second thing on my list, which was to purchase my medicine. All that I had to do was just tell the pharmacist what I wanted and pay for it. She looked at the list, didn't say anything, but left to fill the order. She came back and handed me the sack of meds. I smiled, handed her some money, and said thank you, probably in poor Arabic. She didn't say a thing.

The third on my list was to purchase a lock and key for my luggage. All airlines have their own rules, and I read that Iberia Airlines requires locked suitcases. I've stopped locking them because the airlines since 9/11 have been breaking locks to look inside.

The man who helped me asked another man, a very old-looking gentleman, if he had any locks. He found a lock with a key, and I tried it but couldn't get it to work, and neither could the first man. But he kept working with it and told me it was okay.

However, I asked if they had another one, and the old man handed me another one that worked perfectly.

Later, my stomachache became unbearable, but I went back to the Internet that was opened. The young man there spoke

Italian and French. We went round and round until he finally called his boss to find out what I wanted, and he explained it to the young man. I now have my tickets! I had been in this office earlier with a printing job, so his boss remembered me.

I walked a different way than usual and found the French district and streets lined with upscale shops and classy people walking around. The French are so easy to spot. They beam "class," with men wearing their sweaters over their shoulders, women in high-heeled boots, and both men and women wearing fitted leather jackets.

My stomachache continued, and I stopped in a coffee shop and ordered tea. I told the lady I had a stomachache, and she walked down the street with my notebook and pen and had someone she knew to speak English, write down chamomile tea.

I drank some, and it seemed to help, but not too much, so back to the hotel and my room where I lay down.

The maid knocked on the door to make the bed and clean the bathroom. She saw me and asked if she should clean the room. I told her I just wanted to sleep, that I had a stomachache. I rubbed my stomach and made a face that showed pain. I understood that she told me to drink chamomile tea.

I will do that, I agreed, by shaking my head affirmatively and lay back down on my unmade bed. She motioned for me to get up. I obeyed. It would be too much trouble to argue. She pulled back the blanket and sheet and motioned for me to get in bed. I did, complete with my clothing still on. She then pulled the blankets up to my chin, like a mother would for a child.

Now that is going above her job description, but I thought it was very sweet, and I thanked her. When she left the room, I kicked the blankets off because it was too hot.

After a while, I went downstairs to work on the computer, but the stomachache was still there, so I planned to take it easy the rest of the day.

People in this neighborhood are beginning to recognize me and now wave and smile and do that touch-the-heart gesture.

Waiters are professional and skilled, and it doesn't matter if they are serving coffee, tea, or a four-course dinner; they do it with grace. They all wear either all black or a white smock. Last night, I walked across the street to a restaurant that has a beautiful outdoor garden. I looked inside but decided it was too cold where the waiter offered me to sit. He told me he would take me to a warmer place indoors, so I followed him through the building until we came into a room with tables all set up for dinner. The walls and ceiling were covered in white stucco that was so thick it looked like whipping cream.

The food was served in a *tanjin*. The waiter lifted the lid with flourish, and inside, it was the vegetarian dish I ordered. I'm not certain what herbs and spices were used, but those made vegetables come alive. I should add here that that meal might be to blame for my stomachache. I have a feeling it is food poisoning but am not certain. I have another day to take it easy, and I leave early tomorrow.

Worst day ever

Yesterday challenged me more than any day on the seven-month adventure. I've been sick with what I think is food poisoning, and I slept one whole day and night two days before my trip to Málaga, Spain, where I am now.

I took it easy the next day, the day that I arrived, but since then, I've had very little to eat. Just to look at food makes me nauseated.

However, this morning, I went to a restaurant and had rice pudding.

How did I get here? Two taxis, two trains, two planes, and confusion in the airport. I kept getting different directions from different people, couldn't find my luggage until I was the last person inside the airport, and all the while, I needed to use the restroom—immediately! Restrooms were always inconveniently located, and my luggage was heavy for me to lug around. Carts were available until you get to a certain area; then you cannot take them with you.

At a place where I could get a cart from a man, he said they were not available, that they were going somewhere else.

Go over there, go down there, I think it's way down that way. These sounds were in my nightmares last night.

At the airport, someone at a change window opened it up just for me to change Moroccan money to 20 euros. I got a taxi from the Málaga Airport to the hotel. I had a distance to walk again with heavy luggage, and I didn't have enough money to pay the driver. This driver had gone out of his jurisdiction to help me. It was late, and taxis were limited. I hadn't exchanged enough money.

He let me go on, anyway. He pointed out that he got as close as he could to the hotel, and I had to walk the rest of the way.

I made it to the hotel, with cramping stomach and a need for a bathroom, but the hotel was closed. I rang the bell, but no one answered. I knocked on the door; still no answer. I was past the checking-in hour.

What to do? No place to spend the night, and now it was after 11 p.m. I was miserably in pain.

I heard some voices. I walked really fast to get to the end of the street. I saw two young college students and explained my problem. They are both from Denmark and were working in Spain for one year as part of their education.

"We'll help you. I'm Rasmus, and he's Casper," Rasmus said.

We walked back to the hotel, with the young men dragging my suitcase and carrying the other bags. They called the hotel on Rasmus' phone. No answer. We rang bells, knocked on windows. No answer.

"I know where there is a hotel, and it is not expensive. If you can get in there tonight, then the next day, tomorrow morning, you can come back here," Casper said. He told me that he believed the hotel was sure to have a room.

"Where do I go to find the hotel?" I began to feel desperate.

"Come on, we'll take you there." Casper rolled my suitcase, and Rasmus took the other things. We walked to a hotel for about ten minutes, where we found a man in the reception room. He did have a vacant room. By this time, it was near midnight.

"Oh, thank you both so much. I'm so sick and need the bed. Bless you both."

"You're welcome. Happy we could help you. Maybe we'll see you around town," Rasmus said.

I praised the Lord for that bed.

This morning, I am one hour from checking out, and the big adventure is to try and find the hotel where I'm registered. They will get a piece of my mind for not opening the door after checking-in hour for someone with a reservation.

Tired, not well, frustrated, but glad I'm now on the European continent.

Found the hotel and feeling hopeful

The next day, I got a taxi and walked to the hotel, where the owner let me in.

"Why didn't anyone answer the door last night? I rang the bell and knocked on the door, and no one answered. I had a reservation."

"I got the call, but no one left a message. Had you left a message, I would have opened the door for you." Yeah, right, I said to myself.

"Well, I'm here now, and I'm sick. Do you know where I can get a doctor? I also need to refill my regular medicine."

"I have a friend who is a doctor, but he's way on the other side of town. Would you like something to eat?"

"I'm not feeling well enough to eat anything."

He called to the cook and waitress to make something bland for me to eat for breakfast. I sat in the lobby where other folks were eating. She brought me a dish of food, and I took a few bites, but I just couldn't come up with the appetite, and food just didn't look good to me. I needed a doctor.

The hotel maid was there in the lobby room and overheard my discussion with the hotel owner. She was the maid and hostess, and then she turned nurse.

"If you go down the road and across the street, you'll find a clinic. They will help you," the maid/nurse said.

I went up to my room and slept, instead. I was up every five minutes or so the rest of the day and all night long. The maid kept the wing of the hotel where I slept open, so I had the use of the bathroom without needing to share it. My stomach growled, and I would double over with pain, not to mention the need to get into the bathroom in time.

The next day, I found the clinic and explained that I needed a doctor for the stomach problem and that I also needed to get a refill for my regular prescription.

I showed the prescription to the doctor's assistant who spoke fair English. He told me they could take care of both problems and to come back a few hours later when a doctor would be there. I went back to the hotel and slept until time to go back to the clinic.

When I arrived back at the clinic, a doctor listened to my stomach and immediately agreed that I needed help. She called in the doctor's assistant and told him what to give me. I got a shot of something in my behind and some medicine after I waited in another room.

The next day. Today was the first day after the medicine treatment, and after a wakeful night, I think I'm getting better, although it is slow.

Food still doesn't look that good. From my hotel room, in a tiny alleyway, I have to walk down a wider alley and past a Moroccan restaurant to get to a main courtyard and to the clinic where I got treated. I feel sick just walking past the restaurant. Even the colors are bilious to me.

I went to the clinic again today because I had promised Dr. Slater that I'd get a health review in six months. Well, glad I didn't do that in Morocco! I got some lab work done today, and after one hour, the report was ready. Everything in that area is good.

The clinic is a hospital, as well, and they were all very kind to me. I went back to my hotel room where the lady in charge of rooms said I could wash my clothes in the washing machines that are close by, so I went to look for stores so I could purchase some soap.

Couldn't find anything, and most stores were closed, anyway, due to an impending rally against the current government. I saw groups of four and five cops walking around together.

I did find a place where I could buy some water and went back to the hotel and slept for three hours. A few hours later, there was noise outside, and I went to see what was going on. It was just a few people waving flags and signs, singing, chanting, and blowing whistles. Then it was over.

By now, I was hungry and looked for something open, but just the drinking parts of restaurants were open, with kitchens closed. However, in one place, the manager spoke a little English, and with my Spanish, I told him I just wanted something light.

"Here is something for you." He placed a small casserole of mushrooms in sherry with olive oil in front of me. I'm in olive oil country again. Ate some of it. Then he brought me liquor for free that is from the north of Spain, and placed it on the table.

"This will help you," and he pointed to my stomach. People, as I've said before, are basically kindhearted.

I hope to feel good enough tomorrow to check out my surroundings. I'm just a few footsteps away from the Picasso Museum and some impressive cathedrals.

The streets are narrow and very clean.

I hear chimes from the cathedral. Are things getting better for me?

Still trying to get back on my feet

I'm still under the weather. What an expression that is! It rained here all last night. My room is a tiny space next to a small, open courtyard. I can hear birds chattering away. One sounds like a baby crying. Another sounds like the boss of a gang crew.

I hop out of bed all night long to take care of the problem belly. The belly doesn't ache like it did, but sure wish I could limit the trips to the bathroom. My stomach growls like a family of bears having a picnic in the forest.I tried to find a restaurant this morning where I could get just rice. It didn't happen. Instead, I had chickpea soup with spinach. That was so delicious. Later, I had an urge for mashed potatoes and gravy. Didn't find that, but did find rice in a noodle restaurant.

Again, Picasso waits for me.

Picasso and grotesque exhibit

The rain in Spain fell mainly in the Picasso Museum courtyard as I ventured in to see the Picasso collection, El Factor Grotesco, which featured grotesque art in characterizations of people, either solo or in groups.

Also at the museum are the archeological findings located beneath the buildings that give evidence that the city has roots in Phoenician, Roman, and Moorish life.

The museum is only steps away from where Picasso was born and within eyesight of the cathedral of his baptism. Picasso's artwork has always fascinated me because I wondered what he was thinking when he painted people showing both the fronts and the sides of their heads with eyes off center. How could he not see that eyes are side-by-side?

His own interpretation of his art is that he wanted to shake people up and make them get out of their comfort zones.

Writer Gertrude Stein, one of his ardent supporters and a patron of his work, explained that his work might demonstrate how a baby looks at his mother. A baby will see only part of his mother at one time. He'll see one eye and perhaps her nose, and all very close. This is a summarized statement as I didn't have pen and notebook with me to get her exact quote, but it made sense to me. After I thought about what she said, I began to look at Picasso's work a bit differently.

If you close one eye, you will not see all that the other eye sees, as an example of seeing things in another way. One work that stood out for me was the *Woman With Raised Arms*. It was a painting inspired by Dora Maar, his companion (one of many throughout the years, I might add) and is made of circular motions in blues and yellows.

The museum had rooms full of Picasso collections, both from his early work and the later work, as well.

Another temporary collection made me laugh. It was all about grotesque and humorous interpretations of art. A sculpture with a few men hysterically laughing while sitting on stair steps, and with one man completely falling off the steps onto the floor with his feet up in the air, really caught my attention. I wanted in on the joke.

One that really and truly caught my attention reminds me a bit of my family reunions and our games of charades, where we make up the rules as the game goes on.

I enjoyed the time at the museum, even though I felt very weak. Luckily, I found the coffee shop that sold fresh-squeezed orange juice.

I came back to my hotel room where Monica, the woman in charge of rooms, came in with fresh sheets and pillowcases. She's a dear, sweet lady from the Czech Republic who has been in Málaga for 16 years and considers it her home.

She deserves credit for getting me back on my feet. She often looked in on me.

What I would do?

I observed humanity inside a coffee shop this morning. It was around ten a.m., close to the time the Spanish people begin to wipe their eyes, stretch their limbs, and make plans for the day. I was out on the streets early and did some major window-shopping before going into the only opened establishment I could find.

Inside were five busy men, all dressed in white shirts and black bow ties. One very loud and smiley guy waited on customers in the general area, joking and taking orders. Another was up at the bar, and one large man squeezed churros out of a machine as fast as he could. Churros are like donuts, only they are slender, and they're a hot item here. Two other guys must have been the cooks.

All five kept the place alive with their teasing each other and their talking with the customers.

A small tyke about three-years-old with wavy, brunette hair, wearing a blue raincoat and a fashionable red scarf around his sweet neck, sat at the bar with his doting grandmother. She held his glass in the palm of her hand while the little guy dunked his churros.

Two elderly couples sat in the general area drinking and eating and laughing it up with the waiter.

A beggar came in and went around the room asking for money. One of the couples was about to give him a coin when the churros man told him to get out. That seemed a bit cold, but they are an annoying bunch of people, and as long as I've been here, I've seen the same people begging.

There are also those unfortunates who at least do something—sing, play an instrument, pantomime, or get people into a discussion for a few coins.

The laughing waiter made some loud comments that I think referred to the man as a nuisance, and then he motioned toward his own pocket as if it was loaded down with coins. So, it may be a scam; who knows, and who is to judge?

I'm afraid I overdid my hunger this morning. I saw on the menu potatoes and broken eggs and ham, and after I asked what broken eggs meant and learned they were fried eggs and that they came with fried potatoes, I ordered the dish without the ham. I was disappointed, as the potatoes weren't country-fried but just plain French fries, but it was okay. When I saw the little boy dunking his churros, it made me wonder if he was drinking hot chocolate.

I waved the jolly waiter over and ordered chocolate *con leche*, thinking I'd get hot chocolate. Well, it was chocolate, all right—chocolate pudding in a cup. The first time I experienced this was years ago in Mexico, and now I know where that idea originated.

I asked for a small portion of *leche* and went about making my own hot chocolate.

I started back to the hotel, and within seconds, a downfall of rain poured out of the sky, and when I got back, I was soaked. It was time to rest, anyway.

A few hours later with dry clothes, I went out again to look for a restaurant with Wi-Fi and found the place where I was earlier in the week. The manager had given me a free drink to help my stomach, and I asked him if he remembered me. "Yes," he said and smiled.

I told him I was feeling much better.

"Did you order anything yet?"

"Yes, this." I pointed to the menu of a fruit tart.

"No, you cannot have that. That is not good for you. You need to have this." He turned to the waitress and told her to stop and wait.

"But I'm feeling better."

"No, you need this." He pointed to white rice and some kind of meat on the menu. "And, this drink—with lemon and ice."

"Okay," I said meekly. Actually, I admit to enjoying the attention.

I still wasn't too sure what I'd be served, and when he brought it to me, there were three small pieces of meat with rice.

"Oh, the rice looks good. But I don't want the meat."

"Yes, the meat is good for you. You eat the meat, too." He gave me a look that was meant to make me feel guilty about something.

I ate it and drank the drink. Both were good, and as he walked past me once in a while, he put his head down and looked sternly into my eyes like I was the child, and he, at probably 35-years-old, the parent.

Back to the hotel again to rest, and I'm so full that I hope my stomach doesn't yell out.

Now, here's what I'd do if I got stuck in a foreign country without means. I'd make a sign that said, "ASK ME ANY QUESTION FOR A COIN, AND I'LL DO MY BEST TO ANSWER IT." Then I'd try to be funny. Would this work?

Last night in the heart of Málaga

I spent all three times—morning, afternoon, and evening—on the open, broad, mall-street. In the morning, just a few restaurants were open. By noon, there were more. And as usual, the nighttime brought the hordes of people to the streets with shop doors wide open.

That's not all the night did, for it brought out the old folks, young lovers, parents, children, and solo folks like me. There were weirdos, classy-looking people, and just normal folks. There were fat people eating fat food and skinny folks smoking cigarettes.

There were the street entertainers and that included a holy-looking man. I guess he was supposed to be Jesus. He wore a long white robe, sandals, and long hair. When someone put a tip in his basket, he hugged and blessed them. It all looked so beautiful and sweet, until . . . Jesus took a break, pulled a cigarette out of his jeans pocket, the jeans that he wore under his white robe, leaned against a light pole, and lit up.

There was the couple defying gravity. While one held up the other by just a thin pole, the other sat suspended in the air. That was amazing and drew more of a crowd than Jesus.

A newspaperman was totally covered with newsprint. He simply sat on a chair that was covered with newspapers, wore a newspaper hat, and read a newspaper. I'm not sure what he read, but he was on the same page when I went back to look again. Definitely immersed in the news, this man.

The bullfighter was the funniest. He was dressed in a toreador outfit—hot pink and bright blue, with tights and a traditional red bull-fighting cape. He waited behind a sign until someone got the idea that he would begin his shtick whenever he got a tip. Since I had seen his performance earlier, I dropped a tiny coin, really unworthy of the performance, and he began to fight the bull. The bull was a tiny stuffed toy that, of course, didn't charge, which made it funnier. The toreador would stop and wait again for a tip, and he'd continue until another stop and another tip.

This amounted to my time in Málaga. I didn't get to see much, really, because of my illness. But I'm grateful for what I saw and experienced, and I'm happy I recovered.

I'm couch surfing in Switzerland.

I'm in Winterthur Seen, Switzerland, at the home of the lovely Brigit. Brigit is a college professor, bright and thoughtful and in tune with world politics. Her apartment is in a lovely, posh neighborhood, surrounded by trees and shrubs, and two- and three-story houses.

I left my hotel at 5:30 a.m. in a taxi I shared with a couple from Ireland, and then left Málaga by Vueling Airlines for Barcelona, where I spent six hours waiting for the next flight out to Zurich.

While waiting those long hours, I decided it was time to purchase another suitcase. I found a luggage store and just the perfect small suitcase. The nice salesclerk let me open it up and re-organize my belongings into the new suitcase, and she let me dump the old one with her. I originally had one suitcase, my computer bag, another large bag, my purse, and my camera. Now, I pull two suitcases behind me. I just faced it. Traveling is burdensome.

I walked up and down the airport corridors, looked at the duty free shops, and ate food and drink at various restaurants. Six hours came and went, and then it was time to board for Zurich. I hoped for a seat companion from Switzerland, so I could ask some questions. Lucky me. A nice woman and her husband sat with me and gave me encouragement about how to get where my hostess lives.

Not only that, the woman went with me and pulled one of my suitcases up and down the elevator and escalators until we finally went into a train information/ticket office where I purchased the tickets to Winterthur.

In Winterthur, I asked another lady if she would help me find out where to catch the Winterthur Seen train, and she not only helped me, she stayed with me until it was certain we were at the right station.

At Winterthur Seen, I had to catch a bus for the final destination, which would let me off at the bottom of a hill that I would need to climb to get to Brigit's place. By then it was dark.

The bus driver was a crabby kind of guy and tried to tell me something, and I still don't know what he said.

Off the bus, I wasn't sure if I was on the correct street, and therefore, I stopped at a house that had a light on in a kitchen. I knocked at the door, and a teenaged boy answered. I gave him the address, and he told me the house was further up the hill.

When I got to the top of the hill, pulling my baggage, I found the house, and Brigit wasn't there. She eventually showed up on a bicycle. She rides to work on the bicycle, and in her free time, she rides on long journeys throughout Europe.

She has four longhaired, part-Siamese cats that are guaranteed to sleep with me tonight.

Brigit had made a delicious pumpkin soup and shared several types of Swiss cheese, and I bid her good night. It was a very long day. I slept in a bed near the front door. And yes, a cat joined me there for the night.

Castle steps and one stubborn American woman

I'm in a little town in Goltweg in Switzerland. I went with my hostess on a long walk in the countryside and then to the Schloss (Castle) Kyburg.

We began our walk along trails that took us through the green countryside, fall leaves on the ground, tree limbs like arms reaching out into the space, and past a hippy-looking haven. It's a co-op farm that has a tent and a painted bus, à la the 70s. Brigit explained that it was one man's idea to purchase the property and then sell shares. The residents share in the work. I saw a huge amount of wood all chopped up and sitting like a long wall. Boy, would that have been nice in our Colorado home when we depended on wood to warm ourselves in the winters.

We came to cows grazing and a horse wearing a royal purple blanket. We saw some cute little children carrying leaves strung up on a line. Each child carried its autumn leaf treasure.

At one point, I looked up toward the hills and saw a castle.

"What is that? It looks like a castle?"

"It is. We're going there."

"What? That far?"

"Yes, it just looks far, but we'll soon walk along the river bank, and then we'll climb up to the castle."

We walked on the path along the riverbank. The water was sparkling clean, and according to Brigit, you could drink from it.

We got up to the stairs that would take us to the castle and started climbing. That took a long time, as the steps were high, and my knees had to work hard.

"Are we almost there?"

"See, that's where we want to go. Just rest whenever you want to."

I walked as far as I could go before I had to admit to needing a rest. But rest I did. It must have been 2,000 steps.

We finally got to the top and saw that the museum inside the 1500s castle was closed, so we walked a little bit around the tiny village and found a restaurant. We went in and had apple strudel topped with a delicious white sauce.

The man who waited on us wore a formal white coat of a maître d'. I believe he lives upstairs, as the building is an old home turned into a restaurant.

The original tile oven was still there against the wall with a curtain on top of it. I have read that when people baked inside ovens like this one, the tiles were warmed, which allowed children to sleep on top of the oven.

One huge advantage in Switzerland is the public transportation, and because I was tired enough not to want to walk all the way back, Brigit looked up the bus schedule on her phone, and we waited ten minutes for it. We took that bus to the Winterthur Seen station and then to Winterthur, where we did a little bit of business in the commercial area and then took a train back to the bus station and then the bus back to Brigit's home.

Brigit is a fabulous, creative cook, and she made polenta, a pumpkin stew, and a Chinese cabbage salad. I ate too much, as usual. Homemade food is a treat these days.

Now, for the difficult part. Brigit has traveled extensively and has strong opinions, most of them about how wonderful and perfect Switzerland is and how bad other countries are, especially the U.S. I learned her opinion that people in the U.S. don't know how to read maps; they are ignorant in many subjects, especially math; they don't take an interest in what's going on in the country's politics; they depend on those in power; high school education is many years behind Swiss schools; U.S. citizens are not very bright in general; U.S. people don't know anything about the world in general; the people in the States drink a lot and often get drunk; and the list went on and on the entire weekend.

She blamed the media for showing Swiss teenagers how to binge drink like American teenagers.

I finally nailed her about generalities; I didn't let her get by with it. I can handle a little bit of criticism and can even agree with some of it, but enough is enough.

I'll be in the little country of Liechtenstein tomorrow. It will be a challenge getting to the hotel I arranged through the Internet, but I'll do it. Just wait and see.

Liechtenstein

Three train changes, two bus changes, and now I'm in Liechtenstein, one of the smallest countries in the world. The train cruised quietly past rolling hills and mini-forests that were in fall splendor, and the hills got greener and greener as we got closer to Liechtenstein. All of a sudden, there they were—the snow-capped Alps.

The last bus was in Liechtenstein, and to make certain I'd get off at the right stop for the hotel I had prearranged, the driver agreed to tell me when to get off.

After climbing higher away from the capital city, Vaduz, and arriving closer to the mountains, the bus stopped, and the driver walked back to tell me it was time to exit the bus. He took my two suitcases and put them on the sidewalk. He then got back in the bus and left me standing, wondering where I'd find the hotel.

Then I saw a large yellow van that was a delivery service of some kind. The van stopped at a stop sign, and I waved a note at him, and he rolled down his window.

"Do you know where this is?"

He didn't speak English, but he knew what I wanted and told me to get in; he'd take me there. It was about 500 meters away. I wouldn't have found it by myself.

I trudged into the hotel with my suitcases. It was silent. And the restaurant inside the lobby was also silent. "Hello?" No one answered. Hmmm, wonder what I should do now.

Soon, a small man came in and found me wandering around. It turns out there are two restaurants with two hotels attached, and they are owned by the same people. He didn't speak English, but I understood he wanted me to go with him to the other hotel lobby, where he found my paperwork. I signed the papers, and then he took me to the room that was in the first building.

He told me dinner would be served in the restaurant next door around four p.m. I settled down in the room, a nice, clean place with a soft and fluffy yellow comforter and matching pillow and curtains. I took a nap and then checked out the restaurant that was slowly filling up with noisy people at the bar.

It's strange how in this German environment, I feel quite at home, even though I cannot speak the language. The waitress was dressed in a long skirt with a vest and full-sleeved blouse, which possibly looked like a version of the old costume of the village.

My hotel window looks out to a small farm with cows grazing, and I can see the other side of the mountain range. The Alps are in front of the hotel and seem to never end. There are fall colors all the way up to the snow-caps.

The dinner began with a cream and white wine soup. It was delicious. The second course was a spinach dumpling, a dish with mushrooms and pepper.

Liechtenstein should get more credit as a tourist destination.

Liechtenstein; there is something there.

What is so special about Liechtenstein? People have used this line to discourage me from going to this country.

"There isn't anything there," I've been told, and I have read such opinions in travel forums. But I'm happy to report the opposite of what some have said. This is the most beautiful country with fall colors on massive mountains that jut straight up to the sky on one side of the country, and awesome, snow-covered Alps on the other.

Today, I signed up for one more night in the hotel, as I wanted to discover more of the country. One night was not enough time. I took a bus to the Schaan Station, which is the center of one major town. I was mesmerized by what I saw—awesome, huge mountains; old and new architecture; and spotless, one-way streets that are driven on mostly by large, new cars.

I wandered around and found an old stone church and steeple, with bells beckoning me near.

It's heartwarming sometimes to experience what comes from traveling, especially when you are alone. The massive mountains that border the cities, the fall splendor, and the snow-capped Alps, and because this is all part of a German country, it put me in mind of my German father, Lawrence.

I had an overpowering feeling of his presence in the massive and powerful mountains. He was strict, to say the least, and often used the belt as a whipping tool. I believe in the child-rearing knowledge of today, which might call my father's strict actions child abuse. Because so much time has gone by and because my father became a mellow, funny, and warm man later in life, I long ago excused his style of discipline, viewing it as a part of his cultural upbringing.

But it was today in the mountains and the familiar cold, crisp air like the air I grew up in, in Colorado, that I truly experienced a feeling of forgiveness towards him.

Liechtenstein is a sandwich between Switzerland and Austria, with closer ties to Switzerland. Liechtenstein has a castle. You can climb to the top of a hill and find the dwelling of His Serene Highness Hans-Adam II, Prince of Liechtenstein. It is said the Prince is a casual guy, taking a morning jog and greeting folks. The castle has a broad view of the Rhine Valley.

Politically, Liechtenstein is an independent state. To say it enjoys a high standard of living is an understatement. I'd almost come close to calling it the Rodeo Drive of Europe. The City of Vaduz is the capital city and is the center of commerce and international banking.

"Are you here to get some of the 'black money'?" a man heading up a table of Americans during breakfast one morning asked me.

"I haven't seen any black money yet," I answered, but not really knowing what my answer should be.

He was the owner of a business and was treating his employees to a mini-vacation in Liechtenstein. Later, they whooped it up in the same restaurant.

I learned that low taxes spurred an outstanding economic growth, but banking oversight resulted in concerns about the many banks being used for money laundering and tax evasion, as well. I have also learned the days of folks bringing money-loaded suitcases to hide in Liechtenstein's banks are over.

Prosperity is evident everywhere with buildings going up and stores full of expensive goods. Liechtenstein has never been involved in a battle or a military confrontation and sees its flag as a banner of peace. There is a very low rate of unemployment in Liechtenstein, which is populated by only 35,000 people.

In my walk around Schaan, I came to a theater used for both stage plays and to show movies. There was a children's play scheduled for later in the day.

I also found a Christmas market that was held inside a city-owned cultural building and was a fundraiser for Waldorf School.

The kiosks were full of crafts, the likes of which I have not seen before—wool toys, wool fake fruit that looked real, paper lanterns, books, canned food, dried fruits, candy, and more.

One kiosk made me stop and look further. They were floral arrangements made from a paper product called paper thread. Lidwien, the artist, showed me how the product comes from Great Britain in threads that, when pulled apart, can be used to create flower petals or leaves.

"It's a lot of work," she said, and I can believe it, but they would make a great addition on a holiday table.

Tomorrow, I'll go to Ticino after I have seen the City of Vaduz.

By the way, the people are friendly, helpful, and interested in my journey. I never expect anything other than that wherever I go.

The last of Liechtenstein

The last night in Liechtenstein was a send-off with fireworks. Or at least that is what it meant to me. Birthday parties are often ended that way, I learned, so I enjoyed the display from the bedroom window.

I stayed two days in the tiny country and blew my budget until it now looks like Swiss cheese.

My hotel was in a little village of Nendeln and about a 20-minute drive to the capital city of Vaduz. That was my destination yesterday.

I realized all this time I could be getting a senior citizen discount on the bus system but didn't know how to ask for one, so I came up with, "*Ich been an alt frau*," which, in poor German says, "I'm an old lady."

The bus driver laughed and gave me the discount.

When I asked the nice lady at the hotel, Dagmar, if I could leave my luggage while I spent time in Vaduz, she agreed to give me the key to the hotel to use whenever I came back to get my belongings. The hotel would be closed at noon, and that would have only given me a couple of hours.

So off I went without my luggage to Vaduz. The first place I stopped inside the town with many banks was the Liechtenstein National Museum. It was so well-organized and interesting with commentary available in English. The docents were accommodating and plied me with free booklets about the history and the principality of the small country.

The reigning Prince Hans-Adam II lives with his family in the Vaduz Castle that sits high on a rocky terrace and is accessible on a steep path that puts you at the foot of the castle. Visitors are not allowed into the castle, but it's not unusual, I've been told, to see the royal family in the town at times.

After I toured the museum and went on further to the art museum, observing the tall granite buildings and many banks that match the towering granite peaks surrounding the country, I decided to try the path to the castle.

It was a rocky, steep road, and there wasn't any place I could use as a railing. Once in a while, a shrub on top of a wall would help me gain my balance, but other than that, I struggled up the steep road until it turned and continued on in a rocky, slippery path of fallen leaves.

"My gosh, what did I get myself into?" I stopped where a couple was taking photos and taking their time up the path.

"Yes, and we're not even there yet," the young woman said and pointed toward the top.

I struggled to keep my feet on the ground and to stay on the path, but by then my knees were about to give out. Finally, I saw the castle wall, and that gave me hope.

Meanwhile, people passed me up, and a few people were coming back down from the castle. Some smiled at my struggle.

I will not give up, I told myself. Meanwhile, I saw a road with cars driving down, and it looked as though they were driving past the castle.

"Well, now I know the Royal Family doesn't go up and down this hill," I said to the couple who now had caught up with me and was now passing me by.

I made it to the top and saw the castle with the guardhouse, and then worried about how I would get down the steep path with my weak knees.

Since cars were passing me heading down the hill, I thought it should be no problem to hitch a ride, so I stuck my thumb out and only decided that was useless when three cars stormed by.

So back on the path, I put one foot in front of another one, ever-so-slowly, so that I must have been seen to shuffle as I stepped precariously on the downhill slope with nothing to hold onto.

About halfway down, I began to realize there was no turning back, and there was not another way to get down the hill but to persevere, and that reminded me of my brother, Jack. He was a surveyor and did most of his work in the Colorado mountains, all the while suffering from years of pain from a serious, youthful bout of polio. He never gave up, and neither will I. Just then I looked down on the path and found a heart-shaped rock. Twice now this has happened on this journey of mine.

Rain!

Hello, Swiss-American folks in California's Salinas Valley. I went to Ticino in Switzerland in your honor. I got here yesterday traveling from Liechtenstein. I'm leaving tomorrow for Zurich, where I'll be for three days and then on to Frankfurt for my month in Germany.

I knew if I were to see Ticino, now would be the time, so I just went for it.

I have found the people friendly and with easy smiles, and they were happy to give a comment or two.

The down side is that I am at the end of the second day, and it has rained here both days and nights, and I have found the country extremely expensive. Today, the goal was to take the train to Bellinzona where there are three castles to tour and a lovely city to explore.

I arrived in fog, rain, and chilly air, with the first order of business to find the tourist office and then get directions on how to tour the castles. Yesterday, I did some inquiry by telephone and was told that not all castles were open, but in some, I could see the outside, and the museums would be open.

Note to the world—even with minimal employee training, please teach your employees where the tourist information office is in your town.

With trial and error, I found the tourist office, while I was dripping wet, and the nice lady gave me many brochures about the Ticino area and the castles, and she also opened up a plastic cape for me to wear while outside.

I was given directions to the first castle, after several questions, and found the "lift" that took me to the front of the building. The heavy front door itself reminded me of a fortress. The lobby was inside with a very nice lady ready to sell me a ticket to the museum. The castle itself was closed.

I declined the museum because the price would be nine francs, which meant 11 dollars in U.S. money. I found that an outrageous price for a museum, but that wasn't the last of the surprises about how much things cost.

The lady there told me how to get to another castle where I could go inside but where the museum would be closed. That sounded okay, but once I got outside, the rain came down in sheets, and by then I was tired of walking, so I regrouped inside a cafeteria. I got a cheesecake type of dessert with *cafe latte*. Boy, do they know how to make a *latte*. It's almost like soup; it's so thick with coffee and milk.

I left to find the castle, but the rain discouraged me from trying to find the street to take to get there. I asked myself how necessary it was for me to find the castle. I have seen many castles throughout my traveling life, and therefore, I just talked myself out of it. I couldn't take photos, anyway, since, when I took the camera out of the plastic bag, it immediately got wet, and since the camera already has steam trapped inside the lens, I didn't want to make it worse.

It was lunchtime, and going inside a restaurant would be a cultural experience as would viewing a castle. There was a restaurant handy, and it looked busy.

Inside, there were many tables of two people, some round tables with businessmen, and some long tables with families or shared by several people. There was a buzz in the room of people talking.

I ordered a risotto made with red wine and a bottle of sparkling water. It never arrived, and people who came in later were already leaving. A man came over to me and asked what I had ordered. It seems the kitchen somehow either forgot or just didn't get the message. Anyway, it finally appeared, and I didn't mind waiting. After all, it was a cultural experience.

When it arrived, it was a rice soup-like dish in a bowl over red wine. Interesting. I asked the waitress for *cafe latte*, and that arrived, followed by a dessert that was free since I had waited so long.

The dessert was a spaghetti-type brown noodle over a white, crunchy, sweet, divinity-tasting candy and covered with whipped cream.

Then I got the bill. The dessert and coffee were not on the bill, but here's what a bowl of rice and sparkling water cost—are you ready? Twenty-seven Swiss francs! That is equivalent to 29 U.S. dollars.

Switzerland is a beautiful country, but coming here was a decision that blew my budget way out of bounds. I will be making up for it throughout the next few weeks, beginning by staying in a hostel in Zurich tomorrow.

The villages viewed from the train window made me wish to see those areas up close, but a car would be necessary to get close to a smaller village. Some houses had vineyards attached.

The Ticino experience had pleasant moments, but the rain and expense thwarted the plan. However, I did get to understand where my friends from the Salinas Valley came from.

From Ticino to Zurich. Come along.

Go with me to Zurich from Locarno in the Ticino area of Switzerland.

I just left the hotel about two hours before I needed to catch the train for what the ticket saleslady told me would be a direct trip with no stops. First, I just got a cup of *cafe latte* and will sit for about an hour before heading up to the train station. At the train station and about 20 minutes early, the conductor helped me with my luggage.

"Is it okay if I leave it here?" I pointed right next to the seat where I will sit for a bit over three hours.

"*Sí, sí,* that's okay, *señora.*"

The train is not full. In fact, I'm the only one in this compartment. It is silent here as the train works its way away from Locarno and into the higher regions.

I look up toward the mountains in the rain and see houses way up high. Some have vineyards connected to the property, and some don't. I'm curious about those who live up so high. How do they travel back and forth in all kinds of weather? I cannot see any roads; however, I know there must be some.

It sure didn't take long for us to arrive in Bellizona, not even with the few stops we've made so far.

See the colorful large houses in Bellizona? See the castles up there in the clouds? There is a village way up there, a church, a few houses, and now a waterfall streaming down through the granite, rain-slippery rocks. Where does the water end up?

Now, we're at the stop called Biasca where I can see a huge waterfall, largest among hundreds of them along our way.

"Look at that!" A restaurant called the Colorado Cafe. I was just about ready to say this country reminds me of my homeland of Colorado, and over there is evidence that someone else thought the same.

There is a huge bridge, and I have a feeling we will be on the rail just under it. The rain makes the rocks glisten and mutes the fall colors.

At the stop called Faido, there are stone buildings and a village high on a hillside. How do people live there? I cannot get that question out of my mind.

I feel a bit let down that I couldn't spend some time in a small village and see for myself how people live. But I didn't seem to be able to connect to anyone that way. I'm not thrilled to always be in big cities, but Locarno was kind, and I'm sure Zurich will be, as well.

Doesn't it seem that every time we go through a tunnel that when we come out there is always a surprise?

Now we are near the town of Ambrio Priotti. There is more snow on the ground and covering the pine trees, and we enter another tunnel near San Gottards, then the town of Airolo. And here is the latest surprise.

It's snowing. The limbs of trees that are covered with snow make it look like fantasyland.

Everything is white as we enter the light at the beginning of the town of Göschenen. It's cloudy, and pines are white and close to the tracks.

Below is a stunning scene—white village and houses of three- and four-stories.

Many tunnels and villages we go through, and now the snow is less, and we're going lower where evidence of the rain and snow has turned the hills jewel-green.

The terrain and the houses are beginning to look a little different at the lower altitudes than they did in the higher mountains.

We're passing a beautiful lake. It is loaded with boats, and I imagine people just waiting until the snow melts so they can get back to serious sailing. As we get closer to Zurich, I hear the conversations of people turning to German sounds, and the Italian sounds have gotten fewer.

We pass charming little houses where people grow gardens that have become somewhat of a hobby, I've been told. The houses are simply sheds for tools with comfortable sitting rooms.

The Rhine River offers us an awesome view for quite a long way, and now we're in Zurich, and it's time to gather belongings and find a taxi to the hostel.

It rained the entire time I was in Ticino, and rain has greeted me here in Zurich. I counted at least ten stops along the way.

Switzerland is beautiful but far too expensive. The lady in the hostel said the standard of living is very high, and people can live on minimum wage. However, I couldn't live here on my income.

I'm punishing myself for taking the most expensive side trip I've been on since this long journey began, and now I will be in a hostel for three nights.

I got a taxi here and find the hostel in a seedy-looking neighborhood, and the receptionist informed me, "This is a party area. Oh, the area is changing a little bit. The red light district is moving down there." She pointed to the street and down a block or two.

Well, three nights, and then I'll be with relatives in Frankfurt.

Making mistakes and knowing when to cut losses

A seedy neighborhood it was. I saw ladies of the night (and day) strolling in the neighborhood in their short-shorts and high-heeled boots. I felt sorry for the life they lead and wished I could do something to help them.

The lovely receptionist, who holds dual citizenship from both Switzerland and Canada, informed me there would be a jam session in the lobby, and of course, I would be welcome. The lobby is right next to the street and the general public has access to the bar, whereas the guests have electronic keys that open the door to the front, the room wing, and the bedroom door. There is a closet where we're expected to use our own locks and keys.

The bedroom is small but holds three bunk beds, and the room is stuffy, hot, and steamy. Last night, while music was still wailing away, three of us in the steamy room went to bed, while one young lady sat on her suitcase where she had been since three p.m., surfing the web until way after midnight.

This morning, I woke up to see snow on cars and gently falling down on umbrellas, buildings, and outdoor restaurant chairs.

Switzerland is a lovely country, and the beauty will stay with me in my good travel memories. However, taking the side trip to Switzerland has been a financial mistake, and I attempted to make up for it by staying in the hostel and by watching how I spend money eating in restaurants.

Just to show you how expensive it is here, a cup of coffee will cost at least five dollars, sometimes more. You may be able to find it around four-fifty if you're lucky. Yesterday, I paid 12 dollars for a falafel sandwich that I have never paid more than four dollars for in California.

A pair of boots and a coat are things I need to purchase to make it through the winter, and just for fun, I looked at prices and was blown away.

"I will buy the same thing in Germany for half this much," I told a salesclerk. She agreed.

"A lot of people here go to Germany to shop."

Okay, enough of that, you get the idea by now.

Back to the hostel in the seedy neighborhood, the music into the night, and the steamy, stuffy room. I will cut my stay by one day. I made a reservation for a hotel near the airport and will bite the bullet and get a taxi to take me there. I won't even bother you with the amount of money that will cost. But the next day, I'll be with Juliane and Lenny and Lenny's parents in Frankfurt. I need to be at the airport by five a.m. and rested up in order to be alert when I get to Germany.

I made this decision as I walked back from the train station today. I walked there just to get an idea of what it would be like to take the train to the airport. The train information lady told me to ask at the tourist information bureau, so off I trundled down the street in the snow.

"That is way hell out of town," the information man said when I gave him the address of the hotel.

"What? It's near the airport, right?"

"Yes, it is, but the airport is far away."

"Ok, I get it. So how would I get there by train?"

He gave me the news that, first of all, it would be a ten-minute walk to the train station, then downstairs. He told me where to get off from the first train, get on a second train, and from there, walk about 20 minutes to the hotel. Dragging my luggage, I might add here.

"Or get a taxi from that stop."

On my way back through the snow, I decided to cut my losses and get a taxi tomorrow right from the hostel.

The hostel gave me 50 percent of my initial payment for one night's cancellation, which I figured was fair enough.

The lesson learned here is to do the work before venturing off to a different destination. If I had realized how expensive it is in Switzerland, I would have made other plans. I did know that Italy is the same, and that's the main reason that country is not on the list of places to see.

Sometimes, trying to cut costs actually costs more in the long run, as I have learned in two days in a steamy hostel.

Now I want to share that I came upon a good Christmas market near the train station. There was a mixture of smells—scented candles, incense, wooden items, and international food of many types. It was a pleasure to walk among the creativity that abounds in traditional Christmas markets. I will experience that soon when I meet my friend, Marilyn McCord, in Berlin on December 12.

Chapter Nine

December, 2012

Getting out of the hot house

I left the hot house yesterday morning with folks in the hostel wondering where I was going and why so fast. I couldn't wait to get out of there and into a hotel near the airport. It happened, and I was so fast that I checked into a room by 9:30 a.m., when checking-in hour was two p.m.

When I told one guy back at the hostel, a guy who seems to hang out in the bar, that I just had to leave, his comment satisfied me that I made the right decision.

"Yeah, I understand. This really isn't the right place for you." He and another guy took my luggage out to the street where I waited for the taxi.

Today, I got up at 4:45 a.m. in the hotel near the airport to get ready for the next adventure. I got a shuttle ride to the airport and got checked in with not much trouble and flew on Air Berlin to Berlin. Once there, I boarded the plane to Frankfurt, and outside the window there were great, big, fluffy snowflakes falling. The pilot told us Frankfurt was in the fog, and we would need to wait.

We left about an hour later, and when we landed, I walked as quickly as I could to see Lenny waiting for me with his dad, Wolfgang.

Now I'm in the Schaer residence in Drais, a little village, which is part of the town of Mainz in Germany.

Juliane is the grandniece of my husband, Will. I have known her from the time she was a little girl, and now she is a grown woman with a baby boy.

Juliane stayed with me ten years ago for a few months when I lived in Half Moon Bay. Later, her then-boyfriend, Lenny, joined us there.

Since then, Lenny went on to get his engineering and business management degree, and Juliane became a music teacher. They have been married for five years and are in love with their darling, beautiful, baby boy. He reminds me of a Gerber baby.

He's five-months-old and is the light in everyone's eyes. He has a fetching smile that shows off his round face, blue eyes, and sandy hair. Lenny's mother, Helga, Juliane, and I went walking, with Lenny carrying Jonathan in a backpack on his chest. It is cold, but I got the Icelandic sweater out from the bottom of one of my suitcases, and it feels just as good now as it did back in April when I was in the little village of Thorshofn, Iceland.

Winter has arrived, and soon there will be heaps of snow on the ground. On Monday, I will head to a shopping area and purchase some winter boots.

Last night in the hotel, I purged some of my summer T-shirts to make room for the winter clothing.

When I was in Macroom, Ireland (back in June, was it?), my friends there helped me put my Icelandic sweater in a plastic bag and then sucked the air out with a vacuum sweeper, and that is where it has been sitting for several months now.

My friends, Helga and Wolfgang, are amazing hosts. When Lenny, Wolfgang, and I arrived at Helga and Wolfgang's home from the airport, a beautiful decorated table with cakes and coffee and tea waited for us.

Tonight, we had a dinner using a *raclette*, a type of cooking apparatus with a hot plate on top and a lower level with a small pan that you put under the cooker with your choice of vegetables.

The table is loaded with bowls of vegetables and fruits and plates with types of cheeses and meats for your choice. You put anything you want into the small pan and let it cook there to your desired time of doneness.

After dinner, I asked questions and learned the fascinating subject of the chemistry of ink from Wolfgang, who is a chemist. It is interesting now to look at a package or a label and understand the chemistry that went into the ink that is part of the final packaging process. Now, if the engineers could just figure out how to package products so they aren't so hard to open, I'd be pleased.

A fairyland in Germany

Woke up this morning to beautiful wet snow and great big flakes falling on the village of Drais where my host and hostess, Wolfgang and Helga, live. The snow created a fairyland picture in their backyard. Lenny and Juliane, along with their baby boy, Jonathan, are visiting Drais from their home in Hanover, where we will be in a few days.

Wolfgang and Helga are amazing hosts with a beautiful breakfast table set with Christmas colors and an equally pretty table set for a coffee break. Helga, a school principal, makes everything look easy as she sails through the job of getting everything ready. Her home decorating skills would make a professional decorator envious.

Wolfgang assists her, and together, it makes me feel so well-treated and very much at home. It's been months since I enjoyed such a warm feeling. Wolfgang even took his "fix-it" skills to repair a chain I have been wearing since I began this trip, and he fixed my camera, as well.

The camera had some spots on photos, caused when the camera got wet and trapped moisture inside the protective cover and the lens. I had taken the camera to a photo shop, and they were too afraid to attempt getting the cover off, but Wolfgang found a way and then cleaned the lens, and now I have no excuse for not taking good photos.

Tonight, we all went to a Christmas market in the small town of Nieder-Olm. We saw a small community having fun in a Christmas-decorated courtyard with kiosks of food and craft items. Most of the proceeds went to local charities. There was a range of elderly people and young parents with babies in buggies.

While it was cold, the hot wine we purchased at a kiosk went down well.

Later, after looking at the kiosks, we went to a neighborhood restaurant called Nieder-Olmer Weinstube.

Wolfgang explained that the region is well-known for the vineyards and local wines, and there are many restaurants such as the one we went to that serve their own wine with meals. Some restaurants are found right in the vineyard.

We sat in a small area that was a cozy, warm corner. The ambience made me feel I was back at a time in history.

How did I get this far, people ask.

I got this far with not too many glitches along the yearlong journey, and now I'm in the eighth month. I have been on 19 different flights, eight ferries, trains, and buses (I've lost track), and how many different sleeping places—it's all lost in the span of time. People remark all the time about how difficult it must be for me to take a whole year of travel at my age. I'm somewhat of a pioneer woman, anyway. It doesn't seem unusual to me at all.

I want to mention here how time changes lives. When my great-niece, Juliane, came to visit me in Half Moon Bay ten years ago right after my husband, her great-uncle, died, she was a girl fresh out of high school, wanting to see America before deciding what she would like to pursue as a career.

We had fun together, even though I had to go to work. When my husband died, I found myself in a position where I had to get a job. We had just moved to Half Moon Bay with a plan to purchase a condo, and all that changed. Much of that money went to pay off medical expenses.

When Juliane came to visit, she was on her own during the time I worked, but we had a standing appointment every Wednesday night when I came back from work. That was the night we would sit on my king size bed, eating chocolate and watching *The Bachelor* TV show.

Now, Juliane is a music teacher on a maternity break provided by the German government, and she spends her time being a young mother. This is how time changes things; she no longer watches shows like *The Bachelor*. Now, in her spare time, which is catch-as-catch-can, she reads *Family Magazine*.

This morning, Juliane put baby Jonathan in the hands of his daddy, Lenny, and she and I went to town. The old part of Mainz was holding the annual, traditional, Christmas market, the likes of which can be seen in small towns and cities all over the country.

I was also there last night with Lenny and Helga, and it had a different atmosphere with the lights on above, highlighting the market, with the kiosks lit up, as well.

Today, lots of people were strolling in the market, often in brief moments of sunlight. There are some beautiful handmade items, which could, if I didn't have to watch my luggage weight and budget, find a corner in a suitcase.

We ended our trip to town last night in a restaurant, and today, Juliane and I had potato pancakes, a traditional and very popular snack.

Hanover neighborhood

Lenny, Juliane, little Jonathan, and I left Helga on the sidewalk bidding us good-bye, and we were off on the long ride to Hanover, where Lenny, Juliane, and Jonathan have an apartment. We arrived late, ate pizza, and then crashed for the night.

Today, I went to the local neighborhood Christmas market, with Juliane showing me the way. We stopped and had a traditional treat that Germany borrowed from the Dutch. It is a cone-shaped paper that holds French fries dripping with mayonnaise. The first time I was in Holland with Will, he introduced that snack to me. I still have a photo of us in Delft, each holding a cone of French fries with mayonnaise.

Juliane left me at the market, and I continued on with some necessity shopping. That's all I buy, although I must admit to seeing all kinds of things that would be perfect gifts for this person or that one, but all my American relatives are not expecting gifts this year. They know I love them, and that will be my gift.

The goal I had today was to find a warm coat, and what should I find? A Woolworth store! Can you imagine that the old American institution that has been closing down in the States is thriving in Hanover? I found a coat that will supply warmth throughout the winter here for the inexpensive price of 20 euros. I was so proud of myself for this important find.

Then I began looking for a bakery/coffee shop, but not outside in the market where you have to stand. My legs were asking for a place to sit. The place I found was at the intersection on the street that ends where the Christmas market begins.

I went in and ordered a waffle and coffee. The waffle came with whipped cream and hot cherries on top. I was near a window and watched people walking on the sidewalks covered with snow. Adults and children were bundled up, and the scene looked like a German Christmas card.

Then a bit of waffle didn't make it all the way down my throat, and I began to have one of my infamous coughing fits. These have happened throughout my life, and I finally figured out that if I remain calm and drink lots of water, I will be okay. But the key is to remain calm—the hardest part.

I got up from my seat and walked to where the young man who waited on me watched me coughing, and I motioned to him that I needed water. He handed me a small glass. I drank it, handed it back to him, and asked for more. Three times I drank it fast, and the coughing began to get better, but I felt I should leave because I was getting heated up. I gathered up my coat and other items, said good-bye to the young man, and regrouped outside.

In about five minutes, I was okay again, avoiding an embarrassing moment. The first time this happened, I was about ten-years-old at a piano recital. I began the coughing and couldn't stop. The piano teacher took my arms and held them up over my head. That was too much of the wrong kind of attention for a ten-year-old.

I have found that many people here assume I am German, and they are one-half correct, until I tell them I do not speak German. Most people have answered back in English.

The sun came out on my way back to Juliane and Lenny's apartment, and then I sat at the window marveling at the 1920s-style, four-story apartments across the street.

Lenny and Juliane's apartment has the traditional, big, framed windows with curtains that go to the hardwood floor and other decorative treatments that put you back in the 20s. It reminds me of classic movies of that era.

Later this afternoon, Juliane, Jonathan, and I went way upstairs to the fourth floor apartment where a two-year-old was celebrating his birthday with other toddlers and their parents. It was fun to watch the children play together and to watch how they checked each other out.

Jonathan was in toy heaven, with many toys spread out on the floor. He would crawl to one, put it in his mouth, find another one, and crawl to that one. He was the youngest in the crowd and showed a very possible, active social life in the near future.

German Christmas traditions

Christmas in Germany begins with the Advent wreath of four candles, one of which is lit on each of the four Sundays prior to Christmas. I was in Wolfgang and Helga's home on a Sunday for the lighting of the first candle. This is Saturday, and Juliane will light the second candle in her home tomorrow.

The Advent calendar is another German tradition that involves children in the festivities leading up to Christmas Day. The calendars have 24 small windows, one of which is opened on each day leading up to Christmas. A small piece of chocolate is usually hiding inside the window. Juliane made an Advent calendar of her own for Wolfgang and Helga. Her Advent calendar consisted of family photos. The backs of the photos were covered with Christmas decor, and that is what you see first. When the next day arrives, you turn the card with the design to the backside, so the family photo is displayed, and then you can take your piece of chocolate.

Another tradition happens on December 5th, when children put their clean shoes out on the doorstep with the hope that St. Nicholas will fill them with nuts, fruits, and chocolate goodies the next day. If the children have been good, they will find the sweets, but if they have been bad, they will receive only a switch.

It's also the time neighbors leave little chocolates and sweet gifts at the door, as was the case at Lenny and Juliane's place. Christmas presents are exchanged on December 6th, the same day most Christmas markets open.

Lenny told me about Christmas traditions as we sat for dinner, and then he surprised me with a gift. The gift is unusual, and I love it. It is a world map made in gold leaf. When I get home after this journey I am to scratch a tiny spot in the gold to show every place I have been.

I have walked to the local Christmas market near Juliane and Lenny's apartment, and each time, I see something different. There are kiosks with all kinds of traditional food, including *glüh-wein*, hot mulled wine, and apple cider. There are baked ginger-bread hearts, sugar-roasted almonds, crepes, cookies, stollen, and cotton candy.

I've seen a variety of candle shapes made of beeswax, wooden toys, and handmade wool scarves, hats, and mittens.

Two days ago, I stopped at an Italian restaurant because I wanted to be inside for a while. The Italian hostess was interested in my travels, and because she saw that I had my camera with me, she said she would take a photo of me. I found a bright candy kiosk, and she clicked away with me standing in front of it.

Yesterday, my niece, Maria, Juliane's mother, came to visit, along with Juliane's brother, David, and his little boy. It was a delight to see Maria as a grandmother. We all took a walk to the night Christmas market. It was alive with lots of people, old and young, greeting their neighbors and toasting to the Christmas season.

Christmas Eve is the traditional gift-giving night, where families get together to exchange gifts. On that day, I will be in Berlin with my Colorado friend, Marilyn McCord.

Celle and Hanover family

Today, we woke up to snow on the ground, and snow continued to fall for a long time.

Juliane, Lenny, Jonathan, and I were invited to the City of Celle, where Maria and Otfried had breakfast waiting for us.

Lenny drove expertly in the snow both to get out of Hanover and then on the autobahn and then in Celle, where the snow was heavy on the street, to Otfried and Maria's home. The table was loaded down with good food, and they kept bringing more food in from the kitchen.

David and his wife, Jana, and their baby, Elias, joined us for breakfast. By the time we all got ready to eat, it was around noon. We had yogurt, the best scrambled eggs I've ever tasted, all kinds of bread and rolls, jellies, jams, and then there were planks full of salmon, ham, and other types of meat, cheese of various types, and on and on . . . .

The camaraderie was fun to see in the warm family atmosphere. They got a Skype call from Otfried and Maria's son, Daniel, and his wife, Min Jie, and son, Luka, in Shanghai. Everyone had a chance to be seen and get a bit of a hello from Daniel and his wife and little boy.

Most of us then got into two cars and went to the city for Celle's Christmas market. I noticed this family's favorite place to stop was the wooden toy kiosk. They had fun trying out all the puzzles and games.

It began to rain, so it fell on top of us and on top of the snow on the ground. We headed back home but first stopped off where Maria purchased many types of cakes. Those were devoured later when everyone was home and dried out from the rain.

Yesterday, Lenny took me on a tour of Hanover. We saw the city rathaus (city hall), a park, the building Nord LB (the mother company for whom Lenny works), and a lake.

The lake has some history that involved the early days of Hitler's powerful influence before WWII. The lake, called Maschsee, was man-made by people who were out of work and given a job. Nowadays, during the summer, folks take a beautiful walk around the lake where you can see ducks, swans, geese, and many coffee shops along the way. You can swim and paddle a boat, as well. Lenny and I had cake and coffee inside a coffee shop as we watched the sun set over the frozen lake.

Later, yesterday, Juliane and her girlfriend met Maria, who came by train to the opera house in downtown Hanover where we saw a ballet. It was an avant-garde and very modern ballet. The talented dancers created a story, and they were even more adept at acrobatics and swinging on ropes with hoops.

Fifteen minutes with a baby, better than fame

It's been a long time since I took care of a small child. I almost forgot what that was like all those years ago when my sons and then grandkids were young. Those years came and went way too fast.

Today, I took care of Jonathan for 15 minutes while Juliane took her little nephew to kindergarten. He had arrived with his daddy, David, earlier in the morning.

Everything went fine while Jonathan was happy looking at the little world globe I wear around my neck. He could put his little fingers around it and put it into his mouth, where everything goes these days.

He cried a little bit, but I picked him up and went to the window to watch the snowfall. I sang, "Let it snow." He made me feel proud of my singing when he didn't cry—not even once. He actually seemed to enjoy it. He's the only one so far in the world who doesn't howl like a coyote when I sing.

He got to be too heavy while holding him. But holding him and singing to him seemed to keep him happy for quite a long time, until I had to sit down.

Fifteen minutes went by fast, and Juliane came back and took over. I must say I admire how hard she works as a young mother, as it doesn't seem easy. She packs Jonathan in a buggy and goes for walks in all kinds of weather, every day and sometimes more than once a day.

Everyone should get 15 minutes of fame, Andy Warhol once said. I got 15 minutes of caring for a baby; that's better than fame.

I'm in Berlin.

One bus, two trains, one taxi, one escalator, one elevator, a flight of steps, and here I am in Berlin! I hoisted my suitcase up the steps and wrenched my arm. Once I got up the stairs, I hailed a taxi that took me to the hotel.

Tomorrow, my friend, Marilyn McCord, will be here. She's leaving the snow in Colorado for the snow in Berlin. It's very beautiful here, and it gets dark very early. Marilyn would experience her first Christmas after her companion, Don, died. I thought visiting me in Germany would help her with her grief, and also it would be fun to experience Christmas and New Year's Eve in Berlin with her.

When I got to the hotel, I ate lunch and then took off to the town, which I learned isn't as close as the booking website would have you believe. A nice young lady told me where to get on the tram so I could do some shopping at a supermarket.

I got on the tram and asked around if anyone spoke English. One lady did, but the five or six people standing nearby wanted to get in on the explanation. I learned that I should have gotten on the back of the bus and paid for my ticket. If you don't pay, there's a chance you get dinged by the inspector who makes surprise visits and checks everyone's ticket. A big fine is levied if you can't come up with a ticket.

No inspector, and I was told by three people where to get off the tram and where the supermarket is located. When I got off the tram, I saw good old McDonald's across the street and thought I'd go see if they had free Wi-Fi there. They did.

In McDonald's, I met a lovely lady who is from Portugal. She has lived in Berlin for 18 years. She is a nurse and gave me some help about how to get the next stash of my medicines, which is something I'll need to do within the next few days.

I then went to the supermarket and found that I needed a shopping cart where you have to use a coin as a deposit, a great idea, in my opinion; keeps shopping carts from appearing all over the city. But I just picked up what I wanted and carried it all to the cashier under my arms and under my chin. I had carried a bag with me, a smart move if I do say so myself.

When I got out of the supermarket, I decided to walk back to the hotel, even though the young lady who told me how to get to the supermarket said it was too far to walk. Well, I need to keep up the exercise that I started all those months ago, so I set off down the icy sidewalk.

On the way, I came to one of those cheap stores that sells all kinds of great and cheesy stuff. I purchased a few items that will make it a little Christmassy in the room.

This morning, I left Juliane and Lenny and little Jonathan, who spoiled me royally for a bit over a week. It proved to be a great place to land for a while. They let me sleep as long as I wanted, and then all day long, I was treated in the real German, cozy tradition.

Last night, Lenny and I joined Maria and Otfried to pick up Maria and Otfried's son, Daniel, his wife, and two-year-old little boy from the Hanover train station. They came all the way from Shanghai to spend Christmas in Germany. It was quite fun to see Daniel after many years. Now he's a businessman with a beautiful wife and son. What memories we all have, and now we're making more. It was just a brief moment in time that Daniel and I got to see each other, but here's hoping they will all come to the United States someday.

The first day in Berlin—looking for technology

Woke up today refreshed and took the elevator down to the restaurant in the hotel. The breakfast buffet was over, but I didn't want that, anyway, so I ordered scrambled eggs because the guy who asked me what I wanted was eating that, and it looked good.

I wanted to use the Internet, but to pay for that seemed a bit extravagant, so instead, I purchased a day pass on the tram with the intentions of using Wi-Fi at McDonald's. Most McDonald's throughout the world offer the use of free Wi-Fi.

When inside McDonald's, I asked a worker for the password.

"You have to use a German phone number for Wi-Fi here."

"I don't have a German phone number. Can I use yours?" I asked tongue-in-cheek and with a smile.

"*Nein*," he answered seriously.

"I was kidding."

He said nothing but looked at me with a question on his face, so I asked, "Okay, then. Do you know where else I could go to use Wi-Fi?"

Another worker heard my question and thought she heard I wanted to know where to plug in my computer.

"Over there to set up." The worker went over to the electric outlet to show me where I could plug in the computer.

"Yes, I know where to plug it in. I need the password."

Soon, a manager came out, and I couldn't tell if it was a man or a woman, but again, the message was, "You must have a German telephone number."

"Yes, I know, he told me that." I pointed to the first man to give credit to him in front of his manager. "But I want to know if you know of any other coffee shops where I can use Wi-Fi."

"*Nein*," the manager said.

So much for that bit of communication, so now I'll have to find another place.

Back I went to the tram on the snow-covered, slippery street. While I walked there, I thought about my son, Brad. He seems to know how to handle situations like this. I need Wi-Fi so I can write my notes while they are still fresh and to use the Internet for research and to read my emails, but I cannot pay the huge amount of money that the hotel asks just to log on. What would Brad do, I asked myself, and then came up with a plan.

When I got back to the hotel, up to the customer counter, I asked in my nicest voice if there was a manager on duty.

"Yes," said a lady at the front desk.

"May I speak to him?"

"Yes, I'll tell him you want to see him."

A few minutes later, a nicely dressed, well-groomed, dark-haired gentleman came to where I was sitting in the lobby, told me his name, and shook my hand. I used the attitude my son would use and told him that I was a traveler and writing a book about my journey, and I use the Internet for research and also to book the next places where I will stay.

"I will be in this hotel for 21 days with a friend who will arrive this evening, and I'm finding it too costly for me to use the Wi-Fi to log onto the Internet." I thought my son would then ask him for a discount, but I braved the question and asked for the use of it free-of-charge.

"Of course. I can set it up for you so you can use it whenever you want and as often as you want. Just give me some time, and I'll get back to you."

There is a lesson here. If you find something not to your satisfaction, don't get mad; just politely ask for what you want. That is assertiveness, not aggressiveness. See, you're never too old to learn from someone younger.

Marilyn arrives.

In anticipation of Marilyn's arrival later in the evening, I decorated the coffee table and counter with the Christmas placemats and other red and green items to give a Christmas feel to the room.

Later, I was sitting on my bed, going over the notes from the previous day, when I heard someone using a key to open the door. Quicker than I could get up and head to the door, my friend Marilyn walked in with her luggage. She was a bit earlier than

I expected, so I was happy to be in the room when she arrived. She had taken a taxi from the airport right to the hotel and was bundled up in a long black and white coat. She left cold Colorado for cold Berlin.

Now, we have had dinner in the dining room, lots of conversation, and we're making plans for tomorrow.

Exploring Berlin

Marilyn and I set off for the heart of Berlin early this morning on tram number six. We walked through the slush on the sidewalk and on the way asked a young man which number would take us to Alexanderplatz, a major shopping district and also where many museums are located.

"Excuse me." I surprised Marilyn by stopping the man walking on the sidewalk toward us and asking him a question.

"Do you know what tram to take to the Alexanderplatz?" I pointed to the tram tracks.

At first, the young man said he didn't speak English, but somehow he got us to understand which tram to get on. It turned out he was correct.

Marilyn mentioned how often I get good results by stepping up to ask strangers questions.

"That never bothers me. Most people are happy to help out."

We arrived at the Galleria and did some browsing. This is a department store that I had been in with my nieces and nephews a few years back. It was one place I wanted to see again. Marilyn agreed to go with me, even though we were only going to have a look around. She purchased a black, furry hat that reminded me of Russia. It looks great on her.

We saw displays of fruits and vegetables, which included a small fruit that I had seen plopped on desserts way back when I was in Iceland, and I couldn't locate the name of it. Well, I took a photo so I could remember the name. It's a physalis. Remember that? Wasn't that back in April? Who knew I'd find it again in Berlin?

We stopped first at a coffee shop and had broccoli soup for breakfast. Yes, you read that correctly. We thought the restaurant was having a 20 percent off on soup sale, so we opted for that, and besides, it sounded healthful.

We also had coffee and ordered a second helping. When we paid, we learned that the 20 percent off was for another time. It's the language barrier again, but that is what makes traveling interesting.

We spoke to the short, husky manager who sported a handlebar mustache that I watched move up and down when he informed us that 80 percent of his business was composed of English-speaking tourists. He also said he travels all over the world and especially enjoys Thailand. After that, we walked through the Christmas market and observed kiosks of arts, crafts, food, and drinks. Later, we had *glühwein*.

We headed back to our hotel and got off near a mini-market where we found our oasis. A charming Russian girl named Ann told us about her hard-working mother who cooks fresh food and would be delighted to cook breakfast for us every day, and also lunches and dinners whenever we wanted.

Her mother, who doesn't speak English, came out to greet us. A delightful mother and daughter team with good food and close to our hotel. We purchased some food that we will warm up in a microwave and eat later.

I had mentioned that I wrenched my arm on the first day I arrived in Berlin. Marilyn has been opening the doors for me.

The Gate

Just catch a tram and go anywhere you want in Berlin. Yes, even when you get lost, if you keep trying, you'll get back home. Marilyn and I started out for the heart of Berlin after a bite to eat and some make-do coffee in the hotel. We had an idea on what tram we needed to take to the Brandenburg Gate, a well-known landmark and the remaining old entrance to the city from the 1700s. Since it was a Sunday, our mission was to get an idea for touring the city on a weekday.

We made it to the Brandenburg Gate, and it began to rain. I mind less about getting wet from rain than I do about carrying another burden, an umbrella. There is just too much to take care of while moving around as a tourist. But Marilyn opted to purchase an umbrella.

We found a restaurant where we thought we'd get a little lunch. The restaurant door was covered with a black velvet curtain. That reminded me a bit about what my husband had told me. During WWII, heavy curtains blocked out the light in buildings and homes in Holland to keep the enemy in the dark during nighttime raids.

But the gentleman was friendly and welcomed us in. As we sat in the warm restaurant, we noticed the sky became lighter as the sun gently peeked through the cloudy sky, but it was only a tease.

We left and decided the best bet on a cloudy, rainy day would be to take the hop-on-hop-off bus, my favorite way to see a city and available nearly everywhere. A charming and funny British man who has lived in Germany since the 80s was our guide. As the bus took us from the Brandenburg Gate to 20 popular Berlin sites, he gave factual information and made us laugh.

The Brandenburg Gate is located in the city center. King Frederick II of Prussia commissioned it as a sign of peace in the late 1700s. The Gate was damaged during WWII and restored in the early 2000s.

I thought people visiting the Brandenburg Gate would be quiet and respectful, and that was partly true, especially since before getting on the bus, we observed people taking part in a daily program of meditation. A few people sat in a circle quietly, while more rambunctious activity was going on around them. A mobile cart of some sort, loaded with laughing people, heading right toward me, barely missed me as I jumped out of the way after taking a photo of them. There were other people working the tourists for pay, folks standing as soldiers, one guy holding an American flag, and other street actors.

Back to the bus. We drove by the parliament building, the Berlin Wall, the house where the President of Germany lives, the exclusive shopping area where the guide said you'd need a lot of money to shop, and another Christmas market.

We took a tram back to the hotel and missed the stop, got off, and took the opposite tram back to the right stop. We found a snack shop where we purchased some take-away dinner from some delightful gentlemen who serve international food and who come from other countries, as well.

Walking over the earth

"Take that bridge over there, and walk over the earth to the subway station," said the young man who Marilyn stopped to get directions. She has been convinced that stepping up with a question works nearly every time. On the other hand, I have finally admitted to myself that Marilyn's attention to detail makes her a better navigator. I just put that into her hands. This takes competition out of the game and puts more fun into the day.

"Over the earth" was one man's way of explaining in his best English where we needed to find the next station. We were headed to a doctor's office way on the other side of Berlin so I could get the medicines I'm required to take. Every three months, I need to get another supply, and now I know the rules for purchasing medicine vary in every country. We found the doctor's office in an old building up a flight of curving stairs with a wooden banister. We waited until the room full of people was seen, and then it was my turn.

Prior to seeing the doctor, I was required to show all of my paperwork, but the doctor hadn't looked at it when I went into her office. She just listened to me, and I gave her a list of the medicine I needed, and she wrote a prescription. She apologized that I had to wait for such a long time. It didn't matter, for while we waited, the sun shone through the clouds.

Marilyn, who is expert at nearly everything, even using a chainsaw to trim away tree limbs that are dry and a fire hazard in her Vallecito, Colorado, home, got us everywhere we needed to go, and I got to look at the architecture. From the tram, we passed buildings that were older and some covered with graffiti. Some of it is quite good art, while some is strange, and other is just trash. In the case of walking around Berlin, Marilyn is always two feet ahead of me, while I try to get my legs moving at my best speed.

A guy we met yesterday is, in his own words, "a gypsy." He was looking at some photos in his camera, so when he looked up, I smiled, and he asked me how I was doing. He began to speak English. Turns out, he takes photos of folks and some videos of street musicians and puts them together on YouTube or Facebook.

"I believe that beauty isn't as important as what a person beams out. You must be full of love," he said, and we were convinced he meant it.

We had a good time walking on the earth today.

Touring historical Berlin

Marilyn and I took off toward the Brandenburg Gate for the first stop on a three-and-one-half-hour tour of historical Berlin. Historical is a misnomer, as every inch of Berlin plays a part in the remarkable history, the wars, and the recovery that created the personality of Berlin today.

Our guide, a historian and great teacher, began leading the tour when we all lined up near the Gate during a cloudy and often wet day. We saw sites that explained the events that led to wars, and the aftereffects of war, beginning with the view of the Reichstag, the German parliament building, which had been ruined during WWII but made safe in the 60s, and finally completely restored in 1999.

There were many sites along the way. Some just took my breath away when I learned of their significance. One was the Holocaust Memorial, the name of which is really more appropriately called, "The Memorial to the Murdered Jews of Europe." The artist who designed it never felt a reason to explain his motivation, but to leave it to each person's interpretation.

Our guide told us that you could walk through the memorial, see someone turn a corner, and never see them again. The concrete boxes vary in height, and the pathways are narrow for one person. The path rises and falls. I felt a quiet, respectful silence as I wound around the path within the walls of the structures.

After experiencing the memorial, the guide told us to compare the memorial structure with what she was about to show us. We walked about a block away to where we stood on what was just a simple parking lot covered with weeds, surrounded by apartment buildings. That insignificant space was made as it is by design, for under it was the final bunker where Hitler and his girlfriend-turned-wife, Eva Braun, took their lives when they knew he had lost the war. The German government didn't want to create anything that would be construed as a shrine to Hitler, so they left it as is, with no access to whatever is left of the underground bunker, if anything.

The tour took us throughout the scene of early wars up to the wall that had been created to separate East Berlin from Western Germany, and we saw a portion of the original wall. Many people braved the almost impossible escape to West Germany, and while some were successful, many people perished trying. It stands as a reminder of the times.

Ana's Place and angel wings

The sidewalks were slippery with freshly frozen ice yesterday, so I walked slowly to the restaurant/mini market that Marilyn and I call "Ana's Place."

That was yesterday, while I stayed close to the hotel and Marilyn went by train for a tour of the Sachsenhausen, a concentration camp, now turned memorial.

Marilyn and I dubbed the tiny restaurant and market "Ana's Place" from the first time we stepped inside. A beautiful 20-something woman named Ana waited on us. Her smooth complexion was as flawless as her English skill. Her parents came to Germany from Russia 20 years ago.

"My mother is a great cook. She uses everything fresh and can cook Russian food or anything you'd like." She went further and told us if we ordered something ahead of time she would have it ready for us.

Ana told us this the first day we met her, but it never worked out for lunch or dinner because of the schedule we had. However, we did go back a few times and had her make breakfast for us. We have not seen Ana since the first day, but it remains "Ana's Place."

Yesterday, I went back alone, and found Ana's 15-year-old sister there. She was the interpreter for her parents. I ordered an omelet and talked a bit to her. Ana attends college, so she was always gone by the time we got there for breakfast.

On the way back, I kept telling myself, "I will not fall." I walked wherever I saw snow; others had found the same place as footprints marked the way, until . . . .

There was only ice on the parking lot, and it had a slight slope. How am I going to get down there to the sidewalk covered with snow without falling? I looked around and saw nothing to hold onto, and there was no other way but to head down the icy slope. So I began, one tiny step at a time.

All of a sudden, I found a huge, gloved hand reach toward me. I grabbed the hand and looked up to see a man. He just came from nowhere and helped me down to the snow where I continued on back to the hotel.

I thanked him. He didn't say anything. He just kept walking. Were those angel wings I saw on him or just my imagination?

War museum and Christmas

War. I'm not crazy about dwelling on the history of war or the memorials and artifacts about it, but what are you going to do when, from the beginning of recorded history, humans have been warring?

Marilyn and I weaved in and around the German Historical Museum, each of us carrying a device that interpreted, in English, paintings, artifacts, philosophies, and changing times beginning in 100 B.C. and continuing to 1994. It was just before the exhibition of WWII when we decided to take leave of the museum and go to dinner. Dinner, by the way, was at Einstein's Restaurant. Marilyn questioned if the restaurant chose that name for the genius, or did they just think their food was genius?

But back to the museum. We saw the early cultures beginning around 100 B.C. and up to the Middle Ages when Europe was reaching consolidation with the emperor Charlemagne in the year 800.

Onward, now, to the Thirty Years' War. It was during this time, we learned through the paintings about the teachings of Luther, that the religious brought peace with the Reformation. But differences and political conflicts later led to the war from 1618 until 1648. Nothing new today; we're still fighting over religious beliefs.

Moving quickly from there, not to bore you with details, but there was the French Revolution and then the German Empire and then WWI.

One item I found most interesting in that section was the portrait of a tall warrior who, at six-foot-ten, traveled across

Europe to find other soldiers just as tall as he to form a group of similar stature. Imagine recruitment today based on the requirement that soldiers must be as tall as their leader.

Speaking of the differences between now and then, I observed a photo of a pair of shoes worn by another warrior, with bows on his toes. The shoes were narrow, but squared off like ballet shoes and enhanced with a satin bow.

The portrait of Napoleon really told of his conceit; he liked his portrait so much that he had copies made and gifted them to special people.

The museum was beautifully arranged, and the notes were easy to read. Both Marilyn and I wondered about the empty spaces where pictures were previously hanging but taken down for some reason.

Today, we noticed there wasn't a snowflake anywhere to be seen. The sidewalks and streets were dry, with a once-in-a-while short shower. Aside from that, the air was brisk, but the sun shone through the clouds. Businesses were closed, making us wonder if December 26th wasn't part of the Christmas business holiday. However, restaurants and the Christmas markets were open, and there were many people walking around.

Last evening, which was Christmas Day, we went to the opera. *La Boehme* was sung in Italian with German libretto. Both of us knew the story, so we could follow it, even in different languages, and then we could pay closer attention to the beautiful music.

The Christmas holiday is over, and we're looking forward to New Year's Eve at the Brandenburg Gate. Marilyn is still doing a great job as navigator getting us on trams, trains, and buses.

Well, hello, Dali. You're lookin' swell, Dali.

"The difference between a mad man and me is that I'm not mad." So states artist Salvador Dali on a sign near the way out of the Dali Gallery/Museum in the Potsdam area of Berlin.

Marilyn and I had a day of art appreciation. We went first to the Guggenheim Museum for the "Visions of Modernity" exhibit that featured the art of masters. My favorites were a Paul Cezanne still life and one of the earlier works of Vincent Van Gogh.

You never know whom you can meet in this world. I recognized a woman using a vehicle to tour the museum as a person I saw yesterday in another museum. When she got closer, I told her I had seen her before. I learned she and her husband had been in most of the Berlin Museums, and they are from Utrecht, Holland. I told her one of my favorite artists is Van Gogh.

"I am the last surviving relative of his. His father's brother is my great-grandfather."

"What?" I almost shouted. "Shhh." She put her finger to her lips, as she didn't want others to hear.

While it was exciting for me to meet a Van Gogh relative, it didn't compare with the next large, surrealist painter's gallery, for Dali's works seem to take you inside his brain, and that's not speaking out of turn. A sign on the top of the gallery states, "Come with me inside my brain."

When looking at Dali's sketches, paintings, sculptures, and even some films he produced, you feel like you are experiencing his dreams and quite a few nightmares.

There are some patterns in his work. Take, for instance, the use of butterflies used in bizarre places. Then there is his own look—startling, rolling eyes; long handlebar mustache; black hair; and an almost handsome look—if only he'd try.

The walls on two floors were full of his work, and it takes a lot of time to carefully see inside each picture, as there are obscured sketches inside many of his main pictures.

It was a great escape into the mind of a man who is mad, but not mad.

Heading to one of the museums led us past the Soviet Embassy in Berlin that stretches nearly a whole block. During a tour, a bus guide joked about that when he said, "Here is the Soviet Embassy, here is the Soviet Embassy, here is the Soviet Embassy," and on and on until the end of the block. Guess the Soviets want a large presence in Berlin.

Not too far away, the United States Embassy has an American flag on the side of a modest, clean-lined building. That building is fairly new, and the old embassy building, now vacant, sits unused on another block nearby.

Before leaving the Potsdam area, we found an Asian restaurant. We were talking about asking for an English menu, when two lovely Australian women heard us and handed us their menus. We spoke a bit to them and learned that they both are on thresholds of change. One was a journalist, and because of the changes she is experiencing with newspaper work, she quit and looked for something a bit different. She said reporters were required to write lots of crime stories and gossip. She agreed with me that writing copy for the advertising department was not right for a reporter to be asked to do. I added, "Yeah, especially when we do the work and don't get the commission."

The other lady was in the field of medicine and was also looking for something different and even thinking about going back to school.

It was a nice day with clouds parting to expose lots of blue.

Cross over with the green man.

It's funny how little things will capture my attention. Here's an example of that. The green and red stoplights for pedestrians seem to tickle my fancy.

I call out, "Green Man" when the green light, a stick-figure man, gives us permission to cross the street. The red man doesn't get my attention, for all he does is make us stand and wait. I remember the last time I was here in Berlin, and that green man stick figure caught my attention then, too. Now I have discovered that I'm not the only one who likes the little green man. Marilyn and I found a complete store dedicated to him. In the store there are bags, cups, purses, T-shirts, sweatshirts, shorts, and more with the green man logo.

It was also a surprise to be sitting in the hotel lobby and to look at the Christmas decorations inside the moving door. There, I found that the red and green stoplight was used as decor, along with Santa Claus. So there! I'm not the only person infatuated with the green man.

While on the subject of observations, I have noticed that smokers are not allowed to smoke inside restaurants, but most have designated places outdoors. Because it's cold outside for those who want a smoke, many restaurants provide chairs with blankets. It's not uncommon to see a man smoking his cigar while all bundled up in a blanket outside.

The riches of Potsdam

Marilyn and I met up with Paul near the Brandenburg Gate. Paul was the guide we had on a previous tour, and it was good to see he would be guiding us again on the "City of Emperors," a Potsdam tour. He is a 30ish man, well-studied on the history of Prussia and Germany, and he is a great storyteller. He has a way of entertaining the crowd with facts.

I have previously written about the Brandenburg Gate where tours begin but thought it worthy to mention it again. It was built in 1791, and is one of 17 gates in the Berlin city wall, preserved from the beginning as a gateway into Prussia's most important city. It was built with King Friedrich Wilhelm's spec-ifications—20 reliefs. When, in 1806, Napoleon marched into the city, he took off with the group of figures. A statue returned in 1814, and was transformed by famous architect Karl Friedrich Schinkel into the goddess of victory. On the tour yesterday, we saw another gate that is adorned with gold filigree.

It was a five-hour, six-mile tour, not counting up and down stairs. It took us by tram, bus, and train throughout the Potsdam region where the history lesson we received began.

In the beginning of the tour, with a pain pill, I kept up with the crowd, but as time went on, my position was usually as the caboose. At various times throughout the tour, different people would walk with me, including a woman from Australia, two men from India, and another woman, also from India.

When we got to the King Friedrich II's Schloss Sanssouci Palace in Potsdam, built in 1747, Paul suggested that since there were no railings, he would be happy to lend me his arm to get me to the top of the 100 steps. This is the second time in my life I had to walk those steps. However, the time before was several years ago, and it was my nephew, Andy, who assisted me, but that time it was down the stairs.

Across from Sanssouci is another palace we saw up close, and we learned that this one was also built by King Frederick the Great, and, as was typical for most royalty in those years, it was built to show his wealth.

Frederick the Great built the palace 20 years after Sanssouci, and the new palace was much grander with over 200 rooms. It is a white elephant, in my opinion. By the way, Sanssouci means "without worry."

The interesting thing about the palace is that it was never used. One of the young men from India and I were discussing what should have been done with such an expansive building. I suggested it could be used as a hotel with the proceeds going to charity.

The young man is a master of business administration candidate from a school in Berlin, and he thought my idea was a good one. The building has stood unused for years. We both agreed it was wasteful.

Marilyn reminded me of another unused building—the old U.S. Embassy nearby the embassy row of other embassies, including the new U.S Embassy.

While at Potsdam, we came within view of other palaces, a Chinese teahouse, a Dutch windmill, parks, and lakes.

On the tour, and still in Potsdam, we stopped and took a break within the Dutch area. With buildings of bell and stair-step facades, it was easy to see the Dutch influence.

Today is New Year's Eve, and we'll be back at the Brandenburg Gate where, it is said, all hell will break out.

Chapter Ten

January, 2013

Bombs fell from the sky.

It sounded like bombs, but the magenta, purple, electric blue, white, and gold that splayed close, very close, over our heads were fireworks. They began early on the day of New Year's Eve and could still be heard on into the early morning hours.

I had heard that bringing in the new year at the Brandenburg Gate would be memorable, and so that's where we headed on the tram around ten p.m. Someone told us there would be a band to entertain the crowd. We assumed there would be kiosks with good food and maybe the traditional holiday *glühwein*.

"You want to go to the Brandenburg Gate for New Year's Eve? I would never do that. The crowds are huge and unruly," a young woman told me when I stopped her for directions. Even that didn't impede our progress. Our aim was the Brandenburg Gate, and so, there we stood in back of the roped-off street, about two blocks from the Gate, in about the third layer of people.

We stared at the Gate waiting for the big event. No event. Instead, we were jostled a little at first, while people tried to get up as close as we were. I held my position by holding a wide stance, and I kept my elbows out to mark my space. People kept coming, even though there was no space for even one person, like the old contest—how many people can fit into a Volkswagen?

A group of tall, German-speaking young men with bellies full of booze became aggressive. I began to wonder if this was a safe place for us. However, I felt brave and adventurous, as always. Marilyn was trying to hold her position, as well.

Soon, an older man, probably my age, pressed himself in back of me, too close for even the excuse of an unruly crowd. I pushed him back and turned to give him a dirty look. He said something in German with an aggressive voice. I wanted to tell him that we got there an hour earlier than he did, and we staked out our space. He continued to press himself in back of me, and at the same time, the crowd began moving as one. I alternated between moving a bit forward, and pushing him back. That didn't thwart him.

The crowd continued to move as one, as each person tried valiantly to hold their position.

Well, life isn't fair all the time, and I began to feel that we were in a bit of a quandary. Oh, heck, we were not in a quandary—it was downright dangerous.

"Do you want to get out of here?" I asked Marilyn.

"Yes, let's go."

Getting out was the same experience faced by those who wanted in. We jostled, got jostled, pushed, shoved, and found a tiny clearing where we stopped to regroup.

Suddenly, a man fell to the ground, and people formed a circle around him. Eventually, the police came, and about that time, we decided to venture on further away from the scene.

Fireworks that had begun an hour earlier continued to fall over our heads. The noise sounded like war.

We struggled to where we remembered seeing a space that had been clear. But the crowd again began to move together in collective behavior.

"That place is blocked off. You can't go there," a woman who struggled, moving her arms around above her head like she was swimming and in the process of drowning, tried to warn everyone.

I got the message, and we continued on to the place that was clear. A policeman, not just the local *Polizie* but one with fatigues and a French beret, told us, "You must leave this area; it must be clear." We continued on and around to where we had a little view of the Gate and to where we were in proximity to a man from Brazil and his two daughters.

"It's better to stand here," he said. "The fireworks can't hit us here." He pointed to the fact we were in a covered area, and the fireworks were close by.

He even helped us move to where we had a tiny view of the crane, which he thought he had heard would be the focal point for the counting down of the time. All kinds of languages were being thrown around. That didn't help in the confusion.

Nothing fell from the crane. Fireworks resumed, and soon it was the year 2013.

Being there on New Year's Eve was something I yearned to do, and while I got right in the middle of the action, I wouldn't do it again.

We talked about the event later and decided that just having people show up at the Gate was the program, as nothing else seemed to be happening. Welcoming 2013 was a wild ride.

Here's the headline I imagined—"Two American seventy-year-old women survived New Year's Eve at the Brandenburg Gate."

Pig-tailed, snortin' pumpkin, and fears of deportation

A pig-tailed, snorting, snoring, pumpkin sat next to me inside the tight, six-seat train compartment on the way from Berlin to Prague in the Czech Republic. It was a belly-bulging man wearing a bright orange sweater. His sparse hair was secured with a rubber band. I never got to know him; he slept for four hours. The other four people kept to themselves, reading or looking out the window, being sure not to have any eye contact with me.

It's the strangest human trait. I've asked it before. Why don't humans interact when we are sitting practically knee-to-knee in a cramped place, or when we're in a tiny elevator close enough to rub noses.

I usually break the spell because I have a feeling other people feel the same way. I did break the ice a bit and discovered that three of the others were two sisters and a brother on their way to explore Prague. One young lady got off the train in Dresden, Germany, and in her place a man got on and looked around, being careful not to meet anyone's eyes.

I got up and explored the restaurant car and met Nicky, a young woman on vacation from an intern position in London. She was with her friend, Julianna. Nicky and I discovered we were going to the same hostel, and we got off the train and walked to the hostel together. They were patient with me. We passed customs agents looking past us, not threatening-looking, which gave me a measure of peace, and I'll explain why a bit later.

Now I'm sitting here on the bed looking out at a beautiful apartment building across the narrow street. I'm in a hostel called Fusion. I thought that sounded a bit like disco dancing.

The man who got me settled in is a funny and gregarious guy. I know I'll have some fun with him. It's so nice to come across someone who has an easy laugh and doesn't take everything so seriously.

After getting settled in the room, I explored the city a bit, walking around a few blocks. I came across a window museum of various historical decorating items including furniture, radios, typewriters, lamps, etc. It was interesting to see many items I remember from the 50s, 60s, and 70s.

I found a Christmas market that sold hand-crafted items as in the Christmas markets in Germany, but they are different here since they reflect the Czech culture. Painted eggs, linen objects, and toys are examples.

I saw evidence that America has made inroads into Prague with McDonald's, TGI Fridays, and many other brand names, as well. In a day or so, I'll make some trips to visit the beautiful architecture. This is mainly what I have wanted to see.

The day before yesterday, Marilyn and I saw the temporary display of Prussian architect, Karl Friedrich Schinkel, in Berlin. We both admired his designs in many of the buildings we had seen in that city. Schinkel's exhibit showed his versatility and artistic gifts in not only architecture but in stage design, furniture, candelabras, chandeliers, glass objects, frames, and paintings. Queen Louise of Prussia, the wife of King Friedrich Wilhelm III, commissioned Schinkel to re-design her sleeping chamber (notice it isn't called a bedroom). He used a feminine color scheme of pink, light green, and silver. He said silver was feminine, and gold was masculine. I must remember that, but it won't matter that much because I prefer gold.

The world lost a great artist when Schinkel died October 9, 1841. He had a God-given talent. The impressive collection in the museum had three floors of rooms dedicated to his work.

This morning, Marilyn left for Colorado when I left for Prague. She was working out the details of the last leg from Denver to Durango and learned that her flight was cancelled. I will wait and hear how she got back. We had a great time touring and learning all about Berlin.

I need to back up a bit and explain the Schengen rules that are incorporated in nearly every European country. The rules state that a foreigner, let's say a visitor from the United States, cannot stay longer than 90 days without a visa in any of the Schengen-ruled countries. This means you must leave after a 90-day stay in any one of those countries or even if you move around in several of them, and then you must stay out for 90 days before you can enter back into the Schengen countries.

I discovered in Hanover that as of December 26, I would be over my 90 days. So I attempted to rectify that situation. I wasn't successful in obtaining a German visa and was afraid I'd get deported or fined.

Before I left the U.S., I wrote to the German Embassy and asked if I could get a visa to travel within the Schengen countries, and a person answered, saying yes, I could get a visa when I got to the country. As a matter of fact, I was told Germany is the only country where a U.S. citizen could get a visa outside of the U.S., so that's what I planned to do. I was told a website was available for the paperwork needed to arrange a visa.

When I arrived in Germany, I had a nephew witness and sign the papers, and I provided everything required—insurance, financial records, copy of passport, photo, etc.

I took the papers to the Aegidientorplatz and was directed to the second floor, room two. The gentleman looked at my paperwork and asked why I wanted to move to Germany and how long I had lived in Germany.

I told him I did not want to live in Germany; I only wanted to get a visa so I could stay longer than the 90 days, Schengen rules.

He told me that a visa was not necessary to stay in Germany. He got up and walked across the hall and went into another room. He left me sitting outside of the offices, worrying that I had given him too much information, and a few minutes later, he came back and asked me to go into his office. He didn't offer me a seat but just reconfirmed that I did not need a visa. I felt a need to explain the Schengen rules to him, as he didn't seem to be aware of them. This was an office for foreigners seeking permanent residence, I learned from talking with folks where I waited.

I contacted the American Embassy online, as the gentleman suggested, and got a flashing red note that they would not answer questions concerning a German visa.

A relative contacted the German Embassy and was told that I should contact the German police and then show a ticket that would demonstrate I'd leave at the proper date, out of Germany to the U.S. This is not what I was told originally, and it was not what I wanted to do. I didn't want to leave Germany for the U.S. just then. I had other pastures to roam.

When I was in Iceland, two customs agents, both of whom work in the Dresden station, stayed in the same hotel, and when I asked them about staying longer in the Schengen countries, especially in Germany and Holland, they told me all I needed to do was ask for an extension.

I've been given much conflicting information. I'm now over the allotted time of the Schengen rules but have not yet been questioned by customs officials. This was one reason I was concerned about going to Prague. I will be using only land transportation until I depart from Holland, and flying out of there will be my biggest worry.

The reason I went to Great Britain when I did was to spend the 90 days out of the Schengen area after being in them for the 90-day duration, in order to go back in. Great Britain does not participate in the Schengen rules.

I want to continue on into the Czech Republic and Holland before leaving the Schengen countries. I continue to be a bit worried that I'll be deported and given a fine.

Most tourists to Europe are not aware of the stringent rules because they do not stay over the 90-day allotment. However, I learned the rules are enforced when I spoke to one person who told me, while he waited in line to go through customs, one person he had been talking to about the rules was afraid because he had overstayed. His fear was substantiated when he was pulled away and taken to a holding area.

This same gentleman, himself, had a similar experience. He was taken out of line on another occasion because he was traveling throughout Europe without a visa. He explained that he understood he had followed the rules because he spent 90 days in Great Britain. It was in Great Britain where he was detained for a few hours.

I feel unsettled about continuing on throughout my journey, and as I said, will travel only by land until I leave Holland.

Walking in wonderland

Prague is an open-air museum and art gallery, for everywhere you look, you'll find art, either in sculpture, building filigree, architecture, painting, music, crafts, or dance. There is so much to see that my camera has become part of my body.

There is something to see everywhere. I look up to the top of buildings and find a row of sculptures. I see rows of buildings painted in pastel colors. It's an amazing city full of wonder. Could there be anything to miss if I didn't go on a tour of some sort?

After spending a good part of the day just walking, resting on benches, and eating my lunch on one of those benches, I just couldn't imagine there could be anything I missed.

However, I have opted for two events. One will be a tour on a boat with a dinner in a medieval restaurant, and the other is a walk through the Jewish sector of town, the old and new part of town, and the castle.

Today, while mesmerized by the beauty, I came across a theater where *Swan Lake* ballet is now playing, and I couldn't pass that up, so that will be tomorrow night.

I found some street musicians playing big band music and one thundering drummer using a steel circular object that looked like a hubcap.

I'm pacing myself and probably will miss a lot, but what I'm seeing will be memorable. I'm so fortunate that Lenny and Juliane helped me get to this place. Thank you!

Wow! Prague!

I can't get enough of the buildings and the sculptures. It's just an amazing city full of history and intrigue.

I think the metronome on top of a hill is a statement to the tenacity of the Czech Republic. The metronome replaces the world's largest statue of Stalin, which was destroyed by a bomb in 1962, when the Communist regime was weakening.

Our guide for the six-hour, all-inclusive tour I decided to join said the metronome demonstrates the changes in the Czech Republic, including WWII, then Communism, and then finally its own republic.

Stalin's statue has its own tragic story. The sculptor, Otakar Švec, was under pressure from the government and secret police. He received hate mail from Czech citizens regarding the statue and committed suicide before it was unveiled. It was the Communist party that began the process of de-Stalinization, and it was the new party organization that took the statue down with explosives.

The six-hour tour left me with tired, aching knees after going up and down stairs and hanging onto railings with an occasional helping hand. But the tour wasn't one I'd want to leave out of my itinerary. Our tour guide had an education of Prague with information we might not have learned on our own.

We saw the Prague Castle where I shot a video of the changing of the guards, which had a humorous moment. The guard replacing the one going off duty was caught looking around at the pretty girls who were standing around taking it all in. He stood stiff and still except for the roving eyes.

We saw the St. Vitus Cathedral; a breathtaking viewpoint of the city; St. Nicholas Church; Charles Bridge; astronomical clock; Jewish town with Pinkas, Maisel, and Spanish Synagogues; the cemetery; town hall; and inside the Jewish center.

We arrived in time to see the action on the famous Astronomical Clock when it changed hours, as it has for centuries.

St. Vitus Cathedral was built in 1344, and is the burial place of royalty from throughout the centuries. It's gothic, grand, and opulent.

Our guide said all the gold that is seen on statues and buildings is pure 24-carat gold. Large domes and splashes of gold can be seen all over the city, especially in the old town.

Moe, Joe, and Wonder Woman

After a remarkable few days in Prague, I left this morning by Moe and Joe (left foot, right foot), dragging two suitcases behind me.

"It's a short walk. Just go that way and take the lift to the train, and then go to the bus station." Those were the vague directions on how to get to the bus stop for the long trip to Heidelberg, Germany.

Three information centers were closed in the train station. I asked several people for directions to the bus station, and no one seemed to know it was right up the escalator on the other side of the room.

One guy said he'd help me if I'd give him some money. Another one said the information booths were closed because it was Christmas, and still others had no clue.

"It's right up there," a woman traveler chuckled and pointed to the escalator.

I got inside the 20s art deco-style building that had a high dome with paint falling off the walls. It reminded me of an aging movie star. I found a door that said something like a waiting room, and there I found a woman eating at her desk in front of a computer. The rest of the room had some dirty blue chairs, two coat racks, and a fire extinguisher. The filthy carpet reminded me of my *Soledad Bee* office. I waited there until it was time to catch the bus. She was generous in loaning me a warm place to sit until it was time to leave. I felt more secure being inside the station, not outside where I'd be questioned by security folks. I am convinced that because of my age and looks, I do not appear threatening or like someone who is trying to take advantage of the government.

I was lucky to meet two young women on the bus. Lauren is from Australia and had worked for a world health organization. Her contract was up, and while waiting for another one, she took some time off to travel.

The other lady, Helene Goarzin from France, was doing some preparation for her master's degree in U.S. history. This interesting young lady's emphasis in history is the 50s and early 60s racial climate in the U.S. and also the early women's movement.

I dubbed her Wonder Woman because for our last train change, we had only three minutes to get from one platform to the next, and we worried about that for six hours from the bus, to a train, and to another train.

When we got there, Helene simply picked up her stuffed bag, slung it over her shoulders, and grabbed my suitcases under both her arms and ran like heck to catch the train. I ran as quickly as I could and hopped on behind her.

I don't know if I would have caught the train on time without her. We said good-bye after an eight-hour day.

I wanted to get to Heidelberg on time because my friend, Nathalie Ebikeme, would meet me. She was there, and together we got on another train and then walked a few blocks to her house. Nathalie prepared a great dinner enjoyed by her sons, Pascal and Demsay, and myself.

I met Nathalie and Demsay in Iceland earlier this year. They were staying in the same hostel as I, and we became friends—just like that. She suffered through the British bad boys who were on a weekend bender celebrating a wedding of one of them.

Nathalie is a wonderful cook. We had a smooth pumpkin soup with a salad of tiny leaves she purchased fresh from a farmer in town. I will be here for a few days. Nathalie is a couch surfing regular, and I learned all about that from her.

Bubble hogs

Today, Nathalie made spaghetti and field salad. I've never tasted spaghetti that delicious before. She has a way with spices. The field salad is a cluster of small leaves on a stalk. The leaves are round or oval. Delicious with the dressing she decorated it with.

Together, we went to a spa that has four pools, two indoor and two outdoor. One indoor pool has salt water and is alleged to be good for your skin.

I chose the indoor pool and positioned myself so the water would go clear up to my neck. That was not always easy. I had to try not to float away.

The spa pool reminded me of the movie, *Cocoon*, wherein seniors get into the pool and get younger and younger. There I was in a pool with mostly white-haired people of all shapes and sizes, each vying for a space to soak in the water and rejuvenate.

There were occasional jets that created bubbles in different parts of the pool. Those special sections were taken over by bubble hogs. When the jets stopped in one area, they began in another. The hogs waited for the jets to begin again in the space where they stood for a very long time.

I admit to being a bubble hog, as well. My arm and legs hurt, and so I found a jet and claimed it to be mine, and I worked my body so that the jets worked over my sore parts. Nathalie and I soaked in the pool for a bit over two hours until we decided we were renewed in body and spirit.

I feel so much at home and so taken care of. Nathalie is a fabulous hostess, and I feel that I'm getting rested up after so much moving around.

Queen for a day and more

Nathalie Ebikeme treats me like a queen in her Mingolsheim, Germany, home. Last night, she noticed I was tired and that I had a sore arm, so she set me down on her couch, put a hot lamp on my arm, and served me French cheese and champagne. Could it get better than that?

Earlier yesterday, we went to her parents' home in Honau and had a delicious dinner cooked by Nathalie's mother, Marliese. Now I know where Nathalie got her cooking skills.

Francis, Nathalie's father, is a down-to-earth guy and a delightful Frenchman. He spent ten years in French-speaking Morocco in the city of Marrakech, where his father taught school. He goes back to Morocco on occasion, and sometimes with Nathalie. They are planning a trip there soon.

I told Francis that with the striped sweater he wore, all he needed to complete the French look was a beret. With that suggestion, he left the room and came back with the beret. He grabbed a bottle of wine and a loaf of French bread, and there he was, the complete Frenchman.

He and Nathalie showed me the Moroccan room in their basement. It looked just as I remembered from my time in Morocco—a place to sit with cushions and a filmy net hanging from the ceiling to the floor, where you would rest inside. There were some original remembrances from Francis' father's life in Morocco hanging on the wall and on a long table that is used for Moroccan dinner parties.

On the way to Marliese and Francis' home, we drove through some charming villages, including Rheinbischofsheim, where Nathalie went to school when she was aged ten to fifteen, and Diersheim, where she went to school at the ages of seven to ten.

After eating a wonderful dinner, we left Marliese and Francis and headed to Strasbourg, France, which was only about an hour away from the border with Germany.

We looked around the town and saw the typical old architecture, including the oldest restaurant, Maison Kammerzell, that dates back to the 1400s. Well, I couldn't just stand there and look at it. I needed to go inside.

We went into the newer coffee shop section, and both of us had a cappuccino. After that, we walked up the winding wooden stairs that had a heavy wooden rail, to the third floor that was all set for formal dining.

I can never help but think what it must have been like in the 1400s to climb those steps for a get-together with friends in one of the rooms. Imagine women in long dresses and tall hats, men in long overcoats and probably tall hats, as well. This restaurant was for the upper class. Well, Nathalie and I were upper class for that moment, we told ourselves.

Handball and other action

What a day!

It started with my feeling better today. Then Nathalie and I took Demsay to catch a ride to where his team would play handball. Demsay is the goalkeeper. I think the goalkeeper must be a contortionist to reach the ball, all the while not knowing where it's going to wind up.

It was an exciting game, and I understand it is one of the fastest sports. Really quick action is needed to succeed in handball.

One of the parents on the team where I sat beat a drum, and the other parents clapped in rhythm during the game. The other team's parents sat stoically in their seats.

Demsay's team is ranked fourth in the section, while the team they played is ranked number one. Demsay's team did remarkably well, especially during the second half, and the score ended in a tie.

After the game, Nathalie drove me to Echterdingin where Andy, Ilona, and their daughters, Lucy and Rosalie, would be ready to greet me. Somehow, I didn't have Andy's address. We learned this as we headed down the road, but I knew if we found McDonald's and used their Wi-Fi system, I'd be able to find the address on my computer/address file.

"Where the heck is McDonald's when you want them?" I said, and I can't believe I really meant this, as I find McDonald's in the most obnoxious places. In front of parliament buildings, museums, castles, palaces, and many important sites, there is that annoying golden arch.

Yet when we saw one, both of us let out a cheer, until we went inside and found that this McDonald's doesn't offer Wi-Fi. Nathalie asked some youngster if I could use his phone to access my email account. I got nervous trying to type my password into his tiny phone with my big fingers while four people watched. I quit!

"I cannot do this." It was my first experience using a tiny keyboard, and with people watching, especially the kid whose phone I was using, I just couldn't complete the job.

Then we went to another restaurant, and with the guidance of the young man, Pascal, Nathalie's oldest son, who was on the phone with his mother, we managed to get the address. Then we were on the right road. Nathalie called when we arrived, and Andy came walking out to where we stopped the car. I ran and gave him a hug. I haven't seen Andy and Ilona for six years, and now they have two little girls.

The girls, six and three, speak only German, but they are learning English words and appeared happy to meet me. I'm going to have a great time here with this family.

Andy is my great-nephew by marriage to my late husband, Will, and now, of course, he's mine! He has no choice. We go back around 20 years when he first visited us in Colorado. At that time, he had long blond ringlets and was a wild and funny guy.

Now, he keeps his hair short. He's a family man and shows how much he enjoys his role of daddy.

Memories and making friends in Stuttgart

Modern Germany is on a roll with new high-rise buildings full of glass and class. However, there are still hints of happy memories that linger on in the old coffee shops, bakeries, specialty shops, the cathedral, and the schloss.

One memory was created back a few decades when Poppy, my late sister-in-law, and I would meet for lunch at the Kaufhof Department Store's top floor restaurant where you could, and still can, see the city below. I was there today.

Other memories were made when Will and I went to Germany to get married in 1988. While we were there, we spent time walking up and down the street searching for gifts to take back home to relatives and friends.

In 1998, my brother, Jack, and sister-in-law, Carol, accompanied us to Europe, and we took them to the Königsstrasse. We had a blast watching and listening to street musicians, and at least one of those made us laugh for years about his performance.

He sang the first phrase of, "There goes my baby." And, he would bend way over, as if warming up for the best that was yet to come, and he'd shake a box of matches for rhythm. Then he would just repeat the act. You would just stand there and wait for the real performance. But that was it. People laughed and walked away shaking their heads.

We stood for a while watching and listening because the man was just an unbelievably awful performer. In spite of that, people dropped coins into his hat that was on the ground. He was such a poor performer that someone from a window in a business above poured water on his head. Everyone standing, watching the talent, booed at the person who dumped the water.

Today, my mission was to reminisce about those good times by spending the entire day there, alone. It was cold with snow on the ground, just as it was back in 1985, during my first trip to Germany.

I discovered a store called the American Apparel that sells all American casual clothing. None of it was made in China or Bangladesh.

I saw two huge window-walls that were completely covered with a video of ocean waves breaking and surfers catching the waves. You cannot pass by without looking, as it looks so real you have to stop and watch. On the window it says, Hollister, California.

The surf is up in Hollister? Oh, really?

After a while, I found a flower kiosk and picked out some yellow roses and orange daisies for Ilona. A young man who works in the flower kiosk and I tried to understand each other even with no common language skills. It turns out he is from Slovenia and didn't speak German or English very well.

He took off his hat to show me his blond hair. Don't know why, but that seemed an important message to get me to understand where he comes from. I smiled.

"I like you," he said.

"I like you, too."

He handed me a rose. "For you."

"For me? Well, thank you."

The woman who arranged the flowers was finished with the bouquet and handed it to me.

"Wait," the young man motioned for me not to leave. He turned and wrote something on a piece of paper. "Here is phone number." He handed me a little slip of paper with a name and a number.

When Andy picked me up as previously arranged, I showed him the paper and told him I made a friend.

"How old was the guy?" Andy asked.

"About 19 or 20, or maybe 30 at the most."

Andy had a good laugh about that, but it wasn't the only thing that made him laugh. I had asked a man who sells magazines if I could borrow his phone to give Andy a call to make certain I understood where I was to meet him. The man made the call for me and straightened it all out with Andy.

"You just asked him to call me?" Andy chuckled when he picked me up.

Hey, what can I say? I'm friendly. Can't help it. Turns out the gentleman had been down and out and sells the magazines for a charity organization that helps folks like him get back on their feet. I thought he was genuinely good, and I wished him well.

Nothing lasts forever.

It's time to throw away my original suitcase. I'm not surprised after all it's been through. I had begun my journey with one suitcase, a bag, my computer case, my camera, and a purse over my shoulder. This became cumbersome, so I purchased another suitcase in the Barcelona Airport. The original suitcase had become so beat up from dragging it through snow and water, mud and rain puddles, 12 countries, several islands, and over 20 airplane flights. I can't even count the cars, trams, trains, and subways. The suitcase has done its job, and tomorrow I'll go to the Schlossplatz in Stuttgart to spring for another one. The Schlossplatz is a long, wide mall with shops and restaurants in proximity to the palace. I'm looking forward to that for its many memories.

Meanwhile, there is snow on the ground and grey skies in Echterdingen, a town close to Stuttgart.

Not to get spoiled by sitting in a brand new, warm house, I knew a walk would do me good. I put on my boots and my warm coat and walked toward the business part of town. It's Sunday, so the stores were closed, but the old town is splendid with centuries-old timbered houses.

Some of the houses lean and have needed to be fortified in order to stay standing up, but because of the pride in European history, much effort is put into keeping the old. The old houses do not stand alone, as all around them, new housing makes inroads into the town.

Andy and Ilona's house is an example of a brand new house that even smells brand new. Wooden curved steps take you up to the third floor, past the bedrooms of the two girls, and up to the guest room and the master bedroom. Off of the master bedroom, a deck just waits for springtime, so Andy and Ilona can take their coffee upstairs and enjoy the fresh air.

On the walk and after some window-shopping, I stopped inside a Middle Eastern restaurant for coffee, and there I met a customer, a man from China, who has lived in the town for 40 years.

"I came here to go to school, and I just stayed," he told me. His cute little three-year-old son was with him, a toddler who wanted in the worst way to speak to me.

I didn't have a clue what he was saying, so I just nodded.

"He is telling you that he likes to talk to old people."

Oh well, the news is out—I'm no longer young. Just like the suitcase, nothing lasts forever.

New and old ideas

Yesterday, on my daily walk around Echterdingen, I stopped and had a huge salad in an Italian restaurant. The building is a refurbished house that was born 450 years ago. Some of the old beams join with new beams that provide modern fortification. Brightly colored modern art hung from the ceiling. I love the mix of the old and the new.

Today, the daily walk took me toward a different direction and a mission to find the post office. Whenever I get a pile of papers and books or CDs, I send them off to my son, Larry, who puts them inside my car that is stored on his property. That process is easier than it would be for me to carry stuff all over the place. After finding an ATM and taking more money out of the well, I mailed the package off.

The second mission was to purchase a gift for Andy's birthday.

One more note before I go. Little Lucy, Andy and Ilona's six-year-old, a usually active daughter, has been sick and in bed the four days I've been here. She has been to the doctor once and today one more time. If she isn't better today, she'll go to the hospital. I'm hoping we'll all get the good news that she is recovering.

Andy's birthday with theater folk

It's Andy's birthday. Andy, three of his friends, and I met at a neighborhood restaurant for breakfast in honor of the birthday king. Ilona had to stay home to take care of the sick girl, Rosalie. Lucy, the eldest daughter, was first down with the illness but is back in good form today.

Andy and I walked through the snow to the restaurant and met his friends, all of whom are professional entertainers. Sara Crouch, originally from England, is a dancer. Virginie Donnelly, originally from Holland, is a dancer and singer, and her husband, Nicholas Donnelly, originally from Australia, plays the oboe in musicals.

All three have performed in many shows. Just to mention some of the musicals performed on the big SI-Centrum stage theater in the Möhringen area of Stuttgart are *Mama Mia*, *Elizabeth*, and *42nd Street*.

When Will and I first began visiting his sister, Poppy, and brother-in-law, Walter, back in 1985, the theater/entertainment center hadn't been built yet. Now it sits across the road from where they once lived. I had been inside the expansive entertainment facility a few years ago on another visit. It's huge, with theaters, restaurants, and dance halls, and it stays open into the early hours. People go to the center from all over Germany.

When we left the restaurant, the actors got into improvisation form and said good-bye in a way only actors can.

Yesterday, Ingrid, Andy's mother, visited us here in Andy and Ilona's home. It has been several years since Ingrid had visited me in Half Moon Bay. She was born during the WWII conflict of a Dutch mother (Poppy) and a German father (Walter).

Learning to be a tourist

Andy and I attended the huge CMT (Caravan Motor Tourism) Stuttgart public exhibition for leisure and tourism. It was held inside the 100,000-square-meter space at the Stuttgart Airport. More than 1,900 exhibitors gave information, tips, and anything you would want to know about how to plan the perfect trip or vacation. Elaborate kiosks were set up with nearly every corner of the world represented.

We picked up many brochures and CDs and spoke to people in the know in places such as Croatia and Turkey and many other exotic spots in the world, a world that continues to look smaller and smaller. The U.S. was represented showing the country and where to go to be a dime-store cowboy for a time, for example.

A woman artist showed her artwork at the Serbia booth. She had hand-painted bookmarkers and was trying to give me one. I didn't understand at first. I thought she was trying to tell me to purchase some of her artwork, but I finally understood. It was a gift. Along with the bookmark, she handed me her brochure. Zuzana Veresky was born in 1955 in Padina and now lives in Kovačica. She has painted since her childhood. The first picture was painted on her mother's petticoat. She is an established "naive art" artist and shows her work in Slovakia, Spain, Israel, Cyprus, Belgium, Tunisia, and Germany. The main projects have her participating in Paris, UNESCO, Geneva, UNICEF, New York, Brussels, Strasbourg, European Union, Vienna, Washington, Shanghai, and the World Expo 2010.

Aside from meeting this lovely artist, I especially enjoyed the German booths. Here, they had singers dressed in lederhosen and singing German folk music.

When we walked by the Ireland kiosk, they were getting ready for live Irish music.

I also enjoyed the Mongolia booth. We spoke to a man to whom I mentioned the throat singers; he immediately began to demonstrate his talent as a Mongolian throat singer.

All throughout the space there were ethnic foods and drinks.

We made our way to the Stuttgart Airport and the exhibition by train. It was one stop, and there we were. Europeans have it over the U.S. with transportation that can take you anywhere.

"To market, to market, to buy a fat pig." Well, fruits, vegetables and bread, at least

Farmers bring their goods every week into the town of Echterdingen. You can see trailers of all kinds and tents with plastic walls to keep the goods out of the rain, snow, or sleet, and where it is warm inside. Vegetables straight from the farmer, fruits, canned foods, beans, nuts of all kinds, and dairy products are yours for the purchase.

I was there this morning with Andy. He carried a basket and a bag with him, as in farmer's markets there are no plastic or paper bags. Everyone is expected to be prepared to bag his or her own purchases. Andy waited in the bread line, not the bread line we know for the hungry and homeless but the bread line where Germans can purchase all kinds of breads, rolls, and pretzels right from the baker. Hmmm, so fresh!

We walked back home in the snow. There, Ilona had the table all set for breakfast. We spread out the various types of cheeses, some from Switzerland and some from Germany, and thin meat slices, jam, jelly, and a variety of breads. Then there was that delicious cappuccino. Andy, handy with a frying pan, made to-order eggs, over-easy or over-hard. What a breakfast it was, and oh, so typically German.

While I was in Germany and bemoaning the fact that in California plastic bags litter open spaces and freeways, I received a message from a friend in Monterey County, who said the county has abandoned the use of plastic bags.

Walter

I was so very touched to see my brother-in-law, 92-year-old Walter Frederich. It was at his daughter's home where Andy and I had dinner. Andy's mother and Ingrid, Walter's daughter who was born during the war, were there. Everyone is older now, and the war is just a drop in the pool of time.

Walter was a pilot for Germany, and my husband, Will, was in the Dutch resistance movement when he was a teenager.

Can you even imagine how dangerous it must have been for Walter, a German officer, and Poppy, a young Dutch woman, to fall in love? Complications arose, including when Walter found out that Will was in the resistance. Walter and Poppy were always in love until death parted them. Even a war cannot destroy true love.

I took one last walk around Echterdingen yesterday and discovered a different street by making tracks across fresh snow on a shortcut inside the courtyard of the church on the square. The square is where the town business and the weekly farmer's market are located.

I heard the church bell chimes and sassy birds high up in the tree branches, and I found a wet walkway through an arch of snow-laden bushes. Around a bend, there was a very old house, among other old houses, but this one was reminiscent of the children's tale, *Hansel and Gretel*.

This morning, I woke up to a knock on the door. It was Andy telling me he would be leaving in 20 minutes. You know how I am with traveling transitions? I imagined in my still slumbering mood that Andy was telling me I had to be ready to leave for the train depot in 20 minutes.

I began grabbing my clothing to put on and looking around to see if I had packed everything, until . . . I realized, it was he who would be leaving in 20 minutes and that would be our time to say good-bye. I wouldn't leave for almost another two hours.

I slowed down a bit, and then it was time to say good-bye to Andy, who had stayed home from work for two days due to an illness that everyone in the house came down with, but me. Andy's work takes him all over the world, and this week he will be in Russia. Oh, how I want to go there someday. But for now, I'm in my own personal heaven.

The train itinerary had me going from Stuttgart to changing trains in Mannheim, then a change to Mainz, and then a change to Bingen, my ultimate destination. Ilona drove me to the train station where I bade her good-bye. She was a wonderful hostess in spite of having sickness in the house.

I was early at the platform when a train came in. I saw two women walking toward the train, not knowing they were conductors, and I asked one if that was the train to Mainz and then to Bingen. The tall, scary woman, who I'll call Meany, told me yes, this train went to Mainz. I took her word for it and got on the train. I had previously synchronized my watch to make certain nothing could go wrong. I was about 30 minutes early getting on the train, and I noticed that not many people were boarding.

When it became about ten minutes before the scheduled departure, the train was pulling out of the station, and I knew something wasn't right, so I found Meany again and asked her if she was sure I was on the right train. She looked at my ticket and said something like, "Oh, you're going that route?" I didn't fully understand what she said, but she handed the ticket back to me and said, "We go to Mainz."

"The train goes to Mainz? I don't have to get off in Mannheim?"

"We go to Mainz. This train goes to Mainz," Meany nearly shouted.

"Okay," I said and sat down.

Soon, we came to the Mannheim station, and it was at the scheduled time where I would, if things were normal, get off. I asked myself, should I get off here? Should I wait until we get to

Mainz? Was she paying attention to what I needed to know? My mind was in dithers, but I decided to wait and see if Meany was right and the train would take me to Mainz.

It did, and before I got off, a nice young man, a new conductor, looked at my ticket, said everything would be all right and that I should take the black and yellow to Bingen.

"The next stop is Mainz," he told me. After finding the stop in Mainz for Bingen, I barely had enough time to board that train, and after about half an hour, we arrived in Bingen, yes, on the black and yellow.

I got off the train and began pulling my luggage toward where I thought I saw a crossing road but realized I wasn't getting anywhere but making tracks in the snow, so I turned around and asked a man who looked like James Dean where I should go to get to the town. James Dean said to go down those steps and then up the steps to the town.

"Down those steps?"

"Yes."

"Thank you," I said and walked to the steps, wishing I would find an elevator. Just as I wished it, I saw one that looked as though it took people up to a walkway and then across the walkway to another elevator to the street.

Off I went up the dirty, snowy, slushy elevator that had a floor button that looked as though it was covered with blood. I pushed it, anyway, and up I went. I was soon on the other side of the train station. Isolated. Where to go from here?

I pulled the bags through the snow, through water puddles, through slush, and found a busy street where I stopped a man and asked him if he knew of any coffee shops nearby.

"No, there are none here on this side of town. You have to go over there." He pointed further away.

"Are there any taxis around this town?"

"Yes, but you will need to go down there to the train station."

"I just came from there, and I didn't see any taxis."

He just shrugged his shoulders. I walked into a grocery store and asked the lady at the pastry counter if she would call a taxi for me. She was willing.

Soon, an unsmiling man put my suitcases in the trunk of the taxi and looked at the address I showed him. He didn't say anything but just drove up a hill, up a winding road, up, up, up to a dead end where the hostel was located.

I thanked him, gave him a tip, and got a teeny little smile out of him.

Now I am in a hostel, the only customer in the place, which reminds me that traveling out of season is the best way to go. My bedroom window overlooks the Rhine River, a castle, and an old river lighthouse island that has been turned into a park.

Barges that look like snakes from a distance power their goods down the river. Whole families make their lives on these barges. Right now, it's getting dark out. Across the river, snow blankets miles of vineyards, and now two barges pass one another. A long train that travels across the river between Rhine towns glides between the snowy hillsides and the river.

I'm in the middle of my dream. I have always wanted to spend time along the Rhine River, as I've been in love with the folklore that surrounds this ancient waterway and the castles that have their own stories to tell. I can't wait to get up in the morning, brave the cold weather, and do some exploring.

Lorelei and Hildegard

The Legend of Lorelei, or Loreley, as it is written in some German literature, lives on in the history of the Rhein, or Rhine. The section of the river that claims the folk story is now a UNESCO World Heritage Site, as named in June, 2002.

Lorelei is a feminine water spirit who, as the romantic story goes, was the cause of death to the crews of ships and rafts that passed along a narrow and dangerous path. A rock between the towns of Kaub and Sankt Goarshausen, called the Lorelei, was said to emit ghostly voices through a natural echo. Most of the trouble for the sailors came from the lovely Lorelei, continues the legend. Her enchanting good looks and beautiful voice bewitched the sailors and caused many boat accidents in the narrow curvature of the river.

I saw the rock a few years back with Lenny, and I was enthralled with the folk story. It means even more to me today as I sit at the window and watch the barges, steered by masterful sailors, glide down the river.

The story of Lorelei is a legend, but a real woman with importance to the Rhine was Hildegard von Bingen who lived from 1098 to 1179, and spent years in a nunnery from the time she was eight-years-old. She made a huge impact with her writings on subjects such as natural science and medicine, poetry, and hymns. She was considered a visionary, a shrewd politician, a prolific composer of music, and an unlearned religious recluse whose correspondents included some of the most important politicians and minds of the Middle Ages. She was a sharp-eyed naturalist, a competing orator, and a highly competent farmer. I gleaned some of this information from *The Rhine, A Guide from Mainz to Cologne*.

Now I know why there are so many stores, streets, and products with the name Hildegard. And today, while on my long walk to the center of Bingen, I met Hildegard Willig. Hildegard was standing at a red stoplight talking with another woman, and I asked them for directions. Hildegard stepped right up to help me and even walked all the way to the Information Center with me. She chattered away in English, the whole time telling me how awful her English was, but I understood everything she said. She had thin red hair and watery blue eyes, and because of some distress with her eyes, she was on her way to the eye doctor, but first, she had to show me the way. We went down the street, over the bridge, and under a tunnel that had a mural on it painted by children, until we came out above again on the other side of the river inlet.

Hildegard began to tell me something about herself, and she pulled off a stocking from her arm to show me she had just a stump of an arm.

"It was burned off," she told me. I don't know the story.

She went all the way to the Information Center and told the woman I had some questions. She asked for a pen and wrote her name and address down so I could send her a card when I get back to California.

Now you know the story of the myth of Lorelei and the two Hildegards.

Today, the weather continued to be almost a total whiteout. I don't bother with the camera because the day is just too dark. I'll be here for nine more nights, and some sun must shine on at least one of those days.

I still love it here, however. It fascinates me.

Savoring the beauty of the Rhine

"How often have I greeted the waters of the Rhine with amazement? When, returning from my dealings, I again drew closer to them! It always seemed great to me and quickened my mind and feelings," said Johann Wolfgang von Goethe.

Goethe was, and still is, right about the Rhine. It is a day to savor the surrounding beauty, and I sit at a table in front of the window looking out and below. Over the Rhine River are miles of snowy vineyards that reach up to the tops of the hills. Between a vineyard and closer to the river is a spot where the castle, Ehrenfels, sits among trees and bushes looking out majestically over the Rhine.

The former lookout tower and customs house, the Mäuseturm, rests on an island in the Rhine near the castle. More recently, it serves as a navigation signal station.

Across the Rhine, cars travel between the many towns along the river, and long trains carry passengers and freight.

From my room in the Die Jugendgästehäuser, a family-owned hostel and a restaurant open to the guests, are quaint little houses and small gardens on grounds below. This can be seen all over Europe. People rent or own these spaces and spend summer months caring for the gardens. Above those houses and right below the hostel are larger, older houses that have smoke coming out of the chimneys.

Also on this side of the river, other trains stop at the station, including the same one where I disembarked. You can see not only the train station but also the boat slips that wait and ferry people over to the other town, Rüdesheim.

To get from where I'm staying to the town of Bingen requires walking down a hill, over a bridge, through a tunnel, and on to the street of the town. On this side of town, there are mostly houses, some churches, and a castle ruin.

It is just plain awesome to experience something so different and so out of my own ordinariness that I don't feel I'm wasting time just sitting and watching the day.

Planes occasionally pass overhead, and there are many birds flying low over the river, and some small ones are nearby where I sit. It's cold out, and many tourist places are closed. That doesn't keep me from what I want to do. You can "tourist yourself tired" and still cannot say you experienced it.

My aim is to get a feel for the place by walking through the town every day, and when the museum is open, I'll go there and also over to Rüdesheim by ferry.

I cannot look at this place without imagining what it must have been like in the 1300s to 1400s on the same river, with the same purpose—to ship goods.

One myth about the Mäuseturm goes this way. It was built in the 13th century as a lookout tower, and the name came from *mausen*, which means to be on the lookout, the way a cat is on the lookout for a mouse. But another legend links the lookout to the hardhearted Bishop Hatto who is said to have sought refuge in the tower from a horde of mice; in vain, the mice swam after him and devoured him.

Before the mice got him, I wonder if he savored the beauty that surrounded him?

Changed hotels

I'm still in Bingen but in a different hotel and closer to town. I decided to move. Yesterday, late afternoon, I began the 20-minute walk back to town for the second time. I came upon a man helping an elderly woman into the car, and I stopped him to ask if he knew of a hotel that was nice but not too expensive, and right away, he said, "Yes, I do. It's the Hotel Römerhof." He sketched a little map for me and told me how to walk to it.

I met Michael inside the reception room, and he had a room for me. He told me the Internet would work well, and it was free. Michael speaks good English and German, as well. His father is an American. Michael was raised in Texas and attended high school there, but his home is now Germany.

I went back to the hostel, and the next morning I checked out. No one seemed to care. I got a taxi to take me to the hotel. The taxi driver had spent time in the U.S. and seemed happy to speak some English to me.

I don't have the same views as I did from the other place, but I can see vineyards out of one window, and out of the other, a huge, very old, red stone church. I took a walk down to the museum but found it closed again. I thought today was Saturday, so I'll try again tomorrow.

On the walk back to the hotel, I discovered some interesting neighborhoods—old stone houses, narrow cobblestone walkways, flower plants outside the windows, and on one narrow street on the upstairs windows, I saw clowns looking down at me. I'll take my camera next time and see if I can get a photo.

It is still cold and grey with threats of more snow, but it just adds to the atmosphere.

Before heading back to the hotel, I ate lunch at a restaurant that sits right on an old town plaza, and it was fun spending almost an hour people watching.

Additional news. I had asked if I could buy a cup of coffee a few hours ago, and Michael told me that a large crowd of people would be coming in at three p.m., and I could then go and get coffee for myself. I'm a bit shy and thought that it wouldn't be right to crash a party just for coffee, so I just forgot it.

Then, just a while ago, a woman knocked on my door and brought in a pot of coffee, cream, and two sweet items. Now that is great customer service, and extremely rare.

German history

Carnival times in Germany based on the Easter calendar are from February 11-13, so watch out for silly people in costumes. Clowns seem to be the favorite object to celebrate carnival, as they've been spotted in store windows and on private homes. From what I have gathered, carnival time came to the Rhineland by way of France, which came there by way of Italy and other European countries. It is primarily a Catholic festive season that occurs immediately before Lent. Carnival involves a public parade that combines elements of a circus and a street party. With all the clowns I've seen around Bingen, I can tell it's a popular time for people to escape from everyday life.

Today, I learned more about the Rhineland's Saint Hildegard. As stated before, she was born in 1098. She was the tenth child of Hildebert and Mechthild of Franconian high nobility.

"Say and write what is in your heart," was the God-given advice she felt she had received. Hildegard took that vision to heart and was considered a visionary, a writer of books, music, and plays, and was sought out throughout Europe for advice.

I finally got inside the museum and found the history of Hildegard posted on boards and written in English, as well as German.

After viewing the museum, I went to a restaurant that served typical German food. I sat at a table next to the smoking room. While it was reserved for smokers, I wasn't able to avoid the smell of cigarette smoke that escaped, and when I arrived back to my room, I had to hang up my coat near a window to get rid of the smell.

However, the food and local wine were delicious, so I traded one dislike for an extreme like.

Speaking of exchanging dislikes for likes reminds me of the conversation I had with Michael, the 22-year-old owner of the hotel. He spent a good part of his childhood in Texas.

We talked about how World War II still holds modern Germany captive for the devastation it had on Germany and the rest of the world.

"When I was in school in America, people would call me such names as Hitler's son."

Teachers, he thought, should have told students to stop calling him names and referring to the war as though he had something to do with it. Instead, the teachers used the comments as a teaching moment about World War II.

Michael said people should stop blaming present-day Germany.

"My generation didn't cause the war. We are not responsible for it, and people should not blame us," said Michael.

I have mixed feelings about this because part of me thinks we should teach children what happened so it doesn't happen again, while I also agree that what is behind us is best left there. I look around at what Germany has done since the war, and it makes me proud to see that contrition is ongoing. There are countless ways Germany has paid for the crimes of World War II, even though the war was over in the late 40s.

Right now, it is obvious that Germany is one of the most successful European countries.

Perhaps Michael and his generation have a point we might heed; they should not be held responsible for the crimes of World War II. Look what they are doing now.

Sunday walk

It's Sunday morning, and I wanted to attend church. There are two beautiful churches near the hotel. One is across the street from the hotel, and the other is about one block down the street. The bells ring loud and long; you'd think they were calling people to church. However, when I attempted to get inside, both churches were closed. Guess the bells are just for the tradition. I don't know the reason for the churches' closing, so I just made a walk around the neighborhood, which has become my traveling habit.

One interesting habit the Germans have when moving out of an apartment or business building is to clear everything out and put it all out on the street where it will be picked up by the city. However, there can be some useful items left, and while walking around, I noticed cars and vans stopping to look at the motherlode on the street and taking what they wanted.

I saw some items of personal interest—a large suitcase in perfect condition, sofas, chairs, tables, desks, pottery, cups, and saucers.

Ferry business across the Rhine

The ferry picked up one other lady and me at the Bingen Port to cross the Rhine to the town of Rüdesheim. Christiana was an unsmiling and unfriendly-looking person until I got her into conversation, and I then found her English perfect, her smile fetching, and her knowledge about the area informative. Just give a person the chance to show who they are, and you may be in for a surprise.

For the ten-minute ride across the Rhine, she spoke about the many places I may like to see, both in Bingen and in Rüdesheim. She mentioned Hildegard, the Benedictine nun from nearly 900 years ago who was ahead of her time and who has a serious following even today; people go on pilgrimages in her memory. The chapel on a hill in Bingen is just a short walk away from the Forum of Hildegard and the garden that memorializes her.

Christiana said that Hildegard von Bingen had the ear of the King and other royalties who sought out her advice and vast knowledge. She purchased property and had a second cloister built for the Benedictine nuns.

To be honest here, there wasn't much to see in Rüdesheim, as most of the shops, museums, and other attractions are closed during the winter. However, I did see a busload of tourists get out and walk around as I did. I was not disappointed.

The old town is made up of narrow cobblestone alleyways and streets, with both sides lined with shops, restaurants, and hotels. Some of the hotels are quite old, which makes a visit all the more fun and interesting for me. I like the window shutters and doors, the decor on top of doors, and the window flower boxes. German folks have creative ways of decorating small areas with flowers, leaves, simple twigs, pieces of wood, and pinecones. I always manage to pick up lots of ideas, including cuisine, such as the Black Forest cake. It is layers of chocolate and vanilla cream with one layer of cherries. Hmm . . . delicious, and with a cup of cappuccino—life is good.

Problems with banking today and a donut to ease my mood

I stayed close to the hotel today to receive an important phone call regarding my bank and what they are doing to thwart my getting an apartment in March when I return to California.

It seems that before my credit card is charged, an apartment-hunting company puts my card through by charging only one or two dollars as a test, and then after that goes through, the larger amount is then charged.

A charge as small as the initial one is a red flag for fraud, according to the Bank of America. I have gone round and round with this with emails and phone calls. It's amazing how modern business is so much more complicated as time moves forward. Right when I expected a phone call from the apartment company, the hotel staff left for the afternoon, and I'm stuck in my room with no access to the reception area where the phone call would come through.

It's more complicated than what I'm expressing here, but I'll get through it. I waited all day for a phone call and just found out from reception that there were no messages. I called the apartment folks again, and the guy moaned, "Oh, yeah, I didn't get to that yet."

Just when I was feeling sorry for myself, the nice 13-year-old Daniel, brother of Michael, brought me a pot of coffee with a donut. He's helping his mom tonight—she's in the reception office for the evening. The folks in this hotel are the best I have come across on my nine, nearly ten, months of travel.

Taking a dry run in the rain

I'm taking a dry run in the rain this morning to the *bahnhof*, or the train station, so I'll have no surprises on Friday morning. It's a good thing I walked to the station to get an idea of where I should stand to catch the train because I followed the route that someone pointed out, and it was wrong.

That someone was Hildegard Willig. Today, she was heading back to the eye doctor again. She showed me her new glasses in a case, and she said they weren't working out for her.

I explained what I was about to do, and she pointed to the station. However, when I walked the way she pointed, it was to the old station building that now looks like a haunted house. But it didn't matter, as time is no problem today, so I just continued on the road and up an old stairway that no longer connects to the bridge to the new *bahnhof.* I walked back down the moss and rotting-leaf-covered stairway again and to the road where I had seen Hildegard, and then back down the correct road to the current station.

Isn't it strange what you can see at a place the second time you see it, things that you missed the first time? This time, the station looked well-used, and a fleet of taxis waited to pick people up from the arriving trains. Why I didn't see the station and the taxis when I arrived is amazing, but then we must remember it was a total whiteout that day.

After learning how to navigate my early morning leave-taking on Friday, I walked again to town. This time I walked closer to the Rhine River, which seemed to be moving faster, as the wind was stronger today. Most of the snow that greeted me when I arrived had melted.

Some of what I found today were more brass squares inserted in the sidewalk with the names of Jewish people who were removed from their homes and sent to concentration camps during World War II. I feel sad every time I see one of those, and this time I saw one that represented a whole family.

I also saw a window on the third floor with a pulley that is used to lift furniture up to the apartment above. I've seen these more often in Holland. I also saw a close-up of another castle, this one right in town, and some more beautiful, old, and interesting doors.

I had lunch in a favorite restaurant. It was carrot and ginger soup with fried celery. The celery was de-stringed and then fried.

Good-bye, Germany. It's been wunderbar!

Tomorrow will be my last moment in Germany. I leave in the morning for Arnhem, Holland. I'll be picked up at the train station by Paul Boes and will stay with him and his partner, Dorry, until Sunday, and then I'll leave for the town of Oss.

First things first. My six weeks in Germany have fulfilled more of my dreams than I could ever imagine. I got to renew my friendship with relatives whom I claim as my own, family I inherited from my husband, Will. Every single one of them treated me as if I were something special. I love them and treasure them probably more than they know.

Then there was Berlin and a special time to explore the city with my friend, Marilyn, from Colorado. We celebrated Christmas and New Year's in Berlin, and I will always hold dear those three weeks with my friend.

I have to hold up the city of Bingen as my favorite town in Germany. This is a special place and even more special to me, as it brings back memories of the first time I saw the Rhine River all those years ago. Ever since then, since 1985, I have wanted to spend more time close to the river, and I got to do that this past week. It helped that I found a hotel that will go down as one of my favorites in my ten-month journey, so far. Michael Madden owns and operates the award-winning Hotel Römerhof at the young age of 22. Every single person on the staff is friendly and very capable.

Because of Christiana's information, which was backed up by Michael, I got on a small bus, more like a van, and found the forum and later the Klopp Castle where the Mayor of Bingen has his office.

The van driver was a smiling, happy guy who wanted to be certain that I got delivered where I wanted to go, and when someone got on the bus who spoke English, the driver translated between us, and it worked. I got to visit the forum and the castle, as well.

The Sisters of the Cross sponsor the Hildegard Forum. This is a place for groups to stay for meditation. A kitchen offers great food, and there is a gift shop at the entrance and a place to pick up information regarding Hildegard von Bingen.

I arrived at the forum by walking from the bus early in the morning to find the kitchen closed to outsiders, as they were preparing for a group of folks who were staying a few days. However, a woman in charge of the forum welcomed me to look around.

While waiting for the van back to town from the forum, I saw a nun who was pushing something inside the convent gate. I asked if I could take her photo, and I didn't know if she said yes or no. But she kept smiling, so I thought it would be okay, and I got one of her walking behind the gate.

My stay in Bingen is close to perfection, in my mind.

Chapter Eleven

February, 2013

Now in Holland

I'm now in Arnhem, Holland, being hosted by friends Paul and Dorry. I got here after traveling by trains from Bingen, Germany, with one change in Dusseldorf.

I left early this morning, saying good-bye to Michael Madden. I'll miss him, the good breakfast, and his staff of exceptional people.

Tradition!

Tradition. That's the name of the game.

Forget the musical, *Fiddler on the Roof*, for here is tradition played out in real life. Paul Boes, a career army man and my host in Arnhem, Holland, is the warrant officer in charge of Veterans Affairs and Tradition.

His varied duties involve heading up and organizing medal-awarding ceremonies for worthy men and women of all Dutch armed forces. Royalty and other VIPs participate in these ceremonies.

One of Paul's duties, the Annual Memorial Jump, was held on the very jump zone site where, in 1944, World War II British soldiers were dropped and then marched onto the bridge in Arnhem. The bridge in Arnhem is known for the Market Garden war disaster and the movie, *A Bridge Too Far*.

The Bridge Too Far

During the ceremony last September, soldiers from the United States, Germany, Poland, United Kingdom, and the Netherlands made memorial jumps, according to Paul. I asked Paul about the attitude of the crowd when the Germans jumped.

"Oh, they are very much respected." This gives me more reason to believe we must put wars behind us.

Paul pointed out a nearby sheep barn covered with a grass roof. If you get too close to it, you'll know there are animals living in it.

"Before the ceremony, we take the sheep out, thoroughly clean the building, and then use it as a waiting room for the VIPs."

Another example of Paul's duties was on an annual Veteran's Day when he coordinated a medal ceremony and a parade that involved the Crown Prince of Holland, Willem Alexander. The Crown Prince will soon become King, as his mother, Queen Beatrix, has abdicated her throne. The Veteran's Day event took place on the grounds of the Binnenhof, the seat in Den Haag of the Dutch parliament, and was attended by other important VIPs.

Paul also gives the traditional facts to the graduates of the Eleventh Air Mobile Brigade who wear the prestigious red beret. This is the branch of service of which Paul is a member. There are many traditions of the Brigade, and it is considered honorable to have been chosen to be a member of this branch of the Dutch Army.

Today, I took advantage of Paul's vast knowledge as he took me to the World War II drop site and then along the long road from the site to where the soldiers marched to the bridge. The bridge has been named the John Frost Bridge after the lieutenant colonel who tried to take the Arnhem Bridge.

Paul also took me to an estate, the Bronbeek, which houses the building where veterans live; to an Indonesian museum that shows the history of the Dutch colonization up to the restoration of freedom to the country of Indonesia; and to an Indonesian restaurant.

After going through the informative museum, we then went next door to the Kumpulan, or Gathering, Restaurant. It didn't disappoint. I had *gado gado*, an Indonesian staple of vegetable salad and boiled eggs covered by a peanut sauce.

While Paul and I were out looking at history, Dorry, a pretty and intelligent lady, was home studying for a wine test that is coming up soon for a course she is taking. She already has a degree in art history, and she works in communications for the company, Arcadis. She is now learning all about viticulture. She attends classes, and together the students have wine tasting lessons, just one part of the process of learning the inside business of wine making.

Paul and Dorry's house has a collection of modern paintings that reflects Dorry's fine taste in art.

Scooting to the movie

I got on a scooter with Paul and headed to the Focus Filmtheater in the heart of Arnhem to see the movie, *Hyde Park on the Hudson*. According to Paul and from what I saw on the streets, scooters and bicycles are used by people of all ages and are used more often than cars. Not wanting Paul to go against his wish to make the trip easier and more convenient, I said, "Sure, I'll go on the scooter."

I climbed on and hung onto Paul with a death grip. At first, I tried to straighten myself up when we hit the curves. Paul told me it's best just to go with him and the scooter on the curves. Guess it's easier for the driver, too.

Coming back from the theater, I closed my eyes on the curves, and somehow that made it easier to smooth it out. Or at least that's what my mind was telling my body.

The movie theater is unique in that most of the workers in the small theater are volunteers. There is a restaurant upstairs, and it is quite acceptable to take your drinks into the theater, which has only about seven rows.

We both thought the movie was wonderful, with Bill Murray exceptional as President Roosevelt. There was one touching scene that made me fight to hold back the tears. The King of England and the President were having a one-on-one conversation. You may know from another movie, *The King's Speech*, that King George VI had a stuttering problem, and also from history, that Roosevelt was crippled from polio. King George took out a paper he had written out to be voiced to the President, but his stuttering was so profound that he just gave up and confessed to the President that he wasn't thought of by the people to be a good king. Roosevelt assured him that if George were his son, he would be very proud of him, and as he was speaking, Roosevelt got up and clumsily walked while holding on to chairs and tables to work his way over to his desk chair. He told the King that people will know him by more than his stuttering, that he must not let that stop him from his life as a king.

Queen Elizabeth was shocked that they were to have a picnic the next day, and with hot dogs. Hot dogs? What are they, anyway, they asked themselves. The day of the picnic when hot dogs were served must be a funny scene for Americans who consider hot dogs a typical food item without giving them a thought.

What I didn't know about FDR was that he had a mistress for many years that everyone in his close circle seemed to know about. Back then it was not a news item. When she died at age 100, her letters and diaries about the love of her life, Franklin, were found under her bed, and the secret was out.

The news media at the time was respectful about not mentioning or taking photos of the President while he was pushed in a wheel chair or carried by a loyal employee.

Hyde Park on the Hudson is a good movie, and I recommend it. You don't have to get there by way of scooter, however.

It's a small world in froggy town.

Little did I know when I first met my daughter-in-law, Aleida, how small the world would be and how large my world of understanding would grow.

I am right now in the city of Oss, Holland, staying with Aleida and her mother; Lieke's cousin; and Renzo and his wife, Diet (pronounced Deet). Renzo immigrated to Holland with his family from Indonesia at the age of eight. He met Diet when she and her family moved near Renzo's family.

"You could see her bedroom from my bedroom," Renzo smiled. "She was age 14, and I was 16 when we were in the same school."

They have been married for 46 years and have raised two boys who are now young fathers. Renzo is a charismatic man who seems to not know a stranger. He's also a tennis player who played in a competition tennis match today, while I toured another city.

Diet has a calmness about her, and she creates a cozy, creative atmosphere in her home.

I was inside the home in 1999, when Aleida's mother, Lieke, and our co-grandson, Michael, visited at the time Will and I lived in Den Haag. I remember the time very well.

Yesterday, when I stepped inside the home, I saw the interior as I had remembered, with minor changes. There are Indonesian artifacts on the walls. Some are wooden objects, some are patterned material, some are sculptures and furniture—all typical of Indonesia.

The garden's architecture outside gives a *Home and Garden* example of how to create an artsy area in a small space. The garden right now is in the winter recess but is still beautiful.

For those of you who may not have remembered, here it is again. Indonesia was a colony of Holland for over 400 years.

Indonesia became free, and now the Dutch/Indonesian cross-cultures are represented in Holland in the food, art, and the people.

Diet had prepared a wonderful Indonesian dinner last night, which made me happy. One time I remarked that there must be Indonesian food in heaven because nothing can compare with it.

Today, when Renzo went to his tennis match and Diet went to the doctor (on her bicycle, I want to add here), Renzo took me to the town of 's-Hertogenbosch in the province of Brabant.

Renzo told me to be certain to try the *Bossche bol*, so that was the first thing I did when I was dropped off in front of the cathedral at a nearby restaurant. The *Bossche bol* is associated with the town and is a pastry item with cream on the inside and chocolate covering the outside.

On the way to the town, Renzo gave me a bit of information about Carnival that takes place this weekend. In the spirit of Carnival, the town's name becomes Oeteldonk, and it is said the people make sounds like frogs. "*Hauvel kwaker*" is the sound the frog that sits on top of a hill makes. There are frogs everywhere in the town—in store windows, on tops of buildings, in the town squares, and well, everywhere, frogs are featured.

While walking around town and finding frogs everywhere, I found the St. Jan's gothic style cathedral that dominates the city. It was originally built in 1559. I was struck by the beauty inside with the paintings, the stained glass windows, the chandeliers, and the organ pipes.

When Renzo and I waited for the bridge in town to let a riverboat through, I met some women who were also waiting, and in the town, I saw the two women twice again. We greeted each other. Small world, I keep experiencing.

In front of my eyes, a young man's life changed for the better.

Renzo, my host, is a volunteer with the VluchtelingenWerk Nederland (V.V.N.), an organization for refugees.

Renzo was to meet the train carrying Amer (not using his last name to protect his privacy) at the Oss Railway Station a little after ten o'clock. Renzo said about 99 percent of the people do not arrive on time, so it wasn't a surprise when Renzo came back to the car where I waited to tell me he learned by a phone call that Amer would arrive on the next train.

The next train eventually arrived, and Renzo came back to the car with a young woman on a bicycle and two young Somalian men.

Selena Schouten, an intern with the prettiest green eyes, from the Avans Hogeschool in Den Bosch where she is studying social work, accompanied Renzo and the two men through the process required for refugees.

Ahmed M. Omer, also from Somalia, is the cousin of Amer and, with his fluency in Dutch, translated some of the day's necessary business to Amer. Ahmed has lived in the Netherlands for several years.

Amer, Ahmed, and Selena sat in the back seat, while I sat in the front listening to the process they would be going through with today as day one. Day two would be tomorrow.

First off, we all went to the BrabantWonen, a house-renting agency, where we learned Amer would be able to move into the house in two weeks, and he signed a contract.

The next step was at the town hall where he learned what the financial arrangements would be. He learned that as a single man, he would net 883 euros a month, and from that he would pay everything—rent, utilities, and a 4,300-euro loan that would be payable at 50 euros a month for 36 months. That money is used for furniture, refrigerator, and all that is needed to set up housekeeping.

"You're obligated by the government to have an insurance, and he must pay that himself, as well," Renzo said.

He also receives 1,300 euros for food for the first month before his monthly income is received. This is a gift and is not required to be paid back.

The third stop was the refugee center where we met with another volunteer, Linda, who is from Surinam. This office does what they can to help the new refugees integrate into the city and country.

The fourth stop was at a bank where Amer learned about the loan and his responsibility for it. He requested that he receive the Internet, which the bank would take care of, within the new account.

The fifth stop was the best. Amer was given the keys to his new home. He opened the door and said he felt very happy. He has a new life. There are some requirements refugees must fulfill before becoming Dutch citizens. Some of those are to meet all the necessary conditions, to be an honorable person in his new country, and to learn the language. He has one year to learn the language, and then he must search for a job.

Renzo, when asked about the general feelings about the business of giving money to refugees, said that it is mostly considered an act of kindness and necessary to help people who are in need of leaving a war-torn country.

People trying to get into the country for economic reasons are not warmly received.

Renzo said that over the past three years, the Dutch government arranged a quick assessment of the refugee's status. Prior to that, there was a flaw in the system, and if someone was not legal and stayed without a legal card, it took years to fix the problem.

"Now the government says, 'You have a chance to stay here and abide by the rules.' They now have two months to get everything in order, just as Amer did today," according to Renzo.

Renzo, as a volunteer for several years, said about volunteering, "If volunteers everywhere in the Netherlands said, 'I will no longer do it,' then the whole Dutch economy is dead."

I must say I was touched beyond anything else I have seen on this one-year journey. It was amazing to be part of the experience when one young man's life, just today in front of my own eyes, changed for the better.

Memories begin in Den Haag.

I'm in the land of memories, memories of Den Haag, when my husband Will (Wim in Holland) lived here back in 1998.

I took a few minutes and walked down a busy street, crossed over it, and then back again right during the heavy traffic time. People are ready to get home after putting in a day's work, and it's been hailing.

I found some of my favorite sites—Dutch windows with lacy curtains, cats watching the world from their houses, and stained glass windows.

Renzo, Diet, and I drove from Oss last night to the home of Mike, their son, and Jayah. I was amazed this morning to see Jayah, who from now on will be known in my heart as yet another Wonder Woman. They say it's quite normal for other young mothers to do what she does, but I'm still amazed.

She got up at the crack of dawn, got breakfast for her two older daughters, took them to school on a bicycle, nursed her eight-month-old baby, and then road her bicycle to the train station, left her bicycle there, got on a train, got off the train, got on another bicycle, and went to work for eight hours. She'll do the return trip in the same way, then take care of her daughters and husband, and then start it all over again tomorrow.

Once a month, Renzo and Diet share in her duties, as they fulfill their love of spending time with the granddaughters. They picked up the older girls from school and took care of the little one during the day. Their lives are normal for those living in busy Dutch cities.

On my walk, I saw people on bicycles everywhere. Young, middle-aged, and very old people ride everywhere; it's normal.

I bid Diet and Renzo good-bye, for they now go back home, and I will spend a few days in the home of Mike and Jayah. I'm going to be in Holland until the end of this month, so there are many memories to follow.

More memories

I walked all the way to downtown Den Haag today, and there were buildings I remember, department stores, and outdoor coffee shops. Nowadays, there are more cars, more people, and a lot more bicycles than I remember in 1998.

The first place was a coffee shop that I deserved to walk into after walking so far. And there they were—tulips on each table to remind me that I was, indeed, in Holland. Then I was off to the many department stores I remember and also the big, very old business and high-end store called de Bijenkorf.

There was a time back in 1988 when we tried to put together a business selling American Indian art and jewelry. I had an appointment with de Bijenkorf's buyer and proudly showed him a piece of pottery from the Colorado Ute Indians. He looked at it and said, "No, we wouldn't be able to sell this."

"Why?" I asked.

"Because the Dutch people won't understand it."

"Well, isn't that part of the marketing department to educate people regarding the goods?"

"Yes, but you don't understand, the Dutch want a front row seat for a dime."

So much for that business. However, we did manage to pay our way to Europe a few times, but that's about all.

One funny item I saw in the store today was a hot tub that is heated by a wood stove. It reminded me of cannibalism. Another funny sight that always piqued my curiosity is a bigger-than-life statue of a fashionably dressed couple sitting on top of a wall in front of a hotel. I don't know the story of why they sit there, but I do think the man looks a bit like Mr. Bean.

While walking, I observed a large area where people sit in the sun drinking and eating and socializing. Today, chairs were outside, but people must have gotten up fast when it began to hail.

I found the library and was happy to see that the coffee shop was still there. You can get something to eat and drink and then sit and read books or newspapers if you want. By that time, my legs were tired, so it was nice to find an English magazine to read for a few minutes before starting back on the long walk home.

Chinese New Year and President Lincoln

I got to City Hall just in time for the start of the Chinese New Year celebratory parade. It was a lively group of people ready to become snakes and dragons in the streets, and there were drummers on trucks and lots of colorful, costumed folks itching to get walking.

After I saw that, I hung out in the library for a while and then went to another restaurant for lunch of *oude kaas*, old cheese, my favorite, in a *tosti*, or toasted—a cheese sandwich to Americans.

I then went all over The Hague looking for the American book store, to refresh my memory. Someone told me to go down the street and make two right turns. After walking forever, I asked someone, and he gave me directions just opposite. I realize the first person said two rights when she meant two lefts. It happens in language mix-ups, but I had plenty of time, so it didn't matter.

I found it, and there were hundreds of books, all of them in English. I wanted to see what other products they had. From my memory of 14 years ago, we could purchase such items as Betty Crocker cake mix, Jell-O, and corn bread mix, among other items. Not anymore. I was told that all the items are now available in supermarkets.

After walking around a bit more, I walked by a movie theater and saw that *Lincoln* was playing. This is a have-to-see, and it was a matter of killing three hours, which is very easy in this city, until the movie started. Patrons of the theaters buy reserved seats, which makes it pretty easy to get a good seat.

I loved the movie with Daniel Day Lewis, Sally Field, and Tommy Lee Jones. The latter, I thought, was in a surprise role for him, but he was exceptional.

Church and new friends

I don't know if the pastor smiled at me because he was happy to see that a sinner had arrived to church, or was it because Pastor Tim Blackmon recognized me from my photos on Facebook? Pastor Blackmon and I have been Facebook friends for several years, from the first time I contacted him way back when I lived in Gonzales.

Back then I was reminiscing about my life in The Hague when I lived there. I looked online for the website of the American Church of The Hague. This is where I got the email address of the church and sent a message to the new pastor, Tim Blackmon. I knew someday I would return.

Back in 1998, Will and I were astonished over the music from the choir loft in back of us on the balcony. The choir was directed by Pastor Blackmon's father. We loved the entire service and the many activities generated at the church and by the people we met. Sundays became our day for church. We were never disappointed. The choir was exceptional, with auditions necessary to get invited to participate. I would never have made it up on the choir loft. I sound pretty good inside my own head when I sing, but it doesn't transfer out loud.

One Sunday, parishioners coming from across the world dressed up in their native clothing, and a party was held after church. Will and I dressed in our Colorado western outfits.

So I was there this morning, and again, I was mesmerized by the choir. The message delivered by Pastor Blackmon was about forgiveness. Forgive others, forgive yourself. I needed to hear it. Could stand to hear it again, in fact.

During the social time between the second and third services, I met Wilma who graciously greeted me and did more than that. After church, and when her husband, Ben, was back from singing in the choir, they took me to their home and served lunch. It was *erwtensoep*, split pea soup. It is known to be a cold-weather dish. Good idea, for it has been cold, and there is snow on the ground. "I make *erwtensoep* in all months with an 'R' in them," Wilma said.

Ben is a nurse and left after lunch for his job. Wilma, Benny (the most charming dog I have met in a long time), and I walked from their home to where I am staying until Tuesday.

When I leave here, I will be at an old hotel in Scheveningen. Scheveningen is a popular destination on the North Sea, where Will and I lived for one year. It is close to the beach and other interesting locations.

Meanwhile, I have spent a few days now with fresh eyes experiencing again the sites where Will and his teenaged friends played out their clandestine activities during World War II as resistance workers.

A little of this; a little of that

The only other time it has been as cold as it is today in Holland was when I was in Iceland last year. It's cold. I got back to the house from a long walk with freezing fingers and frosty ears.

While walking around a bit, I looked for a restaurant. I've learned you don't ask for a *Koffee* house because that's usually where pot is smoked and purchased. *Koffee* houses are not unusual here, as people in Holland are allowed a certain number of cannabis plants for their own use.

I looked, instead, for a restaurant. I found one on a cozy looking corner and ordered an *uitsmijter,* or bouncer. I learned about those years ago and understand from what Will told me that they were given to people just before they were thrown out of a bar. A bouncer is simply two fried eggs either with cheese and ham or just cheese, as was my choice, on a slice of bread.

Later, I purchased a beautiful bouquet of pink roses and daisies for the house of Jajah and Mike. I'm happy the flowers didn't freeze before I got them back.

Mike sat with his baby giving her a bottle of juice. It's not unusual to see a father responsible for a baby's care in Holland, either, because as a government worker, he is on leave for parenthood. Male government workers are given three months if taken immediately when a baby is born, or, as Mike opted to do, men can take off four hours a week. This option enables Mike to take his children to school on Tuesdays and Fridays.

He has Mondays off because, as a government official, he works 36 hours per week. Another option, if he chose it, would be to work four nine-hour days each week.

"There is something new that the government is encouraging workers to do, and that is to work at home," Mike said. "It saves money for the government because less office space is needed." It was figured, according to Mike, that space for one official costs the government 70,000 euros a year.

It's heartwarming to see men taking an important role in the lives of their children, especially now that mothers are working, as well.

Changing the subject, I received some sad news yesterday from my daughter-in-law, Aleida. Her 95-year-old grandmother died yesterday in Jakarta. I never got to meet Oma Dien, for when she visited California, I was in Costa Rica. However, I have heard good things about her from all the family, including Aleida's cousin, Mike.

Oma Dien was a school director and strict in her teaching style, which gives credence to the intelligence of her daughter, Lieke, and Lieke's daughter, Aleida, or Debby to the family and good friends. It also explains the good character they both possess.

One fond memory I have of Lieke was when Lieke brought Aleida and our co-grandchild, Michael, at age seven, to Holland for a visit with Will and me in Scheveningen. To keep Michael busy, I gave him the job of pointing out every date he found on top of buildings. And for every one he spotted, I gave him ten cents. Will and Lieke got into the action by helping Michael spot the dates.

Taking it easy today

Taking it easy today with no shame. I'm telling myself I deserve it.

That's probably stretching it a bit for someone who has traveled for ten months and has had an incredible time. But I did feel a need to stay in one place for a bit just to get my bearings before heading off to the last month of my yearlong journey.

So here I am in the Hotel Bor in Scheveningen, watching American TV shows for the first time in many months. Right when I first got here to this hotel, I went to the flower market and purchased some tulips for my room, and they are still looking pretty in front of the mirror.

I received a call from my longtime friend, Dr. Piet Stolk. He will pick me up in front of the hotel tomorrow, and we'll go to his place in Delft. Delft is a beautiful town surrounded by charming canals, bridges, and very old and picturesque shops of all kinds. It is also home to the famous Delft Pottery Factory. I'm looking forward to seeing Piet again after eight years.

So, rest along with me today, for tomorrow, I'll be seeing the sights and taking photos, and I will have many more stories about my stay here in Scheveningen.

Meanwhile, I'll wait for Mike to deliver my two suitcases that I left in his and Jajah's home. I had to take a bus to the hotel, and we all agreed it would be easier for me to find my way without dragging suitcases on and off buses.

On the way here, asking questions about the route to the hotel, I met Monique, who lives close by the hotel, and we will get together for lunch sometime during my stay here.

I want to mention here about the coffee I've made in nearly every place I've been in—hotels and hostels. I purchased an electric water heater that I put into a cup of water. After the water boils, I then pour it into the coffee I had put into a cone-shaped paper filter inside of a plastic cone, and the water drips down to make a great cup of coffee. It's easy to carry this around from country to country. However, I have forgotten the cones in various countries, only to have to look around to buy another one. That has been a challenge at times.

Visit with an important friend

Everyone should have a friend like Dr. Piet Stolk. He invited me to spend the day, beginning at his home in Delft. We had a cup of coffee and then lunch, after which we went on to the city of Rotterdam, and then dinner at his home again.

I met Dr. Stolk nearly 25 years ago when I was in Den Haag for business. He was across the street seeing patients at the hospital. I went to the hospital to ask some questions that had been on my mind concerning mental illness. He was the person I was directed to see, and he was gracious, answered my questions, and then invited me to his home.

That is when I met his lovely wife, Titia, who passed away one-and-one-half years ago. Together, Piet and Titia have acquired an impressive collection of ancient and new pottery and paintings by their favorite and important artists.

We have continued a friendship all of these years. He is an important friend in my life, someone I must see whenever I'm in Holland.

Today, in Rotterdam, after not seeing it for 25 years, I was surprised at the growth—skyscrapers that create architectural art in the sky and also big shopping centers. We walked around a bit in the city and then found a nine-floor bookstore that had an awesome restaurant.

The Port of Rotterdam is the largest port in Europe and one of the busiest in the world. It is amazing to see the city that rose from the ashes of its devastation caused by bombing during WWII. Piet drove me around the city to see the harbor, the brand new bridge, and more unusual architecturally designed new buildings.

Back at his home, he cooked a salmon dinner that was delicious and then drove me back to my hotel.

Piet has two fat cats—Tom, a black and white cat, and Tim, an orange cat. Tim seemed to tolerate me, but Tom didn't quite trust this home invader.

Valentine's Day and memories

Giant red hearts were flying above the Keizerstraat, Emperor Street, in Scheveningen for Valentine's Day. This Valentine's Day was cold, and the snow, sleet, ice, and wind made it difficult for me to recollect my memories of where we lived for one year. However, I didn't give up.

First off, I cannot keep mentioning the name Scheveningen without telling how the word was used during WWII. When a Dutchman would ask someone to say the word, if he couldn't do it, then it was known he was not from Holland and more than likely a German spy. The "sch" part is tricky and comes out from down in the throat.

Will and I decided we would go back to his hometown of The Hague for a year and live close to the North Sea beach and the well-known Kurhaus Hotel and resort. Will was advised by doctors to get to a lower altitude, and that we did, as parts of Holland are even below sea level. We sold our Colorado home and ventured onward.

We lived on the third floor of an apartment house on Badhuiskade, which, translated, means bath house on the path next to a canal. We lived across from a park and a children's farm. I learned what bus to catch to begin my memory walk at the Kurhaus Hotel.

One memory was the radio jazz show in the basement of the hotel way back then, where we heard famous jazz piano player, Pia Beck, stomp out a boogie-woogie medley that included an impromptu riotous beat honoring the Dutch soccer team.

But this building had memories for Will, as well. After he stopped piloting for the Royal Dutch Airforce, he was positioned in an office in the Kurhaus, as it had been temporarily taken over by the Dutch government after the war. He had pointed out the marble steps to his office when I saw the inside for the first time.

The Kurhaus goes back in history nearly 200 years when a German company opened it as a bathing establishment where visitors could take a bath in a tub of therapeutic seawater. It is now an opulent hotel with a grand stairway to the restaurant, painted ceilings, and crystal chandeliers.

I had a cup of cappuccino at the Kurhaus as I watched the snow fall on the North Sea beach and sand.

After I left there and did some walking on icy stone sidewalks around the old neighborhood where I saw the same green grocer, the florist, and other shops, along with new ones and some other changes, I was freezing and needed to get inside.

I found a little restaurant nearby the *Oude Kerk*, or Old Church. This church was built in the 14th century. Will and I with my son, Ronnie, who visited us during the Christmas season, attended Christmas Eve service in the church. It has long been a beautiful memory.

After seeing the old fishing village of Scheveningen and finding the three fish designs embedded in a sidewalk square, designs that symbolize the town, I began to walk back again toward the Kurhaus to catch the bus.

Everywhere I went, people were reinforcing that it was, indeed, slippery. The brick streets and stone sidewalks were so difficult to walk on that I took each step as a one-year-old learning to walk for the first time. The railings that I depend on were slippery, as well.

I decided to head to the restaurants on the boardwalk. It's not like an American boardwalk because it's more on stone and concrete, and on my way up an incline, the wind whipped, suddenly pushing me along fast. I reached out for the railing, and my hand slipped off of it. I almost fell but didn't. I stopped to figure out what to do. I couldn't go back down the incline, but going forward was dangerous. I did continue up the grade inch by inch until I was at the top overlooking the ocean.

I worked my way down again on a different path to a restaurant on the boardwalk and took my frozen face inside to rest. There were cozy little fire stations in the place, and it turned out I was the only person inside except for the nice young man who waited on me. He also stood and talked with me until I warmed up.

I got outside ready to catch the bus, and while I was walking toward it—slowly to keep from slipping—a young woman did fall about then, and the bus left before I could get there. I was inches away, so I had to wait for another bus. Who could get upset at a bus driver when today is Valentine's Day?

I am not alone.

I wasn't alone, for I had a room full of teddy bears to keep me company. That was inside a restaurant on the Scheveningen strand after I had walked nearly as long as yesterday. Teddy bears sat on every available shelf and window ledge. They kept their eyes on me.

Today was a tiny bit warmer; at least it didn't snow, and the ice had melted, so I wasn't afraid to walk anywhere. My destination was the museum ship *Mercuur* on the Scheveningen Harbor, and I had the usual challenge in getting there. First off, I was given the wrong bus to take to the harbor and made a change at the dead end when the bus driver told me where to catch tram number one.

Turns out that the tram number one operator agreed that his tram was the correct one for the harbor but neglected to tell me I needed to transfer to the number eleven.

After making adjustments and getting on and then off the correct tram, a gentleman told me he would be going that way and I could walk with him.

"I'm going that way, and if you would like, I'll walk with you."

"Yes, I would like to walk with you. Thank you." I think he thought I might be wary of walking with a stranger.

After he left, I ended up walking around some construction near the harbor, but I finally found the ship, and guess what? It was closed.

I wanted to see that ship museum because I had donated to it all of the navy papers I had from Will's father, which included his first pay book. He was 14-years-old and received ten cents a week. There were many other papers and photos, as well. I had promised Will that I would donate the items to this museum.

I guess I'll try to find out when it's open and make another trip. At least now I know the correct tram, and by the way, I walked nearly all the way back to the hotel where I began the venture.

I saw the opposite of the Kurhaus where the beach sand was being prepared for the temporary restaurants that would soon be raised for the spring and summer beachgoers.

The famous pier is closed due to the bankruptcy of the company that owned it. It is now for sale. However, I learned it needs a lot of reconstruction. It's a very old structure.

Also along the strand and the harbor, the Scheveningen woman stands in a statue looking out to sea waiting for her husband who didn't come back. She is dressed in the clothing typical of the women in the area. When I lived here 14 years ago, many elderly women still dressed in the Scheveningen costume. I assume when it warms up, those elderly ladies will be seen again.

You cannot fool a brilliant mind.

It was a long and captivating day on Saturday. Piet Stolk drove me all the way to Friesland, one of the 12 provinces in the Netherlands and in the north part of the country.

We had two destinations, or maybe four if you count looking for the Chinese restaurant and stopping for coffee at the d'Oude Waegh Restaurant in the quaint town of Hoorn. Hoorn, situated on the large Lake IJsselmeer, was established in 1357, and still has many of the original buildings, including d'Oude Waegh, which was in its heyday a place where cheese was weighed. The weight apparatuses are still hanging down from the ceiling.

Piet asked the young waitress about some writing on what looked like cupboard doors high above and close to the ceiling.

"I don't know," she said, and added, "We're not allowed to touch them."

Europeans preserve and protect old buildings, and Hoorn is a great example. Many unique and very old buildings like the cheese weighing building have survived through the years. You can walk among them in the old village. Many of the old buildings are inhabited, and some are used as shops.

Later, we were in the town of Franeker to view the oldest planetarium in the world. Eise Eisinga's mechanism is situated on the living room ceiling of his family home, which is now a museum and open to the public. The mechanism shows the current position of planets and the moon.

Eise Eisinga was educated only through a few years of schooling and worked as a wool comber, a person who takes the covering of the sheep and then washes, combs, spins, and sells it to be made into many kinds of articles. But Eisinga had an eye on the planets during his spare time. He took his scientific and mathematical mind and built a complex mechanism. The amazing result, built in the years 1774-1781, is the oldest working planetarium in the world.

Imagine swinging pendulums in front of your face all over your home and even where you sleep. Not much is written about Eisinga's wife, but she must have had an understanding heart. I learned that she did once protest the swinging pendulum near the bed where they slept, and Eisinga made adjustments to that.

Why was this man so motivated to complete such a phenomenon? The story goes thus. People were spreading false stories he thought were just plain ignorant, such as what was to happen on May 8, 1774. On that day, the planets of Mercury, Venus, Mars, Jupiter, and the Earth's Moon would be found in Aries. People were scared that they would collide and that would be the end of the world.

You cannot fool a brilliant mind. Eisinga thought it was time to teach ignorant people about orbits and distances in space. He left all of his drawings and his instructions behind so that after his death, what he taught would not be forgotten. Some of the instructions that are followed today are to set the date ring correctly on the leap day, check the speed of the clock during sudden temperature changes, adjust the orbit of Saturn every year because of a small miscalculation, and paint new year numbers every 22 years in a particular space reserved for that.

The planets orbit the sun at the same speed as the real planets, with energy provided by a gear mechanism that uses 10,000 hand-forged nails as teeth. A pendulum clock and nine weights control the mechanism. As you tour the house, the mechanism can be seen doing the heavy work.

I'm not a student of the planets and would probably be considered ignorant if Eisinga were alive, but I found the museum fascinating, and I delighted that he was such a forward-thinking person to leave notes for the future. Just like time and space, the model of the solar system he built has never failed.

The potter

After spending time at the Eise Eisinga Planetarium, we went to Drenthe Vledderveen after a Chinese dinner and had tea with Hans van Riessen in the home where he and his mother lived for many years. His mother has since died, and he lives alone. Hans is an important potter, and within his home is a gallery of his work. There are vases of all shapes and sizes, and each piece is unique in color and form. Hans showed us where he works every day on his potter's wheel and where each pot goes through a series of three steps—turning, glazing, and firing—which give each object its own character. His work is inspired by Asian pottery processes.

Hans is a tall, quiet, and friendly man with an easy smile. It appears he enjoys explaining the process of his work to anyone who stops by.

I found it intriguing to see how he works each pot to get the desired result. He is an unusual potter in that most potters these days use commercial glazes. Not Hans. He has his own recipe and therefore can control it better because he knows it well.

After seeing the workspace and the gallery, we sat in his living room on big, comfortable chairs and drank tea. The fireplace was crackling, and the room was warm and cozy. What, in the U.S., we'd call a coffee table, is taller, and in the Old Dutch tradition, it was covered with a rug. The teapot wore a tea cozy to keep the tea warm, and we ate cake that Hans made himself. He also bakes his own bread.

Hans' work is collected by people near and far. Piet has several pieces in his collection in Delft.

Driving up to Friesland was foggy a great deal of the way, especially in the area where there is much water on the ground. The Dutch have long learned to work with the large bodies of water through a series of dykes that open and close as needed. We traveled through wide, open spaces where there was an absence of houses—just a few farms, green lands, and once in a while, a windmill and a canal. We saw sheep, goats, and horses. There were quaint villages, each village with its own character as seen in its unique architecture.

Friesland has its own language, and signage in some of the towns is shown with both the Friesland and Dutch words.

Met good people and awesome dogs near Belgium

Piet and his good friend, Dr. Lenie de Groot, drove us up to a town close to the Belgium border to enjoy an evening with Piet's son and daughter-in-law, Eef and Marianne Stolk. Lenie first picked me up at my hotel in Scheveningen, and then we were off to Delft to pick up Piet.

When we arrived, Eef greeted us and asked me if I was afraid of dogs. I told him no. About that time, Eva looked at me through the window. Eva and Nora are females, and the white dog, nicknamed Jake and with the formal name, Don Diego, are all galgos, a little like greyhounds, and were adopted from Spain.

According to Eef, and I checked a website that agreed, this type of dog is hanged to death after the hunting season is over. Gruesome. They need to change that immediately.

When I first saw the dogs, I thought they wouldn't be my pick; however, it didn't take long to get acquainted. They are loving, sweet-natured, clean, and a joy to be around. They love people, love to be touched, and love to sit next to you or on your lap.

Eva sat on Piet's lap for a long time, while Jake sat in a dog bed and Nora in another corner. Once in a while, they would walk to each of us and stare with their big eyes, just asking for a pat on the head or a rub on their satiny, smooth backs. The three galgos aren't the only dogs loved by the Stolks, for there is another older, shorter dog, a longhaired dachshund, who also loves to be caressed. His name is George. They are all gentle creatures and much loved by Eef and Marianne who help people rescue dogs like Eva, Nora, and Jake from Spain.

Eef and Marianne spoiled us well when we were in their home. First off, we were given a rice cake unique to the area where they live. It is baked in a light crust and is filled with creamy rice. Later, we were served crackers with a topping and crispy chips with wine. A bit later, we had dinner. It began with an appetizer of small pieces of toast with anchovies and tomatoes, followed by chicken soup. Then Eef and Marianne served baked chicken, green beans, potatoes baked with rosemary, and a pocket, like a turnover, filled with cooked red cabbage. By that time, I was ready to quit, but in came the dessert—a cake with a center of chocolate, followed up with coffee and Bailey's Irish Cream in a tiny glass.

Needless to say, the day was wonderful with good people, wonderful dogs, and awesome food.

Now you know why I was tired when I got into my hotel room. By the way, I really like the idea of living in a hotel. Every day when I come back to my room, it's been picked up and vacuumed, and the bed is made. I'm worried that I like it too much, as it's easy to let that happen.

The Peace Palace

I have a special memory of the Peace Palace. When Germany invaded Holland, there was a convoy of German soldiers in trucks, singing and drinking beer in front of the Peace Palace.

Will and his buddy Jilles sneaked up to the trucks and let air out of all the truck tires, while another friend, Bertus, kept watch. After the trucks were immobilized, the boys ran like hell, laughing until they fell on the grass. They were spent. It was fun, until . . . each boy walked back to his house silently, thinking about what could have happened had they been caught.

Imagine being a teenager of 15 or 16, when most boys were out having a good time, and being seriously involved with thwarting Hitler's progress. The truck tire sabotage was a dangerous activity but was just the beginning of the boys' work during the war and the Hunger Winter.

The Peace Palace—I just love the name of it—was a dream and a generous gift of American industrial magnate Andrew Carnegie to the Netherlands. It was created by French architect Louis Cordonnier as "a dream palace for world peace."

I stood in front of the massive structure that is a symbol of the ideals of peace and justice. The building that is over 100-years-old houses the International Court of Justice and the Court of Arbitration.

When we lived in Holland in 1998, I remember hearing the story of Will and his two friends. When Will explained the incident to me, we were on tram number one heading past the palace, just as I was today, except today, I got off the tram and took a photo of the palace.

On another trip to the Peace Palace, Will and I were allowed to go inside. That has changed now and is allowed only during special public forums.

After getting off to see the Peace Palace, I got back on number one and headed to the main train station where I purchased a ticket to Amsterdam for tomorrow.

Amsterdam and a gift

Dorry and I did a "Ladies, let's do lunch," date today, and it was lovely to see her one more time before I leave Holland. Dorry, along with her partner, Paul Boes, hosted me in their beautiful Arnhem home three weeks ago. We agreed then that we would get together for lunch, so that was the plan for today.

I met Dorry on the 23rd floor of the Amsterdam skyscraper where she works. Her employer is Arcadis, an international company that provides design, consultancy, engineering, and project and management services for natural and built assets (*arcadis.com*). Dorry's talents are used in the communication department. That seems to me an appropriate niche for Dorry, for she was a key person in the Arcadis Company's art collection.

Later, I met Dorry on the main floor, and with my badge to open the gate, I followed her for lunch in the same building. The restaurant has many choices—warm dishes, a la carte, sandwiches, and more. We both chose the fish dish that was delicious.

Dorry is involved in a huge project with her work, and I felt fortunate to get her all to myself for our one-hour lunch. After lunch, we went to the 24th floor where Arcadis' main office is located, and then to her office on the 23rd floor. Many pieces of the artwork I mentioned are on the walls in prominent display.

When the lunch hour was up, Dorry gave me a gift. It is the book, *Kunst Collectie Arcadis Art Collection*. The book has photos of the major works of art in the Arcadis collection. The book says Arcadis has a goal to find a balance between the company's economic activity and its commitment to enriching the culture. A few years ago, a committee was formed to build the criteria for art and to purchase the collection. My friend Dorry is listed as one of the authors of the book she gifted me, and she was also responsible for the composition of it. She was also a key person in choosing the artwork for the company.

Earlier in the day, I got a train from Den Haag to Amsterdam, following Dorry's description of the building where she works in order to help me locate it. It was easy to find. However, I was a bit early, so I sat in a coffee shop looking up at the building that I would soon enter.

Later, I joined a crowded city center in Amsterdam and walked around the town, viewing what the city is famous for. You cannot miss seeing the "coffee shops" where cannabis is openly sold.

I got on a hop-on-hop-off-bus that would be the last trip for the day, so I couldn't hop off until the very end, but that was okay, as I really just wanted to get an overview of what makes the city so attractive to a huge number of tourists.

I find a possible answer, besides the coffee shops and the red-light district, in the old buildings, canals, boats, and sculptures that all add to make the city unique. The voice guide provided names of famous people and the houses where they lived.

This was my third trip to Amsterdam, and I won't be going back; it's just too busy for me.

However, I will cherish the reason I went to Amsterdam, as well as the lovely book Dorry gave me. Her gift is priceless.

More memories

Memories again popped up when I was in the Centrum of The Hague today. Some memories were of my time in The Hague alone, some with Will, and some from the stories he told me about the years during WWII.

I found the Passage, which Will and his friends walked under to get to their ballroom dance lessons. I walked during the rain to begin with, followed up by standing in front of the Binnenhof complex of stone buildings. One of them is the Great Hall where the Queen holds her annual speech. The complex is also made up of the Dutch Parliament, since 1446. A tower there is known as the Little Tower. Close by is the Mauritshuis Museum, which has been the office of the Prime Minister since 1982.

I wanted to see the Mauritshuis Museum, as the famous painting, *The Girl With the Pearl Earring*, rests inside it. However, due to some massive construction in the same area, the museum was closed.

There are more old buildings in the Binnenhof that have stood in place for eight centuries. A larger modern building, which has been built since the first time I was in The Hague alone, houses the House of Representatives. The courtyard is open to the public, and a gold fountain adorns the square.

The small lake on the side of the Binnenhof was where Will and his friend hid inside an underground shelter close by during the bombing of Rotterdam. When they crawled out of the shelter with many other men, women, children, and dogs, they saw the lake shimmering in reflection from the fires and smoke from the bombing.

I remembered the Indonesian restaurant close by and its top floor reserved for the members of the American Women's Club, back in 1999. This is where our spouses and we women got the best view of Queen Beatrix going to the Binnenhof Ridderzaal in her gilded carriage. Every year on the third Tuesday of September, the Queen delivers a speech, and the Minister of Finance presents the budget to the House of Representatives. The Indonesian food was good, too.

On another walk through the town, I remembered the famous Jamin Candy Store, and I found one that fulfilled my desire to nurture my memory.

Cornelis Jamin was born in 1850, in Boxmeer. He moved to Rotterdam where he started a street trade of candy, and after ten years, he had two sugar factories, one in the Red Sand and one in Crooswijkse Quay. Three years later, in 1883, the Netherlands had its first candy store.

I couldn't resist the Jamin Candy Store. I had to purchase some candy for the memories. I chose what I wanted, and the sales person put it into a cone-shaped bag and tied it with a ribbon. Jamin is famous for its well-loved salty licorice that is unique in flavor, but it's not my favorite. It's just too salty for my tastes.

Just to keep on the sweet subject, another treat are the stroopwafels. These are round cookies with honey and are big enough to put on top of a cup of tea to warm them up. I saw a man in the center of town making them and other sweet items right on the street. Stroopwafels are now available in World Market, but before this, I used to order them from a Dutch mail order company.

A restaurant in the city called The Haagse Bluf uses a typical word that Will had described to me. The Hague had a reputation, deserved or not, I'm not convinced, but a reputation nonetheless, for a dessert made of egg whites and sugar—a bluff. It is so simple with such simple ingredients that it is a bluff for a real dessert. Folks in other Dutch cities thought the people in Den Haag were snobs; thus the Haag bluff was named for them.

Thinking out loud

I came back to the hotel yesterday evening, tired from walking and getting on and off the trams and buses, trying to locate this and that, purchasing shampoo and other items. I found a store with used CDs and DVDs, and for one euro I got a movie, *The Private Life of Henry VIII*. I'll watch that later today. Getting back to yesterday, I was so tired that when I decided to climb into bed, I just put my coat, packages, camera, and purse on the floor.

This morning, I left it all and went down to the breakfast room. Usually, the maid knocks on the door to clean the room and make the bed, or she waits until I leave. But this morning after breakfast, I went to the room to find her there. The bed was all made and the bathroom clean, and all the stuff was off the floor. I was embarrassed to say the least. I'm the person who would clean up a house before a housekeeper comes to clean.

But she put me at ease and told me I had the only room available to clean, and so she went ahead, thinking I wouldn't mind. Of course, I didn't, really. I love being spoiled this way. And then she told me a bit about her life.

She is a young woman and only four years in Holland from Lithuania. She said her dreams of a new life in Holland haven't come true yet. She has a degree in interior design, but like many, she has a million excuses why she hasn't pursued her dream of working in her field of study. I tried to assure her that when the time is right, she'd know it. Meanwhile, she has a job, and that is a giant first step.

This all brought me to my own condition. I have had so much fun on this long journey, and I've learned a lot. I have great notes and photos for my book, but my biggest concern right now is what will I do when I return back to the U.S. in seven weeks? I will need to find a room, generate some income, and work on my book. I'll need to practice some of my preaching, and I know that it will all come into place. For me, the right time begins when I put my foot down on U.S. territory.

Museums—do they really want your donation?

After a disappointment, the situation was rectified, and so far, it's smooth sailing.

This story began when Will and I lived in Scheveningen. We visited the former Naval vessel, *Mercuur*, a ship museum at the Scheveningen Harbor.

Will was impressed with the museum that is run totally by volunteer labor and donations, so impressed that he told the commander he would donate copies of his father's Navy papers.

That would be nice, the commander said, but why not donate the real thing? Will said he thought that would be okay, and he would certainly send the documents after we got back to the States and he had the opportunity to look around for them.

Will became too ill, and I got very busy working and taking care of him, so that we just didn't take care of the donation in a timely way, even though we both talked about doing it.

Will died in 2002. I was living in Costa Rica from 2003 to 2005, and during that time, I took a trip to Holland and asked again if the commander would like the papers. He affirmed that they would be welcomed into the museum.

When I got back to the States and found the paperwork, I had my friend Ellen Korstanje translate the material for me so I would know what I was offering the museum.

After that, a Dutch woman in The Hague, a sister of my friend in Costa Rica, took the papers that I had mailed to her to the ship museum. She and her husband presented them to the commander. They took photos of the transaction and sent them to me. Meanwhile, the commander answered my letter verifying that the paperwork was received with pleasure, and he thanked me for the donation.

Today, I walked in the freezing cold wind all the way to the harbor and to the ship. I wanted to see how the papers were being used and to get a photo.

This was the second trip; the ship was closed the first time. I saw a ramp that goes up to the ship that looked closed, but to the side was another smaller boat with a ramp that appeared to be open.

"Hello? Permission to come aboard? Hello? Is anyone here?" Silence. I continued to walk down the steep and shaky ramp and into the ship. Still, no one was around, so I went up narrow stairs until I could see the deck.

About that time, a man came around the corner and looked surprised to see me. I was equally surprised. I tried in my best Dutch, which is very poor Dutch, to explain that I wanted to see how my husband's father's papers were being displayed in the ship.

He told me to go ahead and go anywhere inside the ship and take all the photos I wanted.

"You must pay my colleague," he added, completely putting aside what I had asked him about the papers.

As I ventured on through the ship, looking inside windows at dummies doing their duties in the various rooms, an elderly woman showed up completely dressed in a Navy uniform.

"Were you in the Navy?" I asked.

"No," she said. That was about all we understood from each other from then on until I left. I kept running into her, and whenever I asked her a question about the ship, she didn't know the answer. I gave up.

Then another man, who had paint splattered all over him, appeared and asked if he could help me. I told him the story about the donation and that I wanted to see the display.

"That doesn't sound familiar to me, but I'll explain all about the ship to you."

He went over the whole history. The ship originated in the U.S. It was a mine sweeper for the U.S. Navy in the Netherlands. After WWII, the *Mercuur* assisted in searching and destroying sea mines in the Dutch harbors.

I listened politely and then asked again about the papers.

"I'll go and ask the commander."

After a few minutes, he came back and said the commander doesn't remember anything about it.

"I need to speak to him. Please tell him I'm here, and I'd like to ask him about my donation."

He came back with the commander, and I explained the whole situation to him.

"What was his name?"

"Diephof."

"Oh, I think I remember now. Wait here and I'll go see what I can find."

He was gone for about 15 minutes and then returned with a note that had the name Diephof on it.

"We are building a shelf to put the papers on," the commander said.

"Oh, well, that's nice. When you finish, will you let me know?"

"Yes. Put your email here, and I'll send you a note when it is finished."

476

The above conversation was all in Dutch, believe it or not! Nearly everyone I encounter with very few exceptions speaks English. He did not.

I left feeling a little bit better, but I wasn't fooled. It doesn't take eight years to build a shelf!

Note to all museums—if you do not want a donation, say so. Do not accept anything and then stash it away. I personally would rather not give it to someone who doesn't want it.

This is the second time this has happened to me, and I've learned my lesson. The first time in another museum, it took years to see my donation put into a glass case, while a more important item was stolen before it was even displayed. Shame.

Searching for a friend

It's cold. "How cold is it?" Well, à la Johnny Carson to his audience's question, "It's so cold, you'd have to jump-start a reindeer."

Even though it's really cold today, there are things to see and do, so I bundled up and went off to the southern part of Den Haag to give my regards to Toosje Van Dyke, who is in the hospital.

Toosje, age 85, is a family friend and former neighbor of the Diephofs. The families' friendship goes way back to the beginning of WWII when the Van Dykes had several children and the Diephofs had two, Will and his sister, Poppy.

I cannot help but feel sorrow for how both families and the entire country of the Netherlands suffered during the cold winter when there was no food, no heat, and limited water. The Dutch burned their furniture for warmth and to warm up any food they might have acquired somehow. Some folks, in desperation, burned asphalt to make a fire for cooking. The smell that came from the burned asphalt was asphyxiating.

It was a rough time, and in getting to see Toosje, those years were on my mind as I walked nearly two miles from the tram to get to the hospital. I was cold, but I would be capable of getting warm soon, and food was no problem.

I had taken a bus to the central station where I looked for a sign that would give the number of the tram I needed to get to Wateringen, where the hospital is located. The station is undergoing extensive remodeling. I knew it would be up to me to take the responsibility, search, and ask questions about what mode of transportation would get me to my destination.

I saw that tram 17 would go to Wateringen, which was verified by the tram driver. It was a long ride, and on the marque that announces the stops, it never showed Wateringen. Soon, the tram driver stopped, turned, and told me we were in Wateringen. There was nothing around—no town, no stores, and no station.

"Where do I go to get here?" I showed the driver a card with the address, but she didn't know. I got off, saw two women in the distance walking my way, and asked for directions. The conversation was all in Dutch. The older one was the mother, and she began to explain, but when the daughter spoke up, the mother slapped her hand and said, "Nay."

Both of us then paid attention to the mother. She told me to walk that way, turn left over the bridge, keep going to the end, then go over a blue bridge on your right, then go straight, and the hospital would be on the left.

The daughter got a word in. "See the church?" She pointed to a steeple barely visible.

"It's across the street from the church."

I walked with them as far as the first bridge, working my legs as fast as I could to keep up, not with the daughter but with the elderly mother who appeared to have motors in her legs. Their friendly directions were great, and I finally arrived at the hospital.

"I'm here to see Toosje Van Dyke," I told the receptionist. She saw only two people with that last name, but they had the wrong first name. She took me to a lunchroom full of residents and pointed to one woman, but I had to say it wasn't her. It reminded me of a prison lineup.

At the next room where someone with a different first name lived, no one answered the door. I was about to give up but went back to the receptionist again and told her the family had said this place was where Toosje was living.

"I'll call Sister and ask her for help."

The nun took me to the second room, and we went inside where a woman looked hopefully up at me—hopeful for a visitor—but no, that wasn't her, either.

"Let's go back downstairs. Maybe she is here only temporarily," the nun said.

She asked the receptionist for the list of temporary patients, and there, right on the list, was Toosje's name and room number.

The nun took me to Toosje's room and left me there to visit. Toosje was in bed but was wide awake and ready to see me.

Toosje's memory is excellent. She remembers practically every time we were together. That was in The Hague and in Colorado where she visited us. Her humor is as good as ever, too; she managed to make fun of my poor Dutch and the big boots I was wearing. She doesn't speak English, so I had to find the words somehow to express myself. I could understand most of what she said.

For many years, Toosje took care of Walter and Poppy's children, who are now parents and grandparents. She is someone the family has treasured throughout the years.

I didn't stay long, as I had to be in Den Haag soon after. I went outside into the cold and jumpstarted the reindeer. Actually, it was bus number 30.

The beach and Dutch customs

Moe and Joe, left foot, right foot, and bus number 23 took me to another North Sea beach called Kijkduin. It was cold, but there were some diehards walking near the shoreline and along the dunes. I stayed back and admired them until I found a restaurant that was warm and cozy inside. There are many restaurants that are open year-round, and the one I chose, Ketje's Mix, was full of people eating and drinking. Everyone walked in with coats, scarves, gloves, and boots, but took them off inside where it was relaxing after being in the brisk wind. I know there are millions upon millions of tiny seashells down on the sand because I have picked many up in other years, so today, I didn't make the trip down to the shore. Instead, I looked down and found a few in the sand near the tall grass. That was enough to make my day.

I don't remember this from the past, but I noticed that the boardwalk near the restaurants and shops is laid down firmly with sand and those little seashells.

While I'm at it and on the last week of my Holland adventure, I thought it a good time to mention some Dutch expressions heard every day.

The expression similar to the American sarcasm, "Yeah, right," is "je, je." However, the "j" is pronounced as the "h" in head.

"So" is heard when someone has accomplished something. I heard that today when a cold-looking elderly lady and a gentleman struggled to get a seat and settled down before the bus lunged forward.

"Lekker" means, "That is really delicious." I hear that often since most of my meals are taken in restaurants.

"Doei" sounds like "dooey." It's an informal way to singsong good-bye.

I may need help with this one. When someone is displeased with something, but it's not worthy of a long complaint, a simple word is said that sounds like "Now."

It's a custom to take flowers to a host, and that is so easy in Holland, for there are many flower stands, stalls, and shops, and flowers are plentiful.

Okay, now let's go to the subject of kissing.

When the Dutch greet or say good-bye, many folks kiss first on one cheek and then the other one, but that doesn't end the greeting, for they then go back and kiss the first cheek again. It takes a long time to greet and say good-bye in Holland.

I remember when living in Costa Rica how people kissed even in business transactions. I was in a travel agent's office, and when most people shake hands, there the manager kissed first and got to know me later. That was a normal way of doing business.

I love to learn about the customs in other countries, and I feel they are a blessing to us. I never want to judge another culture's traditions, for that would be the same as making fun of their family. I appreciate the same in return for the customs and traditions that have developed over the years in America.

Staring at purple tulips

Didn't go far today, as I waited for an airline company's phone call that didn't come. I walked up to the Kurhaus to mosey around and do some light shopping. Before that, I walked to a restaurant for lunch and got a sliced egg sandwich on a brown roll.

On the way back to the hotel, I couldn't resist looking inside a store that said SALE. Who could pass that up? I didn't buy anything, but I did meet a nice lady who has lived in the U.S., both Washington and New York, around 30 years ago. I can see why she had been offered many modeling jobs, as she is still a beauty.

After visiting the Kurhaus and walking around the neighborhood a bit, I sat inside my room, perused the Internet, read all about the Oscar show from *USA Today*, and stared at the purple tulips I have in my room.

Soon, I'm going back to read on my eBook, for I have over 100 books to read.

Taking it nice and easy. Tomorrow will be a busy day beginning at ten a.m. when Piet will pick me up to take me to see more of Holland.

Sand Motor and castle and art

"I'm almost 90-years-old, and you have knee trouble. I think it's time we go back," Piet said. We had just walked in the cold air from a parking lot all the way on a path and then on sand to view a Dutch innovation, the Sand Motor.

By using ships and the latest technological equipment, about 21.5 million cubic meters of sand were dredged up to protect the coast area near Kijkduin in South Holland. Now it is nature's turn to complete the rest. Through wind and waves and ocean currents, the sand will be distributed along the coast to make room for more recreational activities.

As stated on a sign at the beginning of the site, "The shape of Sand Motor will change in the course of 20 years. Eventually, the sand will be completely dispersed across the new dunes and the beach."

It was awesome to see how man and nature work together, and it was great to observe the beginnings of such a project.

The Dutch work wonders with water distribution and dykes that open and close to accommodate rising water and boat traffic. And now, with innovation and engineering skills, they are working on the land and the ocean.

But there I was admiring the magnificent project, and I couldn't help but see the billions of tiny seashells on the sand just waiting for my greedy hands and pockets.

"Isn't it funny how particular you get when the shells are so plentiful?" I asked Piet, as I searched for the most perfect and the prettiest.

After we walked back off the sand and onto the path into the cold wind and got back to the car, we found the restaurant, Haagsche Beek. Beek means small stream. I had *gebakje*, cake, from the baking company, Maison Kelder, known for its hazelnut cake. It's famous in the area. The restaurant was a warm place that surprised us by being full of people. It seems out of the way, but people will find the cozy corners in this country.

The next stop was the small town of Maassluis with its 17th century harbor that was mainly used for fishing boats. Here we found old brick buildings, walkways over bridges, and nice shops along both sides of the canal.

We were hungry by then and found the Frans Vouk's Koffie Shop. I thought I was ordering a pancake with banana topping, but I didn't complain when a pineapple-laced pancake was delivered to me. I learned later that there, again, my misinterpretation of the language afforded another learning opportunity. *Ananas* means pineapple, and banana is *banaan*.

Onward we went over the highways and byways to Kasteel van Rhoon. This castle, built in 1199, is now used as a cultural center where various musical events take place, as do important art exhibits. We were there to see the work of Germaine Sanders: www.germainesanders.nl.

Germaine's creations were displayed at the top room of the castle with many of her works along the walls. They are pen and ink drawings with such detail that you have to stand and study each piece. What drives that kind of patience is a mystery to me.

This artist is one who uses both the left and right sides of her brain. She is an architect with an emphasis on engineering and has taught subjects in college. Now she sketches, sells her work, and has a school that emphasizes creativity.

"I take people outside to draw what they see." She explained that in the busy world, we don't really stop to clearly look at what is before us. "I want people to really see for themselves, and then draw what they see." She went further to say, "It's not the result of the art made by the student, but what the student experiences by seeing."

I found many pieces I could easily live with, although right now I don't have four walls or a ceiling, but I'll take back the memory with me.

After looking around at Kasteel van Rhoon, we traveled onward to Piet's good friend, Lenie, and had dinner in her apartment in Lisse, the town of the famous Keukenhof Gardens. Keukenhof is open during the spring and summer months and is a site every visitor to Holland should see. Every color of tulips makes a home in this garden, and tulips join with other flowers and garden sculptures.

When I said good-bye to Lenie and later to Piet, I knew it would be for the last time during this journey. Piet was most generous with the long time he spent with me touring his beautiful country. I enjoyed all of it, especially learning so much from him and loving his humor.

Chapter Twelve

March, 2013

Moving objects

Saying good-bye a lot lately, including tonight. I visited with my daughter-in-law's aunt and a cousin today in The Hague. This was the first time in 14 years that I had seen Roos and the first time to meet Linda. Roos, Linda, and I had Indonesian food and talked a bit before it was time for Linda and me to catch our respective buses and head for home.

Speaking of buses, it reminds me to tell anyone coming to Holland to be careful of anything that moves. It's an active country with busy cities, with good use of public and personal transportation. I'm not kidding. I look right, left, up, and down before crossing the street or even a bike path. This rule includes birds. Why birds? Because several times now, I have nearly stepped on a pigeon. They are so tame in some areas, and today a goose nearly got so close I could have captured it and cooked it.

Here's a list of moving things to watch out for: walkers and runners, bicycles, bicycles with carts for carrying merchandise or children, bicycles with motors, motorcycles, motor scooters, scooters that kids move with their legs, skate boarders, baby buggies, cars, vans, trams, buses, boats, cranes, tractors, trucks, and . . . did I leave anything out? Probably.

A belly full of poffertjes

You cannot leave Holland without experiencing the delightful dish, *poffertjes*. They are little pancakes made in a special pan and look to be about the size of a silver dollar on steroids.

I met my friends, Mike, Jajah, Aisha, Rania, Farah, Budewyn, Carolina, and Angelina at Paviljoen Malieveld, a *pannenkoeken* (pancake) and *poffertjes* restaurant today. The restaurant sits on a park, and while I waited for the time to meet them, I walked around the park on a path for walkers and bicycles.

While I walked, I remembered being at the same park many years ago with my brother, Jack, sister-in-law, Carol, and my husband, Will. We walked catty-corner across the park to the Paviljoen Malieveld restaurant for *poffertjes*.

I also observed a tower that I remembered. When Will was hungry and tired during the Hunger Winter, he looked at the tower and thought it was standing so strong and stately and without trouble. It made him wonder when his life would change and he would once again be strong and healthy. He needed food and warmth. It was cold today, and the misery of the time he faced was on my mind.

The restaurant Paviljoen Malieveld was built in 1941, and still has the wooden plank floor and familiar lacy curtains, curtains that are becoming things of the past. I still see windows with the lace curtains that either hang down about one-fourth of the way from the top of the window or from the middle of the window. While still seen, views of these lacy curtains are not as frequent as before.

I had a dish of *poffertjes*, and my friends all made their own choices, and when we were through eating, we walked to the center of the city.

It was fun seeing the three little girls, the daughters of Jajah and Mike, cousins of my daughter-in-law, Aleida.

While we walked, Jajah pointed out a big tree from the 1800s. It had been transplanted on the spot to avoid being cut down from where it previously stood.

When I got to the center of town, I made the decision not to stick around, as it was full of people shopping and walking up and down the streets. I observed a sign that told people to watch their belongings as pickpocketers were on the prowl. I had a belly full of *poffertjes,* and it was time to head back to the hotel.

Vaarwel, Holland.

Today is the official last day of my adventure in Holland. I will say good-bye to my old neighborhood. Mike Siegers will take me to Schiphol Airport in Amsterdam tomorrow morning.

Piet Stolk put many miles on his car to show me the Netherlands from the east to west and south to north. I don't think I have missed anything.

My adventure marks the first time I rode on a scooter, thanks to Paul Boes.

It was fun to travel to Amsterdam to meet Dorry Reuling, and afterwards, getting on a hop-on-hop-off bus for a quick refresher course on the City of Amsterdam.

The whole Dutch experience has been a reminder of the many times I visited in the past, and of course, the one year in Scheveningen I spent with Will. My time here also afforded an opportunity to explore the sites, one more time, where Will and his friends played havoc with Hitler's regime. It also reminded me of the Hunger Winter. I experienced the Dutch cold winter and cannot imagine how awful it is to be this cold without any way to get warm, and hungry at the same time. It brought home the WWII experience of Will and his friends and family. Tomorrow will challenge me, for I'll be going through customs after I have knowingly violated the Schengen rules.

Mike picked me up, and along the way, he explained what might happen when I get to customs. He worked for another department in customs and had learned that I was, indeed, subject to scrutiny regarding my stay.

"All I can do is just walk up and give my passport and just be myself."

"I'll wait for you just in case you will be detained."

It was time for me to walk up to the customs agent.

"I think I may be a bit early." I smiled and handed over my passport and my ticket.

"Good that you're early. It starts to get busy." He stamped my passport and bid me good flight.

I waved to Mike and blew him a kiss.

Turkey!

Here I am in Istanbul, Turkey.

I've been apprehensive about this trip since December 21, but now that I breezed through customs when a jolly agent stamped my passport and told me to have a good trip, I can relax and enjoy myself in this bustling, busy city. I am in the Asian side of Istanbul, which makes me on another continent than the one across the river. That side is the European side, and I'll visit there by ferry one of these days.

Mike Siegers picked me up with his baby and another daughter who wasn't feeling well and drove me to the airport. Believe me, it's great when someone knows the route to the airport and can circumvent the airport maze.

After we said our good-byes, I was standing in the customs line where they search your luggage and screen your body, and a woman shouted some directions that I couldn't understand. I asked the tall, three-piece-suited man in front of me what the lady said.

"She said to take all of your clothes off and run through the detector."

"Oh, yeah," I said. "Well then, you go first," I laughed.

He laughed, too, and then the line moved forward until we were at the spot where you dump your coat, computer, bags, and whatever into a tub that then rolls through the peeking-at your-stuff-device.

I then got frisked.

Eventually, I got on the Pegasus Airlines plane and had a great window seat, and then a lovely young lady sat next to me. She is from Istanbul, a zumba teacher, and had been a presenter at a big zumba convention in Utrecht, Holland.

She wrote down several places in my notebook that I should see and also names of typical Turkish food. She was a delightful person with fair English skills.

The gentleman next to her, a Dutchman, works on ships and was off to work on a dredger, which takes sand and places it elsewhere, like in the Sand Motor in Kijkduin.

When Pegasus landed in Turkey, we had to get in line for a visa and then in another line for the passport control. Turkey does not subscribe to the Schengen rules, so I can have a clear mind.

After about an hour of customer scrutiny, I got my luggage and found a bus that said Kadiköy. I sat next to an architect originally from Mexico City but who now lives in Barcelona. An interesting man, he told me his parents live in Holland, and 15 years ago, when they first began living there, he went to Barcelona, and, when back in Holland, he announced he was moving to Barcelona. He's been there ever since.

We had a great time talking all the way to Kadiköy. His mission was to ferry across to the European side, and mine was to find the Konak Otel.

Prior to coming to Turkey, I had sent an email asking how to get to the hotel from the airport, and the answer was that they didn't have a shuttle but to take the bus and walk to the hotel. Well sure, I did that, but now, where in the heck is the hotel? I looked around while the architect I'd sat next to on the bus sort of waited to see what I'd do. I stepped up to a man and showed him the name of the hotel and the address.

The architect looked at me like he thought I was crazy stepping up to ask a stranger for help. I just smiled and shook my head as if to say, don't worry.

The dark-haired and handsome stranger got on his telephone and motioned for me to follow him. He walked in front of cars and buses, motioning for them to stop to let us pass. Some did, but most just closely circled around us. I followed him as best I could, and two times, my suitcase clipped my shoe and my shoe came off. I had to stop and get the shoe back on, while cars were whizzing by me.

When we got across the street and onto a very busy sidewalk with people walking every which way, I felt like I was in Barcelona, running with the bulls.

The man finally grabbed the handle of one of my suitcases and walked fast, occasionally turning to see if I was still behind him. He stopped once again to call the hotel, and he turned back. We had been going the wrong way. So back again the same way, turning at the corner and walking up a hill to the hotel.

When we got there, the two men in the hotel were smiling. Apparently, they had some fun exchange about the man nearly dragging me to the hotel. But I thought it was generous of him, and I thanked him.

Turkish delight

It's a bit overwhelming here in Istanbul. The sounds in the street—cars honking, buses screeching, birds—lots of them—crowing and chirping, Islamic prayer call, people shouting in the street, merchants selling their goods. What you cannot hear, you see—dirty, fat cats waiting for the shops to open; orange, yellow, green and red fruits and vegetables in the stands; women selling flowers; and men selling the traditional strong coffee from kiosks.

In a bookstore to find an English tourist book of Turkey, I heard the most beautiful violin music by Farid Farjad that I purchased and then sent to my son. I never found a tourist book but did find a Turkish/English dictionary.

After this bit of touring and watching the ferries dock at the shoreline, I went to a restaurant and asked for what I saw on a glass shelf. The man on the other side was desperately trying to tell me something but I didn't get it. It turns out he was telling me to sit down, and the waiter would bring it to me. After a while, I understood and did as I was told.

Then a young waiter smiled at me and asked if I spoke German, and I said no, but a little bit of Dutch. He didn't understand the word Dutch or Holland or The Netherlands until a movie-star-looking man sitting next to me, said, "Hollandia." Oh, that he knew, but not the language of that country. He went on to do his work.

The gentleman who helped out learned English in a university, according to what little he told me about himself. I'm just happy he spoke up.

Back at the hotel, I booked an all-day tour on-line, which begins on the European side on Thursday at nine a.m. I asked the gentleman downstairs in the lobby to print it out for me—that I would send it to his email address. That request had three people trying to figure out what I was asking. One man went and got a map, spread it out to show me that I could take a boat from one end of the bay to the other. I insisted I just wanted the voucher printed for my tour.

They finally got it and printed it—in Turkish.

Today, I learned that to be picked up at the hotel, I must go to the European side first, as they don't come to Asia for pick-ups. That led to some more confusion since I am staying in a hotel on the Asian side. I was told to wait for the manager because I had asked them to call the company and get the information for me.

I waited, and then it took two men, two phone calls, and one more call expected tomorrow, and I hope I'll know where to go and when to report. I'll get there.

I find the people here friendly and ready to help a traveler.

Hot pink tie, and Tom never arrives

Today, I left Asia for Europe, and it only took 20 minutes by ferry. When I woke up this morning and looked at my email, there was a note from my friend, Tom Johnstone, of Australia. He's the gentleman I met in Spain who accompanied me to Gibraltar where we met up with three other people. Tom is touring for a year as I have been doing, but he's just a few months into his journey.

He asked me to join him on his last day on the European side of Turkey, and he'd show me some of the sites he had seen.

I jumped up out of bed, took a shower, got dressed, and within an hour, I had purchased a ticket. As the boat screeched its warning to leave and as people were running to catch it, I did the same. The boat was packed with people, most wearing black, and most had black hair. I think my long white hair is unusual. Many women are Muslims and wear scarves covering their heads.

Men walked around the ferry selling tea and orange juice. The tea is delivered in a tiny glass that sits on top of a bowl-like saucer.

When the boat docked in Europe, I walked just a few yards away to a large square where, if you sit long enough, you'll see a cross section of humanity. But first, there were the fancy kiosks and eating areas, all very expensive-looking with many people sitting and drinking tea.

This may be my first adventure with Turkish coffee, I thought, so I went up to a kiosk but was told no coffee, only tea. I think coffee is only an early morning drink because it happened again this afternoon.

While waiting for Tom who never showed up, I saw a fat man wearing a hot pink tie, and he seemed to be waiting for someone, as well. There was also a tiny, bent-over lady who kept shouting, "Hey!" and then she'd let out a witch's cackle. She would creep-walk over to people, look at them, and holler, "Hey!" Some young boys seemed to take a liking to her and had her pose with them for a photo. She seemed to like that.

Meanwhile, the man with the pink tie wandered around.

I sat down on some benches, but one spot had something gooey on it, so a Muslim lady motioned for me to sit next to her. I did. Later, some men wanted to sit at the same place but were also deterred by the goo. One man took the initiative and headed to the nearby tea-drinking place. He got a placemat to sit on.

The man with the pink tie roamed on.

I began to roam on myself, as I was one-and-one-half hours too early to meet Tom. Soon, there were Muslim prayers coming from both mosques. I found that the men's voices, even though I didn't know what they were saying in their chanting, were melodious and easy to listen to. One man held notes for a very long time. I wonder if they audition for the job of calling the invitation to prayer?

Noon came and went, and no Tom. Twelve-thirty, still no Tom. One o'clock, and no Tom. I gave him until 1:30 p.m. and decided something was wrong, so I got a ticket back to the Asian side.

I then went for lunch at my new favorite restaurant and had an omelet because that was the only thing I could pronounce. The detail on the plate made a cheese omelet look gourmet—three green leaves, carrot and cucumber strips.

Again, coffee wasn't available, but tea was, so that was brought in the little glass and porcelain saucer shaped like a bowl. Then I had a rice pudding that was the best dessert I've had in a very long time, so rich and creamy.

Do you think the man in the hot pink tie likes rice pudding?

Great day with fun people

Before getting started on the awesome yesterday, I want to explain what happened with Tom and me missing each other on Wednesday.

Unbeknownst to me and I think to Tom, as well, there is more than one dock on both sides of the bay, and I waited on one of those, while Tom waited on another. We missed each other and both feel sad about that. But we'll always be in touch. You cannot throw away a friendship born while on the road in the world.

Okay, was it the people on the tour that made it a great day? Or was it the sites we saw? You decide. Let's first start with the people. The celebrity, Shay Murphy, a professional basketball player who, right now, is playing in Turkey for the Chicago Sky WNBA. Then there was her cute little brother who is not little. George lives in L.A. and works for a company that sells paint. It's a paint that you cannot paint over, and it sounds like something great for graffiti areas.

There were two lovely ladies from Maryland, Lisa and Patty, who were interested in everything and had great humor all along the way. They were a joy to be around.

There was the bachelor, Ed, from Utah. He got lost from us once, and we accused him of searching for his fifth wife.

Our guide, Tibet Elmalik, is a walking encyclopedia. She gave us details on all the interesting sites and in such a dynamic way, you had to hang onto her words. She also was a great help to me, for she lives on the Asian side where I am staying. A gentleman from the hotel walked with me to the ferry where I met Tibet. This was arranged by the folks in the Konak Ootel and was not the last of what they did for me. Tibet and I boarded the ferry and met the others on the other side. I was in good hands with her from the beginning point, even before we all met for the tour.

Our tour was spent in the oldest part of Istanbul. Formerly called Constantinople, Istanbul is populated by over 13 million people and is considered 8,000-years-old. In 1985, UNESCO named it a World Heritage Site.

We began the tour in a large quadrant that was once the Hippodrome. The space is next to the Basilica Cistern, Blue Mosque, and Hagia Sophia, and is the center of Roman and Byzantine Constantinople time. Still standing are many obelisks and sculptures that have remained since the fourth century.

I will share the treasures that most overpowered me, beginning with the Blue Mosque where we had to remove our shoes. It is called blue from the use of thousands of tiles made in blue designs. The color, turquoise, which was first discovered in Turkey, is also the predominate color. Blue was considered to be the favorite color of Islamic Prophet Mohammed.

The inside of the Blue Mosque is spectacular with high domed ceilings and with chandeliers. Tibet explained that one group of lights hangs closer to the floor because they were originally oil lamps and were easier to light at a lower range, near the place where men knelt to pray.

I couldn't keep my eyes off of the ceiling in wonder at the workmanship created by men in the 1600s.

Hagia Sophia—a Byzantine construction thought to have been built in the year 346 A.D.—was the seat of the Orthodox Church and then became a Roman Catholic cathedral and later a mosque. It was partially destroyed by conflicts, earthquakes, and old age, and through the years, it was rebuilt, restructured, and repurposed, and is now a free museum for all.

What I found interesting is that the building faces the proper way for Islamic prayers, with an additional prayer area for Christians, all made available for the employees of the museum. This fact absorbs my attention due to the recent conflicts modern folks have with the Islamic religion. Here in a predominately Muslim country, the Muslims have made a place available in their house of worship for Christians to pray. This is an example of the best in humanity.

Basilica Cistern is an underground chamber of about 105,000-square-feet that holds 80,000 cubic meters of water. Marble columns sit stone-faced inside the water that gives life to fish. Inside, after we walked down a stone staircase, we were free to walk alongside the water on wooden platforms. It's mysterious and quiet except for the echoes of people. Built in the third and fourth centuries during the Early Roman Age, it was reconstructed after a fire in 476. In our modern age, around the 1980s, mud was removed and the site was cleaned for public access. I found this most amazing and was told it took thousands of people for its original construction.

There was just so much to see and learn that I will need to study more to remember all Tibet told us. I managed to take in the atmosphere and intelligence of the ancient world.

We had a typical Turkish lunch, and I finally had real Turkish coffee that I loved.

During our tour, Shay and George had to leave—George to get ready to catch a plane back to L.A. and Shay to rest up for a game. Read about Shay on *Wikipedia* or on many Internet sites. They were fun to be part of our group. Wish they could have stayed with us until the end.

Later, we were transported to visit Nakkas, where we learned about oriental rugs. Here's the website—www.nakkasrug.com. Mahmut Kaya presented how Turkish rugs are made using a looping of threads that permanently seals the rugs tightly for long-lasting wear.

They were gorgeous in a variety of colors. I swooned over them, wishing I had a floor to put one down on. There were men who whooped up a rug and gently laid it down at our feet. Patty did her best at getting a price she wanted for one large rug and a runner. The men folded up her rugs, tied them up in brown paper, and put them into a bag that she could carry home on the plane. I was impressed with how small the package became after folding it and wrapping it up.

Ed has lived in Turkey as a military man and has several rugs in his Utah home, so he didn't purchase any rugs this time.

The next visit was inside the Grand Bazaar, the largest and oldest in the world. There were kiosks of gold and silver jewelry, cashmere and silk scarves, porcelain, leather, hanging colorful lights, and on and on. A man carried small glasses of tea on a double-layer tray, shoppers walked and bargained, barkers barked their wares, and I just took it all in.

I saw lots of items I would want to take back home for friends, my family, and myself. However, I resisted and conformed to my original vow to not purchase souvenirs on this journey. My souvenirs will be memories, photos, stories, and of course, the people I meet along the way. Tibet, Patty, Lisa, Ed, Shay, George—all made it the most fun day.

I'm just one of many.

What to do on the Asian side? Hmmm, I'm trying to figure that one out. Yesterday, I went for a long walk up, up, up a hill and found a pharmacy to renew one of my medicines. No questions asked—just handed a note and the money, and I was off again up the hill.

Pharmacies, I found out later, are strung along the street facing the harbor, so next time, it will be a very short walk from the hotel.

On my walk, I found a school with kids dressed in uniforms and playing a game in the courtyard. Next to the school was Ali Baba—yes, Ali Baba. Ali Baba is a restaurant. I went in and began to read the menu using my Turkish/English dictionary, trying to figure out which item said chicken kabob, when a waiter came up to me and told me, "We have chicken kabobs." I laughed and showed him the dictionary and where I tried to find the word chicken.

Was he clairvoyant?

Ali Baba brought me a delicious chicken kabob with a salad and rice. The salad seems typical—very finely diced onion, cucumber, tomato, and some kind of green herb, with mild red pepper on top.

After lunch and saying good-bye to the host, the cook, and another customer, all who showed interest in my journey, I took off in another direction, down, down, down a hill. I reached a shopping street where it was amazing to see store windows after store windows, some on the ground floor and some up higher, with white wedding gowns. In a city of 13 million, there must be many weddings. There were also many jewelry shops along the way.

I found a small neighborhood and a store where the woman said she spoke a little English. I purchased a Turkish candy bar and some milk for the coffee in my room.

On the walk, there were cats of many colors, and all seemed friendly. While they were dirty, they didn't look like they were starving.

The mission when walking is to watch the traffic and the uneven stone sidewalks and streets. It's a promise to myself not to fall, ever, on this journey.

Finally, I found the main street that is parallel to the harbor, and then I knew how to get back to the hotel. Turkish people must like to read, as I came across four different bookstores. I purchased *The Pocket Guide to Istanbul and the Aegean Coast*.

Back in front of the hotel at a nearby fruit market, I bought some bananas from a friendly man and pointed to the hotel where I'm staying and to the window of my room upstairs. When I handed the proper number of coins to him, he handed one back. Discount.

One thing I really wanted to explore was the Islamic religion, and that has been possible. I have a pamphlet that explains its origin. I have also learned that young men who have studied the *Koran* are chosen for the special job making the call to prayer.

"It's a woman thing."

It turned out to be an exciting day. Police began to arrive in the streets with guns slung over their shoulders and shields ready at any given notice, and police buses and vans were readied to take the rabble-rousers away if they got out of hand.

The rabble-rousers were all women. It could get dangerous. After all, they were singing and then dancing, and who knows what else they might do. They were dressed in vivid colors and lined up in groups for so many miles that I couldn't see the end of the line up the street.

Loud music played, and a woman spoke for all the women over a speaker so loud that she could be heard many blocks away. Groups of women held banners and marched down to the docks, yelling the "woman's yell" and wearing lots of bling. I played reporter without a press pass and got as close as possible to watch and hear the action. One man standing next to me asked where I was from, and then I knew he spoke English, so I asked him what it was all about. "It's a woman thing," he answered. The "woman thing" lasted pretty much all day.

I walked to a different neighborhood than where I have been going daily, and I found a swanky hotel. I walked in with head up as if I were staying there and rested my tired legs and feet in an overstuffed leather chair. When you're staying in a cheaper hotel, even though it's okay, it doesn't hurt to get off the beaten track and rest a while and pretend.

There are so many bookstores here that I couldn't count them. I mentioned to a bookstore salesman that Istanbul has a lot of bookstores, and his response was curious. He said the Turkish people don't read very much, an observation I had heard once before.

Without doubt, there are many restaurants. It is possible to sit outside now, as it has become warmer.

By the way, I have now seen McDonald's, Burger King, and Starbucks.

Yesterday, I had my hair trimmed a bit. The hairdressers were friendly and did a good job. I found the salon when I looked up at a window and observed a man cutting a woman's hair. He smiled, and I smiled back. Then I walked in and asked if I could get my hair cut. The hairstylist told me to come back in an hour. I did, and I got the VIP treatment. After my hair was cut, both hairstylists asked to have my photo taken with them.

Some of the Turkish culture I observed is the following:

Men often walk arm-in-arm. They also kiss when greeting each other. When a person is not within a hugging and kissing distance, they place their hand on their heart in greeting. The distance between people is closer than in other countries, which could come from the large population, all trying to get where they need to go.

The national drink is tea. The tea is served in tiny glasses held in a saucer shaped like a bowl.

Turkish coffee (in a tiny cup with the grounds settling at the bottom) comes with a small glass of water and often with a piece of Turkish delight candy.

If you don't drink Turkish coffee, then the alternative is Nestlé's instant coffee.

Nearly every restaurant gives a damp hand-wipe that comes along with the drink or food.

You have to ask the waiter for your check, as they won't bring it to you until you ask.

Waiters (so far, I've only seen two waitresses) are usually dressed in uniforms and are professional and attentive.

Women often wear long coats or dresses and head scarves; however, others opt not to wear the scarf. It is up to the individual.

Invitation to prayer is sung over a loud speaker five times a day.

Fruit, bread, and vegetables are plentiful in the street markets.

Cats of all colors live on the streets.

Cars, buses, and walkers do not obey the green/red traffic lights.

I know I'm not in Holland because I haven't seen one bicycle.

People, in general, are friendly and helpful and smile back at you.

I get by with help from friends.

I get by with a big help from my friends and friends of friends, not to mention relatives of relatives who are now my friends.

Gonzales, California Councilwoman Liz Silva has a cousin living on the Asian side of Turkey, and I got in touch with him. Adnan called me this morning and helped me learn how to get a travel ticket that would allow traveling in the city on local buses, trams, and small van-buses. He went above that by calling Engin at the front desk to tell him in Turkish what I wanted. Then Engin went above that and had the go-to person who fixes breakfast and helps everyone, always with a smile, go with me to get the ticket. Sinan is my new friend who walked with me, first to Daisy's laundry where I left two pairs of jeans, then to the ATM machine, and then to the ticket office.

I took my new ticket and tripped around on a local bus, and when it stopped, the driver asked me if I'd like to go somewhere else on a different bus, so I hopped off and got on another one that eventually led me back to where I started. There was much to see and take in on that trip.

Remember, on your travels, don't underestimate traveling on local buses. It's a cheap way to get around the city with the driver doing all the work.

I'm looking forward to visiting my nephew, Andy, with whom I stayed in Germany, when I go to the town of Izmir. He'll be in Izmir on business. I thought it was next week, but lo and behold, he's flying in tomorrow! I got busy and bought a ticket and got a hotel in Izmir. I leave in the morning. I plan to see a Greek island while I'm in the area.

Back to today's adventure. I saw the walkway around the inlet while I was inside a restaurant next to a boat dock. The Turkish coffee came in a tiny cup and saucer and sat inside a paper boat. I oohed and ahhed over it until the waiter showed me how to create my own paper boat.

Then I dodged buses to get my feet safely on the walkway that led me past a mosque and to the train station.

I found a piece of marble that must have come from the steps to the mosque that seems to be under construction. It will go into the seashell bag, for sure.

I found the 1905 train station and took photos of the beautiful detail inside and out. I imagined what it must have looked like during the 1920s when rich American celebrities began traveling in faraway places.

Izmir—finally!

It was a wild night inside the Sisim Restaurant on the harbor in Izmir, Turkey. A soccer game between Germany and Turkey was on, and I'm not sure how many screens there were, but there were plenty, and every time the Turks made a goal, the entire restaurant, filled with men, hollered with glee.

Glee? That's putting it mildly because when Turkey won, it was bedlam. Men jumped up, grabbed each other, circled around and around, arms in the air, hollering and screaming. Soon, cars began to circle outside of the restaurant with horns bleating and flags waving.

It causes me to wonder, how in the heck did I wind up here?

The day for me began early in the morning in a bus on the way to Izmir from Kadiköy, on what I thought would be a five-and one-half-hour ride, but it took twice that long.

I boarded the bus, and unbeknownst to me, that was just the first bus, for we got off at another station and boarded the real bus. We drove through villages and cities, mostly in rain, and then we met snow in the mountains.

A woman in back of me realized I didn't speak Turkish, so when we boarded a ferry to cross the Marmara Sea, she encouraged me to get off the bus for fresh air. She nearly poked holes into my eardrums with her friendly chatter. Her family immigrated to

Turkey from Poland a century ago, which explains her blue eyes and light hair. She was delightful, and I learned a lot, but I'm happy there won't be a test afterward, for I won't remember all of it.

The real answer to the question, how did I end up here, begins with my nephew, Andy. His job as a technical manager for a printing machine company in Germany requires lots of travel, including his favorite place, Izmir.

Andy flew in from Germany at eight p.m. I got into my hotel around 7:30 p.m. Andy and his best buddy and customer, Ozkan Kacemer, with Ozkan's wife, Hatun Gul Kacemer, were waiting for me when I stepped off my hotel's elevator. We got into a taxi and arrived at the Sisim Restaurant to the greetings and hugs from the waiters. Andy is a regular at the restaurant and has been for several years. The waiters treated us like celebrities. I didn't know what was in some of the small dishes they first put on our table, but they were perfectly seasoned.

Andy picked out a fish that the manager of the restaurant showed us at our table. It was grilled to absolute perfection. The waiter carefully deboned it near our table and placed a portion on each plate, along with some vegetables. After dinner, the waiter brought more dishes with a variety of fruit, stuffed dates, a tiny individual cake, and other goodies. Then a very special treat was delivered from the kitchen just for us. It was a mound of something with cream inside and chocolate dribbled on top of it. I honestly do not know what it was, but I'd like some right now.

The night was fun, as it usually is with Andy around. Ozkan speaks fluent German and Turkish, as well. He was brought up in Germany by Turkish parents, and when they decided to return to Turkey, he came with them. He had little Turkish language skills but speaks well now without an accent. He can make himself understood in English, but his wife spoke no English.

There I was among the Turks, listening to Turkish, German, and a bit of English, with a room full of hollering men. While we walked over to get our ride, a man with a drum stopped us and banged on it a few times, while another man with a horn blew it right into Ozkan's face until Ozkan gave him a tip.

What a day. What a night. And my time here isn't over yet.

Attitude adjustment needed!

No Greek island for me this year. It was a change-all morning; you know, those days that seem to go wrong from the moment you wake up?

It took an hour to readjust my attitude, and now I'm okay and will enjoy the experiences that await me the rest of the day.

I bade good-bye to my nephew, Andy, his good friend, Ozkan, and Ozkan's wife, and the many waiters at the Sisim Restaurant last night. Andy was first to say good-bye, for after dinner he went on to his hotel, and Ozkan and wife went with me to my hotel by taxi. Ozkan went inside to make arrangements with the hotel staff to call a taxi for me in the morning for the bus that would take me to the harbor where I would leave to take a ferry to a Greek island. Greece—a long-held dream for me.

Before I went to sleep last night, I booked a hotel on the Grecian Samos Island and a flight out from Izmir to Istanbul (Asian side) where I left the rest of my "stuff" in the Konak Otel. I also booked a hotel near the Izmir Airport, so it wouldn't be too complicated to get the flight out early in the morning.

But this morning, from the moment I woke up until now, I faced obstacles. First, I couldn't find a stocking, and then after a frantic search, I found it. After breakfast, I went to check out, and my credit cards were nowhere in my wallet. I went upstairs and emptied my purse, and there they were. They had fallen out of my wallet. The linings inside the purse that I had acquired in Spain have ripped apart, and now there are more compartments, and I can't find anything in a hurry.

Last night, Ozkan worked hard at getting the folks in the lobby of the hotel where I stayed to understand where and when I needed a taxi, but that didn't happen this morning. The man didn't seem to know anything about it.

And then when the taxi came, I couldn't find my ticket to the bus. It, too, had been trapped inside one of the linings. Oh, did I tell you that I dropped my expensive camera yesterday?

Then the taxi driver kept asking me where I wanted to go, in Turkish, of course. All I know how to say is thank you, and even then I have to think hard to pull it out of my brain. But he did get me there, and when I walked in, about five people were standing there laughing at my confusion about when the bus would come and where I should wait. I didn't think it was funny—not one bit.

I arrived at my destination, Kusadasi, on the bus, where I would go to a travel agent to book the ferry to the island. That's when I learned there would be no ferries to Samos Island until March 23rd.

I went to an outside restaurant and got the computer and the Wi-Fi up and working, through the help of a nice young man, Baris. He wouldn't quit until he had it up and running. He even got some help, and I went to work. I first cancelled the hotel in Samos and learned I wouldn't get all of my money refunded because I cancelled it without a seven-day notice. I picked up my computer and put the translation service to work, and when Baris understood my dilemma, he handed me a card. I needed a place to stay since I wouldn't be going to the hotel on Samos.

Baris' card was about the pension hotel on Women's Beach. Well, heck, that sounds good enough for me. So he called and got the price and a taxi for me. The taxi cost one-half of the amount of one night stay, my first rip-off of the day.

Here I am now up on the fourth floor of a room with a lumpy bed, dirty walls, and curtains that are plastered to a wall by scotch tape. Even the worst hostel is better than this so-called hotel.

But the young lady, Gulay, whose father owns the house, is very nice and helpful, so that makes up for the lack of ambiance. She goes to the university and is studying tourism.

It should be an interesting two days, and who knows, maybe after a 15-minute walk to the shoreline, I'll see Greece from a distance.

By the way, the bus from Istanbul to Izmir cost nearly 70 euros for a ten-and-one-half-hour drive, and the airplane flight, or my return back to Izmir, will cost only 30 euros and will take a little over one hour. It's a special deal right now, I must add.

How did a toilet seat change my plans?

It wasn't the dirty walls, the spikes stabbing me from the mattress, or no top sheet (just a dirty-smelling wool blanket), and not because there was no toilet paper, soap, or a towel.

No, I left the hotel in Kusadasi for the final provocation; I slipped off the toilet seat. The seat wasn't attached. It was just sitting there to fool you into thinking there was one. I slept under three dirt-smelling blankets, wondering how many people before me fell under the smell. And I had one more night to go.

In the morning, I had to ask myself, Is this what I really want? Does this demonstrate the self-respect I have worked all my life to earn?

Besides that, it was pouring down rain, and although that doesn't usually thwart my plans, since the only recreation was to walk 15 minutes to the beach, and with a ghost town beach waiting for the cleanup crew to spruce it up for the summer season, I said, "NO! This is not what I want."

I put everything into my suitcase, stumbled down the four flights of stairs, knocked on the door at nine a.m. when Gulay, the young lady studying tourism, was still asleep, and handed her the key. I wanted to be civil about it, so I simply said I needed to leave.

"I'll call my father about returning your money."

"Okay, I'll wait right here."

She came back about ten minutes later with news from her father.

"He said not to give you your money back because we gave you a special price."

"Wow! A special price?"

"Yes, do you want to stay?"

"No, I want to leave." And then I got my dander up. "The room is dirty, the curtain is taped to the wall, the bathroom needs work, the walls are filthy, and the blankets need to be washed. I cannot stay here."

She looked shocked and didn't say anything. I added, "You are going to be in the tourism business; you must know better."

She and I said good-bye, and I left to catch a bus.

I got off at the bus stop and saw the light change, so I began to walk across a busy street, and from the other side, three rows of cars were coming at me. I stopped, turned, and walked back to the sidewalk. Then I walked the other way to the bus station.

There, I saw a man near just the very bus I needed to take back to Izmir. He smiled and stashed my suitcase in the luggage compartment while I purchased my ticket.

When the bus left, the man who stashed away my suitcase smiled at me and put his hand on his heart. My day just got better.

Plan B would be to go to the airport and see the possibility of changing my flight ticket from Sunday to today or tomorrow. Fussing around at the airport after a 30-minute drive in a taxi, I found the right window. The agent said there wasn't a chance to leave before Sunday.

I got another taxi, with a driver who didn't know where the hotel was but finally got me there, and because I was one day earlier than my reservation, I was lucky to get a room.

On Sunday, it will be five days since I left Istanbul and my hotel there. I've paid for two hotel rooms for five days. The reservationist in the new hotel in Izmir called the guys in Istanbul and told them I'd be there on Sunday, and they said my room was waiting for me and not to worry. I love those guys. The best part is that the toilet seat sits firmly on the toilet in that hotel.

Good customer service makes me happy.

Okay, now I'm over the toilet seat calamity, and onward I go. I'm in a different hotel, which is about 70 percent better than the one I left.

Why are inexpensive hotels dirty? There are maids that clean the rooms, just as there are maids who clean expensive hotels. I've been in both kinds, and now I know the problem. It is called "management." The other two words are called "customer service." If you're a manager, if you're in business, and if you don't have good customer service, then you don't have a thing to boast about.

Okay, enough of that. I got a taxi to a large mall today just to stay busy. I fly out tomorrow, and I'm near the airport and far away from any interesting tourist sites, and it's raining and thundering, as well.

When I got to the mall via a very nice taxi driver, I began to feel dizzy. I found a restaurant and ordered some good nutrition and gulped down two large glasses of water. I think I was dehydrated. It took about 20 minutes, and I was fine again. Good lesson here, again. Stay hydrated!

After I looked at the stores in the mall and didn't buy anything but heard American music with the lyrics, "Oh, Oh, Oh, Oh, Oh" and, "I have a place in mind. I have a place in mind. I have a place in mind," and other jumping and jiving rap stuff, I figured it was time to leave.

I must say, even though the experience in Izmir after leaving Andy wasn't what I expected, it wasn't harmful, and it makes an interesting story. Two out of five days were awesome. Tomorrow morning, I will be back in Istanbul via Pegasus Airlines.

I'm now in my hotel in Istanbul, Asian side, and when I walked in, the front desk man and the three maids were sitting in the lobby, and they were all happy to see me. Before going to the hotel, I stopped at my favorite restaurant, and the waiters greeted me with good humor, as well. I feel as though I made some good friends.

I flew on Pegasus, which is a fairly new airline that covers most of Europe. It is growing larger by adding more stops.

It's nice to be back here in Istanbul.

Finding the city a lot of fun

Sad today. I had dropped my camera, and now the photos are blurry, although the long lens works a tiny bit better than the regular close shots. I have two weeks and three days left until I go back to America, and I surely would like a working camera.

The good news—I'm back in Kadiköy where I started my time in Istanbul. The hotel is small and not too expensive and is kept clean by some awesome maids. One of them knocked on my door and then came in to hang freshly laundered curtains. Then her co-worker knocked on the door, and I told her to come in. We joked about having a party in my room.

I took out the computer, and we began translating back and forth in English and Turkish, using a translating program. It was fun. We laughed a lot. They were sympathetic about my camera and told me to ask the man down in reception for his help.

After they left, I did go down to the lobby and asked the gentleman. He told me I should go to the European side of Istanbul to some shops there. I went up to my room and thought about it. I don't think it would be good for me to spend more money right now on a camera. I'm going to do my best with what I have, but I'm so disappointed in myself.

Yet in the light of that disaster, there is still the city to see, so I took another long walk through a different neighborhood. I find kitty cats wherever I go, and while some look healthy, others look hungry and a bit worn out. There are many engraving and printing shops, cell phone stores, bookstores galore, and several small hotels on nearly every street in the business district, and too many coffee shops to count. Those serve mostly tea and Turkish coffee.

Young men are often seen in the streets carrying two-tiered platters of tea to various businesses in town. It's common to see tea drinkers just about everywhere.

I've noticed that in every restaurant, big or small, they place on the table on a separate dish handy wipes in a package with the company's logo on it.

Bakeries flourish here, with loaves of bread and sweets of all kinds, as seen in the windows.

Kiosks on the streets sell a bread-like snack. Candy stores sit next to the sidewalk with Turkish delight candy, nuts, and other types of goodies.

I've seen people pulling carts of vegetables and fruits to and from their kiosks, probably heading to other neighborhoods.

Cars are everywhere, and drivers are impatient. When they have to wait, someone begins to honk their horn, and then others follow in a chorus. The noise competes with buses and the ferries that come in to pick up commuters. Then there are the five prayer calls a day over a loudspeaker.

Birds of all kinds are plentiful in the city. Pigeons, seagulls, and another kind of large bird land on tree branches right by my window telling people off with their noisy chatter.

Today, when I took a photo of a doorway in the center of a mural, I walked across the street and asked a gentleman if it was a restaurant. His answer in English surprised me.

"It's a church," he said. "It was used by the Seventh Day Adventists and another sect, which I don't remember."

"Are there other churches in Istanbul?"

"Yes, about eight right here in this section." He mentioned that most services are conducted in the Turkish language, but there is one that conducts services in French.

Istanbul is an exciting, bustling city and an interesting place to spend a day.

I can now say thank you without stuttering.

Tesekkur ederim. I have finally mastered the important words, thank you, without stuttering and hesitation. No one laughs now, and everyone says you're welcome right back. I'm thankful that I know how to say it properly because I have much to be thankful for.

Life has been pleasurable since being back in Kadiköy, Istanbul, at the Konak Otel. The folks who keep the Konak running smoothly are so good to me and make me feel welcome, as if we were a family.

Beginning with breakfast—hard boiled eggs, two kinds of olives, two kinds of white cheese, tomatoes, cucumbers, and bread right from the bakery.

My favorite restaurant, Murat Muhallebicisi, is about two blocks away, and in spite of its busy business, the waiters are professional, friendly, and helpful. My favorite waiter greets me with palms together at his chest as if in prayer. This morning, he also high-fived me.

Today, after a long walk the opposite way of my usual path, I stopped at Murat Muhallebicisi and had a rice pudding that was delicious. I wish I knew how to make it as well as they do. Then at the deli, I asked for two dolmas to be packed up to go. The dolmas are grape leaves stuffed with rice and some seasoning I couldn't name, but delicious.

Since dropping my camera, I have looked for a shop that would sell the same camera. Instead of finding a new one, people have sympathized and looked at the camera, but couldn't do anything about it.

I did find a shop with a Canon, but the cost was prohibitive, so I'll continue to do my best with the camera in the two weeks left of this long journey, and I will be grateful for the blessings I've had along the way.

Turkey has so much to offer. The people are friendly, helpful, and appear to be professional. The waiters in most restaurants wear uniforms made up of slacks, white shirts, sweaters, and ties. Many men on the street are dressed in suits and carry nice briefcases.

Cats are plentiful, as I've noted before, and dogs laze around on streets, asleep right in the general pathway.

Today, I heard a young man shouting and carrying a sweet bread-like parcel on his head. He smiled and stopped to allow me to take a photo.

I also took a shot of a man getting his shoes shined. He stopped me to talk a bit, and I was surprised to hear him speak in Dutch. He's Turkish but has a textile business in Holland. He is leaving tomorrow.

The shoeshine apparatus is made of brass, and every shoeshine man has one. I've been told they go back in history and are a Turkish tradition. There are many shoeshine men on the streets, and most always appear busy in their occupation.

On my walk, I was close to a mosque while the invitation to prayer was sung and amplified. I watched as men walked into the mosque for prayer.

It's a busy city with a lot going on, and I'm enjoying every minute.

Destruction—the camera and the street

The streets surrounding the Konak Otel are undergoing street reconstruction. When I came back from Izmir, the streets were mushy with mud under my feet. It was raining, but work must go on.

Today and every day since, big equipment has taken over the streets, and the stones are being ripped out. I don't know the plan for reconstruction, but I do know it's noisy and dirty and dangerous to walk down the street while being chased by a bulldozer.

The good news is the staff in this hotel is awesome, and I like every one of them. Never in my life has anyone ever made my bed, and I'm enjoying the service of the maids. I think I made my point because I have said this many times before. I leave to go someplace, and when I come back, the room is clean, the bed is made, and there are fresh towels.

Today, I took a ferry ride over to the European side of Istanbul and then got into a taxi. I told the driver I wanted to go to the Media Markt. He told me there were several.

"Which one do you want to go to?"

"The closest one." He stopped at a fancy hotel and asked the doorman who was dressed like a prince in tall hat and long coat, where it was. The doorman gave the taxi driver some information. The driver said that would take 40 minutes and that the traffic was bad. I said okay, clearly knowing the taxi driver didn't like the idea at all. I showed him my camera and told him it wasn't working, and I wanted to buy one just like it. He drove on for a bit, and then looked at me and said, "Two minutes."

He turned the taxi around, and back we went. I decided to go along with him, but knowing when we got to where he wanted to take me, I could leave and get another taxi to take me to Media Markt, a German company specializing in electronics. In about five minutes, he stopped the taxi, told me to follow him, and I did. He took me to a passageway that had several camera stores.

I paid the driver, and he looked happy to be relieved of the ordeal.

I went into one shop and caused a great deal of laughter when the salesman showed me an updated version of my camera, and I asked him for a better deal. "For an old lady." That's always good for a laugh.

He told me if I walked down the street and turned left, there would be a Chinese man who owns a store and who could probably fix the camera. Well, I have done the research and have learned that once a camera has been dropped on hard concrete and no longer functions, it can be fixed, but it would be cheaper to buy a new one.

Not wanting to learn anything new with a different camera, I left. However, I saw a camera shop down the street and went in. I showed the camera and told the salesman that I wanted the same camera. He had one. I paid what he asked, and the gentleman gave me a chip along with it. I know I paid a bit more than I would have in the U.S., but I needed it for the two more weeks I have left, so I plunked down my credit card, and now the camera is mine.

The salesman put the strap on the camera and hung it around my neck, telling me not to drop it. I didn't stay long on that side of Istanbul because I wanted to get back and get the camera up and working. The manual is in Turkish—big joke on me. I sent my English manual to my son, Larry, who has been putting all that I send him into my car. I'll have lots of stuff to look at when I get back. But not to worry, the camera is working great.

When I got back to the street under destruction, I caught hotel employee, Sinon, with a pick pulling some rocks away from the hotel, and Engin watching the action.

They were pretending to be construction workers. Nice try.

Nose tweaking

The doctor tweaked my nose. Actually, he leaned over to me and pinched it. I call it tweaked because that's what my mother loved to do to me and what she called it.

It happened this morning when I opted to get breakfast at my favorite place where my favorite waiter works, instead of the freebee in the hotel. That one is getting monotonous. I needed a change.

The waiter asked me what I wanted, and I pointed to a photo of an omelet. When he came back to my table so we could torment each other with our lack of each other's language skills, I got my dictionary out and pointed to the word for post office. He then began to describe how to get there. The other day, he had tried to send me to a bank, and I couldn't get across to him I needed a post office.

This morning, after I pointed to the word for post office, I took the book away from him and pointed to the Turkish word for yesterday, and made a motion that it was while I stood on the sidewalk. Then he got it.

Meanwhile, a woman at a table next to me and a man at a table across an aisle got into the conversation about traveling. I was trying to tell the man that tomorrow I would be leaving, and I was saying good-bye. The lady wrote down how to say good-bye and also a word similar to our "bye, bye."

When I said that, the man from across the aisle, who finished eating, walked over and asked, "Where are you from?"

He said it so loud I jumped. "What?"

"Where. Are. You. From?" he asked louder this time.

"America."

He looked a bit older than the waiter, but they could be brothers, so I asked with the help of the lady and another one at another table who also got involved if the two men were brothers.

"No," the gentleman said, while he and the waiter both laughed, and the two ladies laughed. That went over my head. The gentleman walked back over to me and told me he was a doctor.

"Oh, a doctor?"

"Yes," he said, and then he tweaked my nose and left, while all of us sat laughing.

This morning, when I left the hotel, Sinan, the "go-to" guy at the hotel, was outside in the street shoveling gravel. Why, I don't know, but he saw me and made a motion like he was going to throw it on me.

I just love the Turkish people. I find them friendly and helpful, even if Sinan had thrown the gravel.

I walked around town again to a different neighborhood, a quiet area. I saw a long walkway between two arches and a woman coming out of one. I asked her what it was, and she replied that it was just a walkway between streets, but it was part of the synagogue. Now I've seen churches and mosques, and this was the first synagogue. I was surprised how guarded it was with wire fences on top of a tall, concrete wall. I feel sad that people cannot worship in the way they want without feeling they are in danger.

After that, I walked down to the harbor and sat inside a tent-like restaurant next to the water. The water was moving, with dark and light shades, the dark shades looking like puddles that changed shapes. Seagulls flew haphazardly looking for a meal.

I have noticed on other days that a small boat goes to the shoreline, and a man scoops up garbage, including bread people have thrown to the gulls.

And today, I saw many more cats—tabbies, orange, calico, white, black, black and white, and they make me wish I could take one home with me. I'd at least like to lean over one and tweak its nose.

Finding the post office leads to the market.

To back up a bit, my mission this morning was to find the post office. I got the English/Turkish dictionary out, wrote down the word post office in Turkish, and showed it to Ibrahim in the hotel reception. He slapped the palm of his hand on the top of his other hand. Didn't know what that meant, so I asked him to write down "post office" in Turkish in my notebook. I then went to my favorite restaurant, showed my favorite waiter the notebook with the Turkish writing, and asked him where it was.

"It's here." He said this in Turkish, but I understood his gestures. That restaurant was clearly not the post office, so I continued down the street. I found a young lady who explained it was three blocks away, and she walked part of the way with me until I saw the building. Turkish people are so helpful and kind. I think the gentleman in the hotel had written down the name of the street but not the directions to the post office. No wonder the folks in the restaurant were confused.

After finally mailing the letter, I found an open market I saw for the first time today. There were fish stalls; vegetables and fruits, even some that were new to me; spices and herbs; knock-off perfume shops; toys; clothing; and a long enclosed area with shoes. There were flowers, tea, and coffee shops back-to-back; and candy, bread, and pastry stores.

There was a church at the entrance to the market, and I went inside. A woman was sitting inside and smiled at me. I took some photos, and she kept pointing to other potential shots, so I shot away.

The lady at the outdoor flower stall told me to give her money for a photo. I'm not about to give money to someone on a public street selling goods. I wouldn't take a photo of her inside a shop if she said no, but outside is fair game. I'm certain the street sellers get tired of people with cameras, and I do understand that, but interested travelers can also help their businesses, as well.

I was once an example of being a local character. French tourists once stopped Will and me on the street in Durango, Colorado. They asked to take our photo. It must have been because of our western clothing, including boots and cowboy hats. I wasn't offended.

Again, as I have mentioned before, there are cats everywhere that seem to be well fed. Today, not only did I see cats but two ducks that sat together on the sidewalk. Later, they waddled down the street.

I stopped at a typical kiosk for Turkish coffee, and I finally had a chance to see how it is made. The coffee seller put two scoops of ground coffee into a copper cup with a long handle, and then he poured water over that. Next, he put the little copper cup next to fire coals until it boiled. He then poured it into a tiny cup and served it to me with a tiny box of Turkish delight candy and a small carton of water.

Later, at lunchtime, even though there were kiosks of all kinds, I wanted to sit down inside, eat, and rest, so I found a restaurant with a server who seemed mad and unhappy. He didn't say much. I just pointed to what I thought was chicken kabob and rice. Turned out it wasn't chicken but something rolled in a batter and fried. What I thought was rice was some kind of sauce. It was all a mystery.

While I walked through the town, I came to a street of tall apartments and houses. A gentleman saw me and began a conversation about the street.

"This area consists of very old families that go back 200 years," he said. Some families are from Greece, he told me.

"Are you Greek?"

"No, my grandparents came here from Yugoslavia." The gentleman spoke good English and has lived in Manhattan, New York. He complained about the graffiti on the buildings and said the area is never kept as clean as other neighborhoods. I thought it looked very clean.

He asked someone to bring me a little glass of tea.

"Oh, I didn't ask for that."

"It's our hospitality. Just enjoy it."

When I got ready to leave, he asked one of the street workers to pose with him for a photo. It may get boring to read this, but I must reinforce my belief that most people in the world are good. It is proven over and over to me.

Fatih, not Faith

My discovery on my yearlong journey that most people are good became evident again today. It happened during a transition drama when an Arabic man who speaks French rescued me.

This morning, when I left the Konak Otel on the Asian side, a gentleman who works only on the weekends walked with me to the ferry and pulled my luggage down the street, over an intersection, and then to the ferry. The ferry was about to leave, but it waited for me. The cloudy morning was beautiful and mysterious with views I wanted to remember.

When we docked on the European side, my first goal was to take a taxi to the Faith Hotel. I had an address and a reservation and a phone number. The taxi driver took off but stopped when it was obvious he didn't know where the hotel was located. How many times does this have to happen?

He asked some people on the street and received no answers. Finally, he called someone, and then twisting down stone streets and dodging people, taxis, and other vehicles, he came to the Hotel Faith Istanbul. He dropped me off. I paid him and gave him a tip. When I went into the hotel, I faced a young man who said the worst words—"We have no room."

"What? I have a reservation. See?" I showed him the room number, and he pointed to empty slots where keys would be if there were empty rooms.

"I'm going to sit right here until you give me a room." I sat down with my arms across my chest. He told me to wait for 20 minutes. I did. The manager came down the stairs and gave me the same news.

"It's the wrong hotel," the first man said after he asked to see the paperwork I had in my hand.

"This is number two hotel." He pointed down to the floor.

"Well, then where is number one hotel?"

"It doesn't have a number," he said.

"How do I get there?"

"Walk down the street, turn left. It's a short walk."

In the back of my mind, I felt they were telling me the equivalent of "Take a long walk on a short pier."

I started out as he told me, dragging my life behind me, bumping my luggage over a stone street. I stopped people whenever I saw someone and asked if they knew the hotel.

"No," was the usual answer. But one man told me to walk to the corner of the street, turn right, then left, and "You'll come right to it."

Yeah, right.

By this time, I didn't know whom to believe, and then I saw a real estate business in an old building, and a man was sitting at a computer. That was my hero, Nabil. I showed him the address and did my best to explain the situation. He caught on really fast and let me use his computer. Many of the keys are different from the American keyboard, but never mind; he was patient even though I wasn't successful using his computer.

Nabil then walked to his next-door neighbor at another business where the gentleman spoke a bit more English. He came to Nabil's office and saw my booking right there on the screen.

Zeynettin was my second hero. He was the person who saw the mistake where the American lady (me) switched the letters from Fatih Hotel to Faith Hotel.

Zeynettin made a call to the right hotel and got the directions. Nabil and I walked a block or so for a taxi. He helped me carry the luggage; in fact, he pulled both suitcases. He gave instructions to the driver whom Zeynettin had called, and he told me how much to pay the driver when we got to the hotel.

The taxi driver took me to the hotel, and guess what? There were no rooms.

"I have a reservation." I thought I was experiencing déjà vu.

"Please have a seat," a man at the reception desk told me and pointed to a table by the window that was set for breakfast. Folks were sitting at tables eating, and a lady brought me a plate of food.

"I haven't registered yet," I tried to tell the maid.

"It's okay," the reception maid said. I had my second breakfast of the day.

In about one hour, the owner of the hotel came to me and explained the mistake, but not to worry, he had another hotel and his relative had a hotel, so he would make certain I'd have a room for the night.

"Even if I take you to my house," he added.

"That might be an inconvenience to your wife."

"No, not at all."

He then drove me to the Tulip Hotel, which is near the famous Blue Mosque. The gentleman who owns the Tulip speaks very good English and is an interesting fellow who has taught school and studied religion.

It was a beautiful room, and breakfast in the morning was a full buffet, so my thesis that most people are good was confirmed once again.

However, my question lingers. Why didn't the first taxi driver just look at the address and take me there?

Turkish baths and Turkish taxis

So there I was, lying on a large circle of marble, naked, with several other naked women and scantily clothed scrubbers, splashers, and bathers.

It was in the Cemberlitas Hamami, the oldest Turkish bath located near some of Istanbul's greatest monuments. I found it by walking one hour-and-a-half from the Fatih area to the Hamami that is situated near a mosque, a school, and some tombs. I was greeted at the reception room and paid 70 liras for the traditional experience.

I was led through a door where I was met by another lady who told me to go upstairs, take off my clothing, and wrap myself up in a towel that looked like a dishrag.

I had been handed a chip with the selected service and a bag with a scrubber and a pair of black bikini panties. Well, I thought the underwear was for later when I would be squeaky-clean.

So, when I got inside the steam room and was told to lie down on the marble platform, I couldn't see a thing. My glasses were steamed up. So, I just did as I was told and waited for the next request. A husky woman, wearing a black bra and bikini underwear, handed me some black panties and told me to put them on. I struggled trying to pull them up over my hips because by then my body was damp. She helped me pull them up. This is the first time since I was about three-years-old that someone helped me put my panties on. Then she told me to wait for her. She proceeded to finish up with another woman who knew that the panties were for the duration of the bath.

Then it was my turn. She pushed me and gestured for me to turn over. I obeyed, and she splashed a bucket of hot water all over my back, and a bit later, she came back and told me to lie down on my back. She put a layer of soapy bubbles on me and began to scrub me from neck to toes. It felt like sandpaper. She then motioned for me to turn over onto my stomach, and she scrubbed me again from neck to the bottom of my feet and between my toes.

Sit up, she said, and I obeyed. She scrubbed my arms and neck, and then told me to follow her. When she saw that I couldn't see my way, she guided me to an alcove, and then poured water on my head, then some shampoo, and she washed my hair, neck and arms.

She finished up the process with cooler water and told me to go into another room. There, I received a large towel to wrap around by body and one for my hair. I sat and drank some orange juice, and when I felt ready to hit the street and grab a taxi, I got dressed and gave the receptionist a small tip for the scrubber. I felt rejuvenated.

When I woke up this morning, I had an extensive breakfast in a garden room overlooking the bay, and then I was ready to go to the correct hotel.

"I'm going to walk around a bit before I'm picked up," I told the young man in the hotel.

While I walked, I paid attention to the cars that were driving up and down the narrow streets, thinking I'd see someone who might be looking for me.

Back in the hotel, the reception man pointed to two men who were to take me to the hotel. I knew that one of the suitcases they would be carrying was extremely heavy. So, I took the computer and the camera out to carry myself.

The two men pulled my suitcases up the stone street while I followed with my computer bag, camera, purse, and heavy coat. Up we went, up, up, up, up. "Where are we going?"

Ha, ha, they laughed, not knowing why I was asking. Finally, we were at another hotel.

"What are we doing here?" (It was another hotel owned by the same man.)

"Oh, you must wait here, and a taxi will pick you up and take you to the Fatih Hotel."

The taxi finally came and loaded up my stuff while one of the guys jammed on a helmet and got on his motorcycle. I thought that he was leaving work. When we got to the hotel, he was there waiting for us. I never knew what the heck was going on.

We got inside, and guess what? My room wasn't ready, so that is when I opted to take in a Turkish bath.

After the bath, I got into a taxi, gave the driver the address of the Fatih Hotel so he wouldn't get lost as other drivers seemed to, and I thought he had it all figured out. The traffic was horrendous, so when he said he would take a longer route to avoid traffic and it would save time, I agreed.

He was a flirty guy, kept touching my hair, lifting up my hand and kissing it. Laughed. Raised his hand for a high-five and flattered me to no end. I got suspicious of his behavior and looked down at the meter, and lo and behold he hadn't turned it on. That was a red flag.

"You didn't turn on the meter." I pointed to it. He started it at 40 liras, although the gentleman in the hotel told me it shouldn't cost more than 18 in total.

The driver laughed and told me it was okay because of the traffic. I didn't say anything at that time but worked up my nerve for the moment he would stop at the hotel.

He eventually stopped, and he told me to walk up the hill to the hotel and to pay him 45 liras.

"No, I'm not going to pay you that much."

"Oh, yes, you must pay me. The petrol is expensive, and the traffic is bad. I had to take the long way."

"That is not fair." I handed him 15 liras, and he laughed.

"No, 45."

"No? Okay, here's 30."

"Okay, I'll take 25." He laughed and tousled my hair. He learned he should not have lowered his expectations of the American lady. But he also showed a bit of character for his attempt at misleading me by agreeing to a lesser amount. It was half of his original request but still over what it should have cost. Always check to see the meter is on before you get going.

Palace, the sea, and lost

This time, it was the bus driver and a taxi driver who got lost, with me at their mercy.

But first, let me tell you about the awesome Bosphorus cruise and tour from a boat sailing the Bosphorus Sea, the Golden Horn, and a portion of the Black Sea.

While on the tour bus, we crossed over from the European side to Asia. We observed the walls of Constantinople and other architecture and high-end homes close to the water.

"Now, we are in Asia," the guide told us at the moment we crossed from one continent to the next.

The expert English guide told us fish from the Black Sea are the best, for the cold water makes the fish fat and very tasty.

Every time we had to meet back with the guide, he'd holler, "My group. My group." Some of us nicknamed him My Group.

I sat near the back of the bus where there were several Arabic people entertaining themselves, joking and singing.

From the boat, we also saw the Blue Mosque and the six towering minarets and the Hagia Sophia, all that I had seen inside on another tour weeks ago.

We disembarked to head off to three places, one to a leather factory, one to the 14th century Grand Bazaar, and the last to the inside and outside view of the tour's highlight—the Dolmabahce Palace.

Inside the bazaar, our guide took us to spice kiosks where we were served hot pomegranate juice and a sample of Turkish delight candy. We were given a pep talk about the spices and the fact that Martha Stewart had been there and had purchased some spices, including saffron at $47 for a small bottle. I found all spices in very small jars and very expensive. But hey, if you're Martha Stewart, saffron would be one of your kitchen staples, I assume.

We toured a leather factory where we got another sales pitch and a fashion show. We were herded up to the showroom and met by many salesmen. The salesman that hit me up made me feel the soft sheepskin jacket. I loved it, but I do not appreciate taking a tour when one-third of the time is spent on trying to sell the touring people goods. Not nice. Of course, I looked and admired and then walked back downstairs and waited for lunch.

Our group went inside Dolmabahce Palace where photos were prohibited. It was once the home of the Ottoman Sultans. The building featured the world's largest Bohemian crystal chandelier. It was a gift from Queen Victoria, has 750 lamps, and weighs 4.5 tons. There were other chandeliers in several rooms that also impressed me. Each room had a standard look—a chandelier from the ceiling over a large table with a large vase on top in the center of the table.

The building has 285 rooms, 46 halls, six baths, and 68 toilets. The carpets were made in the famous Hereke Imperial Factory in the city of that name. Antique and historical paintings adorned all the walls.

I was especially interested in a hallway that had a fancy, decorative, cut-out wooden piece that was placed over a window and above the massive hall below. This was where the harem or many wives of the Sultan could peek through the slats and spy on the business going on in the hall. Otherwise, women were uninformed.

I was picked up at eight a.m. and finally made it back to the hotel around 8:30 p.m., when the tour was over at five p.m. After the tour and a ride in several buses and a change in personnel, I was told to get into one bus that would take all of us to our various hotels.

Turkish traffic is a monster on the loose. It was a hectic ride, stopping once for an ambulance picking someone up and then stopping when a car parked partially on the sidewalk and partially on the street blocked us from getting through.

The driver and the guide tried to find out who the guilty driver was, but after several minutes, the bus driver backed out and was on another route. The streets were narrow. The first guide told us the narrowness was from the chariots that were ridden in the streets. They never would have guessed way back then that automobiles would be operated by many of the 15 million people living together in Istanbul.

The driver negotiated the streets to each of the tour takers' hotels, and I was last. He even dropped off the guide, who told me not to worry, that the driver knew exactly where the Fatih Hotel was located.

He finally stopped the bus, got off, and stopped traffic until I could disembark from the bus, cross the street, and follow his directions to the Fatih Hotel.

I walked through a neighborhood that didn't look at all familiar from the two days I had been in the hotel, but I kept walking. Finally, I asked at another hotel for the directions, and that gentleman told me a different way. I tried to tell him that the neighborhood looked different.

"I'm telling you, madam. That is the way to the Fatih Hotel."

"Okay, jerk," I said under my breath and began the way he told me to go. By now, it was dark and raining buckets.

I saw a man closing up a shop, and I asked him if he knew where the Fatih Hotel was located, and he was so kind.

"I'll walk there with you." He took me to the Fatih Hotel all right, but still it was not the right one. Not again.

Inside, we talked with the reception manager. I handed him the address of the hotel I knew to be the Fatih Hotel. He called the number and spoke to the reception man at my hotel and told them he would make certain I'd get a taxi and arrive there soon.

About 45 minutes later, an energetic man came in and told me he had a taxi waiting for me.

"He's a friend of mine," the manager assured me.

The energetic man nearly ran down the rain-slicked sidewalk and several steps to a waiting taxi. He kept saying to me, "Come on, come on, come on."

I did my best and arrived at the taxi and a taxi driver. I thought the come-on man would be the driver. He whispered something to the driver, and we were off.

I felt confident as the driver negotiated the back streets like an expert and seemed knowledgeable of the area. And, we arrived at the Fatih Hotel. Oh, my God, how can this keep happening? It's the wrong hotel!

So, now, I've learned there are not only two Fatih Hotels, but also three of them.

The good driver had to stop and ask where the one with the address I gave him was located.

We eventually got there. I paid him a hefty price and hope the touring company will reimburse me. After all, wouldn't you think that the same company that picked you up would know where to drop you off?

I sent them an email, and we'll see where that takes me. Meanwhile, I woke up with a cold.

Street scenes/taking it easy

How could I get this cold on my very last week? It's a humdinger. I found a pharmacy this morning and gestured that I had a cold in my nose. His return gesture asked me if it was also a sore throat. I gestured back by pointing to my nose again. He handed me some medicine and another box with nose drops. I came back to the hotel, took the medicine, and slept for about three hours.

Late last night, one of the hotel workers knocked on my door to see if I was okay, as no one had seen me the whole day. It's nice that they were concerned.

I took some photos of the area around the hotel. Meanwhile, I've seen enough and will only go out for meals until I feel better.

Some observations and the evil eye

I woke up this morning feeling a bit better and had the usual breakfast—black and green olives, cucumber strips, tomato wedges, two bites of cheese, two kinds of fruit syrup, a slice of some kind of meat that I didn't eat, bread with butter, and tea. I asked for coffee instead of tea. I couldn't make the server understand that I wanted milk in my coffee. One of the reception guys knows that now. You usually have to ask for butter, as that is not always included with bread. As a matter of fact, that was true in Spain, as well. What is bread without butter? Olive oil to drip on bread is the standard in many European countries, and that's okay with me.

Turkish food is good, of course, depending on the restaurant and the skills of the chef/cook. The kiosks have good sandwiches with meat or chicken. The meat is somehow folded together and cooked on a spit. It is shaved downward in thin slices off of the standing roll of meat. It is called *döner*, with those two dots over the "o."

Yogurt is a staple and served with many types of dishes. Vegetarian dishes are easy to find, such as the salad I had yesterday. It was served in a bowl with diced cucumbers, tomatoes, corn, peppers, onion, zucchini, and white cheese cubes. The Turkish meals are garnished with everything imaginable. I've seen tops of carrots, celery, mint, dill, and other sprigs that give the dishes artistic flair. Crushed red pepper is also used a lot as the final touch. There are many bakeries that sell mostly savory types of pastry, but some do have sweet pastry, as well. The one I had the other day was a folded triangle made with layers of flaky crust and loaded with grated dates, nuts, and seeds.

I haven't seen many children's toys, which surprises me. However, in hot tourist spots, there are men selling little spinning tops.

The "evil eye" is also a hot item for tourists. I first saw some of those blue and white eyes in Izmir. They were embedded in a concrete wall. Later, I saw them in jewelry and key chains. The evil eye stems from a desire to keep evil away. However, there are other explanations that contradict one another. I don't get the feeling the eyes are given much importance but are just sold as a traditional object.

Chapter Thirteen

April, 2013

Just an average April Fool; morning in the Fatih Hotel, Istanbul, Turkey

Seen from a bird's eye view in Istanbul, Turkey, I'm upstairs eating breakfast in a restaurant while watching the world go by beneath me. A music video screams while ladies move in suggestive ways with little clothing, and below me, I see ladies modestly dressed in black, covered up to their eyes; billowing capes and long gowns—purple, blue, white, blue and green, turquoise, and lavender and white; green buses stuffed with humanity picking up more humanity; men with skull caps, some with long coats; a man using a cane to cross against oncoming traffic; motor scooters delivering goods; bright yellow taxis speeding (don't you know the faster they go, the more money they make?); scarves of all colors and patterns on 95 percent of the ladies' heads; a stone mosque with long stone steps to the top; stores underneath the mosque; four- and five-story buildings with shops beneath and apartments above; a maroon van delivering vegetables to the restaurant down below; an ambulance with siren blaring and light flashing, begging vehicles to move; a young boy pulling behind him a canvas bag full of what,

I don't know; a helicopter circling above; and birds nesting in trees that are sprouting leaves.

Later, back at the Fatih Hotel, a man knocked on my door and asked if I was okay. "Yes," I said, with a questioning lift in my voice.

Then he asked me to move to another room. Okay, now here's what they wanted. I was in a room with two beds, which gave me extra space for my suitcases. Now they wanted me to move to a room with one bed with barely a space to store myself, much less my luggage.

"It's better for you, Madame."

"How can you say it's better for me?"

"We have people coming and need the room with two beds."

"Oh, so I move to a smaller room, and it's better for me?"

"Yes, Madame. Is that okay for you?"

Well, I told him it wouldn't be better for me (was he kidding?), but I'd do it for him. He gave me a hug. What salesmanship. It's a cheap hotel, and what the heck; I know they are trying to make something out of nothing here.

I'm now in the room that's no bigger than a closet and not even a walk-in closet. I only have tonight and two more nights. I thought about another hotel, but that would involve finding something better and a taxi ride, to boot. I'm doing my part here to portray the good American.

By the way, my room has a balcony, but don't let that excite you. It sits over the utility room where the cleaning lady stores her stuff.

One more event and then . . .

Today is April 2, and I'll be on my way back to California in two more days. Tonight will be the last cultural event in Turkey and will cap off my yearlong journey. I'm going to a folk dance concert late tonight, so I'll have to take a taxi back to the hotel. Hope he can find his way.

It's been an awesome journey. I've been in 16 countries, three continents, three islands, 21 flights. Too many ferries, trams, trains, buses, and taxis to count, one scooter ride, and two camels.

The highlights begin with the interview of me on National Icelandic TV; Christmas and New Year's in Berlin with Marilyn McCord; seeing relatives and friends in Germany, Holland, and the Faroe Islands; and the surprise celebration of my birthday put on by the people in the Orkney Islands. I flew on the shortest booked flight that is listed in the *Guinness Book of World Records* and got to sit in that cockpit and two other times in cockpits of big commercial planes. Another highlight, and there were many, was the Turkish bath. You can't come to Turkey without that experience.

My journey has taught me so much about myself, humanity, and cultural differences. I have made lifelong friends in several countries. One year has gone by fast, and there is so much to remember. I need to spend a bit of time reflecting on it.

I will put it all in a book with awesome photos and will publish it. I will also get my photos enlarged and sell them, perhaps holding a gallery show.

First of all, when I go back, I'll need to find a permanent place to live. If you remember, I gave up a job and my apartment for this journey. I have no regrets.

**Good people in the world? I find my last day
a very taxing one to prove that thesis.**

Do surprises never cease in Istanbul, European side? It's a taxi story again, and my final one.

The same folks in the Fatih Hotel (one of the three in the city) who seemed to want to protect me from taxi rip-offs turned around and ripped me off themselves.

I made arrangements for a shuttle to the airport with one of the day reception men. He, the eldest worker and somewhat in charge, told me a shuttle would cost 60 liras, while a taxi would cost 55 liras. He said the shuttle was much better. "It will take you right there," he said.

"And the taxi won't take me there?" I asked.

"The shuttle is better," he repeated, not really answering my question, but he was adamant about it.

So, I agreed and gave him 60 liras, thinking I didn't want any surprises. I needed to get to the airport. I saw him pocket the money in his wallet.

The next day, I answered an early morning knock on the door. A younger hotel worker was there, announcing it was time to leave. I picked up my bag, and he helped me down the steps with the rest of my luggage and apologized all the way down.

"It is a taxi, not a shuttle. I'm sorry."

"A taxi? Why? I ordered a shuttle from him." I pointed to the reception desk where the older worker served as the concierge. Conveniently, he wasn't on duty this early in the morning.

"He arranged for a shuttle. He called them yesterday," I said.

"I'm sorry." The young man was obviously embarrassed for the lie.

But what choice did I have? I needed to catch a flight.

On the road to the airport, I asked the driver how much he was paid, and he said 40 liras. He showed the order to me. He then put on the meter that registered, when we got to the airport, 30.81 liras.

"I paid 60 liras to the man in the hotel for a shuttle."

The taxi driver shook his head.

So the elder worker in the Fatih Hotel took advantage of me, and this time it wasn't a taxi driver. While I boasted all the while how most people in the world are good, on the very last day, I was lied to.

Returning home

There's so much to do. I'm in Half Moon Bay with my son, his wife, and my grandson. I've got immediate issues to deal with.

When I got back, I found out my health insurance was cancelled by the company my husband worked for, for over 40 years. I have to get that cleared up, and I need to get my medicines filled. And since I haven't seen my doctor for one year, I need an appointment but cannot go to him without insurance. I'm hoping he'll let me have a new prescription until I can get there. He's in Soledad, a two-and-one-half-hour drive from here.

I also have to go to the DMV and get my car upgraded from non-use to use. The car is at my other son's place, also a long way from here.

And on my list of to-dos is to find a place to live and a way to make some money so I can pay for an apartment. I sent one of my favorite photos to have it enlarged. I will get a few more enlarged in due time and figure out a way to sell them.

So here are my welcome back challenges in America. I will meet them head-on.

Getting re-established in my own country

It's surprisingly complicated to get re-established back into the U.S. Who would have thought? I just got up to par with technology. My son, Brad; Aleida; and grandson, Brandon, saw that I got a phone up and running.

As I stated, leaving the U.S. and returning is not easy. There is so much to do, but the familiarity of my country makes it possible. If I had to do what I'm doing now but outside of the U.S.—purchasing health and auto insurance, paying income tax, looking for a way to earn some income, finding a place to live—it would be twice as difficult. At least I can function in my language. I'm hopeful and am taking one step at a time. It is a comfort to be with my son and his family right now, even though I'm a danger near the stove.

I wanted to make dinner and turned on a burner to boil water. I went about doing something while the water boiled. Then

I smelled smoke and heard a popping sound and an explosion. I ran into the kitchen and found I had turned on the wrong burner, and the burning one had a glass lid on it. Glass was everywhere, and the telltale smell left behind still lingers in the air. I haven't been near a stove for so long.

The good news is that I now have car insurance and just need to go to the DMV and show them my insurance paperwork and then pay something; then it's all ready for me to get my car from my son, Larry.

Pharaoh, the cat, keeps me company during the day when I'm alone.

Epilogue

Reflecting over my yearlong adventure, I now realize it was a microcosm of my life; another opportunity to learn about my strengths and creative problem solving skills from the situations I got myself into.

Even though the last day of the journey when the hotel worker lied to me and possibly pocketed the extra money the lie afforded him, I know it was just part of the experience. It didn't ruin my year. Instead, it added to my learning of human nature, which was and still is the biggest part of why I travel.

When I left my photojournalism job to tour the world, it wasn't to run away from anything. I didn't have much of a plan, and my life was going well, but there was and still is a big part of me who wants to see the bigger picture out there in the world. The people, the culture, the food, and everything that makes us all a bit alike and a bit different, as well.

The year accomplished my earnest desire.

If you are one of the scores of senior citizens, or anyone for that matter, who would enjoy having a similar experience, the day-to-day stories you read in *Walking Over the Earth* may inspire you to pack your bags and go.

And in case you're wondering what's next for me . . .

I'm now living in a one-bedroom cottage in the hills of Aromas, California. On one side of the hill across the road, goats of many colors fill their bellies with green grass. Down the road, I walk a bit and purchase fresh eggs from hens that share their space with a feisty rooster. I can hear birds of all kinds, and on the morning I wrote this, there were 13 quail chicks in my yard with their mom and pop. I've seen snakes, including a beautiful California king snake.

How I got here at this moment in time is another story, and here it is.

After arriving back from Turkey, the last country before my return to the U.S., I stayed with my son, Brad; his wife; and my grandson in their Half Moon Bay, California, apartment. I rested up a bit and began to figure out my next move. While searching for a job and a place to live, I found an opportunity that took me back to Monterey County.

I joined AmeriCorps and became the volunteer coordinator for the Arts Council for Monterey County, with the office in the Sunset Center in Carmel.

I lived in faculty housing at California State University Monterey Bay with roommate, Regina Daniels, a sign language instructor. CSUMB was also the post of the Monterey Ameri-Corps office where I was based.

My duties were to line up volunteers for the Arts Council's many activities under the direction of Paulette Lynch. Examples of just a few of the events were the First Night Monterey (an all-day event of art, music, and games); art gallery openings in the Council office and elsewhere; art activity booths for children at community events throughout the county; and for the biggest project of the year, the Champion of the Arts, honoring people in the county who contribute to bringing art and music to children.

After the ten-month AmeriCorps duty, I took my earned stipend and attended a Buddhist Immersion program in Cambodia, under the direction of the Global Service Corps.

Sophak Win, country coordinator for the Corps, met me at the Phnom Penh airport after I had spent a day in the South Korean airport. I took a few days acclimating to the Cambodian weather and culture before the program began. Sophak was instrumental in introducing me to the etiquette required while in the presence of Buddhist monks and nuns at the wat (temple).

Sophak and I were transported from Phnom Penh to the wat on a tuk-tuk (a three-wheeled motorized rickshaw) driven by Koeun Kat. Koeun became the official driver whenever I went into the city from the wat.

During the evenings, I taught English to children at the Buddhist monk-sponsored school. I was guided by the monk, Lokbong Samuth, who introduced me to the children of the school. Samuth also organized the Buddhism study in which I participated.

A local wat driver, Reach, would drive me on a tuk-tuk to the school in the evening. Later, he took me back home in the dark of night, with only flashes of fireflies on the trees and an occasional light from a cook preparing meals in a country house.

While in the Buddhist Immersion program, I took two side trips, one to Ho Chi Minh City, Vietnam, and the other to Siem Reap to see the ruins of Angkor.

When I reflect on my one-year solo journey through 16 countries and the time spent afterwards in Cambodia, Vietnam, and Korea, my memory revisits the people I encountered. The mountains, gardens, oceans, temples, cathedrals, busy cities, and quiet country scenes were lovely to behold. But it's always about the people. My travels confirm my philosophy that there are good people in the world.

There are enduring lessons in life as seen in the goodness of people such as Hildegard of Bingen, for example, who spent a lifetime serving others. But the everyday people who represented the good I found on my yearlong journey were those who stepped up to help from instinctual kindheartedness. While we all know there are rascals in the world, I am profoundly grateful to have been a recipient from folks who proved that there are more who are good.

At the time of this writing, I am preparing for knee surgery in a few days. One knee will be repaired this time, and six weeks later, the other knee. Soon I'll be able to walk without pain and can adventure on to another path. Mongolia, maybe?

Recipes

I am presenting here for your enjoyment some recipes I gathered during my yearlong adventure.

Sunfrid Jacobsen's Fish Casserole

Approximately two pounds of fish (cod was used in Eldrid's kitchen) placed into a casserole dish. Salt and pepper the fish.

Combine the following ingredients:

3 Tbs. oil

1 Cup cream

1/3 Cup mustard

4 Tbs. ketchup

1 tsp. curry

1 tsp. vinegar

Pour over the fish and bake for 45 minutes at 350 degrees. Serve over rice or potatoes.

Queimada

Many recipes for *queimada* can be found on the Internet, where it's often referred to by different names—Galicia Fire Drink, A Galician Fortified Witches Brew, and Flaming Galician Punch, for example. The little clay bowls or cups the Spanish serve it in can be ordered on-line.

I tried making *queimada* when I returned to the U.S. While I was grateful my son and grandson stood by with buckets of water handy, I discovered that substituting a typical U.S. brandy for the required orujo didn't create the desired flames associated with *queimada*. Orujo, made from the residue from wine production, has an alcohol content of over 50 percent (100 proof), while many brandies found in the U.S. have an alcohol content of only 30 percent.

The recipe makes eight servings. This would be a fun item to have at a Halloween party.

You will need a large, fireproof clay pot or bowl that has been seasoned by following the container's instructions. You will also need a long-handled wooden spoon to stir the *queimada*, as well as a ladle.

For safety, have a fire extinguisher or pitchers of water nearby, and it is best to prepare the *queimada* on cement or on a grill outdoors.

Ingredients:

1liter *orujo*

2/3 Cup granulated sugar

The rind of two limes cut into strips

One apple peeled and sliced

Six to eight cinnamon sticks

6 cloves

1/4 Cup whole, free trade coffee beans

Pour approximately 4 Tbsp. *orujo* and 1 Tbsp. sugar into a small glass and stir to dissolve sugar; set aside.

Pour the rest of the *orujo* and remaining sugar into the clay bowl and stir. Add the lime peel, apple, cinnamon, cloves, and coffee beans.

Stir again.

Pour the *orujo* and sugar mixture from the glass into a ladle and light it on fire.

Carefully move the ladle very close to the clay pot until the *orujo* mixture catches fire. Stir frequently until the flames turn blue.

Put out the flames by placing a lid on the bowl. Serve hot in small clay cups.

The Spaniards have put a spell on me!

Tortilla de patatas

This is a versatile, delicious dish and a national staple found throughout Spain. I used several recipes from websites and cookbooks specializing in Spanish and Basque cuisine, added my own creativity, and came up with this version. I like it plain, but other ingredients may be added, if desired, such as chili peppers.

Ingredients:

6 eggs (1 to 1½ per person)

4 potatoes (about 500 grams, or 100 to 200 grams per person)

1 onion thinly sliced or diced

Olive oil to cover bottom of frying pan

Sea salt and ground pepper to taste

Cut potatoes, ideally starchy rather than waxy ones, into thin slices, or dice them into small pieces. Fry the potatoes and onions in olive oil together at a moderate temperature until they are soft, but not brown.

Remove and drain potatoes and onions and mix them with raw beaten eggs to which sea salt and ground pepper have been added. Slowly fry this mixture on one side and then flip it over to fry on the other side. Use the help of a plate or a *"vuelve tortillas"* (a ceramic or wooden lid-like utensil). The plate is placed on top of the pan, and then with one hand on top of the plate and the other holding the pan, both are inverted, leaving the tortilla upside-down on the plate. The other side is then fried.

The tortilla may be eaten hot or cold. It is commonly served as a snack (*tapa*) or picnic dish throughout Spain. As a *tapa*, it may be cut into bite-size pieces and served on cocktail sticks, or cut it into pie-style portions (*pincho de tortilla*). As stated above, other ingredients such as green or red peppers, chorizo, tuna, shrimp, chilies, or different vegetables can be added.

Helga's Christmas Apple Dessert

Try this special treat. Make several at one time.

Core out the middle of an apple and fill it with marzipan, red jam of your choice, and diced almonds.

Bake at 410 degrees Fahrenheit for 15 to 20 minutes.

Place on a dish in the center of vanilla cream sauce. The vanilla cream sauce is a thinly prepared vanilla pudding.

The tour guide in Sahara

Black Faroe sheep close-up

Boat in Komiza

Camel

Cork

Courtyard in Vis

Grotto

Holland in the fog by the lake with two people walking

Inside a house in Tangier

Inside a tent in the Sahara

Seagulls from ship

Turkish slippers

Turkish women protest

Boat in Papa Westray

Majorelle Garden

Trees, Celle, Germany

River Blairgowrie

Acknowledgments

There is a world of folks to thank for this finished book, beginning with my editor, Floy Blair Sitts. I thank her for the tenacity she displayed throughout the editing of this project. She used her expertise and editorial gifts by organizing my words into a readable format, and she cleaned up my grammar and punctuation blunders to make me look good. I would not have been able to accomplish this project without her immeasurable help and support.

Floy and I also extend our gratitude to Jeffrey B. Whitt, Floy's brother-in-law, for his support and technical assistance, and to Floy's husband and an old colleague of mine, Richard Sitts, for his editorial input.

Praises go for technical assistance, as well, to Mark Malatesta, who guided me with utmost patience in the preparation of material required by publishers and agents.

My Colorado friend, Marilyn McCord, has often traveled with me and always teaches me the importance of paying attention to detail.

Thanks to my friend and writer, Dorothy Vriend, for her intelligent critique that made my story better.

Barbara Quin gets a nod for spending lots of time formatting the manuscript.

Suzan Gridley gave me many hours of assistance in getting on board with the Power Point that I have used for speaking engagements.

Two grandsons and their dad also shared their talents. Thanks to Brandon Crocker and Brad Crocker for their technical help organizing a power point presentation and to Michael Crocker of michael@crockervideo.com for his media expertise and for creating my website, www.walkingovertheearth.net.

I am grateful to Klara Hickmanova of the Arts Council for Monterey County for assisting with the book and helping me when I served in AmeriCorps as the council's volunteer coordinator.

My son Larry Crocker organized the massive amount of paperwork I picked up all over the world to store in my car until I got home.

I lift up accolades to my extended family and good friends in Germany and Holland for their fine hosting of me in their homes, feeding me well, and taking me places.

Thank you, too, to the hostels, hotels, and couch surfing volunteers who made me feel welcome and gave me the opportunity to experience their countries' cultures.

I highlight one encourager, my longtime friend, the late Sumi Haru. Sumi sent me uplifting notes all year long. I miss her.

Thanks to Giuseppi R. Slater, M.D., for his third world travel expertise. It helped me maintain good health while in Cambodia.

Good friends Paula and Bud Sarmento always go out of their way to keep me on track.

Matt Arnett, station manager of KRKC radio in King City, California, interviewed me one night when I was in the small fishing village of Thorshofn, Iceland. The humorous interview was streamed for the world to hear.

Stacy Trevenon of the *Half Moon Bay Review* receives high praise for the newspaper spread of my adventure.

Walter Ryce gets a nod for the story of my adventure in the Face-to-Face section of the *Monterey County Weekly*.

Eddy Hamelin, librarian at the John Steinbeck Library in Salinas, invited me to be a member of the Trailblazing Women Series. I was chosen as just one cog in the series and enjoyed giving a talk and power point presentation of my journey around the world, as well as my work as a reporter and photojournalist.

Thanks to the Rotary Clubs of King City, Soledad, Gonzales, and Half Moon Bay, California, for hosting me as their guest speaker.

The Icelandic television reporter, Johannes Kr. Kristjansson, and cameraman, Nickolas Ketilsson, surprised me with a request for an interview, and they deserve my thanks.

A big thank you goes out to KSBW 8 news anchor, Brittany Nielson, who, with a cameraman, showed up at my cottage in Aromas to interview me about my adventurous life.

I am grateful to a myriad of good people everywhere who held the doors open for me so I could hop on a train or a bus; the people who gave me directions, some even walking with me to make certain I got where I wanted to go; the many maids and helpers in hotels and hostels; the tour guides and bus drivers; friendly citizens everywhere who stopped to talk with me; street performers who entertained me and wowed me with their talents or who made me laugh. I thank all the folks with whom I enjoyed a fleeting moment on a plane, bus, train, ferry, or taxi, and in churches, restaurants, elevators, and museums. I thank those I met sitting on park benches and even standing on street corners.

Heartfelt appreciation goes to my children, grandchildren, cousins, nieces, and nephews who accept me as their nomadic family matriarch.

About the Author

Laureen Kruse Diephof, of Aromas, California, was born and raised in Denver, Colorado. She graduated from the University of the Pacific in Stockton, California, with a Bachelor of Arts degree in Sociology. She attended graduate school in education at National University in San Diego.

A photojournalist and columnist for several newspapers, Laureen's work has also been featured in numerous print publications.

She has lived in The Hague, Holland, and San Joaquin de Flores, Costa Rica, and has traveled through the continents of Europe, America, Africa, and Asia. She feels there are more continents and countries to explore to satisfy her adventurous spirit and desire to educate herself about life in other cultures.

Laureen holds a private pilot's license that she earned in Durango, Colorado, while she lived in the mountains above Bayfield, Colorado.

She has three sons, two daughters-in-law, three grandsons, and one granddaughter.

Reach Laureen by email at ldiephof@sbcglobal.net or on Facebook.

This book reflects the events during the years of 2012-2014, and as always in life, family dynamics change and the social climate takes a turn, but the story here is true to the time of my experience.

Made in the USA
San Bernardino, CA
21 January 2020